Alice is half-American and half-German. She grew up in Colombia and attended a French and German school, therefore being fluent in four languages. She has three children and seven grandchildren. After having travelled all over the world, she immersed herself in the spiritual teachings of India and lives by these teachings which have enabled her to serve others thus living her Dharma, or life's purpose. This is her first novel.

Alice Weil

SURVIVAL:
A STORY OF FRIENDSHIP

AUSTIN MACAULEY PUBLISHERS™
LONDON • CAMBRIDGE • NEW YORK • SHARJAH

A CIP catalogue record for this title is available from the British Library.

ISBN 9781528949842 (Paperback)
ISBN 9781528972406 (ePub e-book)

www.austinmacauley.com

First Published (2019)
Austin Macauley Publishers Ltd
25 Canada Square
Canary Wharf
London
E14 5LQ

To my children and grandchildren, who have stood by me all these years, encouraging me to finish telling the story that has now finally seen the light of day.

Table of Contents

How This Novel Came to Be

After being told I was expecting my first grandchild, my thoughts went back in time to when my parents were expecting me, *their* first child. The joy was huge, for it had taken many years for my mother to get pregnant and now that I was on my way, I was their dream come true. My parents gave me a legacy of values, which I have passed on to my children. I, however, wanted to leave this grandchild, and all the others who might come, a special one: A story of their ancestors, written as a novel with all the historical facts, but not too many, for it was not meant to be a history book. Just enough to arouse their interest and inspire them to do their own research.

Whenever I sat down to write, I would imagine hearing my granddaughter's voice in the background saying, "Please tell me more... And *then* what happened?" It has taken me 13 years to write it, but now, having finished, I must say that history seems to repeat itself. The times we are living in are not much different from the ones described in the novel.

The message to them, to future generations, and to all those who read this is: let us never forget, let us always remember that love, gratitude, compassion, generosity and friendship transcend distances and all circumstances.

Introduction

8 August 1918 was a very bleak day for Germany. Having lost the Battle of Amiens, the Military and the Emperor realised they had no other option but to surrender to the enemy. It was not until 14 September, when Austria and Hungary began peace talks with the Allies that General Ludendorff, the head of the German military, was able to persuade Wilhelm the II to ask for an Armistice. The American President, Wilson, offered his services as a mediator in January 1918 but had been ignored. The request was not made until 4 October when the German government sent a note to the American President since the German military needed this lapse of time to come to terms with its defeat.

The reply the German Government received from the American Secretary of State, Mr Lansing, was unacceptable to the military. The Americans demanded military capitulation of the country and the abdication of the Emperor. The German military felt completely humiliated. At the time, both the military and the civil governing parties were governing the country. The Chancellor understood that this situation could not continue and, seeking the best for the country, gave the Emperor an ultimatum: It was either he, the Chancellor, or Ludendorff. Wilhelm the II chose to dismiss General Ludendorff. On that same day, the Constitution of 1871 was changed and Germany became a parliamentary monarchy and the following day, the Emperor left for Belgium, never to return. The military did not accept Ludendorff's dismissal and did everything to hinder the peace negotiations, trying to bring down the new governing order, convinced that the military were historically entitled to govern the country.

Part I – Frankfurt

Chapter 1

Sigmund had been an officer in the Prussian army and was on his way to Frankfurt after an honourable discharge. He had mixed feelings about his homecoming. It was the first time he would be back since the death of his beloved Alice and indeed, he envisioned her beautiful face as his thoughts went back to those cherished and painful memories.

They met on a tennis court in Gstaad, Switzerland on a beautiful, warm summer day. Looking out the window of his hotel room, he was mesmerised by the sight of this beautiful girl. She was laughing and her long, blond hair sparkled in the sunlight. He watched her for a long time, wondering who she might be. He had business to attend too, so he didn't return until late, but she was on his mind the whole time. He had a tennis lesson on the weekend and hoped he would run into her then. He was in luck. She was talking to the tennis pro. He felt his heart skip a beat. She was even more beautiful than he remembered, listening attentively to what the pro was saying.

As he approached, she turned to look at him and gave him a lovely smile. She smiled often and her smile was in her eyes as well. He would never forget that smile. The pro introduced them and upon hearing her name, Alice, he thought how well it suited her. This was to be the beginning of their courtship. They played tennis daily and enjoyed their time together. It was love at first sight. They were married in Frankfurt; it was a huge affair, as she came from a very prestigious Jewish family. Sigmund, being an officer in the Prussian army, was assigned to different posts in different cities, so their courtship had not been easy, but they were both looking forward to settling down and being together.

A year after their marriage, Alice bore him a beautiful daughter whom they named Nellie. She was the image of her mother. Sigmund longed to be home with his little family and looked very much forward to his time off. On those days, they would sit by the fire and dream about their life when they could all be together.

A shiver ran down his spine as he came back to reality, looking at the scenery around him. He closed his eyes. He would never forget the day he received the news that his beloved was very ill. She was dying. He thought he would make it home before, but it was too late. He got there only in time to make the funeral arrangements and to cry his loss.

Alice's mother took Nellie under her wing since Sigmund had to go back to his duties. It had been so painful, so sad, what a loss, what a waste. They were so young and the world was at their feet, but all their dreams were taken from them. Yet, he hadn't lost it all. He had a daughter, and she reminded him so much of her. His mood changed and he felt elated, having something very special to look forward to. No longer feeling sorry for himself, he decided he would do his best to make a home for them both.

The train pulled into the main station, and he caught a glimpse of his brother, Paul, waiting for him, Nellie by his side. She was turning into a lovely young lady and had just celebrated her 14th birthday. Where did the time go? It seemed to him like yesterday that he was holding her in his arms. She looked more like her mother than he remembered. They embraced in silence and walked towards the waiting car. Paul looked a lot older; the years left their mark on him. They drove home, each busy with their own thoughts. Nellie was wondering what her life would now be like, living with her father again. She would miss her grandmother but knew she was welcome any time. Sigmund looked out the window, taking in all the changes and rejoicing now that he would be able to settle down, have a home and tend to the business his father had founded, the import of rubber articles, while devoting some time to his books.

Paul felt very relieved that his brother was back. They had a special bond, and he had missed him very much. He was very tired, having run the business on his own all these years, making all the decisions and carrying the weight of it on his shoulders. Not that he minded the responsibility, for they had both been taught not to shy away from hard work, but it hadn't been easy and it wasn't going to get any easier. But now that Sigmund was back, he had someone with whom he could share the burden.

After a short ride, they pulled into the driveway. Paul lived in a beautiful, large house in a very distinguished Jewish neighbourhood and even though he had never married, he enjoyed people and loved to entertain. Sigmund and Nellie would be staying with him until they found a place of their own. Anna, the housekeeper, had been with him for a great many years and was part of the family. She was in her early fifties, well rounded, not very tall and had something very motherly about her. She wore a light blue uniform with a small white coif on her head. Her hair was blond and curly and her sky-blue eyes seemed to reflect her state of mind.

Anna was absolutely thrilled at having Sigmund and Nellie to care for and it was visible in every little detail. She made a great effort in preparing Sigmund's room for him. The silver frame with Alice's picture was freshly polished and she'd saved all the latest newspapers for him, knowing how much he loved to catch up on the news, and placed them on the little coffee table by the window, next to the fish bowl. He also adored his two gold fish and would watch them for hours while deep in thought. Anna had been caring for them since his wife's passing.

She also went out of her way to make Nellie's room feel like her own tiny kingdom. She had gone over to Mrs Winters, Nellie's grandmother's, to pick up her favourite dolls and stuffed animals. Nellie let out a little cry of joy upon seeing Max propped up on her bed. It had been her mother's teddy bear, and she never let him out of her sight.

Sigmund complimented Anna on how beautiful all the flower arrangements looked and went to his room to freshen up. He stood there, gazing at the picture of Alice for what seemed an eternity, and marvelled once again at how much their daughter looked like her. He felt lonely and sad. He missed her and could not help thinking how different his homecoming could have been. His eyes filled with tears, but he did not allow himself a moment of weakness, it was not in his nature, and, brushing them off with the palm of his hand, he began to rummage through his suitcase. It did not take him long to find what he was looking for. He brought Paul a present, a box of Cuban cigars. One of his friends had received them from his father who had been a diplomat in Cuba and had given them to him as a token of friendship. He, in turn, saved them to give to his brother on a special occasion, and tonight was very special. He was home. His military life was now a thing of the past.

Anna prepared a wonderful meal and Sigmund enjoyed it very much. It had been so long since he'd eaten home cooked food. The conversation was very lively, with Nellie giving a detailed account of all she had been up to since her father had last seen her. Sometimes, he and her uncle would interrupt the flow to tease her a little, but she took it all in her stride, never getting upset and indeed laughing with them. The time went by too fast and, looking at her watch, she asked to be excused for she had to go to school the next morning. The two men wished her sweet dreams and adjourned to the library. Paul went to find his cigars but Sigmund stopped him with a wave of his hand and gave him his gift. Paul let out a whistle of surprise, where had his brother found them? He was deeply touched.

Over cognac, Paul brought his brother up to date with the business. Now that the war was over, there were all these soldiers that had to be employed. The government had ordered the employers to give the jobs back to those who had been on their payrolls until 1 August 1914. In order to accomplish this, a lot of people who were not dependent on a job were dismissed. The women took the brunt of it, which very much contradicted the idea of men and women being equal, so in compensation, on 12 of November 1918, women were given the right to vote. These measures also affected the business and it was with a lot of regret that he was forced to lay off most of the women who had been with them ever since their father started the business. Paul compensated them amply for their service but he could feel things changing…not for the better.

Indeed, he felt that the country was drifting, politically. After the Kaiser abdicated, numerous political parties were formed. A National Assembly was called, which elected Friedrich Ebert as the first President of the Republic. The revolution in Russia had everyone worried as well, but it wasn't until the spring of 1919 in Munich, after the communist uprising, whose leaders had been from Jewish families and the other two had been East Russian Jews, that the hatred of Marxism and Bolshevism turned more fanatic. It also furthered existing anti-Semitism, which would constitute fertile soil for the propagation of the political ideas of the most talented anti-Semite agitator, Adolf Hitler. He would begin his political career in this city in the summer of 1919 as the man of confidence for the commandos of the Realm of Defence.

Sigmund agreed with his brother, life was not getting any easier and only God knew what the peace conditions set by the Allies and the associated governments would be like. They both hoped that President Wilson would keep his word and work out a fair peace deal. Should it be otherwise, they were sure all hell would break loose. But it was getting late and instead of speculating on what could happen, they decided to call it a night.

Sigmund had had a long, emotional day. He lay awake for ages, his thoughts wondering back to his childhood. Paul was the eldest. They were six years apart and as time went by, the age difference diminished, and they became very close. Their parents came from very close-knit families, and they had transmitted the value of family to their children. Paul was tall and lean, his eyes were brown and he wore a moustache. He was very handsome. It was hard to believe that he had not married; the women seemed to flock around him. Sigmund, on the other hand, was short for a man but had beautiful, blue eyes and a stern, serious expression about him. He had very masculine features. He was very secure in himself and what Paul learned to love about his brother was his reliability. He felt a wave of gratitude sweep over him as the images of Nellie and Paul flashed in front of him. He felt very fortunate that they were together.

Nellie awakened Sigmund the next morning when she tiptoed in to kiss him goodbye before leaving for school. Seeing he was awake, she leant over him and told him how happy she was that he was home. Her words made his heart swell. Yes, life had been kind to him. He gave her a big hug and assured her he would be home when she came back. His eyes followed her out the door. What a great girl Nellie had become. She was beautiful, spontaneous, so natural and unaffected. She was very special. Plus, she had a gorgeous figure, even though she was at that age when young girls tend to put on weight. There was a joy of life she had, and one could truly see it in her eyes. Plus, she adored her father. When he came home on leave, she would polish his military boots and while he was busy behind his desk, she would sit on the chair facing it with her head in a book. He had instilled in her, the joy of reading and one day, she would inherit his library. He shot a quick glance at his clock. He hadn't realised it was so late, where had the time gone? He was out of bed in a flash, having promised Paul he would meet him at the office, but was running late so he showered and dressed in a hurry, grabbed the cup of coffee Anna was holding in her hand, gulped it down and left. He hated being late and felt it was a lack of consideration and respect towards the other person. He got in the waiting cab and enjoyed the short drive into the city. On his way, he saw a lot of people, more than usual, standing at the street corners, talking. They seemed to have nothing better to do. These were probably some of the unemployed Paul had mentioned.

Paul met him at the door. "I am sorry I'm late."

"Don't worry, Sigmund, somebody came in to talk to me and you would have had to wait so, it was good timing on your part."

Together, the brothers walked up the stairs. Sigmund looked around, nothing much had changed and he stopped and shook hands with a couple of employees who expressed their happiness at seeing him again. They went into his office and it was just as he had left it.

"So," asked Paul, "did you notice the changes on your way here?"

"I certainly did. I don't remember seeing so many people loitering in the streets."

"Yes, and it gets worse every day." Paul then brought him up to date with the latest figures, and they spent the rest of the afternoon discussing how to cope if the economic situation got any worse. Sigmund was not at all optimistic; he had a feeling very bad times lay ahead.

That evening, Nellie and Sigmund had dinner at Mrs Winters. She'd lost her husband a couple of months back and even though she missed him terribly, for they had been married over 50 years, she was coping very well. She was a very lively lady with a great sense of humour. Very elegant and distinguished looking, she dressed extremely well. Her huge villa was within walking distance of Paul's and since it was such a beautiful evening, they had decided to walk over.

She gave Sigmund a big hug then stood back and looked him over then said, "You have not changed at all."

"No," he said, "except for a couple of more grey hairs, I guess I haven't."

She then hugged Nellie, whom she adored, and told her how beautiful she looked. Nellie dressed with great care, wearing an outfit her grandmother had given her. She looked stunning and she knew it.

The drawing room was just as he remembered and a fire was glowing, which added to the cosiness of the room. He had always gotten along very well with Alice's parents, especially with his mother-in-law, and her loss brought them even closer. "I really enjoyed having Nellie," she said. "She helped me get through the rough times and we had a lot of fun together. Some days, after finishing her homework, we would go out for coffee or visit some of my friends. They all love her. She looks so much like my beloved Alice. I think she even has her personality."

"Yes," said Sigmund, "she reminds me a lot of her mother in many ways and she is just as beautiful."

"Sigmund, dear, what are your plans now that your military life is over? Are you still thinking about going to Munich, or are you going to settle down here?"

"I'm planning on staying in Frankfurt. Nellie has her school, her friends and her grandmother here," he said with a twinkle in his eye. "I also have the business to attend to. Paul really needs a break; it's been a long time since he has had some time off. I have a lot of reading to catch up on, and I would like to devote some time to Nellie as well."

"Well," said Mrs Winters, "I see you have a lot to look forward to, and I am sure everything will work out fine. I'm glad you are not thinking about leaving Frankfurt. That really takes a big load of my mind."

"Don't worry, Oma," said Nellie, "you're stuck with me." Her grandmother squeezed her hand.

Just then, Maria, the maid, came in to say that dinner was served. The big dining table was set with the beautiful Limoges dishes that Sigmund loved and remembered so well.

"I know how much you like this dinner set and it is in your honour that we are using it tonight," Mrs Winters announced.

Sigmund could not help but feel the absence of David, her late husband, and a wave of sadness swept over him. He looked at Oma sitting at the head of the table and their eyes met. Yes, they both felt his absence. Nellie broke the silence by asking her father if they were always going to live with Uncle Paul.

"No, dear, you and I are going to have a home of our own. As a matter of fact, I just spoke to a real estate agent this morning."

"Well," said Mrs Winters, "one of my friends with whom I play bridge, I don't think you know her, is moving to the US. She has a beautiful villa in this same neighbourhood and it's now up for sale. It is very spacious and has a big garden around it."

Nellie looked excitedly at her father, a home of their own, just the two of them, with a big garden around it! "Oh, Daddy," she said, "that is my dream! I can have all my friends over and decorate my room how I want it! I love the mere thought of it. And Oma, if it's not far, I can come and visit you often and we can do all the things we did when I was living with you."

Mrs Winters looked expectantly at Sigmund.

"I could be interested," he said. "And it sounds like the home I have in mind."

"Then I shall call Lina tomorrow and give her your office number."

"That will be fine," he said, and they left it at that.

It was getting late and Nellie had to be up early so, promising to see each other soon and thanking Mrs Winters for a great evening and an excellent dinner, they said their good byes. She watched them walk down the driveway. Sigmund was such a good father, it would do Nellie a world of good to spend time with him, and she felt both happy and relieved knowing that her little sunshine, as she called her, would not be moving away.

On the way home, they talked about the future. Nellie was very excited about her father buying a villa and he shared in her excitement for he had spent so many years living in confined quarters that he really looked forward to having some space and being surrounded by all his memories. Paul was still up when they arrived. Nellie could not wait to tell him the news and he was not surprised. "I'm glad," he said, turning to his brother. "But I will miss you both and so will Anna, even though I know it is for the best."

Sigmund described the villa Mrs Winters had mentioned. "I think I've been in it, Sigmund," said Paul. "If my memory does not fail me, I went to a cocktail party there. It is indeed very beautiful and I am sure it will be to your liking."

"We shall see," said Sigmund, and they bid each other goodnight.

The political unease in the country was growing. The Versailles negotiations regarding peace conditions between the allies and the associated governments were still going on while the German cabinet tried to assess its culpability for the war. The discussions on whether to make the documents public also continued.

Some argued that it would take a lot of courage and that if made public, they would take away what little self-esteem the German people had left, almost like tying a noose around their necks. Others argued that by being honest, they might be able to influence the Entente and get milder peace conditions.

At long last, it was decided that the documents would not be made public since it would be an admission to the people that the leadership of the Empire and the military had misled them for four years. The anguish of having to confront the truth had the upper hand and on 7 May 1919, the German peace delegation in Versailles were given the peace conditions set by the allies and the associated governments. The government was caught completely by surprise and the public was flabbergasted, as they expected a Wilson Peace based on compensation and understanding, anchored on the right of self-determination of all people, including the Germans.

Read at first sight, it seemed as if the agreement had been drawn up—not in the spirit of the American president—but in the animosity of the victors. Germany lost one-seventh of its territory and one-tenth of its population. The economic loss was huge, for it lost one-third of its coal and three-quarters of its iron ore mines. It also lost its colonies. As they could not agree on the amount to be paid for the damages and losses caused by the war, the decision on this issue was postponed. The amounts to be paid for other damages were set immediately.

Germany was to turn over its remote cable, 90% of its merchant fleet and 11% of its head of cattle. Within 10 years, it was to give 40 million tons of coal to France, Belgium, Luxembourg and Italy. The reason for the payment of these reparations was clearly stated in article 231 of the declaration of war culpability which said, Germany and its allies were the culprits of the war and were, therefore, responsible for all the losses and damages the allies and their associates had suffered. The governing parties were divided on whether to accept or refuse the conditions, the hardliners believed that by rejecting them, they were supporting the delegation who were still negotiating in Versailles and that they might thus obtain leniency.

On 16 June, the allies gave their answer to the counter offer made by the German delegation. The most important issue they had obtained was a referendum that would be held in Silesia to decide whether it would become part of Poland or not. As far as the Rhineland was concerned, the Allies would put an earlier end to the occupation, depending on the collaboration of the Germans. The allies rejected the German statement in respect to the war culpability. The German protest had led to a hardening of the allies' position and gave them five days to accept or reject the proposals. The governing parties were again divided, the Chancellor was against accepting them and he let it be known that if the deal were accepted, he would resign—and he did. Had Germany not accepted the peace proposals, the Entente would have invaded and the unity of Germany would have been broken.

In different parts of the country, the separatist movements supported by the French, were gaining strength and there was a possibility that the Poles would attack in the East. The stakes were very high and the country might have found itself in chaos. Due to the political crisis, the Entente gave the Germans two more days to decide. On 22 June, by a vote of 237 for/138 against and 6 blank, the National Assembly accepted the peace proposals. However, due to inner political problems between the German governing parties, the peace agreement was only signed in Versailles on 28 June 1919. Regardless of the peace conditions, Germany remained the most populated country to the east of Russia and the richest economic power in Europe.

The peace agreements were the topic of conversation everywhere, but life continued as usual. It had taken Sigmund some time to adjust, but between the business, Nellie and his books, he kept pretty busy. However, Paul was worried about him. He would watch him sometimes out of the corner of his eye and see a faint glimpse of sadness. He knew that he would never forget Alice, but he could not continue living in the past and had to move on. He tried to discuss it with him once, but Sigmund closed up like a clam. He could be very private at times and also distant. It was too bad his brother didn't enjoy people as much as he did. *Oh well,* thought Paul to himself, *I will have to take matters into my own hands.* And so, he began planning a homecoming party for him. The following day, Sigmund had a meeting with the real estate agent and did not go to the office so Paul took advantage of this and made all the necessary arrangements.

Sigmund spent his day looking at houses. The real estate agent brought a long list with him, but there hadn't been one house he liked. He saw some beautiful villas in the suburbs, and it never ceased to amaze him how many affluent people lived in and around the city. True, Frankfurt was the financial centre, but even so.

He came home late and tired. Nellie was eagerly awaiting his return. Had he seen something he liked? "No," he replied. "Most of them were too far out and the ones I *did* see in the city were either too small or didn't have a garden around them." Nellie was disappointed, but her father put an arm around her shoulders and said lightly, "It takes time finding a house. It's not like buying a sweater, it has to have the right feel to it. But don't worry, sooner or later we will have our little nest."

Paul told them at dinner about the homecoming party he was planning. He turned to Nellie and told her she could invite one of her friends if she wished. It would be a week from Saturday and would be a garden party. The weather should be nice. Sigmund shot his brother a surprised look. "You never hinted about this before."

"Well," said Paul, "since you're all settled in, I thought it would be nice if you could renew the friendships you had and maybe make some news ones. You'll also be able to catch up with your friends. I think it will be a lot of fun."

"You're right," Sigmund agreed. "It will be nice seeing some of my acquaintances again."

Anna came in with an envelope for Sigmund that Mrs Winters dropped off that morning. In a short note, she wrote she had not forgotten about calling her friend and had indeed done so, but Lina was in Munich and would not be back until the following week.

"Well, I guess we will have to be patient," said Sigmund, turning to Nellie and telling her what her grandmother had written.

"That's not too far off, but I hope it is as nice as it sounds," Nellie replied.

"We shall see," said her father.

The next days went by very fast. After debating for a long time whom to invite, Nellie decided on her friend Rachel. They had gone to kindergarten together and she was a lot of fun to be with, a born actress. Sometimes she would stand in front of the class during recess and mimic their teachers, even imitating their voices. What a great show she could put on. There was also complicity between them. They each had other friends and different interests but enjoyed their time together to the fullest. Rachel was half a year older than Nellie and the oldest of three sisters. She had auburn hair and huge brown eyes. Her complexion was very light and she was tall for her age. Absolutely delighted with the invitation, she assured Nellie they would enjoy every minute of it.

The party finally arrived, a beautiful summer day. Nellie followed Anna around the house, helping her wherever she could.

Everything was laid out in the garden.

Chapter 2

Rachel was the first to arrive. She wore a burgundy coloured dress that suited her very well and she and Nellie, who looked beautiful in a new outfit her uncle Paul had bought her for the occasion, retired to a corner of the hallway from where they could watch the guests arrive. Sigmund dressed with much care. He did not relish the party, he would have preferred to have spent the time reading his latest book, but he was fully aware that he was the main reason for it and so, putting on a good front, went downstairs to receive the guests.

Abraham and Sara were one of the first to arrive. Sigmund knew them well, for their fathers had been in business together. He greeted them warmly; it had been so long since they had last seen each other. Sigmund could not take his eyes off Abraham. *He sure has aged,* he thought, even though he was not much older than himself. Sigmund hoped he didn't look that old. When they sat down, Abraham told him that he had not been very well. The whole political situation in the country, along with the unease and tension that could be felt, was causing him a lot of anxiety. Where was this new republic headed? They had really seen better times under the rule of the empire.

Paul interrupted their conversation. A tall lady in her early thirties was standing by his side. Sigmund had not a clue who she might be. Paul introduced her as Helene. Sigmund got up and pulled out a chair for her to sit down and was about to sit down himself when he saw his best friend Jacob make his entrance, and so he excused himself and went over to him.

The pleasure of seeing his old friend again was written all over his face. It had been such a long time. They shook hands, smiling. "Why," said Sigmund, "it seems like ages since we last saw each other."

"Yes," said Jacob, "as a matter of fact, it *has* been a while and under not-so pleasant circumstances."

It dawned on Sigmund the last time they met was at Alice's funeral. "Yes, those were very sad times."

Just then, Nellie and Rachel appeared and walked over to where Sigmund was standing. Jacob was amazed at Nellie. He thought how beautiful she was and that she resembled her mother very much. She was a little girl when he last saw her. Nellie announced that dinner would be served shortly and, giving her dad and his friend a nod of her head, she walked over to her Uncle Paul who was sitting at a table with Abraham and Sara.

Although Nellie knew them both very well, she did not recognise the lady sitting next to them. "This is Helene," Paul said, and asked them both if they wanted to join.

"Sure," was the reply. Nellie and Rachel answered all the questions Abraham and his wife asked while Helene just listened. Their conversation was then interrupted when Anna announced that dinner was served.

The guests made their way into the dining room. It looked lovely. Anna had made a beautiful flower centrepiece of small roses and the candles were lit in the candelabras on either side of it. Everyone complimented her on it. The seating was not a problem, as Paul had placed name cards. Sigmund found himself sitting at one end of the table with Helene to his right. He made small talk with her and soon found out she was a kindergarten teacher and had moved to Frankfurt from Wiesbaden at the beginning of the school year. She had met Paul at a cocktail party and seemed very shy. Sigmund was a little intrigued by her, thinking she was attractive. He would have liked to get to know her better, but he could not ignore the other guests.

The main topic of conversation was the unease in the country. Nobody seemed to know where it was all heading. The economy was in chaos, inflation was very high and the German Democratic Party was rapidly gaining strength. The Jews were also being blamed for the result of the peace proposals. So, all in all, it was a gloomy picture.

The girls were bored to death but had to wait until dinner was over to be excused. When they were finally able to make their exit, they went to their little corner in the hallway. They discussed each guest in turn but it was Helene who had really attracted their attention. A Kindergarten teacher! "Can you imagine something so boring?" Rachel asked.

"Well," said Nellie, "she must like little kids. And she's probably single, don't you think?"

"I'm sure she is," said Rachel, "but I bet she has a boyfriend. Her face is very pretty and she's got a great figure. And I really like her dress. Your father sure did give her a lot of attention."

"What do you mean?" Nellie asked. "I saw him talking to everyone and having a very good time." Rachel made no comment.

The guests began to leave and the girls watched them from their perch. Helene was one of the last to depart, and she and Sigmund stood for a long time talking in the doorway. The girls could not hear what they were saying but shortly thereafter, Sigmund came upstairs and kissed both girls good night. "Yes, it was a nice evening," he said, and hoped the girls had enjoyed it and not found it too boring.

"Not at all," said Rachel, "it was great fun."

They lay in bed going over the day's events but Nellie could not get Helene out of her mind and with her name on her lips, she fell asleep.

After having bade the girls good night, Sigmund went down to the library to join Paul for a nightcap.

"What did you think?" Paul asked his brother.

"It was a lot of fun and I enjoyed seeing everyone again, but I must say, I was really shocked at how badly Abraham looked. Sara doesn't look too well or happy, either."

"Yes," said Paul. "It's such a shame and he takes it all so much to heart. He's so very worried about the political situation and I fear it is making him ill."

"Jacob never changes," said Sigmund, "he has so much wit. I wish I could have spent more time with him, but then I really had to devote some time to everyone."

"I think you did pretty well, to tell you the truth," said Paul. "Everyone commented on how great you look and how well-behaved Nellie and Rachel were and that they acted very grown up. There was something nice said about them by all."

"Yes," said Sigmund, "I felt like a very proud father."

"You should be, she's a great kid."

"I know," Sigmund replied. They were silent for a minute and then Sigmund asked the question Paul had been waiting for. "So, where did you meet Helene?"

"I told you when I introduced you; we met at a cocktail party."

"Oh, yes," said Sigmund, "you did say something about that."

"What did you think of her?"

"I thought she was nice, but I didn't talk to her much. I would like to get to know her a little better, but she seems very shy."

"I saw you speaking to her for a long time as she was leaving. What was that all about?"

"Oh, just the usual, but I did ask her for her phone number so maybe I will get together with her sometime."

Paul made no comment. They finished their cognac in silence, each one thinking about what the other had said. Soon after, they went upstairs to bed. It had been a long day and it was late.

Helene had walked home. It was 20-minute walk from Paul's house and although it was chilly, it was a nice, clear night and she enjoyed the silence and looking at the stars. The moon was half-full and seemed to play hide and seek with the clouds. She mulled over the day's events. What a beautiful villa Paul had, so tastefully decorated. Then her thoughts went over to his brother. He sure was handsome and what gorgeous blue eyes. It was a shame he was not as tall as Paul, in fact, he was half a head shorter than she was. Oh well, that's not important—he really seemed nice and indeed she would like to get to know him better. He'd asked her for her number, so maybe he will call. Helene's thoughts then turned to Nellie. She was at that difficult age, but what good table manners she had and she sure did seem self-assured. Her friend Rachel, though—no, thought Helene, she did not like her much. There was something about her, but she couldn't put her finger on it.

Suddenly, she was home and she walked up the two flights of stairs to her flat, unlocked the door and turned on the light. Standing there for a minute in the entrance to the living room, she felt how cosy and homey it was. She had decorated it herself and succeeded in turning a flat that initially had no character whatsoever into her little nest. It had been a long day for her as well; she got ready for bed and soon after fell into a deep sleep.

Nellie and Rachel woke up late. Paul and Sigmund had just finished their breakfast in the garden when the girls joined them. Paul asked if they enjoyed the party and they both replied that they did very much. They were finishing their meal when Anna ushered Rachel's parents in. They had come to pick her up and were on their way to the zoo. Would Nellie like to come with them? She declined, saying she promised to spend the afternoon with her grandmother. Rachel did not insist and thanked everyone for a lovely time before following her parents out the door.

After lunch, Nellie and Sigmund walked over to Mrs Winters' who had just gotten up from her nap and greeted them with a big smile. When Alice was alive, they always had Sunday lunch with her parents. Sigmund was glad he had broken this tradition, for it took up all his afternoon.

Tea was served in the dining room, as usual. The maid baked a wonderful cheesecake, Nellie's favourite, and as she ate, she gave her grandmother a detailed account of the latest events. Mrs Winters knew most of the people Nellie mentioned and was not surprised to hear about Abraham's ill health.

"If he is so stressed by the situation, why don't they leave? Look at Lina's husband," she said, turning to Sigmund. "He didn't like what was happening and decided to go to the United States. He has family there and is still young enough to start a new business."

"Yes," said Sigmund, "but Abraham is probably older and has no family in the US."

"Yes, that does make a big difference," Mrs Winters said. "And speaking of Lina, she will be back on Monday. I spoke to her on the phone, and she will be more than happy to show you the villa at whatever time is convenient for you on Tuesday afternoon."

Nellie was delighted, she only had to wait one more day. Sigmund had the idea to go over and look at it from the outside. Mrs Winters said they might not be able to see much, as it was all closed in, but at least he would see the location and they might be able to see something of the garden. She then gave them the address and it was within walking distance. Would she like to come along? She declined, it was too long a walk for her, but she would look forward to hearing what he had to say about it. They said their good byes shortly afterwards and headed for what they both hoped would be their ideal home. It was a 30-minute walk.

The villa was on a quiet street lined with trees. Mrs Winters had been right, one could not see the house, but the location was pristine and Sigmund felt in his heart that it was right. He was just as eager as Nellie to see it, but they would both have to be patient. They strolled through the neighbourhood. They saw a small little store on the main street where Anna could get groceries, a florist was just across from it and the baker was on the other corner. The location could not have been better. Night was falling, so they headed home.

"Will you bring me with you when you come on Tuesday?" Nellie asked her father.

"No," said Sigmund, "you will be in school and I do not know at what time I can get away from the office, as I have several meetings. But if I like it, I will come back with you so you can give me your approval. We also have to see if the price is within our budget."

"Yes, father," said Nellie, "I suppose we do. I hope they don't want too much money for it." Then, as an afterthought, Nellie added: "Some of my friends don't live far from here."

The next couple of days flew by and Sigmund had plenty to do. He spent all of Monday morning preparing for an important meeting with his banker to go over his investments. In the evening, as he rummaged through his pockets, he found the card Helene had given him and looked at it, wondering whose it was, until suddenly he envisioned the shy young lady who had sat by his side during dinner. She'd made an impression on him and so he made a point of trying to remember to call her when he had time. He placed the card carefully in his wallet.

The meeting with his banker went very well. He had enough liquidity so as to be able to pay cash for the villa, if the price was within reason. His parents had always preached that one never made a purchase unless one had the money to pay for it. One never borrowed.

On Tuesday morning, Nellie came into his room just before leaving for school. Sigmund was sitting by the window, reading the newspaper. She gave her father a big hug and whispered in his ear:

"I hope and pray that you will like the villa and that we will be able to afford the price."

"I'm sure your prayers will be heard," Sigmund replied, and, giving her a big hug and a kiss on her forehead, he wished her luck with her German paper. He didn't really have to worry much about her grades, she was very intelligent and enjoyed learning, and was also very good at drawing and painting as well as having a wonderful ear for music. With singing in the school choir and piano lessons, her days were pretty much taken up. He, too, had to admit he was very excited about the prospects of finally seeing the house, but it was not until noon that he was able to free himself from a meeting to call Lina Ulrich.

She was home and yes, she was expecting him. "Mrs Winters has spoken so highly of you, I feel as if I already know you," she said to him on the phone and confirmed that 4 pm would be perfect since her husband would be home by then as well. After telling her he looked very much forward to meeting them both, he hung up the phone.

He peeked into Paul's office who was sitting behind his desk, going over some papers. "Do you have a minute to spare?" asked Sigmund.

"Sure," said Paul, "what do you want to discuss?"

"I have just spoken to Lina Ulrich and I am meeting with her and her husband at 4 this afternoon."

"Great," said Paul, "so the suspense will finally be over."

"Yes, but I have no clue about real estate prices and if I really like the place, I will have to make an offer so I was wondering if you could give me an idea."

Paul thought for a minute and said, "The square-metre is pretty expensive in that location, but you also have to take into account that due to the political and economic situation the country is going through, there will not be many people out there looking to buy. I take it will be a cash deal?"

"Yes," said Sigmund. "It's either money in hand or no purchase."

"In that case, I think you could probably take off 30% from the asking price."

"Isn't that a bit much?" asked Sigmund.

"No, in truth it will leave you some leeway to split the difference."

Sigmund thought for a minute then said with a smile, "You are so smart, little brother."

"Thank you for the compliment but it's not being smart; it's just that I have had more experience along these lines than you do. After all, it really is your first real estate purchase."

"It sure is and I have to admit I am very excited about it. I really hope I will not be disappointed."

"Me, too," said Paul. "I wish you all the luck in the world and I look very much forward to hearing how it all goes over dinner tonight."

Sigmund thanked his brother then went into his office to look over some papers but, unable to concentrate on what he was reading, he grabbed his hat and coat and headed for the street to take a walk. He looked at his watch: he had an hour to kill, which gave him sufficient time to get there and scan the neighbourhood more closely. He walked past the grocery store and the bakery then up a narrow street that led to a small park. The whole neighbourhood was so quiet and peaceful and the more he saw, the more he liked it. Then, looking at his watch once more, he saw that the time had finally come for him to walk towards the house.

The gate stood open so he walked up a short driveway lined with trees towards the three-story house then up a couple of steps to the front door. Mrs Ulrich herself let him in. She was tall and very distinguished looking. "Come in, come in," she said, and led him into the living room. Her husband was sitting in a corner reading the newspaper and stood up immediately. Mrs Ulrich introduced him, his name was David, then took Sigmund's hat and coat and told him make himself comfortable.

"What a beautiful afternoon it is," she said.

"Yes," he replied. "I walked over here from the office. There is not a cloud in the sky." He looked around him and liked what he saw.

"Can I get you some coffee and cake or would you rather I show you our home first?" Lina asked and David answered for him.

"If you walked over here, you must be hot and tired, so why don't you have some coffee and you must have a slice, Lina bakes the best chocolate cake."

Sigmund nodded his head and Lina excused herself to do as she had been told. "I hear you are moving to the US."

"Yes," David replied. "I am not that young anymore, but I'm still not so old that I can't travel, but if we don't leave now we'll be unable to do so later. We have family in the States and there are far more opportunities there than here."

"I see," said Sigmund. Just then, Lina walked in.

Overhearing what her husband was saying, she said, "I am really looking forward to going to America. Life is so unsettled here, all the strikes that are going on, all the unemployed. Germany has changed so much since the war."

"Yes," agreed Sigmund, "the war certainly did leave a big scar on the country." When he finished his coffee and cake, he turned to David. "You were right, that really is the best cake." Lina blushed with the praise.

"Let me give you the tour," she said.

The house was just what he had envisioned. It had three bedrooms on the third floor, two bathrooms and a very cosy family room. On the second floor, there was the living room, separate dining room and kitchen. To the back of the house were the maid's quarters and a service entrance. There was a great library on the first floor and leading off from it was a big conservatory. A waterfall ran down to the side of it and ended in a beautiful pond, full of goldfish. Sigmund was very impressed; it was the house of his dreams. He asked Lina if she would mind repeating the tour, and she said she would be happy to.

They took their time. The rooms were bright, and one had a view of the garden from every window, and the house was in perfect condition and needed no repairs. They went back to the living room where they found David, still reading his newspaper.

"Well, what do you think?" he asked.

"You have a lovely home," Sigmund replied.

"Yes, it has been our home for a great many years and we have been very happy here."

"How much do you want for it?" David gave him the amount. It was more than Sigmund had anticipated, but it really was a great house and he could tell it was very well built and the materials that had been used were only the best. "I really like it, but I am afraid the price is higher than my budget."

"You can make an offer and maybe we can come to terms," said David. Lina interrupted, saying that there were so many memories here that she really would not like to sell it to a stranger.

Sigmund thought it over. He said that he would very much like his daughter to see it, to which they answered sure, bring her over anytime. They then asked him about Nellie and made small talk. Sigmund barely listened. He wondered whether to make the offer now or wait until Nellie had seen it, sensing they really wanted to sell and leave. He decided it would be wiser to make the offer before Nellie saw it and they were able to see her excitement. Looking directly at David, Sigmund gave him the amount.

"It's less than I expected," he said, turning to Lina, who agreed that it was a great deal less. "Why don't you bring Nellie over tomorrow and in the meantime we can all think about it? It will have to be late afternoon." Sigmund said that was fine. They assured him they'd be home. Lina brought him his hat and coat and he thanked them for their hospitality before bidding them good night.

It was still early, so he decided to walk home. The house was just right. There was plenty, even too much room for the two of them, and the library! What a great library! I can finally unpack my books. It was all wood panelled and his father's desk would look very nice in there. Nellie is going to be taken aback by the conservatory, what a great idea…a waterfall…he was sure he would be able to hear the flow of the water from the library. And his goldfish would have a big pond to swim in. Yes, it was perfect. He hoped they would come down with the price but he knew that even if they did not, the house would be his.

He let himself in the front door. Everything was quiet, no one seemed to be home. Just then, Anna came into the hallway saying she thought she'd heard a noise. "Why, hello Sigmund, you are home early today?"

"Yes, I got off early for a change. Is Nellie back?" he asked.

"No, she won't be home until later. She has choir practice today."

"Oh," said Sigmund with disappointment in his voice. "I thought she might be here."

"She'll be home in time for dinner," Anna assured him.

"That's good… Well, I have some work to do," he said, starting up the stairs. Anna asked if she could get him anything. "No, I'm fine, thank you. I will wait until dinner."

Sigmund opened the door to his bedroom. Everything was nice and tidy. He was very orderly; it was probably his military training. He hung up his coat and hat, went to the window and looked out. He then walked over to his table and picked up a pencil and paper and jotted down some figures. If they did not come down with the price, he would have to sell some bonds, thankfully the market was not fairing too badly. His thoughts turned to Helene and he decided, since he had some spare time on his hands now, he might as well call her. Looking at his alarm clock, he saw that it was a little after six and she would probably be home by now. If she were not, he could always leave a message. Now where did he put her card? He looked everywhere for it until all of a sudden it came to him; he put it in his wallet, so he opened it and sure enough, there it was. He picked up the phone and dialled the number.

It rang and rang and just as he was about to give up, somebody answered.

"Hello, hi," said Sigmund. "I would like to talk to Miss Helene."

"Speaking…"

"Good evening, this is Sigmund, Paul's brother?"

"Oh yes," said Helene, "I know who I am speaking to. What a nice surprise," she said.

"Well," said Sigmund, "I was just wondering if you would like to have dinner with me at the Frankfurter Hof this coming Thursday?"

Helene was silent for what seemed a long time, then said, "Sure, I would be very happy to."

"Will it be OK if I meet you in the lobby, say about 7 pm?" Sigmund asked.

"That will be fine."

"I look forward to seeing you," he replied.

"So do I," said Helene and they hung up.

Helene set the phone down. He phoned and invited her on a date. She knew he would and was so excited, she immediately went through her clothes, trying to decide what to wear. Not being able to make up her mind, she said to herself, "I'll decide later," and went back to her book.

Sigmund had just hung up when he heard the front door close and thought that it was either Nellie or Paul who was now coming home. He looked at his watch. *It must be Nellie,* he thought. Sure enough, she called his name and walked in, being in such a hurry she didn't even stop at her room.

"Hi Dad, how did it go?" she asked excitedly. "Was it what you expected— did your heart feel it was right?" she asked in one breath.

"Not so fast," said Sigmund. "Relax and I will tell you all about it. Why don't you first go to your room and get rid of all your schoolbooks and freshen up? Then we can talk."

"OK," she answered and went to do as she was told. It was not long before she was back.

"I liked the house a lot," said Sigmund, "but as I promised you, I have made an appointment for us to go over tomorrow after you get home from school. It is big and there is plenty of room."

Nellie wanted a detailed account and he gave it to her as best as he could. "It sounds really beautiful and I'm glad you were not disappointed," she said, giving her father a hug.

"There's only one problem," said Sigmund. "The price is not exactly in my budget."

"Oh," interrupted Nellie, "that's bad."

"But I made them an offer and now we will see if they accept it." Nellie looked a little sad. "If it's meant to be," said her Dad, "something will work out, I'm sure, so let's not get our hopes up too high, OK?" She agreed with him.

Anna announced that dinner was served. They were so busy talking they had not heard Paul come home who also wanted to know how it went. Sigmund told him he liked it and about the very nice library and that it would make a nice home for him and Nellie. Nellie interjected that the price was not in her Daddy's budget. "But I made them an offer and I'm taking Nellie over tomorrow after school to see it. We could go in the evening if you wanted to join us," said Sigmund.

"Sure," said Paul, "I'd love to."

Nellie ate her dinner in silence and then asked to be excused, as she had quite a lot of homework to do. Paul and Sigmund went into the library. Sigmund told Paul the price they wanted and the offer he had made.

"That is pretty high," said Paul.

"I guess it's worth it if you look at the grounds and the size."

"I know," Paul agreed, "but not in these times."

"You are right," answered his brother. "It will be interesting to see what they tell us tomorrow."

Nellie sat at her desk doing her homework, unable to concentrate. Her mind kept wandering to the house. From how her father described it, it seemed perfect. She finally gave up; she would finish it in the morning and decided to go to bed instead. The following day, Sigmund picked Nellie up at school just after choir practice, so they went straight to the Ulrich's home. They arrived at the same time as Paul. Mrs Ulrich set the coffee table and had baked a cheesecake. Nellie took a liking to them immediately and loved the little dachshund, whose name was Gretchen. She was so playful and friendly.

"I can tell you love animals," said Mrs Ulrich.

"Yes," replied Nellie, "I do."

"Do you have any pets at home?"

"No, I don't, but my Dad has a couple of gold fish."

"Oh," said Mrs Ulrich, "we are looking for a home for Gretchen since we can't take her with us to the United States. It breaks our hearts to part with her, but we have to. Maybe she could have a home with you?"

Nellie opened her eyes wide. A dog, a pet! She turned to her father and then to her Uncle who were just as surprised as she was. Here they had come to look at a house and were being offered a very friendly dachshund. Sigmund turned to Nellie. "We don't have to make a decision right now, you are not leaving yet," he said, turning to the Ulrichs. "We can cross that bridge when we come to it."

Nellie liked everything she saw, the house was beautifully furnished and, just as Sigmund had expected, the conservatory overwhelmed her. She also chose her room, her favourite was the one down the hall, and it had a beautiful view of the garden. The grownups headed back to the living room and Nellie asked if she could walk around the garden. Mrs Ulrich opened the door for her and Gretchen promptly followed her.

"What a delightful young lady she is," said Lina, turning to Sigmund.

"Yes," he said, "she is a great girl."

David spoke up for the first time. He had given Sigmund's offer a lot of thought. As he had told him when he made it, it did not meet his expectations, but in all honesty, he had to tell him that somebody had been over to look at the house that morning and really liked it. He wanted to wait and see what offer they made before making a decision. Sigmund looked at Paul and said, "I think that is fair. I am in no hurry so do take your time and let me know what you decide."

Nellie came in from the garden just then, closely followed by Gretchen. "There are some very old trees out there."

"Very old indeed," David confirmed, and they said their good byes and left.

"What happened?" asked Nellie. Her father brought her up to date. She said she really liked everything about it and that waterfall was really something.

"I knew you would be stunned by it."

"What a great idea," said Paul, "and you are absolutely right about the library, what a delightful room. The price they are asking is high," he went on, "but I firmly believe you made a right offer."

"What do you make about somebody else being interested?" Sigmund queried.

"It could be possible, or he may have just made it up to put pressure on you. He seems to be a very sharp businessman. I am glad you gave him the right answer," said Paul.

"I looked at you and I could read it in your eyes: don't panic, take your time."

"I have a feeling they will get back to you sooner than you think."

"We shall see," replied Sigmund.

"Daddy, what do you think about Gretchen, can I keep her? You really liked her and I have always wanted a dog but it has never been possible, first living at Oma's and now at Uncle Paul's."

Paul looked at her. "You never mentioned wanting to have one," he said. "That's true, but I had never run into one as friendly and cuddly as this one."

"If we get the house," said her father, "you are more than welcome to keep her. She will be in her own surroundings and hopefully will not miss her masters much."

Nellie was overjoyed. But was the house going to be theirs? She wondered how long she must wait to find out. They had an early dinner and as Sigmund bade Nellie good night, he mentioned matter-of-factly that he had a dinner engagement the following evening.

Chapter 3

Helene came home from work quite late, as she had to attend a meeting. She was unable to concentrate on what was being said for her thoughts wondered back to her telephone conversation with Sigmund and that evening's date. After finally choosing her outfit, she dressed with utmost care then looked in the mirror and was pleased with what she saw. Would he be there on time, what would they talk about, what if he did not show up? *I'm really nervous,* she thought to herself. "He'll be there, no need to worry, just take it all in your stride," she said, trying to calm herself. Everything will be fine. She did not want to be late but she did not want to get there too early, and she could not bear to sit at home so she hailed a cab and got out a couple of blocks from the hotel right in the middle of the posh shopping neighbourhood. The short walk had a soothing effect on her and she enjoyed taking her time and doing some window-shopping on the way. Upon getting to the hotel's main entrance, she looked at her watch: 7 pm, right on time. *There sure are a lot of people here this evening,* she thought, *they must be having some kind of a convention.*

She made her way to the lobby and was just about to sit down when she saw Sigmund walking towards her. He was even more handsome than she remembered in his blue suit and, if anything, it made his eyes look bluer than ever.

"You haven't been waiting long, have you?" he asked, shaking her hand.

"Not at all, I just got here," she replied.

"Good, I hate to keep people waiting." Sigmund booked a table in the gourmet restaurant, which was small and very intimate. The waiter brought them the menus and Helene had a hard time trying to decide what to order since she wasn't a big eater. Sigmund made a couple of suggestions and she gratefully took them. They talked about the weather, the party where they had met, and Paul then over dessert, Sigmund asked her to talk a little bit about herself. She blushed, saying there was nothing much to tell, but slowly started answering his questions.

She was born in Frankfurt, but her parents moved to Wiesbaden when she was a baby, and was the third of five girls. "No boys?" he asked.

"My father was the only man in the house," she replied.

"It must have been hard for him being surrounded by six women."

Helene smiled at that. "Oh, we all got along quite well, I must say. Do you have any sisters?" She wanted to know.

"No, I come from a very small family; it's just me and Paul."

Helene moved to Frankfurt because she had been offered an interesting job and this was a much more exciting city than Wiesbaden. Sigmund nodded his head in agreement. She came from a mixed marriage, her mother was Jewish, her father was a Christian and the children were allowed to choose their religion. Helene and one sister were Christian while the other three Jewish. Her parents were very liberal and they always believed one could suggest, not impose, so were given the option. Sure, they had been brought up in both faiths, so at the end of the day, each of them was able to make their choice according to her convictions.

What a great idea, Sigmund thought, his parents were both Jewish and very strict. Helene said she chose to become a kindergarten teacher because of her love of children and had not been married but was once madly in love and engaged, but unfortunately, her fiancée was killed during the early stages of the war. It came as a great shock to her, but somehow life had to go on and one has to bury the past to be able to keep on living.

"Yes," said Sigmund, "I could not agree more with you on that issue." He could understand her loss for he, too, had been married and lost his beloved very early. Nellie was just three years old when her mother passed away.

"How sad," said Helene, "what a beautiful child she is."

"Yes," said her father.

"Who took care of her while you were in the service?" she asked, and Sigmund told her about Mrs Winters and what a blessing she had been.

They felt very comfortable in each other's company. *How easy it is to speak to him,* Helene thought, *he's so easy going.* They had so much to talk about. Then Helene looked at her watch. "Sigmund," she said, "I have really enjoyed my evening with you but I must be getting home. I have to be up early in the morning."

Sigmund looked at his watch, "Why, I hadn't realised it was this late. I'm sorry," he said.

"Not at all, it has been a fun evening."

"Yes," said Sigmund, "I really have enjoyed it." He then asked for the check and after settling it, helped Helene into her coat. "I will see you home." He hailed a cab and during the short ride, thought about what a nice neighbourhood she lived in, then he walked her to the front door, saying he would call her soon, then said goodnight.

She let herself in. What a nice evening it had been, it was so long since she was out on a date. She needn't have been so nervous about it all, she scolded herself, he was really such a gentleman and she hoped they would see more of each other in the future. Maybe life would give her a second chance. Time would tell.

The house was in darkness when Sigmund got home. He quietly let himself in and, trying not to make any noise, walked up the stairs then tiptoed into Nellie's room. She was covered up to her chin, sound asleep. He kissed her good night, she did not stir and he stood looking at her for a minute, thinking how lucky he was to be her father, then slowly turned towards the door. As he got ready for bed, his thoughts went back to Helene. She really was very nice, and the one thing he really liked about her was she did not talk much and was also a good listener. She was, of course, 20 years younger, but seemed very mature and what difference did it make? She was full of life and he would see her again, for he had really enjoyed being with her.

What would Nellie think of her? he wondered. Since being home, he devoted practically all his free time to her. *Well,* he thought, *she will just have to accept that I must have something more than her and my work.* He was half-awake when he heard Nellie walk quietly over to his bed; he opened his eyes and said that she was ready to leave for school.

"Good morning, how did you sleep?" he asked.

"Just fine, thanks," Nellie answered. "I missed you at dinner. I hope you had a nice time."

"As a matter of fact," said Sigmund, "I did. I had dinner with someone you know."

"Oh," said Nellie, "who could it be?"

"Well, I will give you a hint…she was at the party." Nellie frowned. "I don't know…" Then all of a sudden, her face lit up. "You mean the lady who came by herself?"

"Yes," said her father. "Her name is Helene." Nellie knew exactly whom he was talking about. She leaned over and kissed her father on the forehead then told him she needed to get going as she headed for the door. Sigmund thought she sure was in a hurry. Nellie raced down the stairs. Helene… Helene… What was it Rachel said? "Your father sure seems to like her." She got to school just as the bell was ringing and would now have to wait until recess to tell Rachel and try as she might to pay attention, it was hard and her mind wandered off. Her father had dinner with Helene. Would anything come of it? She hoped not. As soon as class was over, she went straight to Rachel.

"What's up?"

"Oh," said Nellie, "guess who my father had dinner with last night?"

"How am I supposed to know?" asked Rachel, laughing. "Oh wait, yes, I know!" she said, turning serious. "I bet it's that lady, the kindergarten teacher."

"Yes," answered Nellie.

"I told you your dad seemed to like her, but you didn't believe me when I mentioned it, so now who is right?" she asked.

"I guess you are," said Nellie. "But it doesn't mean much, does it?"

"Yes," said Rachel, "that's the way friendships start, then they develop into relationships and just think, Nellie, you might someday have a stepmother. Helene as a stepmother!"

"Rachel, stop," cried Nellie, "my father would never remarry."

"Who says? I know, we shall see," said Rachel. "There is no need to get so angry, Nellie, you can't change things anyway, so why don't you just calm down? How many times have they seen each other?"

"I guess just once," Nellie replied.

"That's a beginning," said Rachel.

"I thought you were my friend," said Nellie.

"I am," replied Rachel, "I put you wise to it, but you didn't believe me."

The bell rang just then, and they both headed for their classrooms in silence. Nellie decided to forget the whole matter and concentrate on what the teacher was saying. She knew her father, she was sure nothing would come of this friendship and Rachel would be wrong. The days went by fast; summer was at the door and with it came the end of the school year. Nellie's time was filled with preparing for final exams, which would take place in a couple of weeks. She'd made up her mind to forget about Helene and she had.

Helene had not heard from Sigmund since they went out to dinner, but deep in her heart, she knew he would show up again someday. She was looking forward to the holidays and was thinking about spending some time in Brussels, she had family there and it would be a nice change. Sigmund had not heard anything from the Ulrichs. The house was still in the back of his mind and he sometimes felt tempted to call but refrained from doing so, knowing too well nothing would come of it. He would just have to bide his time.

Helene hadn't left his mind, either, but he had just been too busy to make time to see her. He was thinking of taking a week off and going somewhere with Nellie. They had never been away together and it might be a lot of fun. He didn't want to go too far, somewhere in the countryside, he thought and decided on Bad Durkheim. His family had come from a little village called Friesheim, which was about a half an hour's drive from where they would be staying. He talked to Nellie about it, saying he thought it would be a nice week for both of them, and interesting for Nellie to see where his part of the family came from.

"Yes," said Nellie, "but what else is there to do?"

"Oh," said her father, "there's lots to keep us busy. We can go for long walks and there is a delightful city close by, but most important of all we can relax, sleep late and enjoy our time together. I am sure you will not be bored."

"Not with you, Daddy," answered Nellie with a smile, and knew her father would try and show her a good time. "So when are we leaving?"

"I thought about taking the first week in July off, is that good for you?" he asked.

"Yes," said Nellie. "School will be over by then."

"Good, then I shall go ahead and make the reservations."

He felt guilty about not having called Helene so the next evening before leaving the office, he gave her a call.

"What a pleasant surprise," she said.

"I have been meaning to call you, but I have been very busy. I just wanted to let you know I am still alive."

"Well, that sure is a great thing," she replied. He wanted to know how she had been getting on and what her plans for the summer were. She told him about going to Brussels to visit some family for a couple of days then spending time with her family in Wiesbaden. He listened attentively to all she had to say, thinking the entire time how nice it would be to have dinner with her again.

He had several meetings scheduled, but thought he might be able to squeeze it in the following evening. He had been so immersed in his own thoughts that he had not realised Helene had finished speaking. Her voice calling his name interrupted his thoughts.

"Are you still there?"

"Yes, yes, I am," he replied, "I was just about to ask if you would like to join me for dinner tomorrow night."

Helene hesitated. "No, Sigmund," she said. "I am sorry, but I can't, I have a prior engagement."

"That is too bad," he said, "maybe another time."

"Sure," said Helene. He then told her he was going away for a couple of days with Nellie but promised to call her when he returned. She wished him a good time with Nellie, and they hung up. She did not move, but instead looked about the living room then stood up and arranged the porcelain figure on the small table by the couch. It was not true, she was free tomorrow night, but her mother had always taught her it was better not to be too available. She now regretted it, for she was sure she would not see him for a couple of weeks since he was going away and she was also leaving. *Oh well, if something is to come of it, it will,* she thought, and she smiled to herself. She had to wait and be patient, but he had called and she was sure she would not have to wait as long for the next one.

Nellie could hardly wait for her father to come home. She met him at the front door and handed him her grades. They were excellent; it was no surprise to him, for Nellie really applied herself. "They are very good, I am proud of you," he said, handing them back to her. Just then, the door was flung open. It was Paul.

"A family reunion at the front door!" he said with a twinkle in his eye.

"Yes, kind of," said Nellie. "Today was my last day of school for this year," she said, looking at him. He asked how she did and Nellie handed her grades over to him.

"They are really very good. It was a tough school year as well," he added.

"I am so happy, I can forget about getting up early and doing homework and now I can really enjoy myself."

"You sure have earned it," said her father, "but I'm afraid you won't be able to sleep in tomorrow since we are leaving. I would like to make an early start."

"But," she said, turning to her father, "I thought it wasn't a long drive."

"It's not, but it would be nice if we could leave early, the scenery is really beautiful."

Nellie was not looking forward to this trip. To see where her father's family came from and to go for long walks all sounded so boring, but as it was only one week, she resolved to make the best of it and packed her bag before going to bed; she did not need much. She remembered to take a couple of nice outfits with her, just in case.

Sigmund woke up early. It was a beautiful, sunny day, perfect for what he had in mind. He read his newspaper and then woke Nellie who was sound asleep. Not a morning person, she could stay up until all hours of the night, but when it came to getting up, it was quite a fight. She was very good about being on time for school, though. Slowly, she stretched opened one eye, then the other and looked around her, groaned, stretched and finally greeted her father, who was standing by her bed, smiling.

"It is a gorgeous day outside, just perfect, so let's try and get a move on so we can enjoy it," he said. Nellie shot him a look as if to say, I will do the best I can, as she sat up in bed. Anna had a big breakfast waiting for them when they came down. One never knew what to expect on the road these days, she said, and Paul agreed with her. Sigmund was impatient to be off but he did not rush Nellie through her meal. While she finished, he packed the car. Anna handed him a basket with some sandwiches she'd made for them. One never knows, she said, with a twinkle in her eye. Sigmund knew better than to argue so he thanked her and set the basket on the back seat then went back into the house; Nellie was coming down the stairs. They were finally ready. Paul and Anna stood in the doorway, waving at them as they drove off.

They drove in silence and, being Saturday, there was not much traffic so they soon reached the outskirts of the city. It was warm and not a cloud in the sky. Sigmund looked at his watch. "We should be at the hotel by 4 pm if all goes well," he said.

"Is that counting a lunch stop?" Nellie asked. Sigmund nodded.

"That's not too bad!"

"I told you it would be a short drive," he replied. The different shades of green on the countryside sparkled in the sunlight and flowers were blooming everywhere. There was something soothing about the colours. Sigmund called his daughter's attention to it and explained how no one has been able to duplicate the colours of nature. Depending on how the sun hits them, they become a shade lighter or darker and one can see it very well by looking at the trees and the grass. Nellie looked and saw what he meant. "It really is quite amazing," she remarked, then continued to drive in silence.

Nothing escaped her father's eye. Why don't I see the little things like Dad does? I guess it's a talent one develops as one grows older, she answered herself. Her father's voice interrupted her thoughts. He was telling her that he had received a phone call from Lina Ulrich the day before. "What did she want? Did they accept your offer?" Nellie asked excitedly.

Lina had invited him over for coffee and was surprised to hear that he and Nellie were going away for a week. He did not mention his offer nor did he ask any question, just that he would call her upon his return.

"All I seem to do in life is wait," said Nellie, exasperated.

"What do you mean?" asked her father, taking his eyes off the road to look at her.

"I had to wait until I was old enough to be able to stay up late, I had to wait for you to come back to have a father and now I have to wait to have a home of my own."

"Well, that's life, Nellie. If everything were just the way we wanted it when we wanted it, if we just had to move our little finger to get it, don't you think we would take it all for granted?" her father asked, and without waiting for an answer continued, "The things we appreciate the most, and you will realise this more and more as you grow older, are those that have cost us effort and time."

Nellie thought for a minute. "I guess you are right, as usual," she said.

"I told you this once and I am saying it again, when the time is right, we will have our home." They were driving south on a narrow country road, the River Rhine was to their right and one could catch a glimpse of it behind the vineyards. Sigmund brought the car to an abrupt halt. Nellie, who had been dozing, opened her eyes and looked about her.

"Why are we stopping?"

"It's time for lunch," replied her father. "And it will do us both good to stretch our legs." Nellie nodded her head in agreement then Sigmund came around to her side of the car and helped her out, having parked the car alongside what looked like a quaint inn. "I think you will enjoy the food here," said Sigmund. "I have eaten here before and the place is really very cosy."

It was a nice, warm summer day and tables had been set up in the garden, but Sigmund chose to eat indoors. They sat at a table by the window from which they had a great view of the river and ordered their lunch. Sigmund pointed out to her that it was owned by a couple, she served the guests and her husband did the cooking. The meal was wonderful, but what Nellie enjoyed the most was the dessert. They had freshly baked fruit pies served with fresh cream on the side. She ordered an apple pie and told her father it was the best she had ever eaten.

Sigmund chatted with the owner for a while. Business was slow, people were hard pressed for money and preferred to eat at home. Before the war, farmers from the neighbouring villages would bring their families for a meal, usually on a Sunday, but now everything had changed. The cost of living had gone up so much that everyone was having trouble making ends meet. Several times they thought about closing down the restaurant, but they really enjoyed what they did and there were, of course, the occasional travellers who stopped by who were a welcome distraction and always had some news. In addition, they sold the land they had inherited from their parents and invested the money in the restaurant, so their only option was to look for work on one of the farms. But, having been self-employed for so long, they could not see themselves working for somebody else.

Nellie listened politely to the conversation going on around her but her father could tell she was getting bored. He looked at his watch and said that they must be on their way, asked for the bill, paid and left. "She sure does like to talk," Nellie commented once they were in the car.

"One has to be tolerant, they probably don't see many people and they must get pretty lonely," her father said. She agreed.

Nellie was quiet and looked at the scenery; it was really very beautiful countryside. "Are we almost there?" she asked after a while.

"We do not have much further to drive." Sigmund pointed out a sign by the road that read Friesheim as well as a small narrow road that led up a hill. "My great, great grandparents came from that little village," he informed her.

Nellie opened her eyes wide. "Have you been there?" she wanted to know. He had. She made a motion with her hand, let's drive up to it! But Sigmund hesitated for a moment, reasoning that it's getting late and that they were both tired and they could come back while they are still there. She nodded her head. About half an hour later, they pulled into their hotel.

It was a small country inn with a huge garden around it. The owner herself came out to greet them. Apparently, she knew Sigmund well.

"It's been a long time since I last saw you," she said, shaking his hand. Sigmund agreed and introduced Nellie to her. She gave her a big friendly smile and commented on how she was the image of her mother. Nellie made a mental note of it. Their rooms were side by side on the second and last floor, overlooking the garden. They were simply decorated but sparkling clean. The bed, with its fluffed out eiderdown, looked especially inviting. "Do you like it?" asked her father.

"I love it. It is so nice and cosy."

It was almost dinnertime, so they agreed to meet in an hour. Nellie walked around her room looking at everything and then stood by the window. She would have to ask the owner about her mother. Nellie hardly remembered her and there were so few people she knew who had known her. Did her parents come here often and what brought them here? This would be a question she would ask her father at dinner.

She unpacked her suitcase, hung up her clothes and then, looking at her watch, decided she had time to take a bath. Sigmund lay on his bed and looked around him. It was just as he remembered it. *So many memories,* he thought to himself, and drifted off to sleep. He did not sleep long. He dressed for dinner and knocked on Nellie's door. She was ready. This was something he really appreciated about her, always being on time, and he told her so. The restaurant was just as cosy as the rest of the house and they were shown to a table in a quiet corner. After their order had been taken, Nellie turned her blue eyes full of unspoken questions on her father. He took a deep breath and, going back in time, gave her the following account.

The day after the wedding, which had taken place in Frankfurt, he and Alice drove down here for their honeymoon. They both would have liked to spend it in Gstaad where they met, but it wasn't possible, for he had only been able to take a couple of days off so they decided to drive down the Rhine Valley and stop midway between Germany and Switzerland. They stumbled on this small country inn and were immediately taken by it; the vineyards, the river, what a romantic setting: the perfect place for a honeymoon, far away from the crowds and noise of the big cities.

The landlady had been so kind and friendly and she gave them her best room, going out of her way to make their stay unforgettable. They went for long walks along the riverbank, fed the ducks and geese and enjoyed just being together with the sound of the flowing water. After a wonderful time, when they returned home and celebrated their first wedding anniversary, Alice was pregnant with Nellie. After Alice's death, he came back several times on his way to Frankfurt, finding peace and comfort here. Now Nellie was here with him and he looked very much forward to showing her around, ending his story with a smile. Nellie listened in silence, not once taking her eyes off her father. "You must have loved mother very much," she said. He just nodded his head and took her small hand in his.

There were not very many guests and as they were leaving the restaurant, the owner came up to them to wish them goodnight. She turned to Nellie with a smile and said, "Remember, if there is anything you need or I can do, just call me." She returned her smile and said she would.

Nellie woke up early the next morning to the sounds of the birds singing. Her room was flooded with sunlight. After stretching and looking around she thought, *What a beautiful day.* And decided to get up and explore. She went to the window looked out, the garden looked so inviting, then bathed, dressed and went downstairs but just as she was about to walk out the front door, she heard her name called. It was the owner.

"Child, you are up early, did you sleep well?"

"I have never slept better," Nellie replied and told her she was going out to explore the garden.

"Why don't I come with you? I have some time to spare and I could show you around." Nellie agreed, saying it would be fun and the owner said, "Please call me Brigitte," as she walked up to her. "Everyone calls me by my first name."

They walked around the garden; everything was in bloom, what a variety of colours and flowers. They could hear the river in the distance. Brigitte showed her the vegetable garden, which was her pride and joy, saying that everything she served in the restaurant came out of this garden. Nellie agreed it was all so tasty. They then walked down to the river and found a beautiful spot between the trees from where they could see it and listen to the flowing water. Nellie mentioned what a beautiful place it was and Brigitte agreed. They sat down on the grass and stared out on the water. Nellie broke the silence.

"I was only three years old when my mother passed away, so I do not remember much of her, could you tell me what she was like?"

The question took Brigitte by surprise. "She was very beautiful and looked a lot like you, with a great figure and always smiling. Your father and mother were a beautiful couple. I must say, I only saw her on two occasions, when they spent their honeymoon here and a year later, but they were very much in love and your father took great care of her. They would go for long walks and were always laughing. It was such a joy to see them, seeming not to have a care in the world. I am sorry I cannot tell you more, but I really did not have much contact with her, it was all so short."

"I know," said Nellie. Then she glanced at her watch and stood up. "I must be going in, Daddy is probably already up and waiting for me to join him for breakfast. It was very nice talking to you."

Brigitte gave Nellie a hug. "I enjoyed sharing my river with you," she said. They walked together in silence towards the house. Sigmund was sitting in the lobby, reading the morning newspaper, and looked up as she came in. Nellie told him where she had been while making their way to the restaurant. After discussing all their options, they finally decided to drive to Friesheim. Nellie was very keen on seeing the village where her forefathers had come from.

It was a half an hour drive from where they were. Vineyards lined the road all the way up to the village, which they partially hid, and the houses were all well kept and flowers were everywhere. It was really very picturesque. Sigmund parked the car on a street off the village square. "What a nice place this is," said Nellie.

"It is indeed. Can you imagine what life must have been like several hundred years ago?" Sigmund asked.

Nellie frowned. "It must have been very peaceful," she replied, as they made their way back towards the village square. The very old church was right across from it and they strolled through the square, taking their time before sitting down on an inviting bench to take in their surroundings.

"People led a very simple life in those days," said Sigmund, continuing the conversation. "This place has not seen much change and just like today, the vineyards were the most important agricultural activity. Now, everything is done with machines, in those days it was all done by hand."

"So, your great-great grandfather must have been a vineyardist," said Nellie.

"Yes," said Sigmund, "he was. As time went by, some moved to nearby towns, but this is originally where my father's side of the family comes from. Many years later, my grandfather decided to move to Wiesbaden but in order to do this, he needed permission from the king."

"Why? What king?" asked Nellie.

"The King of Hessen, for this part of the country belonged to that kingdom," replied Sigmund and continued on as though he had not been interrupted. "You have surely learned this in school, but in those days, Germany did not exist as a state. It was made up of different kingdoms and it was only under Bismarck in 1847, if I remember correctly, that all the different states were united into one country, which is the Germany we know today. Although that is not exactly right either, for it has suffered a lot of changes. This part of the country has changed hands very often during the centuries between the French and the Germans, so sometimes we were French and sometimes we were German, which is why most of the people from this region speak both languages."

"That's quite amazing," said Nellie.

"It really is and one cannot realise what it means until one sees it written, for instance on death-or birth certificates. One member of the same family could have his birth certificate written in French while the other member could have it German, which meant one was French and the other was German. Even today, Germany is not what it was before the war. You have surely heard talk about the reparations?" Sigmund asked.

"Yes, I have. As a matter of fact, we analysed their meaning in school not so long ago and, come to think of it, Daddy, some parts of the country no longer belong to Germany even today. They now belong to Poland."

"That's right," said her father. They were silent for a while, as Nellie took it all in. There were not very many people around; everyone seemed to be out in the fields. Her father interrupted her thoughts. "Shall we continue our walk?" he asked, and Nellie nodded in agreement.

They headed towards the little graveyard that lay behind the church. The gate was unlocked; it made a groaning sound as Sigmund pushed it open. They walked along the small alleys and he pointed out a couple of tombstones to her. "See here," he said, "this one is written in French and here, this one is in German. So, if you look at the dates, you will know exactly when this part of the country was occupied by the French, which usually happened after a war. The French were especially keen on annexing this territory, for the river gave them access to the North Sea."

"I see," said Nellie. "Look Dad," she said, turning towards her father, "here's one of your great grandfathers' tombs, our family name is written on it."

"So it is," he replied, looking at the date. "I'm sure if you look around closely you will find some more." Nellie looked around and sure enough, they were all close by. "This must have been the family plot," Sigmund continued, as he took a closer look at them. He became thoughtful. "We were such a big family and now there is just Paul and myself and, of course you."

"It's sad, but I guess that's life," said Nellie.

"Shall we go?" asked her father, striking a lighter tone. "Are you ready to do some more exploring?" she said she was and so they retraced their steps, Nellie heading in the direction of the car. Sigmund stopped her. "I would like to show you the vineyards up close, do you mind? It is not a long walk."

"Not at all," she replied, and they turned left and walked towards the end of the village. As her father had said, it really was a very short walk to the vineyards, starting right where the graveyard ended. There was a bustle of activity. Men, woman and children were busy in the fields. "So here is where everybody is," said Nellie.

"This is a very busy time of year. If you look closely at the vines, you will see small little clusters of grapes." Nellie moved up closer and saw what her father was talking about. "These will grow and later on, when they are big and ripe, will make excellent wine. From this stage on, they have to be protected from the birds so, even though as you can see there are scarecrows everywhere, they are not enough so everyone is out here helping cover the clusters."

"It seems like a lot of work," said Nellie.

"It is," her father replied. "Not many realise how much work goes into making a good bottle of wine," he said with a smile. Walking on for a short while, then turning back towards the village, they felt dusty and thirsty, so they got into the car and headed back towards their quaint little inn. Nellie was also hungry and tired.

What a great day they had, thought Sigmund to himself, and Nellie really seemed to enjoy herself. Then his thoughts went back to an issue he had not been able to deal with: Helene. He wondered who she had a date with that she was unable able to accept his dinner invitation. He was really intrigued, but knew he would never know the answer. The next days went by fast. Sigmund took a lot of pride in showing Nellie around, taking her on the same walks he had taken with her mother and sometimes even felt Alice's presence. On one of these occasions, a Jewish saying came to his mind:

"As long as the dead are remembered, they have not died."

He finally understood its meaning.

They were having dinner on their last evening and enjoying their meal when all of a sudden Nellie broke the silence by asking, "Dad, would you ever remarry?" Sigmund was taken completely by surprise.

"Why do you ask?" he wanted to know, "I haven't really thought about it."

"Well," replied Nellie, "I was just wondering. You have taken me back in time to when my mother was alive, and I have had the impression all this week that she was with us. Not only was she with us," she continued, "but that you loved her very much and you miss her. So I was just wondering."

Sigmund did not reply immediately. "You are right, I did love your mother very much and I have also felt her presence. I have not thought about remarrying, but I have not ruled it out either. Let me explain," he said, seeing a look of surprise on Nellie's face. "I'm still young and although I have you, you have to become your own person. One of these days you will fall in love, get married and have a home of your own. That is life. I'm not looking for anyone, even though I feel very lonely sometimes and think it would be nice to have someone to share my life with, but if I were to meet someone and fall in love again, yes I would marry. Does that upset you?" he asked, looking her directly in the eye. Nellie swallowed hard.

"It does surprise me," she said.

"I hope that if the question should ever arise, and that is a big if," he said, giving her a broad smile, "that you will be understanding."

"To use one of your expressions, Daddy, let's cross that bridge when we get to it."

"I could not agree with you more," replied Sigmund, and then, changing the topic of conversation, he told her how much he had enjoyed her company this week and felt he had really gotten to know her better, she had been so much fun to be with. "I hope it hasn't been too boring for you."

"Not at all," replied Nellie, for she too had gotten to know her father better and felt much closer to him, especially since he had shared his memories with her.

They were up fairly early the next morning, as Sigmund wanted to be back in Frankfurt by mid-afternoon. Brigitte was sorry to see them go and told them how much she had really enjoyed their company, adding that she looked forward to seeing them again someday. She handed Nellie a small paper bag. "I have filled it with herbs from the garden so that you may garnish your salads with them," she said, and Nellie thanked her then Brigitte gave her a big hug and shook hands with Sigmund. She felt sad. Maybe they will be back someday, she thought to herself, and went back inside.

Neither Nellie nor Sigmund were in a talkative mood, so they drove in silence. Neither of them was hungry after the huge breakfast they had eaten, so they did not stop for lunch and were home by mid-afternoon. Paul looked up from his book, startled. *It's too early for them to be back,* he thought, getting up to check the front door. He collided against his brother. "Why, what a surprise," he said, "I was not expecting you home till later. Did you have a nice time?" he asked Sigmund.

"We sure did," replied Nellie, going on to explain that her father had wanted to be back by mid-afternoon.

"I have lots to catch up on," he said, turning to Paul.

"Well, nothing much has gone on in the office this past week but before I forget, Mrs Ulrich called this morning and wanted to know when you would be back. She asked that you contact her as soon as it is convenient for you."

"I will," replied Sigmund. "That was one of the things I had on my mind since I really want to decide on this house once and for all. If it is not meant to be, I can just forget about it. I am sure we can find another one that is to our liking."

"I hope you won't have to," Paul said, watching him go upstairs. *He sure is in a hurry,* he thought to himself before going back to his reading. Sigmund was, in fact, in a rush. There was one call he wanted to make before it got any later and it was not to Mrs Ulrich.

Chapter 4

Sigmund set his small suitcase down by the bed and found what he was looking for in his wallet. He picked up the phone and dialled the number on the card. He hoped there would be an answer. The phone rang and rang and at last, he gave up. *Where could Helene be?* he asked himself, then all of a sudden he remembered: she said something about visiting family in Brussels and then spending the rest of the holidays in Wiesbaden. "Oh well, at least I tried," he muttered to himself, then he rang Mrs Ulrich's number. She answered almost immediately, inquired about their trip, then asked if he would accept an invitation to coffee and cake the following day. He accepted, saying he would be over as soon as he could leave the office. It was not until late afternoon that he was able to free himself. In order to gain time, he hailed a passing cab. It was rush hour and traffic was bad. He should have known better but as he was running late, he thought unwisely that he could save some time. As it turned out, it seemed to take forever.

The driver was in an unfriendly mood, complaining not only about the traffic but the whole political and economic situation; jobs were very scarce, the cost of living went up with every passing day and it was almost impossible to make ends meet. Only a revolution like the one taking place in Russia could change things, in his opinion, but the government was very quick in putting an end to the slightest uprising. He was convinced that under the traditional parties nothing would ever change. His and the hopes of many others were in this new party that touched the soul of the people with its nationalistic ideas: Germany for the Germans.

Sigmund listened with interest. How much the country has changed, he thought to himself. He read about this new party and felt a growing unease. He finally reached his destination and let out a sigh of relief. He knocked and Lina opened the door almost immediately. Gretchen recognised him and barked a happy welcome. Everything was just the same. David was in the living room with his face in the newspaper. The news gets worse and worse as the year goes on, he said by way of greeting.

"I know," replied Sigmund. "I am afraid there is not much one can do, except bury one's head in the sand like an ostrich, but what good would that do?" he asked. Lina came in just then saying she remembered how much he had liked her chocolate cake and had baked one that very morning.

David set his newspaper down and told Sigmund he really appreciated him being patient and not pushing him for an answer. The couple who had been interested in the house had made an offer, it had been a little better than his, but they needed the house vacated within a month and that was out of the question. "When would *you* need the house?" Sigmund replied that he was not desperate, that he had a roof over his head, and David went on to explain that they would only be able to turn the house over to him in three months' time. If this was acceptable to him, the house was his.

Sigmund could not believe his ears. His offer was being accepted and he would have three months to get everything ready... What great news. He stood up, but David silenced him with a wave of his hand. There was still one more issue and that was the payment—half the amount now and the rest upon taking possession. Sigmund shook David's hand and said, "You have a deal, sir. And Nellie and I have a home."

Lina was overjoyed; she gave Sigmund a hug and told him that now she would finally be able to give the movers and the family dates. "What about Gretchen?" she asked, stroking the little dog's head.

"Don't worry about her," said Sigmund. "She will have a home with us." Lina was happy and relieved, the endless uncertainty finally coming to an end. After taking down all the information he needed to make the money transfer, Sigmund took his leave. Lina told him he should feel free to bring Nellie over at any time as she escorted him to the door.

His heart was bursting with happiness. Paul had been so right, three months was no time at all and he needed time to get all his furniture out of storage anyway. He could not wait to give Nellie the good news. It was still early so he decided to take a detour and walk by Helene's building; he had tried calling her again late last night but received no answer. What if she were back? The windows on her floor were dark but just as he was about to walk away, he saw somebody walk out the entrance.

"Are you looking for someone?" asked the stranger.

"Not exactly," replied Sigmund, "I just wanted to pay a friend of mine a call, but she does not seem to be in."

"Who are you talking about?"

"I was referring to Miss Helene," replied Sigmund.

"I am her neighbour and she is away, but she will be back Saturday. May I introduce myself? My name is Birgit, would you like me to give her a message?" she asked. Sigmund hesitated for a minute and then, taking a card out of his wallet, handed it to her.

"If you could just give her this," he said. Birgit was all too happy to oblige. *Now at least she will know I have not forgotten her,* he thought to himself as he headed home.

Nellie had been at her grandmother's and returned a short while before. Suddenly, she remembered her father say something about having a meeting with the Ulrichs, so she left in a rush, telling Mrs Winters that she just remembered something and needed to leave right then and there. Her grandmother gave her a surprised look but did not pursue the issue further, knowing how private her granddaughter was.

Nellie walked back as fast as she could but was very disappointed not finding her father at home. Where could he be? He should have been home by now, absolutely positive that the meeting could not have taken that long. She paced up and down her room, going from one window to the other. "Why is he not home?" she asked herself time and time again, when at last she saw him turn the corner: Finally!

She raced down the stairs and opened the door just as he was looking for his keys. "Why hello," he said, looking very much surprised. "Are you going somewhere?"

"No, no," she replied, "I have been waiting for you for hours. I saw you come around the corner and came down to let you in." She could not wait any longer. "How did it go? Do we have a home?" she asked.

Sigmund gave her a big happy smile. "Oh, so *that* is what has been on your mind."

"It sure has and I have done nothing but dream about that house all day."

"Well, it's no longer a dream—the house is ours," replied Sigmund.

"I am so happy," she said, giving her dad a big hug. "When do we move in?"

Sigmund interrupted her. "I can answer that question once I have gone inside, washed my hands and relaxed." Nellie had not realised she was blocking the entrance.

"Sure," she replied, moving out of the way. Overjoyed, she went back to her room, starting right away to go through all her things. She would have quite a lot to move, but she had no furniture. Would her father buy her some, and if so, she asked herself, what would she really like? Unable to come up with an answer, she dismissed the thought and started getting ready for dinner, confident her father would give her all the answers at that time.

Paul and Sigmund were in the living room, waiting to be called to the table. Nellie looked absolutely radiant as she walked in. "Why, don't you look beautiful tonight," said her Uncle Paul.

"Thank you," she replied, blushing. "I guess it's all the excitement over the house. Has Dad told you about it?" she asked.

"I was just about to tell him and now, since you are here, I will only have to tell the story once," he replied with a smile. Then Anna came in to let them know dinner was served and Nellie waited impatiently for all to be seated and served then, unable to wait any longer, started prying her father for details. He told them all about the meeting and yes, they were keeping Gretchen, the only hitch was the three months delay. Could they not take possession sooner? That seems like a terribly long time. "I am afraid not," said her father. "But time will go by very fast and we will be busy finding everything we need so we can move in."

Now that he had mentioned it, Nellie wanted to know what she was going to furnish her room with and what about his bedroom—and the rest of the house? Sigmund patiently explained that the furniture was in storage and he was sure that they had more than enough to furnish the whole house with. Nellie gave a happy sigh, at least the uncertainty was over, she said. Paul was happy for them, but he also felt a little sad. It had been so wonderful having them and Nellie sure brought a lot of life into his home. He would miss them both very badly but he hoped they would come and visit him often. Their rooms would always be waiting for them. Sigmund gave his brother an affectionate look and returned the sentiment.

Helene had a great time visiting with her family in Brussels and they had all gone to Knokke Le Zout for a week. The water was a little too cold for her to bathe in, but she walked on the beach and ate the freshly caught baby shrimp that were a delicacy. She would watch the fishermen's wives walk up and down the shore, calling out that they had fresh baby shrimp for sale to the passers-by.

The women fascinated her. They did not seem to get tired, their wide skirts billowed in the wind and their faces were rugged from the elements. Sometimes they would have their small children with them who would follow their mothers barefoot, stopping to play in the sand or stick their toes in the water. Upon hearing their mothers call, they would quickly stop what they were doing and, with a mischievous look on their faces, run to catch up with them. They looked so innocent and neither offspring nor parent seemed to have a care in the world. She had also gone to Bruges and had taken a boat ride down the canals, thinking that the city was absolutely charming. She stood for hours watching the women make lace. What patience they had; the lace was a work of art, no wonder it was cherished all over the world.

Even though it was not one of her favourites, she stayed a couple of days in Brussels then spent the rest of her time in Wiesbaden and enjoyed being with her sisters, whom she had not realised how much she missed. Her mother, who worried about her not eating properly while being on her own, went to no end of trouble preparing her favourite dishes. Helene ate mindfully, for she did not relish gaining weight. Her summer had been a very happy one indeed and now that the time had come for her to return to Frankfurt, she thought about her flat, her work and the people she knew. She thought of Sigmund once or twice, curious about how his trip with his daughter had gone and asked herself if he would call her again.

Helene regretted not having accepted his dinner invitation and even though she felt she did the right thing, she would be sorry if he did not give any sign of life, for she really cared about him. As teary-eyed as she was bidding farewell to everyone at the station, her sisters promised to pay her a visit in Frankfurt and she promised to return as soon as she got some time off. It was mid-afternoon when she arrived home. It was raining. She walked into her home; it looked so inviting, thinking with a smile how nice it was to be back in her own four walls.

She had just finished unpacking her suitcase when there was a knock at the door. Who could it be? It was Birgit. "May I come in?" she asked.

"Sure," replied Helene. Birgit told her about meeting Sigmund and handed her his card. Helene stared at it in her hand without uttering a word. Birgit felt she had to break the silence. "He is very handsome," Birgit said to Helene who replied, "Yes, yes he is." Her heart was racing; he had not forgotten her and was not offended. She turned to Birgit and thanked her coming to relay the message.

"That's what friends are for," replied Birgit and Helene muttered something like, yes I guess so, without paying much attention to what she was saying. "I have a dinner engagement, so I must be going," said Birgit.

"I hope you have a great evening and thank you again," replied Helene, closing the door behind her. She sat down on the couch. He came by, he has phoned and he has not forgotten me. Should I call him? "No," she said to herself, "I will wait. I'm sure he will call."

She was getting ready for bed when the phone rang. She knew immediately who it was and she was not disappointed, the caller was Sigmund. After inquiring about her trip, he invited her out to dinner the following evening. He said he hoped she was free, hinting at his last invitation. "I am," said Helene and he told her he would be by to pick her up about 8 pm. She was overjoyed and it seemed as if life was going to give her a second chance after all.

Sigmund made a point of leaving the office early in order to have enough time to go home and change before going to pick up Helene. There was no sign of Nellie or Anna. *They may have gone out,* he thought to himself while he got dressed. He ran into Nellie just as he was leaving. She gave him a surprised look; you look so handsome Daddy, where are you going? He told her he had a dinner engagement and would probably not be back until late then gave her a goodnight kiss and jokingly told her he hoped she would not miss him too much. Nellie giggled and said she thought she might be able to survive dinner without him. He gave her a hug and let himself out.

He arrived at Helene's right on time and she was ready. As a matter of fact, she had been ready for the last thirty minutes. After trying everything on that she had in the wardrobe, she finally decided on a burgundy dress, knowing the colour suited her very well and the style very becoming. She opened the door and invited him in, and Sigmund thought how beautiful she is as he followed her in. The living room was small but cosy and he looked at the pictures placed on one of the tables while she went to fetch her purse. She found him standing where she had left him. "This is my family," she said, picking up one after another and introducing him to them.

"You sure do resemble your mother," he said with a smile.

"Yes," Helene replied, "we are very much alike in many ways."

"It must be nice having a big family," Sigmund commented.

"There's never a dull moment," she said with a smile.

Sigmund looked at his watch. "Our dinner reservation is in twenty minutes, I think we had better be going." They hailed a cab and Sigmund gave the driver the name of the restaurant. Helene had never been there before but she'd heard a lot about it. It was one of the best known in the city. They were given a table in a quiet corner. The décor was simple yet very elegant and there was not one empty table. The food was excellent, too, and so was the bottle of wine Sigmund ordered to go with it. After tasting it, he told her the name of the region where it came from then mentioned his visit to the village of his ancestors and to the vineyards, remarking how much hard work and time went in to making a good bottle of wine, which was usually taken for granted. They talked about themselves and their plans for the future, and fully enjoyed the evening.

As they were leaving, they ran into Rachel's parents. There was no way Sigmund could avoid them and so he greeted them with a smile and introduced Helene. Rachel's mother gave her a penetrating look and informed them that they were celebrating their wedding anniversary. Sigmund congratulated them. She then inquired about Nellie and said she would have Rachel give her a call, for now that they were both back, they might be able to do something together. Sigmund agreed and said he would tell Nellie about their encounter, then took his leave.

As it was a lovely evening, they walked part of the way, afterwards they took a cab that he dismissed upon arriving at Helene's, for he wanted to walk home. He saw her to the front door, she did not invite him in, so he bade her goodnight and thanked her for a lovely evening, promising to call her later in the week.

It was a twenty-minute walk, there were people on the street and the moon was shining bright. In his mind, he went through the events of the evening. The food had been excellent and Helene really seemed to enjoy herself. She was more beautiful than he remembered and it was so easy to be with her. He really enjoyed her company and they had a lot in common. Then he recalled his encounter with Rachel's parents. "Oh, well," he thought to himself, making a mental note not to forget to tell Nellie with whom he'd had dinner. He thought about how it would not be proper for her to hear it from Rachel and of one thing he was sure, that was the first thing Rachel's mother was going to mention to her.

The light was on in the living room, an indication that Paul was still up. Sigmund walked in and asked his brother if he might join him in a nightcap. "Sure," said Paul. Sigmund remembered all of a sudden that he had forgotten to let Paul know that he would not be home for dinner. He started to excuse himself, but Paul waived him off saying he was lucky he had a very good secretary. Sigmund raised an eyebrow, not understanding what he meant until he realised that Nellie took care of it.

"You look as if you have something on your chest," remarked Paul. "Would you care to talk about it?" It was amazing how both could understand what was going on in the other. Sigmund told him about his evening with Helene.

"She is really beautiful and has a wonderful figure, as well. I like her a lot but I am a little worried about getting emotionally involved."

"Why?" Paul wanted to know.

"She's 20 years younger than I am, and that is a very big age difference. Then there are my memories of Alice and, of course, Nellie."

Paul listened without interrupting, then a long silence. "I do not understand what is worrying you," said Paul, finally. "She is beautiful, intelligent, young, single, you get along well, you enjoy her company—and you are afraid of getting emotionally involved? I think you are very lucky to have met someone like Helene and if I were you, I would take the chance destiny has given you. Age is irrelevant, what matters is how old your heart feels and yours is young. I have met men in their 30s whose hearts are over 70 and you certainly are not one of them. Also, it would be nice for Nellie to have a mother figure since she hardly knew her mother. She is almost an adult now and will be leaving home sooner than you think, so I see no problem there. If Helene is as intelligent as you claim she is, and with her background, I am sure she will win Nellie over in no time. And, as an afterthought, you might want to start a family again. I certainly could do with a little nephew," he added, smiling mischievously at his brother.

"I guess I should just let time take its course," replied Sigmund, and decided not to mention the conversation he and Nellie had about the subject.

"I like Helene a lot," said Paul, "and I sure do look forward to seeing a lot more of her."

"I guess you will," replied Sigmund. "Time will tell." Then he headed upstairs to bed, feeling relieved at having shared his emotions and uncertainties, knowing in his heart that Paul was right. He also knew that he was falling in love. He decided before dropping off to sleep that he would leave a little later than usual for the office the next day and join Nellie for breakfast, who was surprised to find him still home when she got up.

"I thought I would have breakfast with you, to make up for my absence last night at dinner," he said, smiling as she came in to the room. She walked over to him and gave him a hug then asked him over breakfast about his dinner engagement. "It was actually very enjoyable," and added matter-of-factly, "I had dinner with Helene."

Nellie looked at him in surprise. "You had dinner with Helene?" she repeated in disbelief.

"Yes," replied Sigmund.

"You seem to be seeing quite a lot of her," said Nellie in the tone of voice she used when she disliked something.

"What if I am?" replied her father, getting defensive and giving her a stern look. "I think she is very nice, I enjoy her company and have you forgotten what I told you at dinner not so long ago?" he asked.

"No," replied Nellie, blushing, "I have not and I understand that you have to have a life of your own."

"So what worries you?" asked Sigmund and without waiting for an answer. "You're not going to lose me and I will always be there for you," he said, trying to comfort her, for he could see she was very upset. "I am sure once you get to know Helene, you will really like her and find that she is a lot of fun."

Nellie did not reply and Sigmund wisely decided to change the subject. He told her about running into Rachel's parents and suggested she give her friend a call. Nellie said she would and finished her meal in silence. Her father left for the office as soon as they finished eating.

Nellie was on her own. Her father and Helene. She could not think of anything else. The sound of the doorbell interrupted her chain of thoughts and she wondered who it could be. It was Rachel. "What a surprise," said Nellie, "I was going to call on you a little later."

Rachel had spent a couple of weeks with her parents in the south of Spain and had gotten a beautiful tan that really was very becoming. She explained that her parents had told her about their encounter with Sigmund and she had decided to come and see her. She was dying to know what Nellie thought of what was going on and sensed that her friend was not in too good a mood so decided not to bring up the subject, even though it had been the main reason for her coming. She was sure that Nellie would eventually discuss it with her and she did not have long to wait. Rachel was in the middle of a sentence trying to describe somebody she had met when Nellie interrupted her somewhat rudely.

"So what did your mother think of Helene?" Nellie asked. Rachel told her how surprised her parents had been; they never expected Sigmund to date anyone, especially someone so much younger than he, but she wanted to know how Nellie felt about it.

Nellie thought for a minute and replied that she was also very surprised. Rachel went on to tell her that she should not be, that she had warned her and, giving her a cruel smile, said with a sneer, "You will have Helene as your stepmother. She will come first, she will be the queen of the home and everything will revolve around her, just you wait and see. Speaking about houses, what ever happened to the one your father was going to buy?"

"Oh," said Nellie, very much relieved that Rachel had changed the subject, "Daddy bought it and we will be moving in less than three months' time. He and I will decorate it and I have already chosen my room. And of course, Gretchen will have her basket just outside my door."

"Who are you talking about?" Rachel asked.

"Oh," said Nellie, "that's right, I haven't told you, but Gretchen is a dog and she comes with the house."

"I see," said Rachel. "But I don't think things are going to work out the way you have them planned. With Helene in the picture, she is going to be moving in as well, and she will decide whether you can keep the Gretel or whatever the name of the dog is, and she will assign your room to you and your father will let her have it all her way."

Nellie could feel her pulse racing. "Daddy would never let anyone boss me around and make me unhappy. I am the only one he has and he has always told me he will be there for me and look after my interests. Besides, he, too, is entitled to having someone to share his life with. He's been a good father and I have no objections whatsoever. Why are you being so mean to me? I thought you were my friend. I know now I was wrong, so please leave. I never want to see or talk to you again."

Rachel was taken back. She never expected Nellie to defend her father, or to kick her out. "You don't have to tell me twice," she said angrily. "I am leaving." And she opened the door and walked out, banging it behind her.

Nellie let out a sigh of relief having stood her ground. She had never felt so much hate as she just did, listening to Rachel, but wondered why she hated her and why was she trying to create animosity between her and her father. It might be envy, she said to herself, but she could not find an explanation that really satisfied her and felt miserable. She had considered her a friend but now she realised she'd made a mistake, no true friend would create such hostility. She needed to go and get some fresh air. But where to? She made a mental list of options and finally decided she would go pay her grandmother a visit. She might be able to answer her question.

The walk had a soothing effect on her. Mrs Winters was a late riser and was having her breakfast when Nellie walked in. "It's been a while since I have seen you child, how nice of you to make some time for me," she said. Nellie walked over to her and kissed her on the forehead.

"I know, it has been quite some time, but you are always in my thoughts," she said, pulling out a chair. She answered all her questions about everything she had been up to and mentioned what a lovely time she had had with her father.

"Oma, could you help me find an answer to something?" she asked.

"It all depends on what it is, but maybe, between the two of us, we can come up with an answer," she replied.

Nellie thought for a minute, trying to frame the question without mentioning Helene or her father. "How would you define a friend?" she finally asked.

Her grandmother looked at her thoughtfully. "Let's start by differentiating a friend from an acquaintance, that might make it easier," she replied. "An acquaintance is somebody with whom you have fun, but it is all very superficial, and a friend is somebody who shares in your joys and sorrows, feeling them as if they were their own. It's called empathy. There is no envy, no jealousy, just trust. A friend is something very special, indeed, and that is why there are not many around. No war, no distance will break up a real, honest friendship; it transcends everything, no matter what the circumstances might be. You have to remember something child," said Oma, taking her hand, "all friendships start out as acquaintances. As one gets to know the person better, one will find maybe some common ground, or some similar circumstances, which could be the seed from which a friendship will grow."

"I see," said Nellie. "Well, I guess I just have acquaintances and I have not yet found a real true friend."

"You will someday. It's not easy, which is why one can count one's friends on the fingers of one hand," replied her grandmother. She wondered what triggered this conversation but knew better than to ask. "Are you satisfied with the answers?" asked her grandmother.

"Oh, yes," replied Nellie, "I am. I guess I had better be going," she added, "I have to get ready for school."

Mrs Winters had not realised that the beginning of the school year was right around the corner. "It won't be long before you move into your new home," she remarked.

"No, it won't, but even though the time has gone by very fast, it is still very far off," said Nellie, getting up from her chair. She gave Oma a hug, thanked her for her help and said she would try to come and visit her soon before heading for the front door.

Mrs Winters was very thoughtful. She knew her granddaughter very well and even though Nellie tried to conceal it from her, she could tell that something had upset her terribly. She must have had an argument with one of her friends, but which one and what could it possibly have been about? She went through the names of the girls she knew, then looked up, startled, so deep in thought that she had not heard the maid enter or call her name. "Maria, you scared me," she said.

"I'm sorry, I did not mean to, I just wanted to tell you that Mrs Ulrich is on the phone."

Mrs Winters got up and went to take the call. She told Lina that she had been thinking about her and hoped all was going well with her move. Lina assured her that everything is going according to schedule then went on to tell her about running into a friend at the hairdresser's early that morning. "I am sure you know her, it's Mrs Weiss, Rachel's mother," she added as an afterthought.

"Well, what about her?" asked Mrs Winters, unable to conceal her impatience.

"She only mentioned that your son-in-law seems to have fallen in love." Mrs Winters took a deep breath and the puzzle began to come together.

"I'm glad," she replied, then changed the subject.

Lina was disappointed at not getting any juicy gossip and cut the conversation short. "So, it was Rachel," Mrs Winters mumbled to herself, putting the phone back on its cradle. She always hoped Sigmund would find someone to share his life with someday and if he had, she was genuinely happy for him. It looked as if life was moving on in giant steps.

Nellie settled into her school routine and ignored Rachel completely.

Sigmund made a point of seeing Helene at least twice a week. It was not always easy for him, but on the rare occasions where he could not make it, he really missed her. At first, they would go out to dinner, Sigmund introducing her to the best restaurants in town and she really enjoyed the different foods, but she could also see the effort he was making. He would come by looking so tired sometimes that she really felt sorry for him, having to sit through a long meal, for the service, no matter how renowned the restaurant, was generally very slow. So, one evening she decided to surprise him.

It was a Wednesday and pouring rain. Sigmund arrived not only looking tired, but wet as well. "I think we should be going," he said greeting her.

"Oh," replied Helene. "I decided to prepare dinner here. I thought it would be nicer if you did not have to go back out in this weather."

He looked surprised. "Are you sure?" he asked.

"Of course," said Helene, "I have everything ready." Sigmund went to dismiss the taxi, thinking how considerate she is on his way to the door. She had set a beautiful table and bought his favourite wine. The food was excellent and he complimented her on it. She blushed with pleasure. "My mother taught me to cook," she said.

From then on, they ate at Helene's and went out to dinner only on very special occasions. They were becoming closer and closer, Sigmund found in her a real companion and she gave him back his joy of life. There was also a complicity between them that he had not known with Alice. Helene knew she was in love, she tried fighting it at first, the age difference had been an issue, but she finally gave up. She felt a deep gratitude to life for giving her a second chance.

Nellie was very much aware of her father's relationship. He had made it all too clear to her that he needed to have his own life and she resolved to respect his privacy. Rachel's comments still lingered in the back of her mind and she hoped that they would never materialise. Still, it came as a shock to her when her father announced one evening at dinner that Helene would be joining them for lunch the following Saturday. Sigmund gave her a look. Nellie bit her lip and made no comment.

Helene had mixed feelings about this encounter. Sigmund spoke about his daughter for the first time a couple of evenings before and Helene sensed that she was very possessive of him. She also realised, however, that her relationship not only involved Sigmund, but his daughter as well. She would do her best to try and become Nellie's friend.

Nellie took the 'wait and see' attitude and could only hope that nothing would come of it. Sigmund made a point of having breakfast with her on Saturday morning and they spoke about school and a new girl in her class, then he inquired about all her friends but she never once mentioned Rachel. He thought it kind of odd but did not pursue the matter further. They also discussed their new home. In just a month's time, the house would be theirs. "It's been such a long wait," Nellie remarked, but her father reassured her that it was almost over and there was a lot to be done. Nellie wanted to know what.

"Well, the furniture has to be sorted out, which means going to the warehouse and seeing what's there," he replied.

"When are you going to do that?" Nellie asked eagerly. Her father said it would probably be the following weekend. Nellie thought for a minute. "Could I come with you?" she asked, and her father said with a smile that he didn't see why not and that he always enjoyed having her with him.

"I have to pick up Helene in an hour and am going to walk there. It's such a beautiful day, would you care to come with me?" he asked. Nellie did not answer immediately. She might as well go she thought, it would make her father happy and her not going would not change anything, anyway. She said she would and, beaming with pleasure, he told her she'd better get ready. Nellie said she would hurry.

Paul overheard the end of the conversation as he walked into the dining room. "Did I hear her say she was going with you to pick up Helene?" he asked.

"Yes, I am quite surprised myself, maybe things won't be as difficult after all," said Sigmund.

"You have really fallen in love, little brother. Are you planning on getting married?" Paul asked. Sigmund told him about how he was torn between his loyalty to Alice and his own feelings, but he realised with every passing day that life was really a gift made up of a great many choices. One was either aware of them, took them or let them go by, but once they were gone, they never came back. He had been given the choice of living his life as he had up until then or sharing it with someone. The decision had been placed in his path and he had chosen.

It would not be easy for Nellie, but he knew she would eventually come to terms with it. He had not yet proposed, but purchased an engagement ring once it was clear to him that this was what he wanted. He hadn't met her parents yet, but they were planning on going to Wiesbaden in the next couple of days. "I am happy for you," said Paul. "And maybe I will have a nephew after all."

"I don't know about that, but you will definitely have a sister-in-law," said Sigmund, getting up from the table. "I had better get ready, I do not want Nellie to have to wait for me," he added.

Paul finished his coffee and stared into space. He was happy for his brother, but it was also going to be very hard on Nellie. He was sure Sigmund did not realise what a big change this would be for her. He recalled several conversations with her about the house and Gretchen and how she looked forward to decorating it and having a home just for her father and herself, but now that she and her father would be sharing it with a complete stranger, her dreams would be shattered. Yes, hard times lay ahead for her. Paul loved his niece very much and he resolved to give her all the support he could.

Nellie dressed in a hurry. She was conscious of the thought behind her decision to accompany her father, having recently read in one of her books the following sentence:

"It is always wise to look the enemy in the eye."

She'd made a mental note of it and considered Helene her enemy because she was taking her father away from her. "How pretty you look," said Sigmund when she joined him.

"Thank you, you look very nice yourself," replied Nellie. She wanted to say sarcastically: 'I dressed in honour of the occasion' but wisely held her tongue in check. Paul said good-bye to Sigmund and gave Nellie a big hug, telling them he would see them again at lunch. They walked in silence. It was a gorgeous day. Sigmund asked her if she had seen or spoken to her grandmother lately, she replied she'd had breakfast with her a couple of days ago.

"I really want you to see a lot of her, she is growing old, and she is so wise. You can learn a lot from her," said Sigmund. "You are right, Dad, she is a fine lady and she always finds the right answers."

"Why don't you come to me?" he asked.

"Well, Dad, a lot of the time you are not home and there are some things you would probably not understand anyway." She hesitated for a minute, asking herself whether she should tell him about Rachel, but decided against it.

"Like what?" he asked.

"Oh, like girl stuff," she replied. "How much further have we got to walk?" she then asked, changing the subject. Luckily, it was just around the corner.

"You can see the back of the building from here," Sigmund said, looking at his watch before ringing the doorbell. "We are right on time," he said.

Helene opened the door almost immediately. She was wearing a suit that was very becoming. Sigmund kissed her on the cheek and she shook hands with Nellie. "Do come in," she said. Nellie looked around. Her living room was very cosy, indeed. Sigmund told her that they had walked over, it was such a beautiful fall day and there were probably not many left. "Yes," replied Helene, "winter is not very far off." She turned to Nellie. "You must be thirsty; can I get you something to drink?" she asked.

"I would love a glass of water," Nellie replied and Sigmund said he would have the same.

"These are pictures of her family," Sigmund told Nellie, noticing she was looking at them.

"Oh," said Nellie, "she must have a big family."

"Yes," replied Helene, overhearing the conversation, "I do." Then proceeded to tell Nellie briefly about her sisters, as she served them their drinks. Nellie listened attentively then, when Helene was finished, remarked how nice it must be having brothers and sisters.

"As you know, I am an only child," Nellie said.

"Yes, I know," replied Helene.

"I take it you have not been out today?" Sigmund asked. Helene told him she had not and would really enjoy walking back with them if they were not too tired. Sigmund turned a questioning look at Nellie who said that she was not at all tired and added that they might walk back through the park. They left shortly afterwards.

Her father and Helene walked side by side, Nellie trailing behind them. She had not noticed how much taller Helene was than her father but aside from that, they did make a handsome couple. The walk through the park was beautiful. The leaves were turning and they sparkled in the sunlight, standing out against the green of the pine trees. It was not long before they were home. Paul had been on the lookout for them and Sigmund was holding his key in his hand when the door was flung open.

Paul gave Helene a hug. "It's been quite a while since I last saw you," he remarked.

"It has indeed," she replied. He then led them into the living room where they made themselves comfortable. An awkward silence ensued. Paul finally broke it by asking Helene how she had spent her holidays. She told him about her trip and then turned to Nellie asking her if she'd had a nice summer. Oh yes, she replied, she had, then she went to great lengths to describe the week she and her father spent together. Helene listened politely but could not ignore the message. Nellie was making it quite clear to her that she was not only close to her father, but that they also enjoyed being and doing things together.

Sigmund listened to the conversation going on around him, feeling very relieved that all was going so well. Nellie was being very sociable, he thought, then Anna interrupted his chain of thought by announcing that lunch was served and everyone followed her into the dining room. Before sitting down, Sigmund made a point of introducing Helene to her. "She is the heart of this household," he told her, "and everything revolves around her. I really don't know what we would do without her," he added. Anna replied that they would all surely survive.

"How long have you been with Paul?" Helene asked. Paul answered for her that it has been so long, she has become a member of the family. Anna felt a little embarrassed and excused herself. Paul kept the conversation flowing. Anna had cooked a delicious meal and everyone enjoyed it. Nellie was quite bored. She could tell by the way her father and Helene looked and spoke to each other that there was a lot more going on than met the eye. She tried, without succeeding, to silence her inner voice. It kept on repeating: Rachel is right, Rachel is right. Sigmund sensed that Nellie was not enjoying herself so he excused her as soon as she finished eating her desert.

Nellie ran up to her room and flung herself on her bed and asked herself: Why was life so unfair? She had lived so long without a father and now that he was finally home, and it was just the two of them and they could do all these things together, he had to fall in love. Where did that leave her? How she wished her Uncle Paul had never held that garden party. That's where it had all started. If only—there were so many 'ifs', but she knew that she could not change anything. She drifted into a restless sleep until her father's voice woke her up.

"You must have been exhausted," he said. "Anna came up to ask if you would care to join us for coffee and cake, but you were sleeping so soundly she decided not to disturb you."

"I am sorry," replied Nellie. "I did not hear a thing."

Sigmund told her that he was going to take Helene home and invited her to join them. She could tell he really wanted her to come so she said she would and that she would be down in a minute. Helene greeted her with a smile. "I must have been very tired, it was not my intention to be gone so long, but I fell asleep," she said.

"Don't worry," replied Helene. "You should always listen to your body." Helene said goodbye to Paul, thanked Anna for all the trouble she had gone to and as she was leaving, Paul told her he expected to see her soon. Helene smiled.

This time, she made a point of walking at Nellie's side and hoped that she would someday get to know her, breaking the silence by telling Nellie all about her sisters and all the pranks they used to play on one another while they were growing up, describing each one of them in turn. She said she admired her mother for putting up with them, for they were always so full of fun that a day never went by without one of them getting into some kind of trouble.

Nellie listened to her attentively and at one point was unable to control her laughter. Helene described it all so vividly that Nellie had no trouble picturing it. Sigmund smiled from time to time, overhearing some parts of the conversation since he could tell Helene was trying to build a bridge between them. "I wish I'd had some brothers and sisters," said Nellie when Helene had finished. "Growing up as an only child couldn't have been easy," Helene stated.

"You are absolutely right," Nellie agreed.

"It does have some advantages, though. You get to wear new clothes all the time and not hand me downs," replied Helene. "My oldest sister got everything new and we would only got something new to wear on our birthdays."

"That is true," replied Nellie. "But then, you always had someone to do things with. I have friends of course, but it is not the same, for you either have to go to them or they have to come to you and just that little factor of not living under the same roof creates complications. So basically, I just have my dad, but he is not always around and he does not always have the time, either. I must say, though that he has always made a point of finding the time so that we can be together. It was not always this way when he was in the military. I lived with my grandmother and I really did not see much of him, being stationed in different parts of Germany, so it really was not easy for him. But on the rare occasions when he managed to come home, we had a great time. My grandmother tried to make up for it as best she could. She is a lot of fun to be with and is so very wise. She can always find an answer for the most difficult question."

"You must love her very much," said Helene. "You are very lucky to have her. I only have vague memories of mine. I never met my grandfather."

"I was lucky," replied Nellie. "My grandfather passed away not too long ago, he was a lovely person but a lot stricter than Oma and he did not spoil me as much."

Before they knew it, they arrived at their destination. Helene invited them in but Sigmund declined. He kissed her on the cheek.

Nellie shook her hand. "I enjoyed talking to you," said Helene.

"So did I," replied Nellie, then added: "The walk felt so much shorter."

"It sure did," replied Helene.

"Well, goodbye," said Nellie. "I am sure we will see each other again soon." Then she asked her dad, catching up with him, "Are you in a hurry?"

"No, why?"

"I was just wondering," she said.

"Because I declined Helene's invitation to come in?" he asked.

"Yes," she replied.

"It is still early and I thought it would be nice to have some time just the two of us, so what would you like to do?" he asked. "Why don't we go to my favourite café? I would love a slice of cake."

"That sounds like a good idea, I could do with a good cup of coffee."

"You're right, Dad, she *is* a lot of fun."

"I told you so. You have to get to know a person before judging them."

"I think she loves you," said Nellie.

Sigmund looked at her in surprise. "What did you say?" And Nellie repeated what she had just said. "What makes you think that?"

"I can tell by the way she looks at you, by the way she talks to you."

"Interesting," replied Sigmund.

Nellie thought for a minute. "Dad, do you love her? You enjoy being with her, but do you love her?"

Sigmund hesitated. He had never lied to his daughter, but he knew it was a little early for her to know the truth. "Let's put it this way," he began. "I miss her and I look forward to seeing her."

Nellie thought over what he had just said. "That does not answer my question."

"What is love?"

"I guess it is a lot of things," said Nellie.

"You are right, there are different kinds of love but this is going to lead us into a very long discussion and we have reached our destination," said Sigmund very much relieved. "We are both tired, so why don't we just sit down and enjoy our coffee and slice of cake."

"You've got a deal," replied Nellie. The place was crowded but luck was with them and they were given the last table. Nellie enjoyed watching people. Sigmund was waiting for his check when he caught sight of Abraham and his wife who were waiting for a table.

"Look who's here," he said to Nellie but she said she didn't see anyone she knew. He told he would be right back and Sigmund went and walked up to them.

"What a surprise," Abraham said, "it has been a long time since we've seen or spoken to each other."

"Yes," replied Sigmund. Sara asked about Nellie and Sigmund replied that he was here with her. "Why don't you join us?" They followed Sigmund to the table. Sara commented that Abraham had not been at all well and had had several medical check-ups. Abraham cut her short.

"Since we last saw each other," he told Sigmund, "life in this country has not gotten any better and if anything, it has gotten worse. The military says it wants peace and a republic, but they are not at all happy with the conditions set by the Allies and will never accept their loss of power. Just you wait, mark my words; they are going to find some way to rearm themselves again."

"Do you really think so?" asked Sigmund.

"I am convinced of it."

"I hope you are wrong."

"What is your view on the political situation?" Abraham then asked.

"One issue that worries me a lot is the clause in the constitution concerning the presidential powers, which, as you know, enables the President to govern by decree. I find it extremely dangerous because if enforced, the President can govern without a parliament and it could lead to the end of democracy and to a totalitarian state. It is something to bear in mind for the future. We have so many parties right now and getting them all to agree, or to form a coalition, is not going to be an easy task and that is when the use of this presidential decree could come in handy. In the wrong hands, I hate to think about the consequences but with Ebert as President, I don't think we have much to be concerned about. He has a lot of integrity and I strongly believe he only has the country's best interest in mind."

"You have brought up an interesting issue," said Abraham.

Nellie and Sara were having their own conversation then Nellie gave her Dad a look.

"I'm afraid we must be leaving. Paul will be wondering where we are as we told him we would be back shortly and we have been gone longer than we intended," said Sigmund.

"I do hope we will see each other soon," said Abraham, shaking Sigmund's hand.

Sigmund and Nellie had no sooner left than Sara turned to her husband. "You were so busy talking to him, you did not give me a chance to confirm the rumour about him and Helene," she said.

"I am glad you did not; it certainly would not have been very prudent to do so in front of Nellie," he replied.

"I had not thought of that," said Sara, "but you are right."

"Sigmund brought up a very interesting point," he said, and told Sara about it. "I don't think many people realise the potential danger of that clause."

"I am sure they don't, they only see the positive aspect of it," replied Sara.

"Oh, well, just one more thing," said Abraham.

"Now don't get all stressed out," replied Sara. "Let's try and enjoy life while we can," she added, then changed the subject. "This cheesecake is delicious. And Nellie is such a smart and nice kid, if the rumours are true, I really hope Sigmund knows what he is doing and that he has prepared her for it. Nothing and no one can replace a mother's love. Nellie is practically an adult and I do hope Helene will have sense enough to treat her like an equal." Abraham did not answer. "You are not even listening," mumbled Sara.

Tired of walking, Sigmund and Nellie were home in no time after hailing a cab. Nellie went straight to bed. Sigmund told Paul about his encounter and conversation with Abraham.

"I am afraid Abraham is right," said Paul.

The week went by fast. As promised, Sigmund took Nellie to the warehouse to see everything that was there. He told her that most of the furniture had been in their home when her mother was alive and after she died, he put it all in storage. "How funny life is," he said, then changed the subject and showed her his desk, mentioning that it had been his grandfather's. Nellie said how nice it was. "Yes, it also brings back many memories."

They spent a lot of time looking around and there were several boxes stacked one upon another. "What's in them?" Nellie wanted to know.

"All of my books. I am looking forward to organising my library. You probably do not remember it, do you?" he asked.

"I do, vaguely," answered Nellie.

"I guess we have everything we need. And look, there is your bed and night table," he said, pointing at them.

"So, I *do* have furniture for my room," said Nellie, looking pleased.

"You sure do," replied Sigmund.

"I can't wait to move into our own four walls," remarked Nellie happily.

"We may have to do a little work on the house before we move in, so you might have to wait a little longer," he told her.

Nellie gave him a surprised look. "I thought you liked the house the way it is," said Nellie.

"I do, but I have been giving it some thought and I believe it might be worthwhile to have the house repainted, as well as some minor things done to it before we move in. It makes life so much easier if they are done before hand," replied her father.

Yes, Nellie was right, it had been his intention to move in right away but now things had changed. With Helene becoming a part of his life, it would be her home as well and he knew that she, like any other woman, would want to give it her own personal touch.

A shiver ran down Nellie's spine. She put two and two together since there could only be one reason for his change of heart, and that could only be Helene. Why had she not believed Rachel? She tried to calm her inner voice, she might be wrong after all.

Her father was staring at her. The look on her face anguished him. Should he tell her the truth? He asked himself if it might be the right timing and hesitated, but decided against it. He had still not proposed to Helene and what if she turned him down? There would be many more occasions to do it.

Nellie broke the silence. "We have been here long enough," she said. "I think it is time to go home. There is nothing more left for us to do."

"Let's go," said Sigmund, and they drove back in silence.

Nellie opened the door before the car had even come to a full halt. She barely greeted her Uncle Paul, whom she met on her way to her room. Paul took one look at her and knew that something was terribly amiss but would hear about it soon enough. Sigmund went straight to the library and was making himself a drink when Paul came in.

"Nellie nearly ran me down as I was coming downstairs," he said. "She looked as if she were about to be sick. Is anything wrong, Sigmund?"

Sigmund took a deep breath. "I do not know what to say or what to think," replied his brother. "Everything was going fine, she was happy and excited looking at the furniture until I happened to mention that we might not move in right away. I can still see the look of anguish on her face," said Sigmund. "I don't understand what could have caused it."

Paul gave his brother a long look. "Are you serious?" he asked. "What about?"

"Nellie is not stupid," said Paul, "and she knows you are dating Helene; she can put two and two together. Have you told her about your intentions?" he asked.

"No," answered Sigmund. "I have not. Once I have asked Helene to marry me, I will tell her and not before. I am going to ask her on her birthday; it is just in a week's time."

"I have something to tell you that might be helpful," said Paul.

"I can't wait to hear what you have got to say."

Paul related the conversation he had with Anna a couple of days before where Anna told him that Rachel had come over the very next day after her parent's encounter with Sigmund and Helene.

Sigmund interrupted Paul. "Nellie never said a word to me about Rachel's visit. As a matter of fact, she mentioned all her friends to me when we were discussing school and I found it odd that she never once talked about Rachel. Did they have a quarrel?"

"Let me continue with my story and you will soon find out," replied Paul. "Anna was upstairs putting away the linens when she heard Rachel telling Nellie that Helene was going to be her stepmother, that she would be the queen of the house and that Nellie would not even be able to choose her room, and that if Helene decided she did not want to have a dog, Nellie would be forced to give it away. Nellie was in a rage, she screamed at her saying that her father would never do such a thing and he would never let her down. Rachel must have said, 'just wait and see' for Nellie, now on the verge of hysterics, told her to leave and that she never wanted to see her again. Rachel left immediately banging the front door behind her. Anna's first thought was to intervene, but decided she had better stay out of sight."

Sigmund turned pale. "That explains everything," he said.

"Thank you for telling me, I just wish you had told me sooner."

"What are you going to do?" Paul asked.

"I do not know, but one thing is certain, I am not going back on my decision. It is my life and I, too, am entitled to happiness," he added with some bitterness.

"You can count on me," said Paul, "but I hope you do realise how hard all this is going to be on that little girl, she will need all the support she can get."

Sigmund ended the conversation by saying he was tired and he needed time to think. He lay in bed unable to sleep. Every time he closed his eyes, he could see that look of anguish on his baby's face. Why had she not told him about her encounter with Rachel, he wondered, and was that the thing she discussed with her grandmother? Then he remembered her mentioning something about her grandmother being able to find the answers to everything. Did Mrs Winters know about his relationship with Helene? She probably did, women loved to gossip and in the Jewish community, they all moved in the same circles. Would she understand? He did not want to lose her as a friend. He decided it would be best if he went over to see her and broke the news to her himself. Yes, that would be best. But he would wait until after Helene's birthday.

Sigmund tossed and turned, then got up and walked quietly into Nellie's room. She was sound asleep. He stood by her bedside, looking at her for a long time; he hated to hurt her, she was all he had of his first true love and he loved her so. He resolved to find the right time to have a talk with her and counted on Helene being understanding. Then he bent down and kissed her lightly on the forehead. She did not stir. He went back to bed, then fell into a deep, restless sleep.

The next day, he left the office earlier than usual since he was unable to concentrate, trying hard to get Nellie out of his mind but now and again that look of anguish would creep up on him like a ghost taking over his mind. It was useless to fight against so he finally gave up. "I will go for a walk," he said to himself, for he did not want to go home and face Nellie just yet and Helene would still be at work. He paid no attention whatsoever as to where he was going and was completely lost in his own little world, going back to the time when Alice was still alive. She had been so calm and always seemed to find the right words when a difficult situation arose. He could feel her presence. It was as if she were walking by his side. All of a sudden, he heard her voice: "Go see my mother," it said. He looked up, startled. There was nobody around. He knew now what he had to do—he would go and see Mrs Winters. Why had he not thought about it before? He looked at his watch. From where he was, it would take him 20 minutes to walk to her house. Deciding against it, he hailed a passing cab. It never crossed his mind that she might not be home.

Mrs Winters had just gotten back from her weekly game of bridge, having taken it up a long time ago, and she always played with the same group of friends. It was the one thing she fully enjoyed, it was so challenging. She heard the sound of the doorbell. Not expecting anyone, she wondered who it could be. There was a knock on her bedroom door. "What is it, Maria?"

"Mr Sigmund just got here, he is in the living room," replied Maria.

"I will be right down. Oh, and Maria, please set the table for two."

Sigmund stood up to greet Mrs Winters. "Why, Sigmund, what a lovely surprise," she said. He gave her a hug.

"I have been meaning to come over for a long time but something always comes up," he said.

"That is life," said Mrs Winters. "How is Nellie?"

Sigmund told her she was fine and very busy with school. Mrs Winters said she had seen her recently, but did not mention the conversation they'd had. "So, what is new?" asked Mrs Winters.

"Quite a lot," said Sigmund. He always felt so comfortable in her presence, the unease was suddenly gone and he started telling her about Helene. The words just flowed; Mrs Winters was an attentive listener and did not interrupt him once.

"I am so happy for you, Sigmund," she said beaming. "I have prayed all these years you might find someone to share your life with and my prayers have finally been heard. Helene must be a very fine woman and I look very much forward to meeting her. Has Nellie met Helene and have you told her you are getting married?" Mrs Winters then asked with a note of concern in her voice.

Sigmund told her that they had already met, but he was waiting to tell her of his plans until he proposed. He then gave her the full account of Nellie's quarrel with Rachel.

"Things are beginning to make sense," said Mrs Winters.

"What do you mean?" Sigmund asked, surprised. She then told him about Nellie's visit and their conversation. A long silence ensued after she had finished until Sigmund finally broke it.

"You know how much I love my child," he said. "I wouldn't want to hurt her for anything in the world. I just wish I could somehow make her understand that even if I marry Helene, my love for her will never change."

Mrs Winters interrupted him. "A parent's love transcends everything but you have to make her a part of your new life, she cannot feel excluded. I hope Helene will be understanding and loving towards her. It is not an easy task she will be taking on. Being a mother to a child that is not your own is extremely difficult, and Nellie is too old and has been on her own for too long to be mothered. If Helene could just be a friend to her," she finished.

Sigmund mentioned the look of anguish on Nellie's face and what had caused it. *She is resenting Helene already*, thought Mrs Winters, *but she kept it to herself.* Maria then announced that dinner was served. Sigmund looked up surprised. "I did not mean to stay this long," he said.

"You had a lot on your mind and I appreciate you sharing it with me. Let's get a bite to eat," said Mrs Winters, taking his arm and leading him to the dining room.

Mrs Winters made him promise he would drop by sometime with Helene. Sigmund left right after dinner, he wanted to get back before Nellie went to bed. Walking home, his heart was filled with gratitude. Nellie was in her room, finishing her homework.

"Hi, Dad," she said, looking up when he came in. He walked over to her desk and gave her a hug.

"I had not planned on being absent for dinner," he said, "but I was at your grandmother's and you know very well how she is, she would not let me leave," he added, smiling.

"I know how it is," replied Nellie. "She must feel very lonely eating by herself and I think even though she does not admit it, it is during mealtimes that she misses my grandfather the most."

"I had not thought about that," replied Sigmund. "But I am sure you are right." He then inquired about school and about her friends.

She mentioned the new girl, her name was Bettina and she was an excellent student. "She must do nothing else but study," Nellie said. "I think there is more to life than just studying for school."

"You certainly put that into practice with all the extracurricular activities you are involved in," replied her father. "But tell me, Nellie, what has happened to Rachel? I have noticed you never talk about her anymore. Has she left school?" Nellie's expression changed and she looked very unhappy.

"Oh, no, she is still here," she answered and tried to change the subject.

"Are you no longer friends?" inquired her father. Nellie thought for a minute. She decided that she might as well tell him.

"It's a long story," she said, sitting down on the bed beside her father. She told him everything and Sigmund listened in silence. He would have to allay all her fears. Tears were running down her face by the time she finished. "Rachel's wrong, isn't she?" she asked, taking her dad's hand. "You're not going to marry Helene, are you?"

Sigmund was very troubled, but even if he hurt her, the moment of truth had come and he could not postpone it a second time. He put his arm around her shoulders and held her close to him. Nellie repeated her question. Sigmund looked her straight in the eyes. "I want you to listen to me without interrupting," he said, and reminded her of their conversation at the inn. He had not been looking for anyone but destiny had put Helene in his path and they had fallen in love. After fighting it for a long time, he realised time and time again how lonely he was and how much meaning she had given to his life. She had become such a part of it that he could not imagine living without her.

He knew that it would not be easy for Nellie, that all three of them would have to adjust to their new life, but, he added, pulling Nellie closer to him, "Nothing is going to change between us. You and I are bonded and nothing can break or destroy that. You were asking me the other day about love," he went on. "There are different kinds of love; there is the love you have for you parents, which is very different from the love a man and woman profess for each other. There is the love between grandparents and grandchildren and it, too, differs from the others, but the love of a parent for his child is unconditional, it is always forgiving and it knows no boundaries. It is unique, it is very, very special, and what makes it so special is the fact that a child is a part of its parent. One love does not exclude the other. I will never love Helene the way I love you, I could not even if I tried, because of all the reasons I have just stated. You do not have to compete for my love either, as I said, and remember, you'll always have it until the day I die. So, you see, there is no reason whatsoever for you to resent Helene, for she is not taking anything away from you, quite the contrary she might be adding something to your life as well."

"Is Rachel wrong, then?" Nellie asked in a small voice.

"She is," replied her father. "And I think she is not a nice and true friend. You will have the room you choose and there is no question about Gretchen. One last thing I would like to add before we say good night. We will all have to be considerate of each other. All I wish is for us to live in harmony."

Nellie's mind was racing. "Do I have to call her mother?" she asked.

"Not at all! There is only one person one can call mother and that is the woman who brought you into the world. You can call her Helene as you do now."

"Dad, one last question, when is the wedding going to be?" Sigmund told her they had not yet set a date but it would take place soon. It is late, he then said, we should be in bed by now; we both have to get up early.

"I know," replied Nellie. "But I promise, this is really the last question. Have you told Oma?"

"Yes," replied Sigmund. "She was very pleased about it. She would very much like to meet Helene, so maybe the three of us could have tea with her sometime." Then he got up feeling very much relieved. Nellie gave him a bear hug.

"Thank you, Daddy," she said.

Sigmund fell asleep before his head hit the pillow. Nellie was tired, too. It had been a very emotional evening for her and even though she had not finished her homework, she decided to go to bed… There was so much to think about. Being confronted with reality and having mixed feelings about it all, she knew that her father had made his decision and there was no turning back. A new chapter in her life was about to unfold.

Chapter 5

Helene came home after a long day. Working with children was never uneventful and she really enjoyed them, but today had been particularly stressful. One child was very restless and had incited the others, so she'd had her hands full. She relaxed on the couch, the colours of the room had a soothing effect on her and she gave her thoughts free-reign. She was happy, or better said contended, with life. It had treated her well in spite of all the sadness she endured during the early stages of the war. The only thing missing in it was a husband and a child. She was very much in love with Sigmund and knew he also cared about her, but she doubted that his feelings were as deep as hers. She longed to have a child, but the hopes for one were diminishing with every passing year. Her thirtieth birthday was in two days' time and, as usual, the weather was cold and bleak. It was November. Would Sigmund ever ask her to marry him? They had been dating for some time, but he seemed quite happy with the relationship the way it was. He hadn't been intimate with her up until now and so it took her completely by surprise when he discussed Nellie with her, that being the first time he allowed her in to his own private world. Would she ever become a part of it? Her family was also pushing her since three of her sisters were married and they asked every time she came home if he had already proposed. She dreaded the question more and more and always got defensive when they would say that he probably would have done so by now, had she led him on.

Her mother was planning a big family reunion to mark the occasion of her birth and scheduled it for the coming Saturday.

Helene hadn't mentioned anything to Sigmund about it, but decided it would be the perfect time to introduce him to her family. They were all very intrigued by him and could not wait to meet him. She attached a great deal of importance to her birthday and had always done something meaningful on that important date. This year would be very different from the rest, for she now had a sweetheart to celebrate it with.

Sigmund was well aware of how much meaning she attached to her birthday, so on Wednesday night, just before turning out the light, he set his alarm clock for midnight. Helene was dreaming; it was a very happy dream for she was dreaming she was getting married, but what was this loud ringing in her ears? It went on and on and on. Then all of a sudden, there was silence and she realised the sound was gone, that it had stopped just as abruptly as it began. She was in the midst of the wedding ceremony when it started up again and suddenly she realised it had nothing to do with her dream. Startled, she sat up in bed. Then it was gone. Just as she was about to lie down again, thinking she must be hearing things, she heard the ringing again. How foolish of me, she scolded herself, it's the phone. She got up to answer it and it was Sigmund.

"This is a wakeup call to announce that your birthday is here," he said, "so happy birthday, dearest." Helene was speechless. "Are you still there?" he asked.

"Yes, I am," Helene said, "how sweet of you to call. What time is it?"

"The clock has just struck midnight," he replied.

"You mean to say that you have been awake all this time just to call in my birthday?" she asked.

"Nothing could be more important to me than being the first to wish you a very happy birthday and I'd like you to know how happy I am that you exist."

She could not believe her ears, was this really Sigmund? The Sigmund she loved? All she managed to utter was, "Thank you so much, you have already made this day very special."

"It has just begun and there is more to come," replied Sigmund. "I look forward to seeing you this evening, and I will try to leave the office a little earlier in honour of the occasion."

"I'll be home," answered Helene. She returned the phone to its cradle and went back to bed, Sigmund's words still ringing in her ears. She did not want to think, all she wanted to do was go back to sleep and return to her dream. The next morning, she awoke to a bright, sunny autumn day. She took her time getting ready and enjoyed a leisurely cup of coffee, going back over the night's events in her mind. Sigmund had never spoken to her the way he had last night, there was so much tenderness in his voice. She did not want to dwell on it and instead wondered what life was going to be like for her now that she had turned thirty. Answering herself, she said it would probably be the same as when she was 29, the only thing that could change it would be if Sigmund were to ask me to marry him and that, she was sure, was not going to happen during her lifetime. She felt a pang of sadness, for she really loved him and knew she would have been a very loving and caring wife. In addition, she would have so much liked to have his child. But she scolded herself for thinking about what she did not have and reminded herself she should be happy with what she does have, to count her blessings and to realise that she is very blessed. All she had to do was look around her to remind herself of them. Then she looked at her watch; if she did not hurry, she would be late.

Sigmund was nervous. He opened the little box and looked at the ring one last time. It was beautiful. Paul came into his office just as he was placing it in his pocket, so he took it back out and showed it to him.

"That is quite a stone," he said admiringly. "She is going to love it. I had completely forgotten that today is the day." And clapped his brother on his back.

"It is, indeed," replied Sigmund, "and I have to admit, I am a little nervous even though I am not a novice."

"Everything will be fine. She is not going to turn you down, why, she is head over heels in love with you."

"What makes you think so?"

"Even a blind man could tell," said Paul.

"I hope you are right, for I have never discussed my intentions with her."

"Well, then, she is in for a huge surprise. But you must be on your way, so good luck." And he gave his brother a hug.

Sigmund stopped at the florist to pick up the flowers he had ordered. They had put together a beautiful, yet very simple bouquet of blood red roses. Traffic was light so the cab he hailed made it to Helene's in no time. After ringing the doorbell, there was no answer. So he waited, then thought, *I told her I would be there earlier than usual, where could she be?* He rang again, but there was still no answer. Growing impatient, he decided something must have happened since it was not like her to make him wait, then felt a growing apprehension.

Just then, the door was flung open and Helene stood at the threshold. "Have you been waiting long?" she asked, out of breath. She'd caught a glimpse of him from a window and ran down two flights of stairs.

"Not at all," replied Sigmund, letting out a sigh of relief.

"One of the neighbours called me over and—" He did not let her finish her sentence.

"Let's go inside, it's pretty cold out here," he said taking her arm. Once in the living room, he turned to her, kissed her and handed her the flowers.

"I have never seen such beautiful roses," she exclaimed, taking a closer look at them. "I'll be right back; I'm just going to put them in a vase."

He went over to the bar and poured himself a drink. She was back in no time. "I have a surprise for you," he said.

"Oh, what is it?" Helene asked. She loved surprises but could never keep a secret herself.

"If I told you, it would no longer be one."

"May I guess?" she asked.

"You can try, but I know you will never find out."

She gave it three tries and Sigmund was amused, listening to the things she came up with, but just as he had predicted, she did not find the answer. "I suppose I will have to wait, then," she said, turning to him smiling.

"I might as well tell you so you can get it off your mind. I have booked a table at the restaurant you have wanted to go to for so long and we haven't been able to get in."

Her face lit up. "You must have read my mind," she replied.

"It's exactly where I was hoping to go on my birthday."

"Your wish has come true then," he said, beaming. "I made the reservation several months ago." He did not mention the time and she did not ask. Changing the subject, he asked her how her day had been and if she heard from her family.

"Oh," said Helene, "you have just reminded me of something." Then she told him about the celebration her mother was having for her and invited him to accompany her.

"I would be delighted to," he replied. "Would you like a drink?" Helene very rarely drank and declined, saying she would wait until dinner. Sigmund got up and poured himself another drink then walked over to the window, looked at the

71

roses and finally came and sat down by her side. Helene watched him and thought that he didn't seem to be in any hurry to leave and so dinner might be a late affair.

Sigmund took a big sip of his drink then turned to her. "I was going to give you your present at the restaurant," he began, "but I have changed my mind. Happy Birthday," he said, handing her the gift he'd wrapped at the florists while he was waiting.

"What beautiful paper, what can it be?" she asked.

"Open it and you will find out."

Her mind was racing. It was such a small package, it could only be jewellery. But…could it be? Would it be? What if it was? Her hands shook but she forced herself to take her time and unwrapped it very carefully so as not to break the paper. Taped to the lid of the box was a card. She broke it loose and read it:

I hope you will say yes. S.

She took the ring out and held it in the palm of her hand. "What a beautiful diamond, I have never seen anything like it." Sigmund took the ring from her and saw that her eyes were moist. She turned to him as he slid the ring over her finger. There was no need for words; he had read the answer in her eyes. Helene was ecstatic. She'd waited so long, remembering the dream—had it been a premonition? She was not even listening to what Sigmund was saying and when she came back to reality, she heard him say it was time to leave. She excused herself to get ready. Her inner voice kept repeating: he asked me to marry him; I'm engaged to be married.

Their table was waiting for them when they arrived. Sigmund ordered champagne and toasted her birthday and their engagement. She was at a new beginning. They discussed the house, which would now be her home, and she was excited about it, agreeing that whatever refurbishing needed to be done, it was best carried out before they moved in. Sigmund told her the Ulrichs would be vacating the house in a couple of weeks, but he would call Lina to see if they could come over before.

Nellie was the main topic of conversation. Sigmund told her that she was in the picture, that she had taken the news very well, but had mainly been concerned about what to call her, for she did not want to call her mother. He said she could call her by her name, just as she had up until now. Helene listened carefully to everything he said and told him she would give her a lot of space. She knew it would take a while for them all to adjust to the new situation and was, however, very confident that they would both get along. Helene had not quite realised it up until this moment that she would be assuming the role of a mother as well as that of a wife at the same time, and spoke her thoughts out loud. He agreed with her.

"That is life," he said.

"And I am sure I have found the very best," then she took his hand and kissed it.

The food and the service were excellent. They had so much to say to each other, so many plans to make and agreed not to wait too long to get married. It would, however, depend largely on the house being ready. Sigmund was excited about meeting her family, he had heard so much about them. Helene wanted him to stay with her for the whole weekend but he thought it best to attend only the celebration, as he needed to spend some time with Nellie. He explained that it would not be fair to her since he had been so busy all week and hadn't seen much of her. Helene was not too happy about it and asked herself if she would ever have him all to herself but her inner voice answered for her: never, for she would always have to share him with Nellie.

It was very late by the time Sigmund dropped her off and he was exhausted. All he wanted now was some rest. The house was in complete darkness and he looked in on Nellie who was, as usual, sound asleep, then went into his room. He laid his wallet on the night table and a paper caught his eye. He picked it up. Nellie had written him a note: I missed you, Daddy. He felt guilty. He had forgotten to tell her he would not be home for dinner. *Oh, well,* he thought, he could not think of everything.

Helene lay in bed, unable to fall asleep. It had been a very exciting and emotional birthday. Too many thoughts were going through her mind: She was getting married and she would now be able to have the child she longed for. Nellie was not going to be easy and she would probably always come first. Helene tossed and turned; finally falling into a restless asleep.

Chapter 6

Sigmund woke the next morning feeling very much refreshed. He was happy and whistled while he got dressed. Nellie heard him as she went past his room.

"Dad must be in very good spirits. I bet he had dinner with Helene," she thought, then suddenly remembered him mentioning something about Helene's birthday coming up and was now sure that had been the reason for his absence. She was finishing her breakfast when her father came in.

"Good morning, Nellie," he said, giving her a pat on the head.

"You must be one happy man today," she said. "Why?" he asked in a surprised tone of voice.

"Because you only whistle when you're happy," she replied.

"You are right, I am happy."

"Is there a special reason for it?" she asked.

"Is not being alive a good enough reason?"

"I guess so," replied Nellie, spreading some honey on a thick slice of black bread.

"Thanks for the note you left me last night, I must say that I have missed you as well, I have been so busy all week, how about we go out for dinner tonight, just the two of us?"

Nellie's eyes lit up. "I would love to, Dad."

"Is there any particular restaurant you would like to go to?" She thought for a minute.

"The Frankfurter Hof might be nice, they have a good selection of desserts," she said.

"Frankfurter Hof it shall be," answered her father.

Nellie looked at the time. "Oh, my, I am late, I have to go." And she went over to him and kissed him lightly on the forehead, calling over her shoulder that she looked forward to the evening, then ran out of the room.

Nellie was right; he was in an excellent mood. The uncertainty was over, Helene had not turned him down and his life was getting back to normal. It wouldn't be long now before he had a home of his own and a wife and daughter to come home to.

Paul was an early riser and always the first to arrive at the office, having to open up for the employees. His father always stressed the importance of maintaining a good relationship with one's employees and Paul indeed enjoyed talking to them and listening to what they had to say, mornings being the only time he had during the day for this. By the time he walked into his office, he usually had a list of things that needed to be tended to. Sigmund arrived just as Paul was finishing a conversation with one of them, greeting them both then continuing on his way. Paul soon caught up with him and followed him into his office.

"It's amazing how difficult life is for most people," said Paul, settling himself into a chair. "The chap I was talking to when you came in has a daughter who is ill and now his mother-in-law has had a bad fall and fractured the hip bone. She needs surgery and they are trying hard to make ends meet. As is our policy, we will help them out with a sum of money, but sometimes one cannot help but wonder how people manage to live and pay their bills. It truly is a mystery to me how the jobless survive and the number is growing with every passing day. The government is trying to pass some laws that would protect the worker, but with so many parties and so many different points of view, the President does not have an easy task of getting them all, or a majority of them, to agree, which makes it very hard for Parliament to legislate." He did not wait for Sigmund to voice in his opinion. "So…did she turn you down?" he asked teasingly.

"No, she loved the diamond and the ring fit her engagement finger perfectly."

"Have you set a date? And what about Nellie, have you informed her?" Paul asked.

"No, we are going to wait until the refurbishing of the house is finished. It really should not take longer than a couple of months," replied Sigmund. "I will break the news to Nellie during dinner tonight. She wants to go to the Frankfurter Hof, of all places, so that is where we are going."

Paul told him he would have to be very considerate and tactful. "Don't forget, Sigmund, she has never had to share you with anyone, so this is going to be a drastic change for her. Be sure you tell her, and make her feel, that she is, and always will be, very important to you."

"I have told her that so many times."

"It does not hurt to repeat it. And don't forget to put it into practice once you are a married man or else you will have a very unhappy young lady on your hands. You are not getting yourself into a bed of roses, that is for sure," Paul added.

"I love your encouragement," replied Sigmund, a trace of anger in his voice.

"I'm just being realistic. And now I have to do some work."

"Thanks for the good advice," said Sigmund, this time earnestly. Paul was right, as usual. He knew he would have to have a lot of patience, but love overcomes everything, he said to himself, smiling and decided to put his personal life behind him for the time being. He had a busy day ahead of him, which would be taken up by several important meetings, leaving him no time whatsoever to think about what was foremost on his mind: What would Nellie's reaction be to the news?

He assured himself on his way home that he had prepared her for it to the best of his ability, but resolved to try and break it to her as gently as possible. Nellie was on the lookout for him and flung the door open as soon as she saw him get out of the car.

"I see you are ready. I will be down in a minute," he said. She looked beautiful in the two-piece outfit he had bought her some time back. *Her grandmother sure has done a very good job of teaching her how to dress according to the occasion,* he thought, changing his shirt. He was ready in no time. It was raining so he decided to drive.

"I see we are going in style," said Nellie, getting in the car.

"With such a beautiful young lady by my side, how could it be otherwise?" replied her father. He looked at her out of the corner of his eye. *She always blushes when I praise her,* he thought, *just like her mother.* He had not thought of Alice for some time and asked himself what she would think of Helene and was sure she would be very happy, even relieved. But would she be worried about Nellie? Nellie was talking to him and he had not heard one word she was saying.

"Daddy, you are not listening."

"I'm sorry Nellie. I was concentrating on my driving. What were you saying?"

"A lot of my classmates are sick," she replied.

"I hope you don't get sick, too," he replied, parking the car then went around to her side and opened the door for her. Nellie took her time looking around the lobby. There was something grand about it. As she walked to the table, she glanced at the desserts. "You were right," said her father, "they do have a great selection."

Once they placed their order, Nellie gave him a detailed account of everything that was going on, not only at school but with her friends as well. He would interrupt her once in a while with a question, giving her the impression that she had his undivided attention, even though he was preoccupied with finding the appropriate time to break the news to her. Nellie paved the way for him, however, by asking him, out of the blue: "Has Helene already had her birthday?"

"What made you think of that?" asked Sigmund, surprised.

"I remember you mentioning it the day we went to look at the furniture," she answered.

"Yes, it was yesterday."

"Oh, I see," said Nellie. "Did you go anywhere special to celebrate?"

"As a matter of fact, we did. I also asked her to marry me. I am sure it comes as no surprise to you, for I had discussed my intentions with you beforehand, remember?"

"Yes," Nellie said in a small voice, taking a long drink of water. Sigmund took her hand. "Helene would like me to go to Wiesbaden this weekend and meet her family, whom I have never met. Her mother is planning a belated celebration for her. I would very much like you to come with me, if you haven't any other plans, but you do not have to give me an answer right now."

Nellie was thoughtful. "I do not think it is a good idea for me to come since you are meeting her family for the first time. I will come some other time."

"Nellie, you are a part of me. I am bringing you into this marriage and I do deem it important you meet my future family."

"I know," she replied, "and I appreciate your taking me into account, Daddy, but I honestly believe it is not the right timing. I will meet them some other time and besides, whether I like them or not, it is not going to change anything, is it?" She was right it, would not make any difference whatsoever.

"Have it your way. I will be back Saturday evening and we can do something together on Sunday."

Nellie told him that she would spend Saturday with her grandmother since it's been quite some time since she's seen her and will have a nice time, as usual. "Have you set a wedding date?" she inquired.

"Not yet, but now that you bring it up, I would very much like Helene to see her new home, and I'm afraid I must insist that you come along with us," said Sigmund.

"I will be more than happy to come with you and I can introduce her to Gretchen, maybe they will become friends," she added with a smile and in the tone of voice she used when she disliked something or when implying something else. Sigmund ignored the meaning behind the words.

"That is a good idea," he replied. "But coming back to your question, it depends on what and when the refurbishing of the house is finished, for we would like to get married and move into our home. I know you can't wait to move in as well."

Nellie thought to herself, *That was before,* but she did not speak her mind out loud. "Daddy, when is the wedding going to take place?"

"If everything goes according to my plans, it should take place in a month, or a month and a half from now," replied her father. The waiter interrupted their conversation, and they ate their meal in silence.

I guess that's pretty well it, thought Nellie. How fast my life is changing. Her father's voice interrupted her thoughts. "What time do you get out of school on Tuesday?"

"I am home about half past six," she answered, "why?"

Sigmund told her he could leave the office earlier, Helene had Tuesday afternoon off and if she could get out of school earlier as well they could all go and see the house that evening. Nellie said she would skip choir practice and Sigmund said he would call Mrs Ulrich to make an appointment for that evening.

He was explaining that, since it was their last week in the house and they were surely going to be extremely busy, he hoped Lina would be able to accommodate them. Nellie was not paying any attention to what her father was saying and no longer cared about the house. She had been looking so much forward to it ever since her father had come back but now she had lost all interest, feeling a great emptiness as if something had been snatched away from her, and wished she could live with her grandmother again. She knew better than to share her thoughts with her father. He would give her one of his stern looks, which she dreaded, and a piece of his mind as well.

Sigmund was very tolerant about a lot of things, but one thing he would not put up with was her behaving like a spoiled child. She had given up long ago trying to play the part, for she only accomplished the contrary, and learned instead to go with the flow. The waiter came around with the dessert cart and they all looked so inviting she had trouble making up her mind, but finally decided on the cheesecake while her father had some strawberries with cream.

"I always end up eating the same desert," said Nellie, laughing.

"I know," replied Sigmund. "I enjoy watching you try to make up your mind. You open your eyes wide and there is a look of expectation and excitement on your face and then—"

Nellie interrupted him. "I just know that I can never go wrong when I order my favourite."

"If we were to apply what you just said to different situations in life, one would say it is better to stay with the known than the unknown," replied her father.

"You are right," said Nellie. If she could only apply it to her current situation, but she knew it was impossible as she would hurt him terribly if she did not move in with them. She had not realised it, but her father was staring at her.

"Is anything wrong?" he asked, concerned. "From the expression on your face, you look like you're on another planet."

"No, I was just thinking what a nice dinner we have had and how much I enjoy going out with you," she replied.

"It's been a long day for you and you must be very tired, let us be on our way," he said. Indeed, she had not realised how tired she was until she got into bed and within seconds, she was sound asleep.

Sigmund picked up Helene early Saturday morning. She tried to persuade him to stay until Sunday, but she did not succeed in making him change his mind. Had Nellie accepted his invitation to come, he would have stayed. Helene made no comment but—was he planning on taking her everywhere, including their honeymoon? Somehow, she would have to find a way of making it quite clear to him that his relationship with his daughter would no longer be his top priority once they were married and would have to lay the groundwork as soon as possible.

Sigmund broke the silence, telling her he had made an appointment with Lina Ulrich for Tuesday evening. He was sure she would like the house and that she would be able to make any changes to it she pleased.

"I will try to make it a nice, comfortable and cosy home," she said.

"I know you will," he replied. Helene could not keep the note of excitement out of her voice as she exclaimed they had arrived at her parents' house. Sigmund brought the car to a halt in front of a large two-story villa surrounded by a big garden.

"We live in that garden in the summer," said Helene, as she led him up to the front door. They did not have to knock; a stout woman in her early sixties was standing in the doorway. "Mama, mama," cried Helene, rushing towards her, hugging and kissing her then, taking Sigmund's hand, said, "Mama, this is Sigmund." She shook hands with him.

"Do come in, please," she said, and they went into the living room where the rest of the family were assembled. Helene introduced him. "Do sit down," said Helene's mother.

Sigmund looked around. One of her sisters asked him if he came from a big family to which he answered no, then told them all about him and Nellie. Helene proceeded to describe her birthday, giving them all the details, the ring was passed from hand to hand. They agreed they had never seen a bigger and more beautiful diamond and everyone seemed excited about the prospects of a wedding. A lot of questions were asked and Helene and Sigmund answered them to the best of their ability. Her eyes glowed with happiness. He could feel the complicity between the sisters. It was a very happy family he was being welcomed into. Helene's birthday took second place, but her mother, who had been listening to the conversation and observing Sigmund out of the corner of her eye, reminded them of the main reason for the family gathering by bringing in the cake. She had baked it and decorated it herself and it truly was a work of art. The gifts Helene received were all hand made by her mother and sisters, a family tradition, having been taught at a very early age to make their own presents for it constituted a way of giving of oneself.

The day went by fast. Night was falling and it was time for Sigmund to take his leave. They all tried to talk him in to staying but he was adamant, assuring them he would another time, then left alone and Helene would take the train back the following day. No sooner had he turned his back, each one of the sisters began commenting on him. Helene listened patiently and then turned to her mother. "What did you think of him?" she asked.

"I like him," she replied. "I do not worry about the fact that he is much older than you, even though right now the age difference is irrelevant, but when you are fifty and he is seventy, it will be a completely different picture. You will be in the prime of life with an old man to take care of. My main concern right now is his daughter. I can tell he is very much attached to her and she probably is as well. I hope you will be able to win her over because I am afraid she is going to see a rival in you and that is not going to make life easy for any one of you. You all are going to suffer, but she is the blood of his blood and blood forgives everything and there is no tighter bond than blood. You are the outsider and I just hope you will be able to deal with the situation when it arises and that you are very much aware of what you are getting yourself into."

"I have thought about it and I am sure I will be able to handle it, Mama," replied Helene, trying to allay her mother's fears but making a mental note at the same time of what her mother had just said. Her mother could tell she was head over heels in love and it would do no good now to try to make her face reality. She brought up five girls and it had not been an easy task, but they had all given her a great many joys and it was thanks to them that she had discovered the clue to happiness a long time ago, which lay in 'live and let live'. She did not expect them to live her life, nor could she live theirs, so knowing that Helene would have to find out for herself, she changed the subject.

Nellie slept in on Saturday morning and woke up in excellent spirits. She bathed and dressed and it was almost lunchtime by the time she was ready. She decided to skip breakfast, as it would ruin her appetite since she was sure her grandmother would have told Maria to cook her favourite meal. Nellie always looked forward to her time with her grandmother, but this time she could barely wait to see her. After reflecting on the reason for it, she concluded it had to do with the latest developments. She would have a good long conversation with Oma, and Oma was such a good listener.

She ran down the stairs and was about to open the front door when she heard Paul call her name. "Hey Nellie, where are you going in such a hurry?" he asked, coming towards her.

"Hi Uncle Paul, I am on my way to see Oma."

"I am sure you will have a nice time with her, but how have you been? It has been a while since I have seen you to talk to, how is everything?" he asked.

"I guess everything is OK," she answered in a small voice.

"You sure don't sound too happy," he said.

"I know you will not tell Daddy, but you are right, I am not happy about so many changes in such a short time."

"I understand what you are saying, Nellie," he said, putting his arm around her shoulder, "but time is the best adviser."

"What do you mean by 'time'?" she asked.

"Everything is a matter of time. You will get used to the new situation, everyone is going to have to adapt to each other but, as they say, there is no pain that lasts 100 years and you can always come to me, you know that, don't you?"

"I know, Uncle Paul, I can always count on you." She looked at her watch. "I really have to be going," she said. "Oma does not like to be kept waiting." She broke away from him and was out of the front door in a flash, arriving at her grandmother's as Maria was getting ready to serve lunch. "I am sorry, Oma, my Uncle Paul held me up as I was leaving," she excused herself.

"That is quite all right, child, you are just in time." Maria had prepared all her favourites. Mrs Winters could tell by one look that Nellie was not happy; she looked pale and had lost some weight. "Have you not been feeling well?" she asked, making herself comfortable in her rocking chair in the living room. Nellie settled herself down on the footstool beside her chair. It was her favourite seat and she would put her head on her grandmother's lap who would then stroke her head. When she was little, and would fall sound asleep like that, her grandfather would pick her up in his arms and set her down on her bed.

"No, I haven't Oma, but a lot of my classmates have. Why?"

"It might just be my eyesight, which is failing me, but you do look a little pale," she replied. Nellie put her head in Oma's lap and her grandmother stroked her head. There was something very soothing in the way Oma's fingers ran through her hair. She was almost half asleep when she heard Oma ask about school and life in general.

Nellie sat up with a jerk. "School is fine," she said, "but has Daddy told you he is getting married?" she asked.

"He has indeed," replied Oma. "Are you happy about it, Nellie?"

Nellie described Helene to her and also told her how disappointed she was about the house. Her grandmother knew how much she had been looking forward to having a home of her own, with only her father, and now everything had changed. Nothing was working out the way she had planned. Oma listened to her without interrupting. She could tell her granddaughter needed to get it all off her chest. Nellie was finally being able to voice her feelings and emotions, knowing she would not be judged or punished.

Once she had finished her story, she felt as if a heavy burden had been taken off her shoulders. "I am so lucky to have an Oma who listens," said Nellie, squeezing her hand.

"And I am so lucky to have a granddaughter like you," said Oma, giving her a big hug. "I can tell you are hurting, but usually things never work out in life the way one expects them to. That is one of the things that makes life exciting. When one is looking forward to something and there is a change, one tends to get upset and angry at life, but when something comes up that one did not dare to hope for, one feels elated and joyful. Those are the contradictions in life. How boring life would be if everything went according to schedule. You know, Nellie, you will become aware of this as you grow older, but one tends to think that we hold all the power in our hands, and it takes an act of nature to show us how wrong we are."

"Like what, for instance?" asked Nellie.

"Let's take a nice, warm, summer day. You and your friends have planned to take a swim in the river, you have been looking forward to it all week long and are about to leave when in a matter of minutes, the blue sky has vanished and dark clouds roll in, the sun disappears and a wind comes up. You hear the roar of thunder and see lightning in the distance and you have a change of heart. It was not you who dictated it, but nature, right? And yet you bow your head to it and do something else. Being flexible and open minded does not come easy, but it is a very important part of life."

"Oma, are you trying to tell me you approve of Daddy remarrying?" asked Nellie.

Mrs Winters thought for a minute. "Your mother and father were deeply in love with each other and they were a very happy couple. But your mother would never have wanted Sigmund to spend the rest of his days by himself, bemoaning his loss. She would have wanted him to get on with his life, to live it to the fullest and to be happy. She would also have wanted the very best for you."

"In other words, you approve."

"Yes, Nellie, I do, and I trust his good judgment. I am sure Helene must have some good qualities."

"Dad says she is a lot of fun to be with."

"I am sure she is. I know it is not easy for you, but child, look at it from this point of view, your Dad will have a companion, someone to share his life with and you will have much more freedom."

"What do you mean?"

"Be patient and let me explain," replied Mrs Winters. "One of these days, and the day is not far off, you are going to want to have a life of your own, maybe travel, maybe get married. Won't it make the decision much easier knowing that your dad, whom you love, is not left by himself, that he has someone to care for him and to do things with?"

"Oma, you are right! I had not thought of that. You are so wise, what would I do without you?" asked Nellie, hugging her.

"Wait, Nellie, let me finish. This is the price you have to pay, but is it not worth it? Be nice, get to know her before you judge her, give her a chance and one last thing…try placing yourself in her shoes. Just imagine you were the one getting married and having a teenager to cope with. How would you feel?"

"I guess I would not be too happy about it, but I would try and make the best of it for my sake as well as for the others."

"Well, that might just be what Helene is planning on doing. One more thing before we close this chapter, give her a lot of space, let her come to you, let her invite you out, you might even find you have something in common. Summing it up, don't be prejudiced against her and try to have an open mind."

"Oma, you have given me wonderful advice and I will try hard to follow it. I feel so much better about it all and I do want Daddy to be happy." Nellie could see her grandmother was tired, her face was drawn and she was having trouble keeping her eyes open. She knew she was used to taking a nap right after lunch and had skipped it in order to spend time with her. "Oma," said Nellie, "I think I should be going. I need to do some homework and I would like to get it out of the way so I can spend tomorrow with Daddy without having to worry about it. I do not recall telling you, but he went to Wiesbaden today to meet Helene's family and wanted me to come with him but I did not think it wise, so he is only staying for the day, even though I am sure Helene would very much have liked him to have spent the weekend."

Mrs Winters covered a yawn with her hand. "Just remember what I told you when something goes wrong and you start feeling sorry for yourself. You will always be your father's top priority. Not only has he told you this, but he has also proven it with actions. But now, I do think I will go lie down for a little while." She walked Nellie to the door. "I hope to see you soon," she said.

"You will," replied Nellie, giving her a big smile.

Mrs Winters went straight to bed, hoping that she had set Nellie on a good path. It was not going to be easy for her, but at least she would be able to guide her on her way.

Sigmund drove back, deep in thought. There was something about Helene's family he did not like. Try as he might, he could not place his finger on it. The sisters gave the impression of putting on a show, it all seemed so artificial. And the mother… Quite the opposite from Mrs Winters, she was hard and she had no sweetness in her whatsoever, lacking the refinements of life and somehow reminding him of a hawk. Those beady eyes of hers had watched every one of his facial expressions, every movement, like a hawk ready to jump its prey. It would not be an easy family to get along with, but he would not have to see them very often, either, and he was lucky enough that they did not live in the same city. "One mistake I will not make," he said out loud, "is committing to having lunch or dinner with them once a week. Once a month is fine and if Helene wants to see them more often, I will make sure she feels free to do so."

He was home before he knew it, the house was in darkness, and he tiptoed into Nellie's room to check on her and she was smiling in her sleep. He stood by her bedside looking at her, "May everything in life give my child a reason to smile," he spoke his wish out loud. Nellie stirred in her sleep and opened an eye. "Is that you, Daddy?" she asked.

"Yes," replied Sigmund, "it's me."

She rubbed her eyes and sat up in bed. "It must be very late," she said, "did you have a nice time?"

"I did. And what about you?" he asked.

"I had a lovely time with Oma," she replied.

"Go back to sleep, we can talk in the morning." Nellie nestled back against the pillows and Sigmund bent down and gently kissed her on the forehead. She heard him tell her to sleep like an angel, then he was gone.

Nellie was up and dressed when Sigmund came down for breakfast. "You must have gotten up early," he said.

"I did," she replied, "but I slept in yesterday."

"Have you got anything special planned for today?" asked Sigmund.

She gave him a big smile. "I am spending the day with the most wonderful father in the world." She then asked about Helene's family and he told her about them, then mentioned she was eager to see the house again and hear what Helene thought of it. Sigmund was more than pleased; she was back to her old self and what a change in attitude! He was sure her grandmother had a lot to do with it, as he knew Nellie discussed everything with her. They must have had a very long talk and he was certain that he, but mostly Helene, must have been the main topic of conversation. They went for a stroll in the botanical gardens and then to the Zoo, one of Nellie's favourite places. They spent most of their time there, watching the monkeys as they were so entertaining. "I could stay here forever looking at the babies. They are so cute and I love the way they cling to their mother's stomachs," she said.

"I know," replied Sigmund. "But it is getting cold now and I could do with a nice cup of hot tea and I am sure you—"

Nellie finished the sentence for him, "Would like a big slice of cheese cake."

"We agree, so let's go," said Sigmund, laughing. The tension between them was gone and it was just like old times, both of them enjoying the day to the fullest. They were on their way home when

Nellie took her father's arm.

83

"Daddy," she said, "I just want you to know I do understand, and I want you to be happy." Those words were like music to his ears, that being Nellie's way of telling him he had her approval, and he gave her a hug right in the middle of the sidewalk.

Chapter 7

Nellie kept her word. On Tuesday morning, she went up to the choir director and asked to be excused from rehearsal, saying she had to attend an important meeting with her father. They agreed to meet at the house and it was a good 30-minute walk from her school, but as she had time to spare and it was not raining, she decided to walk the distance, arriving just as Helene and Sigmund were getting out of the car. She approached Helene and shook hands with her, giving her belated birthday wishes, then kissed her father on the cheek.

"So, this is it," said Helene. "Your Dad drove me around the neighbourhood and I like it very much, it is so quiet and the shopping is close by."

Sigmund rang the doorbell. Mrs Ulrich answered his summons almost immediately and greeted Nellie. Sigmund introduced Helene to her as his fiancée. "I'm so happy to meet you," she said to Helene." Looks like the rumours that have been going around for quite some time are true," she added, smiling at him.

"I guess they are," replied Sigmund, following Helene into the house. They went into the living room and Sigmund looked around. The furniture had been removed. "When are you and David leaving for the States?" She informed him it would be at the end of the week. "That is earlier then you intended, is it not?"

"It is, indeed," she replied. The move had gone so well, they were able to bring their departure date forward. She apologised for David being unable to join them but something unexpected had come up and instead he sent his best wishes.

"Where are you staying?" Helene asked.

Lina informed her that they were spending the last couple of days at the Frankfurter Hof. She had finally come to terms with the decision they had taken, having had mixed emotions all along, but now, since moving out of her home, she was beginning to look forward to a new life in America and her husband, David, could not wait to leave. "You must be eager to see your new home," she said addressing Helene, "so let me show you around."

Helene took her time, looking at everything. Sigmund could tell she liked what she saw. Taking more time than usual in the bedrooms, she walked to the windows and peered out, assessing the view. "They all look out on the garden," said Lina, "so they have a lot of light."

"Yes," said Helene, "and they are a good size as well." On the landing, she turned to Sigmund. "I love the master bedroom and I think Nellie should take this room, it has the best view of the garden," she added. "I will turn the room across the hallway into my sewing room."

Nellie gave her father a horrified look. "Helene," she said turning to her, "Daddy told me I could have my choice—"

Sigmund did not let her finish and took Helene by the arm. "This will have to be your sewing room," he said, "because that particular room will be Nellie's bedroom."

"But that was before—" Sigmund interrupted her as well.

"That is the way it is," he said, in a very determined tone of voice.

It had begun to rain so Lina excused herself to let Gretchen into the house and the little dog came running up the stairs. She was soaking wet and as soon as she saw Nellie, went straight to her and stood up on her hind legs. Nellie stroked her head while Helene gave the dog a look of disgust. She turned to Lina, "One does get so attached to a pet," she said.

"One does," replied Lina, "but Gretchen will be staying here. It was so fortunate that Nellie and the dog took to each other immediately."

"The dog, yes," replied Sigmund. Helene reprimanded him for not telling her. "It slipped my mind, I am sorry, but she is so friendly."

Gretchen sensed that they were discussing her and so she wagged her tail and went from one to the other, but flashed her teeth at Helene. Nellie had a hard time holding back her laughter.

Helene was very much impressed by the conservatory and agreed with Sigmund that the library was more than perfect. They went over the house once more. Lina had to leave, so she handed Sigmund the keys. "You are the new owner," she said, "so, you might as well keep them."

"That is not so," said Sigmund. "I have to see David in a day or two to pay him the rest."

Lina bade her dog a very tearful farewell. She explained that living in a hotel had been hard on her so Nellie might as well take her home with her. "What about Uncle Paul?" Nellie asked.

"I am sure he won't mind," replied her father. They walked Lina to the door and wished her all the luck in the world. The house really didn't need much work but Helene wanted to have it repainted and Sigmund wanted the woodwork in the library professionally polished. The curtains would have to be changed, but Helene was sure her mother and sisters would help her make some up.

"We could probably move in two months at the most," said Sigmund.

"I guess we could, but don't we have to have a wedding first?" Helene asked.

Nellie wandered off. She was proud of her dad; he stood up for her just as he had promised. Her worries were gone; she could now face the prospects of a new life with no misgivings. Entering the living room, she heard Helene say under her breath: "I am sure it will be a lovely wedding."

"I think we should be leaving. We don't want to keep Paul waiting," said Sigmund. Gretchen climbed onto the car seat just as soon as Sigmund opened the door, clearly she was used to going for a ride, and Nellie got in beside her. No sooner had she sat down that Gretchen got into her lap, put her face on Nellie's arm and fell asleep.

"Poor little doggie," said Nellie, "you must be worn out. It must have been a very emotional day for you as well."

Paul asked Sigmund to bring Helene back to the house, as he wanted to celebrate their engagement with a family dinner. The idea had flashed through his mind when he woke up: It would just be the five of them and he would ask Mrs Winters to join them as well since it provided a good opportunity for her to get to know Helene. She was probably eager to meet Nellie's future stepmother, as well, and it would be in Sigmund's best interest. He rang her and she had accepted without hesitating.

Sigmund had misplaced his house keys so he rang the doorbell and Paul went to answer the door. He was not expecting anyone, for he had told Mrs Winters he would pick her up, and when he opened the door, Gretchen whizzed past him. "Do we have another family member?" he asked Nellie.

"The Ulrichs can no longer care for her and I know you will not mind having little Gretchen around for a month or two since she would have been homeless if it had not been for me," said Nellie.

Paul smiled and said, "I don't mind at all, but she is your baby, you worry about her and clean up after her."

"You have a deal," replied Nellie.

He greeted Helene warmly and welcomed her, saying how pleased he was at having her as a sister-in-law. Helene blushed as she followed him into the living room.

Sigmund went into the dining room on his way upstairs and the table looked very festive with the candelabras and a flower arrangement in the centre. Anna had outdone herself as usual. "But why has she set the table for 5? There are only four of us," Sigmund said out loud to himself. "Paul has probably counted one too many," he mumbled, and he went back to the living room with the intention of making Paul aware of his mistake.

But, no sooner did Paul see him that he said, "Sigmund, I forgot to tell you, I have invited Mrs Winters to join us and I must go now and pick her up. Would you mind serving Helene her drink?"

"Not at all," he replied, giving his brother a surprised look. That was Paul, one never knew what to expect.

Nellie was overjoyed. "You will love my grandmother," she said happily to Helene. "She is so wise." Helene said she was looking forward to meeting her and Nellie excused herself. She wanted to see about Gretchen and found her sleeping soundly on her bed. As she happily stroked the dog's head, she thought about how nice it will be to have a bedmate from now on. Gretchen barely opened her eyes and wagged her tail for a moment, but it was too much of an effort and she went back to sleep.

"Did you know Mrs Winters was coming?" asked Helene, as Sigmund handed her the drink.

"I did not," he replied, "but I am sure you will like her, she is so very nice."

Nellie came in just then. "I found Gretchen sound asleep on my bed," she said, laughing.

"She may sleep in your room tonight, but as of tomorrow, she will have her own bed in the hallway. I have never approved of sharing beds with dogs," said Sigmund.

Nellie heard the garage door close with a bang and rushed out to greet her grandmother. "Oma, how happy I am to see you, you have to meet Gretchen," said Nellie excitedly, leaving to go and fetch her.

Mrs Winters gave Paul a puzzled look. "You will soon have the answer," he said grinning. "Let's go join the others."

Mrs Winters made a grand entrance. She was petite, but there was something royal about the way she carried herself and Helene thought she had much class as she got up to greet her. "I have heard a lot about you," said Mrs Winters warmly, shaking her hand. However, she was unable to get any further for Gretchen came in as fast as her legs would carry her, Nellie following right on her heels.

"You have just met Gretchen," she said, laughing at the perplexed look on her grandmother's face. Nellie had a way of giggling when she laughed that was very contagious and it was not long before everyone joined in the laughter. The ice was broken. Paul opened the bottle of champagne he had been saving for the occasion and they toasted the happy couple. It was a very enjoyable evening, Anna had prepared a wonderful meal and she would be sorry to see Sigmund and Nellie move away, for she had become very attached to them.

Helene praised her cooking several times and Anna offered to give her the recipes, telling her she would be glad to be of assistance should she require any. Mrs Winters could not help but compare Helene to Alice. One thing was certain, she did not have her daughter's class or upbringing and it was not going to be an easy relationship for Sigmund. He and Alice had not only been well suited for each other, but they also shared the same background, which was so important. Class and background were the two things that could neither be bought nor taught and had seen no end of marriages drift apart for this very reason. It was obvious Helene was madly in love; her eyes followed him everywhere, but in the end, she hoped Helene would not see Nellie as a rival—yet only time would tell.

The conversation was very lively with Paul doing most of the talking. He was such a great entertainer. Nellie seemed at ease and happy. It had really been a great evening and wonderful dinner. Sigmund dropped Mrs Winters off on his way to take Helene home.

"What a great lady she is," Helene remarked.

"She really is and she has been such a good teacher and practically a mother to Nellie."

"Yes, I can see Nellie dotes on her and there is a complicity between them."

"You are absolutely right, there sure is," replied Sigmund. "I will always be grateful to her, for I do not know what I would have done had she not been around." He kissed Helene at the door and said goodnight, it had been a long day and he was very tired and at this point, all he wanted was his bed.

Sigmund went over to the Frankfurter Hof the next day to keep his appointment with David and was surprised at how much older he looked. It seemed as if he had aged overnight. David stood up to greet him and he was taken aback by the profound sadness that he could see in David's eyes. Once they were seated in a quiet corner with their backs to the bar, David ordered a whisky for himself and a Brandy Alexander for Sigmund.

"I would have never believed bidding farewell to my homeland would be so hard," he said as soon as the waiter had taken their order. "This is the only country I have lived in. I was born and raised here, as you know, and I have so many memories. Of course, they will be with me, but they can never make up for the smell of the forest, with all its different pine trees, and that I will never bicycle along the Main River again. I am giving up everything and I sometimes wonder if it is really worth it. I have lived through so much happiness and sorrow," he stopped to catch his breath.

"I understand what you are saying," replied Sigmund, "but you have been very unhappy with the path the country has taken."

"I know," said David, "and I like it less with every passing day, but that does not make it any easier. I am practically uprooting myself and Lina. She has come to terms with it and it is amazing how her attitude changed once we moved out of the house, as if she had broken loose from that which was restraining her. Now she is actually looking forward to starting a new life in America. Tell me, Sigmund have you ever been to America?" asked David.

"No, I have not, and I have no desire to go," he replied. "I have been there once. It is very exciting and if you're willing to work, you can make a lot of money. It is a country with a lot of opportunities, you just have to take them."

"You have made your choice," said Sigmund.

"Yes, I certainly have, and only time will tell which one of us was right," said David. "America will become my new homeland whether I like it or not and I know, Sigmund, that once I leave Germany this coming Saturday, I shall never, ever return."

"I am very much aware of that, David, and it saddens me. I have gotten to know you in this short time and I admire your integrity, you are a man of honour." The waiter then brought them their order and they toasted to the future, whatever it might be. Sigmund handed him the check.

"I hope you and your bride will be as happy within those walls as Lina and I have been," said David. "Are you going to make a lot of changes to it?" Sigmund explained briefly what he had in mind. "You are so right, the house does need redecorating, but it won't take long to do if you find the right people," David added.

"I have them lined up and will be starting work next Monday. They should be finished within a month." Sigmund stood up. "I must be going, David. I wish you all the luck and the happiness in the world, and do please say goodbye to Lina for me, she is such a nice lady, you are a lovely couple and I am very proud of having met you."

David had tears in his eyes. He stood up and gave Sigmund a big hug. "Good luck to you, too. And who knows, you may need it more than me," he said, smiling sadly. Sigmund looked back at David before exiting the bar as he sat there where he left him, staring into his empty whisky glass. David's words still rang in his ears as he headed home.

Chapter 8

It was a very exciting time for Helene. Her sisters and mother were busy making up the curtains for her new home as the conversation revolved around the upcoming wedding, which was only a month and a half away. There was so much to be done in such a short time and she much would have preferred to wait until spring, but Sigmund was really eager to move into their new home and she didn't want to disappoint him. It was to be a small affair, but when they each made up their guest list and sat down to discuss it, they realised they were talking about one hundred guests and none of them could be excluded, for they did not want to hurt anybody's feelings.

A couple of weeks after getting engaged, Helene took a week's leave from work to go to Brussels with her mother. Nicole, the seamstress who had made her sister's wedding gown, lived in a small village not far from the city. There was never a doubt in her mind that if she were she to marry, it would be Nicole who would continue with the tradition started by her mother's family to make her dress. Nicole's mother had sewn both her grandmother's and mother's dresses and now her daughter was doing the same for the younger generation.

Helene knew exactly what she wanted. The dress would be very simple and yet elegant and exclusive: it would be made up entirely of the famous handmade Bruges lace. Her relatives were all happy to see her and overjoyed at the prospects of the wedding and understood that mother and daughter needed to spend time together, accepting quite readily that they stay in a hotel. After having met with Nicole the very day after their arrival, they continued on to Bruges to choose the lace. It was a long train ride. She had been to Bruges the previous summer and could not help remarking to her mother about how different it looked in winter. "You are right, Helene, but regardless of the season, it never loses its charm," she replied. They spent most of the day looking at laces; there was so much to choose from. She finally decided on the finest and most elaborate. It was absolutely beautiful and the quantity she required was available. Helene was overjoyed.

They stayed at a small and quaint hotel in Bruges and were up early the following day. Despite the sunshine, it was cold and damp, but the weather could not deter them from taking a boat trip down the city canals. Bruges was such a romantic town. Her mother was a little sad and she discreetly wiped a tear or two from her eye, hoping Helene would not notice, but nothing escaped her, silently taking her mother's hand until she finally spoke. "I am very happy for you, Helene, and even though Sigmund is a lot older than you are, I am sure he will be a loving and caring husband and a good father. It is always sad to see one's child leave the nest, but that is the law of life and I would not want it otherwise. I have seen you blossom and grow since you met him and that is what love is all about, in other words, it is about helping each other become a better person. I will welcome him into our home as another son."

Deeply moved, Helene listened as she watched the scenery drift by. Her mother did not express her emotions easily and she was very much aware of the effort she was making. "Thank you," she said, hugging her, and enjoyed the rest of the ride in silence. Late the next evening, they went back to Brussels and time just seemed to fly by. There they went shopping and bought some gorgeous outfits for her to wear on her honeymoon.

Still undecided about where they were going to spend it, they did agree it would be close to Frankfurt. Helene was sure it would be somewhere special but Sigmund could not take a lot of time off. Paul had not been well and the business needed their full attention. In addition, she herself only had one week's leave.

Sigmund actually wanted her to stop working altogether, but she could not see herself sitting at home so they came to a compromise and she would resign at the end of the school term.

They went to the theatre and to the opera, her relatives threw several parties in her honour and she was the centre of attention, which she enjoyed every minute of. It was a wonderful week. When they returned to Frankfurt late Friday night, Sigmund was at the station to meet them. He, too, had been very busy, not only with his business but overseeing the redecorating of the house. It was going really well and he was very pleased with the workers he had hired. David had been so right: Only the best. Now and again, his thoughts would go back to him and the last sentence that still echoed in his ears:

"Good luck to you, who knows—you may need it more than me."

His future mother-in-law greeted him warmly and would be staying with Helene, leaving for Wiesbaden the following afternoon. Sigmund insisted she stay until Sunday so that they could all have lunch together and introduce her to his brother Paul and meet Nellie but she declined, saying that although she really appreciated his invitation, she felt she had been away long enough and really needed to get back. "I have to see how the girls are coming along with the curtains. I also have some other things to tend to and time is running out. I am sure we will all meet some other time before the wedding," she said, turning to Helene.

Even though it was late, Sigmund accepted Helene's invitation to come up for a drink. She looked tired but happy.

Helene's mother joined them with a glass of sherry and soon after she finished it excused herself.

They made themselves comfortable in the living room. She gave him a full account of all she had done and bought but never mentioned her dress or the trip to Bruges, for it would have given it away. He could not help thinking how happy she looked. Her brown eyes sparkled as she spoke and he took her hand in his. "May your eyes always sparkle, like two big stars," he said tenderly, looking her in the eyes. "It really is a shame your mother cannot stay, it would have been the perfect time for her to have met my side of the family."

"I know," replied Helene. "And I could not agree with you more, but you will learn with time that once she makes a decision, she abides by it. I am sure there will be another time." He could tell Helene was tired, so he did not stay too long. As he drove home, he thought about Helene's mother and how different she was from Mrs Winters.

Nellie was busy with school. Word had spread about her father remarrying and her friends were all very curious about it. One day Rachel, with whom she had not exchanged one word since the day she had asked her to leave, came up to her. "Well, Nellie, so I was right after all. I hear Helene and your father are getting married," she said.

Nellie blushed, having thought often about Rachel and how unfair she had been to her. She felt guilty and resolved many times to speak to her and apologise, but she always found one pretext or another for putting it off. Now it was too late. Rachel was confronting her. She felt ashamed and at the same time relieved. "Yes, Rachel, they are getting married and you were right. I am sorry I got so angry with you for speaking the truth; I should have known better," said Nellie.

"It's all a thing of the past and anyway, I did not know for sure, I was just speculating. But do tell me about Helene. Have you come to terms with her?" she asked.

"I guess I have, it's no use fighting something that is not in one's hand to change," she replied, then added, "I do hope we can be friends again."

"Sure, Nellie, as I said before, what came between us has long been forgotten." But they both knew that the friendship as they had once known it would be no more.

She saw very little of her father and of Helene, for their time was taken up attending all the different social events in their honour. It was as if the entire Jewish community wanted to be a part of what they called 'The Wedding of the Year'. Nellie went with them to the dinner that Abraham and Sara gave in their honour. It was a very intimate and informal affair and their daughters, who were a little younger than she, were also present.

On their way home, Sigmund invited her and Helene to go over to what would be their home the next day to see how the redecorating was coming along. Nellie was thrilled with the prospects, for she had not been back to the house since Helene's first visit. They arrived right after lunch and Nellie was impressed with all the changes. Helene took her time describing to her what it would look like once it was all furnished and the curtains were hung. She had seen the furniture Sigmund had in storage and had agreed to his taking some of the pieces that seemed to mean so much to him and with the exception of his desk, which had been his grandfathers, they would be a constant reminder to her that she never would be his first love.

It hurt her deeply, for even though he was tender and very attentive to her, she could at times feel that his heart was, and always would, belong to Alice. She tried not to show it, but once in a while, the hurt would reflect in her eyes and it never went unnoticed. Sigmund would have given anything for things to be different but he knew that it was not in his hands to change what once had been.

They had discussed Nellie several times and he stressed the importance of them getting along, so it was with a look of satisfaction that he trailed behind them, listening attentively to Helene's explanations. Nellie was very impressed and told Helene that she was looking forward to moving into the house, which would be a home to them all.

The wedding arrangements were in full swing. To Sigmund's relief, Mrs Winters offered to see about Nellie's dress, which also gave her a pretext to spend more time with her dear granddaughter. Even though Nellie was very good at hiding her emotions, her grandmother could tell that there was a lot going on underneath the surface. A couple of days later, on their way to the seamstress for a fitting, Nellie mentioned her visit to her new home. Mrs Winters listened to her account without interrupting but when Nellie was finished, she asked her what she thought about it all.

"Oma, I am trying hard to accept and adjust to this new life that is about to begin, but to tell you the truth, I have very mixed emotions. It was Daddy and I who were going to decorate the house, but Helene has taken my place. I'm sure it will look beautiful and I probably could not have done as good a job of it, but it is just the fact that I no longer count," she said, her voice breaking.

"You do count and you are important," replied her grandmother. "Your daddy has been so busy lately that—"

Nellie interrupted her, "It's OK, Oma, really, you do not have to make excuses for him," she said. Mrs Winters made a mental note, however, of having a little word with Sigmund.

The week of the wedding was upon them. As expected, it was a very busy and intense week, indeed. Helene's family decided to spend the last couple of days in the city, staying at the Frankfurter Hof to be closer to Helene and to attend the parties and the day after their arrival, Paul and Sigmund threw them a dinner. They had debated for a long time whether to include Mrs Winters and had decided to invite her, for as Nellie's grandmother she was a very important member of the family and would also be attending the wedding.

Anna outdid herself as usual. The whole house looked immaculate. Nellie was curious about Helene's family, especially about her mother. This would be the first time they met and she did not know what to expect. The dinner itself was long and drawn out. The two families were worlds apart from each other. Mrs Winters did her best to keep the conversation flowing. She did not like Helene's mother or her sisters and could tell that, even though Nellie went out of her way to be nice and sweet, none of them liked her.

Just as they were finally taking their leave, Gretchen managed to sneak in from the kitchen and went from one to the other, barking and wagging her tail in the friendliest manner. Helene's mother lost all composure and cried out over and over again, "I hate dogs," while ordering someone to get the dog away from her. Helene, who was standing by her side, put an arm around her and tried to calm her.

Gretchen was in her element, standing up on her hind legs, barking at her all the while. It was a funny sight. Nellie had a hard time keeping a straight face and finally, at her father's urging, picked Gretchen up and took her upstairs. As she left, she heard her father and Paul apologising for the inconvenience. Paul was in the sitting room when she returned looking for her father. He told her that he had gone to take Mrs Winters and Helene home and so she sat down next to him.

"Did you enjoy the evening?" he asked.

"I only enjoyed the end of it," she said, giggling. "It was so funny. And what boring people they are!" she said when she could finally speak. "I cannot imagine somebody hating dogs," she added.

"Yes," said Paul, "it sure was boring. I'm sure they did not like me and, in fact, I don't think they liked any of us. But they are Helene's family, so we have to be nice and accept them for what they are," replied Paul. Nellie agreed.

After they dropped off Mrs Winters, Sigmund told Helene where they were going on their honeymoon. "Schloss Kronberg!" Helene repeated, ecstatic. "I have always dreamt of staying there. I have seen pictures of it and you could not have chosen a lovelier spot," she said, smiling at him happily. She almost said that she had the perfect wardrobe for it, but kept that to herself.

The wedding was to take place the coming Saturday 20 January 1920. Sigmund had his hands full, mostly overseeing the last minute details of the redecorating. The work was finished right on schedule, but as he went through the house with Helene one last time, she pointed out some minor details that needed doing. He added them to his list and spent a lot of time at the house making sure that none were overlooked. They also debated whether to furnish the house now or wait until their return. Helene did not relish spending a couple of nights in Paul's home and Sigmund did not want to stay in a hotel, so it had been agreed that they would move in before the wedding.

In addition to having her family with her and all her other duties, Helene was far too busy to help with the moving, which was a blessing for Sigmund since he was able to do it all his own way and with no one interfering. He had no trouble placing the furniture in its place for Helene had drawn him a plan of where everything belonged. She was so meticulous; she must have gotten it from her mother. The curtains were absolutely stunning and were all hand sewn. He walked through the house one more time, admiring everything. His study looked wonderful and having all his books neatly arranged in the bookshelves made such a difference. The woodwork looked spectacular. "It's amazing what a good polishing can do," he thought, standing in front of it and hoped everyone would be happy here. Even the two gold fish in the pond seemed to be enjoying their new surroundings. "Well, when I return, I shall be a married man again," he spoke out loud, locking the front door behind him.

He arrived home with enough time to change and pick up Helene on his way to the dinner her family was offering in their honour. He ran into Paul at the front door. "You sure look as if you need a holiday," said Paul, taking one look at him.

"I am beat. Between the office, the workers, furnishing the house and partying, it is taking its toll on me. You can't imagine how much I am looking forward to next week, not having to do anything, but rest."

"I can imagine," replied Paul. "I guess we better get ready, we sure do not want to be late tonight."

Just as they were heading upstairs, Anna called to them. "You might want to take a look at the dining room. I have never seen so many presents and I am really running out of space." It was customary to send the wedding gifts to the bride's home and that the family view them the eve of the wedding, but since Helene's family was staying at a hotel, they decided to have them sent to Paul's home instead and would open them upon their return from their honeymoon.

"I can see Helene is going to be quite busy," said Paul, walking around the room.

"We really should get ready," said Sigmund, heading towards the staircase.

They arrived just in time. All their closest friends had been invited and it turned out to be a great evening. Helene's mother had seen to every detail. A couple of Helene's friends, who had known her since early childhood days, read a poem they had written about her and once they finished, handed her the original with a lot of pomp. She was very touched, for it brought back many memories.

Paul and Abraham composed a song about Sigmund and his encounter with Helene, describing their meeting and courtship, singing it accompanied by an accordionist. Needless to say, it was a great success. Nellie fully enjoyed herself and it was very late when they decided to call it a night.

Chapter 9

Helene was exhausted and could hardly wait to get into bed. She worked her usual hours and had just taken Friday off. It was the one time in her life when she wished the days had more than 24 hours, cramming her packing into whatever free time she had, of which there was certainly not much. It was amazing how much one could collect in such a short time. Since she could not afford the time to travel back and forth to Bruges, Nicole arrived in Frankfurt at the beginning of the week, the fittings taking up more time than she had realised but so worth it. The last one took place late that afternoon and the dress was a dream.

She looked around her room once more before closing her eyes. It would be the last time she slept in this bed. Deciding to keep her dressing table and desk, the rest of the furniture would be sent to Wiesbaden and would find new homes with her sisters. A couple of times during the night she woke up, so many thoughts going through her mind: What would it be like to be married? Would she and Nellie get along? It was only in the early morning hours that she fell into a deep sleep.

The sound of the ringing phone finally awakened her and she got up like a sleepwalker and went to answer. It was Sigmund, sounding extremely worried. They were to be at the registry in an hour and she had given no signs of life. It was the third time he called and had she not answered this time, he would have gone over there immediately.

"You woke me up," she said, now wide-awake. "Don't worry, Sigmund, I will be there on time." She bathed and dressed in a hurry and was ready when her mother and sisters arrived to pick her up. Just the families would be attending this ceremony.

They were the last to arrive. Sigmund looked stunning in a dark suit. Nellie handed her the corsage, a small duplicate of the bridal bouquet she would be holding at the Synagogue later that evening.

"Flowers are a must for a bride," Nellie said, handing it to her. She gave Nellie a hug. Sigmund walked over to them and, taking it from her, pinned it on her jacket.

"You look beautiful," he said tenderly and added, "I thought some flowers would make the occasion more festive," he replied after she thanked him for it. She was touched by his thoughtfulness. Love was made up of all those small little details.

The ceremony was very brief and to the point. When it was over, they went back to Paul's house where champagne and hors d'oeuvres were waiting for them. They toasted the newlyweds. Sigmund told Helene about all the gifts and she could not refrain from peeking into the dining room and letting out a gasp. Sigmund, who had followed her, said: "You are going to have quite a time opening all those presents when we return." She glanced at a couple of cards and was about to open a big package when she heard her mother calling her.

"Helene, we should take our leave now, we don't want to keep Nicole waiting."

"We better go back to the others," Sigmund said gently, and she put it back.

"Too bad," she said. "It will have to wait with the rest." They arrived at her home just as Nicole was getting out of the cab and as the afternoon wore on, Helene became increasingly nervous. Nicole helped her get dressed and did her hair for her; she looked absolutely beautiful, as her mother looked on proudly. Before leaving her flat, she walked around it for the last time. She had been very happy here, so many memories, and the nice thing about memories was, they go with you everywhere.

They were only ten minutes late. The synagogue had been decorated with flower arrangements that matched the colours of her bridal bouquet. Her sister's husband ushered her down the aisle where Sigmund was waiting for her, Nellie standing by his side underneath the nuptial canopy. He smiled at her warmly as their eyes met and hers went moist, Helene's most ardent wish about to come true.

She joined Sigmund and Nellie. The canopy symbolised a home, the home she would now be making for the three of them. As she looked down at all the people, she felt a deep surge of gratitude; they were family, friends and acquaintances who had come to share in their happiness. Life was good to her, it had given her a second chance and she resolved to make the most of it as she turned her attention to the rabbi. They left the reception right after dinner and went to Kronberg.

Paul drove Nellie and Mrs Winters home. He tried to urge Nellie to stay at the house, but was unable to persuade her, for she had promised her grandmother she would spend the week her father was away with her and they were both very much looking forward to it. As he kissed her good night, he felt a mounting sadness, having gotten so used to having her around and now… "Oh well," he thought, "life has to go on." He then said to Nellie, "Make sure you don't forget your Uncle Paul and come around anytime," he said, giving her a hug. "Anna and I will always be happy to see you."

"Don't worry, Uncle Paul, I will come see you," she said, striking a light note, for she could hear the sadness in his voice.

He bade Mrs Winters good night and headed for the car and as they watched him drive off, Mrs Winters said, "It's too bad he never married and had a family."

"It is," said Nellie. "But I am sure he will get used to having his peace and quiet once more."

Before retiring, they discussed the wedding. It was beautiful and Helene's mother had seen to every detail. The guests had a wonderful time. "It's too bad Daddy and Helene did not stay till the end, but I know Daddy was very tired and I am sure Helene was as well, with all her family here and having to go to work."

"Plus all the excitement," Mrs Winters added. "Everyone was remarking about her dress, so simple and yet so elegant, she really is beautiful."

"She is so lucky to be so tall," said Nellie.

"Your father looked very distinguished and handsome," said Mrs Winters.

"And they really do make a beautiful couple."

"Yes, they do. Now, my dear child, I know you would love to stay up and talk but it is way past my bedtime and I am ready for my bed."

"I understand, Oma, we have the whole week ahead of us," said Nellie, giving her a hug.

Nellie was the centre of attention at school on Monday; everyone wanted to hear about the wedding, what she wore, as well as a detailed description of Helene's dress. Rachel remarked it must have been a dream of a dress for she had seen a picture of the bride and groom in the social column of the 'Frankfurter Allgemeine Newspaper'. "It was," replied Nellie, and she went to great lengths to describe the lace's pattern.

The week was over in no time and it seemed to Helene that they had just been married the day before and here they were on their way back to Frankfurt. Sigmund was well rested and happy, he had loved all her outfits and she enjoyed seeing the heads turn whenever she walked into the restaurant, which had not gone unnoticed to Sigmund, for he commented on how lucky he was to be escorting the most beautiful and glamorous lady in the hotel. She beamed with pleasure.

They were very much looking forward to settling into their new home after Helene finally convinced him they spend the first night in the house by themselves. He had given in reluctantly, he didn't think it fair to exclude Nellie for she was a part of the family, but he finally agreed when Helene mentioned that she was sure she would be all too happy to spend one more night at her grandmother's.

They arrived home just as the sun was setting. It was a beautiful, cold winter day and the sky turned various shades of pink as the sun faded away. "What a gorgeous sunset," exclaimed Helene, getting out of the car.

"It must be a good omen," replied Sigmund, teasingly.

"It must be," Helene said seriously, then he carried her over the threshold and sat her down on the couch in the living room. "You sure did a wonderful job!" exclaimed Helene, looking around her.

"It was no big deal, you deserve all the credit, I just did as I was told," he said, smiling. They walked around the house hand in hand, admiring everything. Sigmund opened a bottle of champagne in the library. "Here's to us," he said, "may we be as happy here always as we are right now and when little sorrows cross our path, may we remember how lucky we both are at having been given a second chance."

"Let us never take it for granted," Helene added, putting her arm through his. Sigmund and Helene went to work the next day and Sigmund left the office a little earlier than usual to go and pick up Nellie. He rang Mrs Winters in the morning to let her know he would be coming.

"Would you and Helene care to join me for dinner this evening?" she asked, but he declined the invitation, saying that he would be coming by himself. *Good,* thought Mrs Winters, hanging up the phone, it will give me a chance to speak to him in private.

Nellie wasn't home yet when he arrived. "Where is my darling daughter?" Sigmund asked after greeting Mrs Winters warmly.

"She is still at school. I heard her mention something about having to stay a little longer today."

"I see," replied her father. Mrs Winters remarked how rested he looked. "We had a wonderful time in Kronberg, it is so beautiful there and the forest makes the air so pure. And I was exhausted."

Maria came in just then with a tray of sandwiches and some tea. Sigmund mentioned they were his favourite and watched as she set them on the table.

"Nellie and I had a very nice time. She is such a loving and caring child."

"I think she has adjusted to the new circumstances quite well," said her father.

"No, Sigmund, she is getting *used* to the idea but she will only begin to live the new reality once she comes home with you tonight, and it is not going to be easy for her."

"I realise that," replied Sigmund.

"One last word of advice; make her a part of everything. She was hurting pretty badly because her opinion was not asked for once as far as the decorating of the house was concerned, and she felt very much left out. Remember, it is her home as well."

It was true, neither he nor Helene had thought of making Nellie a part of it and he felt guilty. He was about to reply when Nellie walked into the room. "Hi, Dad," she said. "The week sure seems to have agreed with you, you looked so tired when you left."

Sigmund got up and gave her a big hug. "I missed you, little one, but I understand you had a great time with Oma."

"Yes, Oma took me out to dinner last night at a restaurant that just opened. I will have to take you there."

"It is the one that has had many write ups in the newspaper," added Mrs Winters. Nellie finished her tea and excused herself to go fetch her things. She packed a bag for just the week and her father had moved all her belongings to their new home.

Sigmund turned to Mrs Winters, "You are right, we should have thought about that, but from now on, I will make a point of seeing to it that we do not leave her out."

"Your room is always ready whenever you want to come and spend some time here," Mrs Winters said when Nellie came back in the room.

"I know, Oma, I will be back."

Mrs Winters watched them leave and was happy with the thought she was able to make her point, as she went back into the house.

They did not go home immediately. Sigmund mentioned that Paul had not been feeling well that afternoon and he wanted to check on him. Nellie stayed in the car and Anna let him in. "How is he?" Sigmund asked.

"A little better," Anna said. "It must have been something he ate. After working at his desk for a while, he went back to bed. Maybe he's awake."

"No, I will not go upstairs, sleep is the best medicine. If he does not leave for the office tomorrow or should you need anything, Anna, please call me. I will be home."

"Do not worry, Sigmund, he will be all right."

"Is he better?" asked Nellie, as Sigmund got into the car.

"Anna believes he is, but I am a little worried about him. He really has not been well for a long time and the doctors cannot put their finger on it." They drove the rest of the way in silence.

Helene heard the car and went out to meet them. She gave Nellie a warm welcome and they both gave her a tour of the house. "It is so beautiful and homey," said Nellie. "I love the conservatory, and the sound of the water makes it so special," she added, as she stood watching the goldfish for a moment. "And now, if you will excuse me, I have to say hello to Gretchen." Her father went with her. Gretchen was in the garden and as soon as she heard Nellie's voice, she came out of her little house to greet her. "This is a new beginning for you as well," said Nellie, taking her in her arms.

Chapter 10

It took Nellie almost the entire week to get her room in order. Helene, who was extremely organised, had a hard time controlling her temper and thought once or twice about complaining to Sigmund but decided to keep quiet for the sake of keeping the peace. Nellie did not seem to care about Helene's feelings. No sooner was she home, she would let Gretchen into the house, which was another cause of conflict. Helene had spoken about it to Sigmund, but he told her in very clear terms that Gretchen was Nellie's dog and she was there to stay, the condition being that she was to sleep outside. Nellie had been very careful not to break that rule.

She tried hard not to let her stepmother upset her too much, but they both resented each other. Helene would have given anything to have Sigmund to herself and Nellie was convinced she had a rival in Helene. Nothing she ever did was good enough for her and try as she might, it was Helene who received the praise. Nellie spent a lot of time at her grandmother's, pouring her heart out to her. Mrs Winters would inevitably try to point out the positive side of everything but was well aware of the antagonism that lay between the two women and decided only something out of the ordinary could overcome it.

Sigmund could feel the tension between them, knowing they both resented each other and sometimes, especially when he caught a glimpse of one of Nellie's unhappy looks, would blame himself for having created this situation. He, too, had to adapt but he was all in all a happy man, the only shadow being the rift between the two women he loved. He tried hard to ease the tension, but when it became too much, he would disappear into his study and find solace among his books. There were times when everyone was happy and had a lot of fun together and Sigmund cherished these moments, wishing they would last forever.

Paul was doing fine, just as Anna had said, it had been nothing serious and he was back at work the next morning at the usual time. Nellie had been over to see him several times and he always enjoyed her company. The gifts were still in the dining room waiting to be opened, and every time she came home, she would ask Sigmund and Helene when they would finally make the time. They decided on the following weekend.

Paul and Sigmund left the unwrapping to the girls. From the living room, they could hear their giggles. "It sounds as if they are having a lot of fun," said Paul.

"It sure does sound like it. I wish it could always be this way," said Sigmund.

"I surmise it has not been easy."

"No, it has not. I am forever waiting to see when one is going to pounce on the other."

"Nellie has been spending a lot of time at Mrs Winters' as well as here," Paul added. "Are you happy?"

"Yes, I am, as far as I can be with this little cloud hanging over me," replied Sigmund.

In May, Helene announced she was pregnant. The news took Nellie completely by surprise. They were having breakfast when she told them, she was sure it had come as no surprise to her father, knowing Helene she must have told him the minute she found out. Nellie nearly choked on her toast and when she was able to speak again, she said, "Why, that is wonderful news, Helene."

Sigmund remarked that the timing could not have been better since Helene was quitting her job at the end of the school term so she would have time to take rest and take care of herself.

"*And* get everything ready for the baby," Helene added happily. "What would you like it to be, Nellie?" Helene asked.

"I have no preferences," she replied. "I have no experience with babies whatsoever."

"I will teach you," said Helene.

This may be the bridge I have been hoping for, thought Sigmund as he listened to their conversation. Nellie had to leave for school so she got up, kissed her stepmother for a change, said congratulations and told them she better hurry or she'd be late. "It looks as if she really liked the news," said Helene.

"Yes, I am sure she did," said Sigmund. "We, too, had better be going. I will drop you off," he said, taking her arm and leading her to the front door.

Helene did not have to worry about clearing the table for Marga the maid, who had been with her mother for many years, offered them her services and they accepted without hesitation. When the time came, she would be able to entrust the baby into her care.

Nellie arrived at school with a big smile on her face.

"Somebody looks very happy and pleased this morning," said Rachel. "Do you want to share?"

"Sure," replied Nellie. "Helene is pregnant."

"That *is* news!" said Rachel. "You better start getting used to the idea that you will no longer be the centre of attention once the baby is born," said Rachel. Nellie thought, *I no longer am,* but she did not voice her thoughts out loud. It was not long before everyone was discussing the new event. Helene was blissfully happy; life was fulfilling every one of her wishes. Sigmund took the news in his stride. So much time had gone by since Nellie had been a baby that it would be a whole new experience for him as well. Hopefully, it might be a boy this time, he thought, but he never mentioned his preference to his wife.

Nellie was right, they had both known of the happy event for a couple of weeks. With the exception of the usual morning sickness, Helene was doing just fine. Paul was absolutely delighted when Sigmund broke the news to him that very same morning. "So it will be a little nephew after all," he said, beaming at his brother.

"I hope it is, but what if it is a little niece instead?" asked Sigmund.

"She will be just as welcome," replied Paul.

The political situation in the country had not improved—on the contrary. Not only was the new republic being confronted with the settlement of the Treaty of Versailles that had been imposed on it without negotiations, but inflation was on the rise as well. There had also been a series of political threats, which came from the far left, as well as from the radical right. The Kapp-Putsch for one, in which Mr Kapp and Mr Luttwitz tried to seize power in Berlin. The Military, despite having being ordered by President Ebert to take action, just stood by. Further uprisings in the Ruhr, Saxony and Thuringia were the cause of a lot of unease as well and a lack of commitment towards the republic was also an issue. Support for the parties of the coalition had dropped considerably between the years of 1919 and 1920 and there was absolutely no cooperation from the DNVP, the German Nationalistic People's Party, in the Reichstag or Parliament. This fact put a lot of pressure on the moderate parties. There were a lot of elements that opposed the Republic, trying hard to bring it down. The uncertainties were huge, but people went on with their lives as usual in the belief that the situation had bottomed out and could only get better.

Due to Helene's pregnancy, and mostly to the difficult economic environment, Sigmund made no plans to leave Frankfurt during the summer months. In did not bother Nellie much as most of her friends were in the same predicament. She could hardly wait for the school term to come to an end. She was tired and looked forward to her free time. The last few weeks had been very stressful, as she had had to prepare for oral and written examinations. Needless to say, she passed them with flying colours.

Helene had no regrets when her last day of work came around. Her colleagues had a farewell lunch for her and everyone brought a little gift for the baby. She beamed with pleasure. They were the baby's first clothes and all so cute and small. They teased her about having to get used to having so much free time on her hands, but she reminded them that she had plenty to do looking after Sigmund, Nellie and preparing the baby's trousseau.

Sigmund had not forgotten Mrs Winters' words of advice and had a long conversation with Helene, not only about including Nellie in everything, but also about making her feel she was a part of the preparations for the baby's arrival. Time just seemed to fly past and soon Helene's figure took on the roundness of motherhood and the sparkle in her eyes gave her a radiant look. There was a serenity and peacefulness in her that reflected on those around her. She enjoyed going about the household chores and took a lot of pride in preparing the family's meals with Marga's help. Now that she and Nellie had something in common, the bickering between them ceased, to Sigmund's relief. She taught Nellie how to knit and embroider and Nellie was absolutely thrilled with all the compliments she received after showing them the little sweater she knitted for the baby.

Her father also decided it was about time she learned something about the family business, so she spent three mornings a week in the office learning the ropes. They would drive to the office together, Sigmund making a point to take his time getting there. Sometimes they would drive in silence or one of them would bring up a subject of conversation and they would discuss it at length. On one of these occasions, Nellie asked whether her mother had made similar preparations while expecting her. "Oh yes," replied her father eagerly. "We both were very much looking forward to you."

His mind went back to that evening almost 16 years ago when, after dinner, Alice mentioned that he was soon to become a father. He could still recall the look of happiness and love in her eyes. They both had been so excited about it; he got up from the table and scooped her up in his arms. "Be careful, be careful, Sigmund," she said between giggles. "You do not want to upset the baby." And he gently set her back down.

Nellie's voice brought him back to reality. "Daddy, you are not listening."

"I was just recalling how elated your mother and I both were when we found out you were on the way. I am sorry, what were you saying?"

"I wanted to know if you'd had a preference."

"Yes, I did. My dream was to have a daughter and you sure did fulfil it!" he said, smiling.

"And what about my mother?"

"She also wanted a little girl and prepared for your arrival with a lot of love and care, putting so much work into everything she made for you. It all had to be perfect. Every garment was a work of art. I must say, your grandmother also added her little touch to your wardrobe. Believe me, your outfits were absolutely gorgeous and you were such a beautiful baby that your mother received many compliments on you wherever she went. Even before you were among us, you were loved by a great many persons and your following has certainly grown," he finished.

Nellie was thoughtful for a moment. "I guess that love is everything, Daddy."

"Love is a very important part of life but it is not being at the receiving end of it that is the most rewarding. You will find as you walk down the path of life that being able to love unconditionally, giving of oneself to others selflessly, is by far the most fulfilling, since it enhances your growth as a person. Your mother was a great giver. Her greatest joy lay in being able to provide for others and she never expected anything in return. The day she was laid to rest, even I was surprised at how many hearts she had touched and you, Nellie, are very much like her. You have her sweetness, her caring and her generosity. May you never change, even if adversity were to come your way, remember those are qualities that are yours and nobody can take away from you."

"Thanks, Daddy," she said. "I am really going to miss our morning drives once school starts again."

"We will still find time for our little conversations," Sigmund said, as he parked the car.

Even though the summer was uneventful, it went by very fast. Sigmund suggested to Helene she invite her family over so that they could see the house and spend some time with her. They came up for lunch on a Saturday and to Sigmund's great relief, they returned to Wiesbaden that same evening. They were all very impressed with their home and each one brought whatever they had ready for the baby. Her sister offered to lend her the crib her niece had outgrown, but Sigmund would not hear of it. His child would have its own brand new crib, which would be made to order, there was no need for hand-me-downs and tried hard to conceal his disgust—the very thought! For Helene's sake, however, he went out of his way to be nice to them but it was no easy task. "I guess tolerance is a virtue that not many have, for it does not come easily," he mused to himself.

Nellie had just begun her last school year when, late one night, Sigmund received the call he had been dreading for quite some time. It was Anna. She tried to control her voice but all Sigmund was able to hear was sobbing. "I will be right over," he said, setting down the phone. He turned ashen and did not need Anna to frame it in words, he knew what to expect. The sound of the phone had woken up Helene and one look at Sigmund said it all. "It's Paul," said Sigmund. "I will be back as soon as I can." Helene offered to go with him but Sigmund said no whilst dressing. He was ready in no time, and Anna was at the door waiting for him when he arrived.

Her eyes were swollen from crying but she was more in control of herself. "Is he…?" Sigmund asked tentatively.

"Yes, he has left us. He called for me and I came running."

"Did he say anything?"

"He complained about being in great pain and was breathing heavily. I called Doctor Rubens, who lives just across the street from us, but when he got here, it was too late. It was a heart attack."

They went up to Paul's room. Tears were streaming down Sigmund's face. Paul was lying in bed as if he were sleeping, he looked so peaceful. Sigmund sat down by his bedside and took his hand in his, it was already cold. He did not hear Anna leave and close the door behind her. "Little Brother, I see you have decided to take your leave. I had a feeling this was coming, but the last couple of months you hadn't complained and indeed looked far better than you had in a long time. The little nephew, or niece, you were looking forward to will have no Uncle Paul to tease and I will be very lonely without you, little Brother, for I have not only lost a brother but a partner and best friend." Sigmund broke down and wept.

Nellie was devastated. All the men she loved had been taken from her; her grandfather, her Uncle Paul, would her father be next?

Paul was buried at the Jewish cemetery in the city of Frankfurt. All his friends and business acquaintances made themselves present to bid him goodbye and as Abraham pointed out in his farewell address, here was a man who had distinguished himself for his wit, humility and honesty. He was a gentleman and a man of his word who had earned the respect and admiration of all those who had been lucky to know him. His memory would live on in his friends and as long as those who have left us are remembered, they have not died.

Helene worried about Sigmund. It seems as if he'd aged overnight. It had been such a blow to him, for even though he had anticipated it, Paul's sudden death caught him completely by surprise.

It was not long now before the baby was due and its arrival would surely be a welcome distraction. Nellie, too, sensed her father's unhappiness and tried her hardest to please him, going out of her way to be nice and considerate towards her stepmother. An air of tranquillity permeated their home and Sigmund was very grateful for it, as he was under no end of stress. Not only did he now carry the entire responsibility for the business on his shoulders, but he had to execute Paul's will and wind up his affairs. Anna would live in the house until it was sold and then she would move in with them. Helene had not objected to it, quite on the contrary.

Anna would be in charge of the laundry and kitchen and Nellie and Sigmund were delighted at the prospects of having Anna prepare their meals for them. No one could beat her cooking. At first, Helene thought she might be bored at home, but it was not the case. She was a wonderful homemaker and getting everything ready for the baby took up a lot of her time. Now, as her pregnancy was nearing its end, she did not have the same stamina and tired easily, so she was grateful for all the help she could get.

On the weekends, Sigmund would see to it that she rested and they would go on long walks. Nellie would sometimes join them, but mostly it would be the two of them.

If Paul's passing had not brought Helene and Nellie closer, it at least had led to a tolerance between them, for Sigmund's sake.

Chapter 11

On one of her walks, Helene's attention had been drawn to a couple. The woman was pregnant and a few years older than she, her husband was short and seemed to be the same age. There was something special about the way she carried herself and they had seen each other so often now, they would smile at each other as their paths crossed. Helene was intrigued by her and wondered if it was her first pregnancy as well. It was a gloomy afternoon, the beginning of February. The days were longer and the sun was warmer and one could feel the cold winter months would soon be coming to an end. Helene was very restless. She was tired, so she lay down but she could not find a comfortable position; her belly seemed to always be in her way. She tossed and turned and finally gave up. "I will go for a walk through the park," she said to herself, getting up, then put on her warm winter coat, got her gloves and shawl and told Marga she would be home in an hour.

She headed for the park and was enjoying the peace and quiet when she saw a familiar figure walking towards her. It was the unknown lady she had seen so often. "It's either now or never, so now I will talk to her." It was not in her nature to speak to strangers but she was so curious and intrigued by her and as they came abreast of each other, the stranger smiled at her. This was Helene's chance and she smiled back and said, "Even though it is pretty cold, it really is a nice afternoon to be out."

"It is," replied the stranger, "and going for walks is so important in our present condition."

"Is this your first?" Helene asked.

"Oh, no," said the stranger, "it's my fourth. By the way, my name is Martha, what is yours?"

Helene introduced herself and told her she was expecting her first. "That is very exciting," said Martha. "When the fourth comes along, one is already so experienced; it's not nearly as romantic."

"I guess it is like that with everything in life," replied Helene, and invited her to join her on her walk. Martha was delighted.

As it turned out, Martha lived just around the corner from Helene and was very sad at Lina and David's departure, for ever since she'd gotten married, they had lived on the same street. She did not befriend Lina directly, but every once in a while, if they met at the store or on the street, they talked and even enjoyed a cup of coffee together. "Have you heard anything from them?" she inquired.

"Not one word," replied Helene. "I only met Lina once but found her very nice indeed."

Martha told Helene that she lived in a small building with six flats and she and her husband were the caretakers. It was really *her* job since her husband worked at the Frankfurter Hof as a handyman. Her dream was to one day to own a big villa like Helene's, for with three children and now a fourth on its way, they were pretty cramped for space. But with the cost of living rising steadily and no wage improvement in sight, a person could count themselves lucky nowadays to even have a job. So many people were being laid off that her dream would probably never come true, but she knew how very blessed she was: she had a roof over her head, a job, a caring husband and three gorgeous and healthy children, two boys and a girl. What else could one want from life?

Helene listened and nodded her head in agreement. Martha went on to say that her in-laws had a home out in the country, about a two hour train ride from the city, and the children spent all their summers with them while in the winter they were all at school.

"How old are they?" asked Helene.

"They are eight, ten and twelve."

"You look so young to have such grown children," said Helene.

"What a nice thing for you to say," replied Martha, smiling. "But looks can be deceiving and I am a good deal older than I look. We started a family immediately after we were married and this baby is a surprise, but it will be just as welcome as the rest," she added. "It does not make it any easier, you know, one more mouth to feed, but I am sure the Lord will provide."

"When is the baby due?" Helene asked.

"In a few more weeks," replied Martha.

"Mine is also due towards the end of the month."

"What if we gave birth the same day?" said Martha, smiling.

"Now, that would really be a coincidence," replied Helene, looking at her watch. "I was only going to be gone an hour and it's been about two, so I should be heading home. I had not realised it was so late."

"Neither had I," said Martha. "Time goes by so fast when one is having a good time."

"It is always the way," replied Helene, then thanked Martha for a nice time and told her that they would probably run into each other again before heading home. However, she did not see Martha again for a while. The weather turned and winter was back with all its might, putting an end to her walks.

It was not long after their conversation that Helene woke Sigmund up in the middle of the night. She was drenched in sweat and felt miserable, describing her symptoms to him. "You'll feel better in a couple of hours," he said tenderly. "It sounds to me as if the baby is announcing its arrival." He picked up the phone and called the doctor who told him to bring Helene to the hospital, then went in to Nellie's room. She was sleeping soundly and he did not want to wake her so he scribbled a note telling her their whereabouts.

Just as he had foreseen, Helene gave birth a couple of hours later to a baby boy and Sigmund was beside himself with happiness. Now he had a son and an heir, someone who would carry the family name. Overjoyed, he went home to give Nellie the good news, leaving Helene with the baby sound asleep in her arms.

Even though Helene was tired, she could not take her eyes off the child. The nurse came in several times and offered to put the baby in a crib that was beside her bed so she could get some rest, but she would not hear of it, not bearing the thought of parting with him. It was her own flesh and blood, the product of love, her baby, and she was a mother at last. Her eyes would close and she would open them immediately to make sure she was not dreaming.

Nellie was just finishing her breakfast. She had seen and read the note when she got up and was beside herself with excitement. She wondered if she would know anything more before leaving for school when her father walked in and gave her the good news. "It is a darling little boy and both mother and child are doing well," he said, giving her a happy hug.

"That is wonderful," replied Nellie. "I cannot wait to see him."

"I will take you to the hospital as soon as school is out," said Sigmund, happily. True to his word, Sigmund was waiting for her when she came home and she ran up to her room, dropped her school bag, barely washed her hands, ran downstairs and got into the car. It was a short drive.

Helene was in a private room in the maternity ward. As they walked in, she was finishing nursing the baby and gave them a happy smile. "Your timing could not have been better," she said. Nellie kissed Helene on the forehead and looked down at the tiny bundle in her arms.

"What a beautiful baby," she said. His face was small and all his features were so delicate, his head perfectly shaped and the little hair that covered it like a patch was almost black. Helene noticed her gaze and told her it would fall out in a couple of weeks and that it was very probable his hair would be much lighter. The same is true for the colour of his eyes, they, too will change in time. Nellie looked at her father, "He is so small, so helpless," she said. "To think that I was once just as small."

"It really is amazing," said her father. "Of all the creatures on this earth, we humans are the most helpless when we are born.

Look at a horse for example, he can walk just minutes after his birth."

"Would you like to hold your little brother, Nellie?" asked Helene.

"I would love to," she replied, beaming, and Helene gently put him in her outstretched arms. Nellie sat very still looking down at him. All of a sudden, he opened his eyes and stared at her and Nellie let out a gasp. "He is looking at me," she said full of awe. Helene and Sigmund, who had been watching in silence, smiled.

"As he grows older, he will sleep less," said Helene. "You are very precious to me, little one," she said under her breath, smiling happily. Just then, the baby started crying and Sigmund took him from Nellie and gave the baby back to his mother.

"Is something wrong?" asked Nellie.

"Oh, no," Helene replied, "he may just be a little uncomfortable, it is his way of communicating."

"What are we going to name him?" Nellie wanted to know. "We have thought of calling him Alfred, do you like it?"

"I do! We can call him Freddy for short," Nellie suggested.

"Well, then, Alfred it shall be," replied her father, looking at Helene who nodded her head in agreement.

Helene spent three days in the hospital and Nellie went with Sigmund every evening to see her little half-brother. Helene was eager to go home and be in her own surroundings and, although she had a lot of visitors and her mother and sisters took turns spending time with her, time just dragged on and on. She looked forward to the evenings with her husband and Nellie. Finally, her stay at the hospital came to an end. Sigmund got there around midmorning to take her and his son home and it took forever for the doctor to arrive and sign her release form. She was bathed, ready to go and filled with impatience when he finally showed up, just minutes ahead of Sigmund, worried that she might not be ready by the time he arrived. Helene was well aware of Sigmund's busy schedule and did not want him to be late on her account.

The private nurse escorted them to the door and waited by her side while Sigmund came around with the car. It was hard for her to conceal the relief she felt at finally being able to leave. Alfred was sound asleep in her arms; nothing seemed to disturb his sleep, as she gently lay him in the basket on the back seat. He opened an eye for a second as if to acknowledge his new surroundings then closed it almost immediately. Sigmund whistled happily behind the steering wheel, feeling elated at having his family reunited and under the same roof.

Marga came out to greet them as soon as she heard the car drive up and helped Helene out while Sigmund, the proud father, unloaded the basket. "Take a look at our new member of the family," Sigmund said to Marga.

"What a gorgeous baby!" she exclaimed, taking a peek at him. Helene smiled.

Sigmund set the basket on the bed in their room. "I could put him in his crib but I'm afraid I will wake him," he said to Helene.

"That's fine, just leave him there until he wakes up."

Sigmund turned to his wife and, taking her in his arms, said, "I have missed you these last days, you do not know how happy I am to have you home again." He kissed her and added, "But I must be leaving, I do not want to be late. I will try and be home early tonight." Helene returned his kiss then went to the window to watch him drive off.

Helene was so busy she had all but forgotten about Martha until one day a couple of weeks later, she happened to run into her in the park, sitting on a bench with a baby carriage by her side.

"Why, it's Martha," she said to herself, walking up to her. "Hello!" Martha looked surprised at first but finally recognised her.

"Helene, how nice to see you. I've thought of you often and wondered…but now I see."

"Yes, it is a boy. And what about you?"

"It is a boy as well," replied Martha, proudly. "Helmut was born the 31 January."

"Alfred," said Helene, "was born on 25 February."

They admired each other's babies and after exchanging some of their experiences said good-bye, promising to see each other soon.

Nellie loved her little stepbrother and was not shy about showing it. She read him stories and sung to him and even wrote a poem about him, doing all the illustrations to go with it. Helene taught her how to care for him and thus a wonderful relationship developed between the two siblings that would last a lifetime.

Chapter 12

Martha lay in bed next to her husband, so worn out she was unable to fall asleep. As she stared at the ceiling, her day's activities unfolded before her eyes. She did all the washing and ironing and Helmut had not made her life easy. He was a content and quiet baby and as long as he was fed and kept dry, he was no trouble whatsoever, but today for some unknown reason, he kept her busy. Every time she set him down, he would cry and whimper so her tasks had taken twice as long and her nerves were on edge. The picture of Helene and her baby flashed through her mind. How rested and serene she looked. How could it be otherwise, when one has maids to do the housework and to help look after the baby? And what a beautiful baby Alfred was. She forgot to tell her husband about her encounter, so much had happened since then. "I have to tell him," she told herself and laying still, listened to his breathing. She didn't think he was asleep. "Peter, are you awake?" she asked softly.

"Yes, I am, what is it?"

"I just remembered, I forgot to tell you about my encounter some weeks ago with Helene."

"With whom?"

"Helene," replied Martha and, after telling him again who she was talking about, gave him a vivid description. As Peter listened, he felt the rising anger in him. Life was so unfair. He had four children to clothe and feed, he and his wife worked hard to make ends meet and she seemed to age with each passing day, and here were the privileged without a care in the world. Martha finished her account and was waiting for him to say something. "Peter, did you listen to what I was saying?"

"I sure did and that child will never have a care in the world. Born to a rich family, he will never know what it means to worry about the next meal or having to get the money together to pay the rent, or losing his job."

Martha interrupted him. "And he will never know what it is to wear hand-me-downs because he will always have the best of everything. Those are the injustices of life," she continued bitterly. "But I have learned to live with them; I try hard to overlook them and to accept what is not in my power to change. What do we know? Maybe our children are the most fortunate, growing up in a big family where all we can give them is love and instil in them the importance of family and the love for nature. That may well be worth a lot more someday than all the money and carefreeness in the world."

"I hope you are right," said Peter, yawning. "Let's try to get some sleep; I do have to be up at the usual time."

Just then, Helmut started crying and Martha got up to tend to him, hearing Peter say under his breath, "If we could afford a maid, we might be able to get a full night's sleep for once."

Martha smiled and said, "Maybe someday," and kissed him gently on the cheek. Helmut quieted down and lay happily in his mother's arms suckling at her breast.

"She said someday," Peter said to himself, but he did not think he would live to see that day. There had been so many changes. Not only had Germany fought a long war that it lost, but it also had to accept the terms of the Treaty of Versailles, which the Allies had agreed on and were set taking three priorities into account: 1. Guarantee Germany against the possibility of future German aggression, 2. Revive the economic infrastructure of the Allies and 3. To ensure the stability of the new nation states in central and eastern Europe. Last but not least, there was the War Guilt clause, which provided the justification for the war reparations.

Peter overheard people at work saying that the republic was to blame for that because this new government had signed what the media called 'a disgraceful document'. To make matters worse, a couple of months before, the Allied reparations commission set the bill at 132000 million gold marks of which 12000 million would be paid in advance, 2000 million yearly and 26% of the value of German exports would be paid to the Allies. In order to avoid antagonising the population further, the government decided to print notes instead of raising taxes, but of course, that caused a spiralling inflation.

On the political front, there were the activists who opposed the republic and produced specific crises, adding to the political malaise and lack of commitment by the vast majority of the population, which was reflected in the drop of support for the three parties of the coalition from 76.2 to 47.5 between 1919 and 1920. And of course, there was the attempt to take over Berlin and overthrow the republic by Wolfgang Kapp and General Luttwitz. The government had withdrawn to Stuttgart and a general strike paralysed the essential services of the city, forcing Kapp to give up the attempt while President Ebert made full use of the presidential powers under article 48 of the Constitution.

Peter felt sad. The future of his children looked bleaker than ever. Maybe that new party someone mentioned at work not so long ago could be the answer. He resolved to find out more about it and with that thought on his mind, finally drifted off to sleep. With the intention of getting the information he sought, he left for work a little earlier than usual and was about to enter the lobby when he saw the guy standing by the main entrance.

Peter vaguely remembered his name…was it Max? He was in his early thirties, very tall and his eyes matched the colour of the sky while his blond hair framed his face with its very masculine, well-defined features. He was very handsome indeed. Peter walked up to him and commented on what a pleasant morning it was. Max agreed and then Peter said, "I don't know if you remember, but a couple of days ago, I overheard you mention something about a new political movement. I wonder if you—" Max interrupted him.

"Sure, we could meet at the bar across the street this evening and talk about it if you want."

"Great, I'll see you there," said Peter, heading for his office.

Later that day as he was putting on his coat to leave, his boss asked him to find a file for him. Peter looked at his watch. Every time he was about to leave and needed to be somewhere on time, his boss would want something at the last minute and he would invariably be late; today was no exception. Peter did as he was told, having no trouble finding the file and handed it to his boss. He said goodnight and was gone in a flash.

Max was not alone at the bar when Peter walked in. Two other persons Peter had never seen before were at his table. "Well, you finally got here," said Max, getting up to greet him. "Let's get down to business," he said, once the introductions were over. "I will now talk to you about this new movement."

In January 1919, the German Workers Party was founded in Munich. It was one of a number of völkisch, or radical fringe groups, that were established immediately after the end of the First World War. Hitler, an Austrian who had served in the German army, joined the party in November 1919. He was placed in charge of the party's propaganda and was largely responsible for renaming the movement the National Socialist German Workers Party (NSDAP) in 1920 and drafting the 25-point program, which contained both nationalist and socialist elements. "I will now mention the most important points of the program," said Max, taking a sip of his beer.

Article 1: The Union of the Germans in a Greater Germany
Article 2: The revocation of peace treaties Versailles and
Saint-Germain
Article 3: The acquisition of land and territory to feed our people and settle our surplus population
Article 4: Jews are to be excluded from German nationhood
Article 8: All non-German immigration must be prevented
Article 10: Emphases on physical and mental work
Article 11: the abolition of incomes unearned by work
Article 12: the confiscation of war profits
Article 13: extensive nationalisation of businesses
Article 14: Profit sharing in large industrial enterprises
Article 15: the extension of old age insurance
Article 16: The creation and maintenance of a healthy middle class
Article 17: land reform
Article 19: The replacement of Roman law by German law
Article 22: The formation of a people's army
Article 23: Non-Germans should be excluded from any influence within the national media
Article 25: The establishment of a Central State power

Max looked up from his notes and Peter was about to speak but Max silenced him with a look. "I have one more thing to add and then I will answer whatever questions you might have," he said.

"We have just bought a newspaper called the 'Völkischer Beobachter' [People's Observer) that appears twice a week, and I am very proud to say that comrade Hitler, as we call him, has just recently become party leader."

"How many members does the party have?" Peter asked.

"By the end of last year, membership increased from two hundred to two thousand and party branches have extended outside of Munich and Bavaria to all over Germany. I forgot to mention it, but we have just finished creating our own strong-arm squad called the 'Storm Detachments' or SA."

One of the strangers spoke. "This is at least one party willing to fight those treaties and the present government along with them. They are the ones to blame for our misery. My friends who are members and have been urging me to join are absolutely right. This party is the only way out; it will redeem us and our country."

Max turned to Peter. "Where do *you* stand?"

"I would like to think about everything you have said and study the whole program before making a decision," he replied.

"Fair enough," said Max, getting up and asking for the check. "You know where to find me if you need more information or want to join, feel free to contact me."

Peter shook hands with everyone and was the first to leave. "Sooner or later, you will be one of us," he mumbled under his breath, as he watched Peter open the door, then turned his attention to the others. "What have you all decided?"

"We are joining," they replied in one breath.

Max gave them a pleased look. "I can assure you, gentlemen, you will have no regrets."

Peter made his way home deep in thought. Martha was still awake when he got home. "Have you eaten?"

"No, I just had a beer." She warmed up his dinner for him while he went to wash his hands. "How come you are still up?" he asked, sitting down at the table.

"Helmut woke up wet and hungry and I thought you would not be long so I decided to do some chores until you got back. Did you find out anything of interest?" she asked.

He told her about the meeting and mentioned some of the points of the Party's program. "It sounds pretty good," said Martha, who had listened with the utmost interest.

"It does if you overlook the following two points: Jews are to be excluded from German nationhood and all non-German immigration must be prevented."

"I don't understand what those two points mean, do you?" Martha asked.

"I am not sure," replied Peter, "but I think it means that the Party does not want foreigners in the country and that as far as Jews are concerned, the Party does not recognise them as German citizens."

"How can they not be German citizens if they were born here?"

"I do not have the answer to that," replied Peter, "but to put your mind at rest, I did not join the Party. I told them I needed to think it over."

"Well," said Martha, "I certainly do not think it is right for a Party to exclude its own citizens."

"It's late, Martha, why don't I help you do the dishes then see if we can get a good night's sleep for once," Peter said, getting up from the table.

Chapter 13

Sigmund watched the latest political developments with growing unease. Some of his customers were having a hard time paying their bills and he was indeed forced to close down the credit of one of his oldest clients. It had made him sick to his stomach but business was business and he surely was not running a charity institution. He, too, had commitments to fulfil and he always honoured his word.

Little Freddy was like a ray of sunshine in these gloomy and uncertain times. Even though he felt quite helpless around him, and could not bring himself to making all the cooing sounds Helene and Nellie made, he would take his little hand in his and hold it. How small it was compared to his, to think that someday, not too far in the future, it would become as big as his. He was absolutely thrilled at having a son, he felt so lucky and could hardly wait for the time to come when they could do things together. He would never forget the day he walked into the nursery and over to the crib where Freddy lay awake and as soon as he saw him, had given him a toothless smile and stretched out both his little arms to him. Tears sprung to his eyes and he'd turned to Helene, who had come in behind him. "He knows I'm his dad," he said, his voice full of emotion.

"Yes," she replied, taking the baby out of the crib. "He sure does."

The proud father stretched out his arms and she gently placed the baby in them. Freddy was almost 6 month old and it was the first time he held his son, awkwardly at first, and felt his little heart beating against his chest. Helene was well aware of all the emotions that were going through him. She stood in the background, taking it all in.

Suddenly, Sigmund turned to her and, at the sound of his voice, Freddy starred at him out of his honey coloured eyes. "I don't think he is very comfortable," he said and Helene walked over to them and took Freddy from him.

"It is time for his bath," she said, starting to undress him.

"I will leave you to it," said Sigmund, making his way to the door. He peeked into Nellie's room and saw her sitting at her desk.

"Hi, Dad," she said, looking up from her work. Sigmund sat down on the bed.

"Can you spare a minute?" he asked.

"Sure," she replied, as she sat down beside him. He told her about Freddy. Nellie listened to him, smiling. "You are kind of scared of babies, aren't you?"

"It is not being scared, it is just that he is so small and so vulnerable and all he cares about is eating and sleeping, right now we have nothing in common."

"But pretty soon you will, as soon as he learns to walk and to talk," said Nellie.

"Ah, then, my child, it will be like it was with you," said Sigmund.

"I don't think you will have too long to wait," replied Nellie. "I know you have been studying hard," Sigmund began.

"Yes," said Nellie, "my time in school is almost over."

"Are you happy about it?"

"I have mixed emotions."

"Finishing school means a period of your life has come to an end and another is about to begin," added her father.

"Yes, Daddy, it is a change and there is an uncertainty about it, even if one knows what one is going to do."

"Are you telling me you have made up your mind?" asked Sigmund, surprised.

"I think I have. I have decided to take your advice and go to business school."

"That is a wise decision, and I do not think you will regret it for one day. You will have to be my successor in the business, you know, and one has to know the ropes in order to be able to tell others what to do."

"I know, but Daddy, I do have something that has been on my mind for a couple of days now."

"And that is?"

"It is my grandmother, have you seen her lately?"

"I hate to admit it, Nellie, I have been meaning to pay her a call but I have been so busy, you know the situation. But what about her?"

"Well, I have neglected her a little as well, with Freddy and school, you know how it is. But I went over to see her last week, it had been a little less than a month since I last had lunch with her, and she looked so frail. She was not herself, either. Normally, I am as tall as she is but, well, what I want to say Daddy is that she has become smaller, and she did not have her usual spark and there was indifference about her as well. At first, I thought I was the cause of it but then, just before leaving, the maid came up to me and said she was worried about her, that her whole attitude towards life has changed."

Sigmund took Nellie's hand in his. "I can tell you are worried so I will go by and see her tomorrow."

"Thank you, Daddy," replied Nellie. "Maybe you can do something about it, you know how much she means to me."

"I know," said Sigmund, getting up. "Are you joining us for dinner?" he asked.

"Yes," she replied, "I am."

"I will see you in the dining room," he said and left the room.

Nellie felt very relieved now that she had spoken to her father about what was foremost on her mind and was sure he would find out what was ailing her grandmother and be able to do something about it. She went across the hallway and peeked into the nursery. Everything was quiet. She glanced over at the crib and saw Freddy sleeping soundly. All of a sudden, a smile swept over his face.

Nellie thought how beautiful he was and how much he has grown. Just as Helene had said, the colour of his eyes changed and his hair was now a beautiful golden hue. This tiny being brought a ray of sunshine into all of their lives and distracted them from their grieving over Paul's passing as well as giving Nellie and Helene something in common.

Sigmund was true to his word and he called Mrs Winters around half past ten in the morning, slightly surprised not to hear her voice when someone finally picked up the phone. "Mrs Winters' residence," he heard the voice say.

"Hello, yes I would like to talk to Mrs Winters, is she in?"

"May I ask who is calling?"

"It is Sigmund."

"I will see if she is awake," replied the maid. Sigmund glanced at his watch. Mrs Winters was always up and about at this time and it seemed a long time before the maid picked up the phone again. "Just a minute, please," she said.

Sigmund waited. He was very relieved when he finally heard Mrs Winters' voice. "Is that you, Sigmund?" she asked.

"Yes, it's me, how are you?"

"I guess I am all right," she replied. "Am I ever going to get to see you again?" she asked.

Sigmund was startled, this was not like her. "That is the purpose of my call, I was thinking of joining you for dinner tonight if it is convenient to you."

"That will be just fine," she replied, "but try not to be late. I go to bed very early, as you know," said Mrs Winters.

"I will not be late," replied Sigmund.

"Good." Sigmund was about to say something but he realised the phone had gone dead. "I'm afraid Nellie is right, she sure does not seem to be herself. I hope it is nothing serious," he mumbled to himself, picking up some papers. Then he called Helene to let her know he would not be home for dinner, which suited her just fine for her cousin who lived in Brussels was in town and she could have a nice evening with her.

Sigmund left the office at five o'clock sharp. Maria opened the door. "Come in, do come in," she said. "Mrs Winters has been looking forward to your visit all day."

Just then, he heard her voice say, "Sigmund, I'm here in the living room." She was seated in her usual chair and looked as beautiful as ever. He walked over to her and, bending down towards her, gently brushed his lips against her cheek.

"You do not change, do you?" he said straightening up, but he noticed almost immediately that the gleam in her eyes was no longer there. What had happened? Where had it gone? She looked so frail, and small, yet her presence still filled the room.

"It's been a long time since you were last here, Sigmund," she said.

"I never intended for it to be so long," he said.

"I know a lot of things have changed for the better in your life and I can see in your eyes that you are happy."

"As happy as I will ever be," he replied.

"I also heard you are the father of a darling little boy."

"Yes, indeed," said Sigmund and, taking out his wallet, retrieved a picture of Freddy and handed it to her.

"He sure is a beautiful baby," said Mrs Winters. "I have heard so much about him, Nellie dotes on him and she keeps me up to date," she added, smiling.

"He really has been a ray of sunshine."

"He has helped you forget the sorrows and has brought Nellie and Helene closer, has he not?"

"Oh, without question," said Sigmund, "the tension between them is a thing of the past."

"I'm so glad," she replied.

"But why don't you tell me about yourself, how have you been?" asked Sigmund.

"There is not much to tell, life goes on as usual, but everything around us has changed. The world we live in is no longer what it was. But I do not want to bore you with this." Just then, Maria came in and announced that dinner was served. Sigmund helped her out of the chair and was surprised to see her using a cane. She noticed his look. "This, too, is part of life, you know," she said, smiling sadly. "As you grow older, you tend to lose your balance and a cane does help to steady you."

"It sure is a smart looking one," said Sigmund, lightly. The meal was excellent, as usual. He had been so busy at work he forgot to eat the sandwich Helene had made for him and didn't realise how hungry he was until he started eating. Sigmund took up the conversation. "You were saying that everything around us has changed…"

"Don't you see the changes?" she asked.

"I do see, I have customers who can no longer pay their bills and I see prices rising every day."

"And what about the political instability, have you read about this so called Nazi movement?" she interrupted him.

"I have," said Sigmund, "and I do not like it, but I do not think anything will come of it, it is small and the Nazis will never come to power."

"I would not be so sure," replied Mrs Winters, "we Jews are getting blamed for a lot of things and even our own countrymen are turning against us." Sigmund was pensive. She was speaking the truth. "I am old. I have seen a lot of changes and have adapted to a lot of different circumstances during my lifetime, having lived through one terrible war. But I am tired. Indeed, I have had the best of everything and lived it to the fullest, I've enjoyed every minute of it, be it in happy times or in times of sorrow, and have grown as a person being able to give back. But the time has now come for me to let go. David is beckoning to me and it is time I left this world to be with him." Sigmund listened to her in silence. He was sad, but he only admired her all the more, knowing in her heart that her time was up and she was not going to put up a fight. She would leave this world like the lady she was. They were both silent for a long time.

Sigmund was the first to break it. "I understand what you are saying and it takes a lot of courage to admit to oneself that time has run out. I admire you for it. The changes that are taking place are even harder for us to accept and comprehend, but we have not yet reached the end of our path and we must, therefore, go on seeking our way with every passing day."

"That is the law of life," she replied with a smile. Sigmund looked at his watch.

"I guess it's way past your bedtime," he said with a twinkle in his eye, "and I really should leave now."

"I do hope you will find the time to come see me again," she said, as he helped her out of her chair.

"I will, I promise."

She leant on his arm and on her cane and escorted him to the front door where he gave her a hug and held her close for a minute. How much weight she has lost, he could feel her bones and felt his eyes grow moist, then he opened the door and walked out before she could see the tears running down his cheeks.

Maria heard the front door close and came to help her mistress up the stairs. She found her staring at the closed door. He has left, but he will be back to say good-bye. The conversation drained her of all her strength and she fell into a deep sleep just as soon as her head touched the pillow.

It was late by the time Sigmund got home. Helene was already in bed, sound asleep. Only Nellie was still up. She had waited impatiently for her father's return, eager to hear about the outcome of his visit. "Did you have a nice visit with Oma?" she asked as soon as she heard him walk into her room.

"It was very nice indeed."

"And did you find out what is ailing her?" Sigmund looked pensive.

"I did."

"What is it, is it very serious?"

"Your grandmother is very depressed. You know the whole political situation, all the changes that are happening in this country, it is not the Germany she has known."

"Yes, Dad, but why didn't she get depressed when the war was going on, why now?"

"While we were at war, Germany still had its old institutions, the Emperor still ruled, there was stability within the country and everyone looked up to him for guidance. This is not the case today. The political structure of Germany has changed, it is no longer a monarchy, it is a republic with a parliament where the parties make the decisions. But, with so many different parties, it is almost impossible to get them to agree on something, or at least to have a majority, so the task of governing has become very difficult. Then there is the fact that prices are rising from day to day. This creates a lot of uncertainty as well, especially for people who, like your grandmother, have a fix income to live on. Their living expenses rise but they still have to make out with the same amount of money, thus becoming poorer with each passing day.

And last but not least, there is this new party—"

Nellie interrupted him, "The Nazis."

"Yes, the Nazis, whose policy is directed against foreigners and us Jews."

"I can see that it is not a happy picture at all," said Nellie.

"It is a very unsettling one and it is hard for old people to accept, or adapt to change and uncertainty, which is the thing that is ailing your grandmother."

"Is there anything we can do?"

"We can only devote as much time to her as we possibly can, realising that one day she will no longer be with us." Sigmund looked up at Nellie. She was so calm, so in control of herself and although he knew how much this last sentence would hurt her, he felt he must prepare her for the inevitable.

Nellie gave him a hug and nestled her head on his shoulder. "Thank you, Daddy," she said in a broken voice. "I will try and spend as much time with her as I can before it is too late." Nellie's shoulders shook as she sobbed and Sigmund pulled her closer to him, stroking her hair.

Nellie did not have much time to brood about her Grandmother. School was coming to an end and she had to prepare for both written and oral examinations. The oral exams were conditioned on her passing the written ones and so she devoted her time to preparing for them and whenever she took a break, she would go into the nursery and play with Freddy. By now, he had learned to sit up and roll from one side to the other, a strong baby who enjoyed all the attention he received.

Between the two exams, students were given one week off school. The purpose of this was to give the teachers time to correct the papers and the students time to prepare. The results were posted on the school board after 3 pm on Friday afternoon. Being nervous all day, Nellie got there early, she could hardly wait to get them. She had had lunch with her grandmother, who did her best to distract her, and now she was standing in front of the message board looking desperately for her name. She didn't realise how many students there were whose last names began with W.

"Hurray!" she exclaimed out loud after finding her name. She read it several times to make sure it really was her then she looked again at the list, hoping to find all her classmates names on it. Everyone had passed except, and she could not believe her eyes, Rachel. Rachel's last name was nowhere to be found. She stared in disbelief. Rachel, who had always been one of the best students. What happened? It could not be possible that she, of all people, should have failed! Even though she and Rachel had not become close again, she felt very sad about it and made her way home deep in thought, and could feel so many emotions waiting to surface.

Helene was home when she came in. Nellie had been on her mind all day. When she heard the front door close, she came out to the hallway to greet her. "Hi Nellie, I have been thinking of you all day, how did it go?"

"It went well," replied Nellie. "I have been invited to the oral part."

"That is great news," said Helene, giving her a hug, "but I must be honest, there was never a doubt in my mind that you would not succeed. Did anyone fail?"

"Yes, one did," said Nellie, "and you will never guess… Rachel."

"Who? Rachel of all people? I feel so bad for her. It may have to do with all the stress she has been under, you know her father has not been well and I heard someone say that they were not doing too well financially either," said Helene.

"That really surprises me, for Rachel never mentioned a word about it."

Nellie expected the oral exams to be more difficult than they were. She was very nervous at first, having to face 12 teachers seated behind a long table, but as soon as she heard the first question, she felt more at ease and was able to answer them all correctly. When it was over, the teachers stood up and congratulated her. As usual, she passed with flying colours and felt relieved, happy and sad, all at the same time.

Sigmund left the office early and was standing in front of the school entrance, waiting to escort her home. He'd meant it to be a surprise and what a surprise it was. Nellie had not seen him and was about to walk right past him when she heard a voice say, "May I escort you home, miss?"

She looked up and said, "Why, Daddy, it's you, how nice of you to come."

"It was the least I could do on such an important occasion," he replied. "I do not even need to ask, I know the answer."

"Yes, Daddy, I passed," and she told him her grades.

"I am so very proud of you," he said, giving her a big hug. They walked home arm in arm. The diplomas were handed out that evening and she had been asked to make the farewell speech for her class. As she spoke, she looked at all the parents and students listening to her and her eyes finally came to rest on her parents who were beaming proudly at her. Her happiness would have been complete if only her grandmother had been able to attend but she was too weak to leave her bed.

On their way home, Sigmund stopped at Mrs Winters' so that Nellie could show her the diploma. She was still awake. "I knew you would come by," said her grandmother, as Nellie entered her room. "I have a gift for you," and, reaching over to her bedside table, handed her a beautifully wrapped gift. Nellie unwrapped it carefully and opened the box. She let out a gasp of surprise…it was a ring, but not just any ring; it had been her grandmother's engagement ring, her favourite. "You have always admired it and now, when you wear it, it will bring back memories of our time together and of what hard work can accomplish," said Oma.

Nellie was speechless. She gave her grandmother a gentle kiss and was about to take her leave when she heard her Grandmother say, "Why, hello, Sigmund, the proud father."

"I could not very well drop Nellie off and not come in and say goodnight," he said, taking her hand.

"Where is Helene?" she asked, and Sigmund told her she was in the car, "Why did you not ask her to come up with you?"

"We did not want to wear you out and besides she is eager to get home and see about Freddy."

"Yes, I know what it is like when there is a baby at home," said Mrs Winters.

"I will come by next week and pay you a longer visit," he said.

"I look forward to it," replied Mrs Winters, closing her eyes.

They both kissed her good night and left.

"She tires so easily," said Nellie sadly.

"What a lovely gift," said Helene, admiring the ring Nellie had on her finger.

"I will always treasure it," she replied.

To celebrate the occasion, Sigmund uncorked a bottle of champagne. "This is to you," he said, toasting his daughter.

Nellie walked over to her parents and, taking their hands in hers, said with a voice full of emotion, "Without your encouragement and support, I might not have succeeded."

Nellie was so tired that all she did was eat and sleep for the first few weeks after her graduation. In the late afternoon, she would go over to her grandmother's, usually taking a book with her to read at her bedside. Once in a while, Oma would open her eyes and say something, assured that her beloved granddaughter was by her side, then drop off to sleep again. These visits were really very hard on Nellie, for she could literally see her grandmother fading away like a candle with every passing day. She would come home looking sad and tearful but for her Oma, she always put on a happy front, cracking a joke now and then or giggling when they both remembered some funny episode they had shared.

Sigmund worried a great deal about Nellie, but he admired her tenacity. She was standing by her grandmother just like her Oma had stood by her during Nellie's difficult times. Yes, as he reflected on the whole situation while enjoying the peace and quiet of his library, life boiled down to giving back what one has received. He also learned that when one has done his duty towards the loved ones and one has nothing to regret, one tends to accept the inevitable much more readily after they are finally taken from us. His thoughts were interrupted by a knock on the door. "Come in," he said. It was Nellie.

"Hi Dad, I have looked all over for you, I should have known I would find you here," she said, laughing.

"You should have known," he said. "Is there anything I can do for you?"

Nellie sat down on the chair facing his desk. She always looked at the portrait of her grandfather that hung on the wall above it before making herself comfortable. Sigmund followed her gaze. "You always look at your grandfather," he said.

"Yes," replied Nellie, "I can't help wondering what he was like. I sure do wish I could have known him."

"He would have been very proud of you," said her dad.

"Maybe someday when you have time, you can tell me more about him," she said.

"I promise," replied her father. "But is there something special on your mind?"

"I have been thinking," she began. "I am well-rested but now getting a little bored, so what would you say if I were to come to the office with you in the mornings? I could help you out and still have my afternoons to be with Grandmother," she said.

"I think that is an excellent idea," replied Sigmund. "It will give us some time together, as well. When do you want to start?"

"Tomorrow, if it is all right with you."

"Sure," he said.

"Business school does not start until another month," she said matter-of-factly.

"You will get paid for your work, Nellie," said her father.

"It really is not necessary, I have everything I need, Dad."

"No," replied her father. "It is only right and it will give you a little extra money. I am sure you can put it to good use." Nellie stood up and thanked him. "Have you been over to see your grandmother?" he asked.

"No, I am going to go see her now."

"Do you mind if I come with you?"

"Not all, I am sure Oma will be delighted to see you."

It was raining and cold, and Sigmund got up to get his coat and let Helene know where he was going. When he came down, Nellie was already seated in the car. "That was quick," she said, as he put the car in gear. Maria opened the door for them. "How is she?" Nellie asked.

"I have not been able to get her to eat all day, all she does is sleep. I will bring up some ice cream and maybe she will listen to you," she said to Nellie. Father and daughter went up the stairs. Mrs Winters opened her eyes as they walked in.

"Why Sigmund, how nice of you to come," she said, almost in a whisper. "Where is Nellie?"

"I am here, Oma," she replied, taking her hand. Sigmund walked over to the bed and brushed his lips against her cheek. She was fast asleep. Nellie settled herself on the bed and Sigmund sat down on the chair. Neither of them spoke, busy with their own thoughts. Then Mrs Winters opened her eyes again when she heard the door open. "Sigmund, Nellie? Are you still here?"

"Yes," they replied in one breath. Comforted in the knowledge that her loved ones were with her, she drifted off back to sleep. "Oma, how about a little ice cream?" Nellie asked, as she dipped the spoon into it. She repeated her question one more time but her grandmother did not stir. She looked at her father. "Daddy?" Sigmund walked over to the bed. "Daddy, Daddy, something is wrong," said Nellie, shaking his arm. He turned to her like in a trance.

"Nothing is wrong, Nellie, everything is as it should be; your grandmother is finally at peace," he said with his voice breaking. Somehow, he always managed to be by his daughter's side when she needed him the most. He took her in his arms and held her tight and she cried as if her heart would break.

Mrs Winters had made all the funeral arrangements herself; she chose the music and the flowers and had written a message for all her friends, placed in a sealed envelope, which Maria handed over to Sigmund. In it, he found a note addressed to him that read:

Dear Sigmund, when you open this I will no longer be among you. I am taking the liberty of asking you to read the note included to all my friends at the Synagogue.

He read out what she had written:

I want to thank each one of you for having contributed in one way or another to helping me become a better person. I do not want you to grieve or be sad, I want you to be happy and live your lives to the fullest and from where ever I might be, I will be keeping an eye on all of you.

Sigmund did as he was instructed. What a great lady and how lucky they all had been to have befriended her, were the words on everybody's lips. Sigmund, Helene, and Nellie were about to leave the cemetery when Abraham and Sara walked up to them. They greeted Helene warmly. "What a lady she was," he said to Sigmund.

"She sure was," he replied.

Sara turned to Nellie, "I know it is a great loss to you," she said.

"Yes, it is," Nellie replied, "but I was very fortunate to have had her for as long and to have been able to spend as much time with her as I did," said Nellie, tearfully.

"Yes, you were very lucky," replied Sara.

"I have been wanting to get together with you," said Sigmund, "but time just seems to fly."

"How about having dinner with us next Thursday?" Helene asked, looking at her husband.

"As far as I can remember, we have nothing scheduled," Sara answered and, turning to Helene, said, "I really am looking forward to seeing the darling baby I have heard so much about."

Abraham took Sigmund aside and said he had something of interest to discuss with him and Sigmund asked if it could wait until the following week. "Sure," Abraham said, "it is nothing urgent."

Everyone took their leave and on the way home, Sigmund told them he had some urgent matters to tend to at the office. "Have you thought about what you might like to do this afternoon, Nellie?" Helene asked. Nellie did not answer immediately; she was trying hard to choke back her tears.

"Grandma is no longer and it does not make sense for me to stay home and mope. What she would have really liked is for me to get on with my life and not be sad, so if it is all right with you, Daddy, I would like to go back to the office."

"Fine with me."

Helene glanced at her watch. "We are almost home and it's almost time for lunch. How about stopping for a bite to eat before continuing your way?" she suggested.

"I am really not hungry," said Sigmund.

"Neither am I," said Nellie, "just the mere thought of food makes me sick."

"Well, then, have it your way," said Helene, opening the car door. "I will see you all this evening." Then she got out of the car.

"We will be home early," said Sigmund, and father and daughter drove in silence. All of a sudden, he spoke his thoughts out loud. "I wonder what Abraham wants to see me about."

Nellie looked up, startled. "I haven't a clue," replied his daughter, but I'm sure you will find out in due time.

They climbed the stairs to the office side by side, and Sigmund headed straight for his office as he had some very important meetings scheduled. The day's events receded into the back of his mind as he went about his business.

Nellie, whose only wish had been to seek solace and comfort in these walls she had gotten to know so well, was constantly reminded of her loss. The employees kept coming into her office, offering their condolences and saying beautiful things about her grandmother. She knew they all meant well but it only exacerbated the pain and with it, this terrible void she felt as well. She was exhausted and relieved by the time her father came into her office to take her home. He did not have to ask as he could tell she had had a very rough time.

"I should have known better," he said.

"About what?" asked Nellie.

"About you coming here," he replied.

"Don't worry, Daddy, they all meant well and they just wanted to be a part of my sadness."

"I know, but you do look exhausted."

"Helene's food and a good night's sleep will do wonders," she said, trying to strike a light tone. Needless to say, she did not make it to dinner that night. As soon as she entered her room, she lay down on her bed and within minutes was fast asleep. Sigmund checked in on her before going downstairs.

"She is sound asleep," he reported to Helene.

"I'm glad. Sleep is the best thing for her right now."

Nellie was happy with her work. Now that her grandmother was no longer, she was working full time but could not help feel a flash of pain when she looked at her watch mid-afternoon, remembering that just a couple of days ago at that very same time, she had been vigilantly at her grandmother's side. It was especially hard for her to understand how a person could be and then all of a sudden be no more, as if she just vanished into space, and yet one knew that the person had once been just by looking at or remembering little things. She would wake up at night, bathed in sweat, and sit up in bed, hearing a voice telling her she is no more, which would be followed by a pang of pain. Then she would hear another voice reply, "You are lying, you are lying, she has not left." Nellie would cry out loud between her sobs, "Yes it's true, Oma is no more, but from somewhere high above in the sky, she is keeping a watchful eye on me." And thus comforted, she would go back to sleep. She was wise enough to know that time, and time alone would heal her open wound, and she was grateful for all the little things that distracted her from that feeling of loss and loneliness.

Her father also saw to it that she be kept busy, sending her from one department to another, learning the ropes. What she liked the least was accounting but she tried hard to understand it. Slowly but surely, time, as expected, did its work and the wound began to close.

Chapter 14

Helene had been busy all week preparing for the dinner party. Sigmund suggested they invite one other couple as well and Helene had been all too happy to oblige. On the day of the dinner, Helene gave Freddy a long warm bath after lunch then slept most of the afternoon. She dressed him in the new outfit she bought especially for the occasion, and he looked absolutely adorable. As usual, she took great pride in her own outfit and Sigmund held her in his arms and whispered in her ear: "You are the queen of my heart." A deep feeling of gratitude swept over her. Everything had worked out better than she had ever dared to hope. She adored her husband, she and Nellie were getting along better than ever expected, and she had the son she wanted—all her wishes had come true. Life was so very good to her.

The ringing of the doorbell interrupted her chain of thoughts and, with Freddy in her arms, she went down to greet their guests. Abraham and Sara were the first to arrive. "So this is Freddy," said Sara, taking him from his mother's arms. He gave his mother a look, but she spoke soothingly to him and thus let himself be taken from her without uttering a sound. However, he never once took his eyes off his mother, as they made their way into the living room. "So darling," said Sara, "and he sure is no lightweight," she added. "He must have a hearty appetite."

"I guess he takes after me," added Sigmund, proudly.

"He must be a year old, is he not?" asked Abraham.

"Two months from today, we will celebrate his first birthday," replied Nellie, overhearing the conversation as she made her entrance with Jacob and Viviane.

"I am so happy you were able to join us," said Helene, getting up to greet them.

"I trust your mother is feeling better," Sigmund asked, as he shook her hand.

"Yes, we are so fortunate as it could have been a lot more serious, but nowadays, with the right medical care—"

Freddy's cries interrupted Viviane but subsided as soon as they started when Nellie took him from Sara and laid him down on the floor. Now, as he crawled all over it, all eyes were on him. Knowing he was the centre of attention, he started showing off, to the delight of the adults. Holding on to the side of the table, he tried to pull himself up. After three tries, he managed to stand erect.

"He will be walking before you know it," Sara remarked.

"I hope so, for he has become so heavy it will make it a lot easier for me," said Helene.

Sigmund served some drinks and the men retired to a corner of the room, leaving the ladies to themselves. They made light conversation and more than once, the room echoed with laughter as they recalled some happy experiences from bygone times. Just as he was about to ask Abraham what he wanted to discuss with him, Helene excused herself to put Freddy to bed. He gave everyone a kiss and waved his chubby little hand as he left the room.

Anna was in the nursery waiting for them. Helene kissed him good night then handed him over but he gave her such a sad look that she took him in her arms again. No sooner had she done this did a smile light up his whole face. She kissed him one more time and, saying she needed to get back to her guests, left him in Anna's capable hands. *That child is really going to be something,* she thought, going downstairs. She then peeked into the kitchen and saw that dinner was ready to be served. Upon returning to the living room, she invited everyone into the dining room.

Over dessert, the conversation turned to the economic situation. Jacob brought up the subject. "These reparations we have to pay are going to ruin this country, there is no way the government can continue printing money as it has been doing. Our currency is becoming worthless with every passing day and I am sure the Allies have to realise that the sums they set are completely beyond our means," he continued. "It's creating a lot of unrest among the population and a lot of antagonism against the government, not to mention this new party, these so-called Nazis, who are trying to take advantage of all the havoc."

"Maybe the Allies will come to their senses," said Abraham.

"I do not think so," Jacob lamented, "they just want to ruin us."

"I don't agree with you," Abraham said. "I think they just want us to make good the damage we did. It is their way of taking revenge. They may be well on their way to helping create a monster," Abraham then said thoughtfully.

"What do you mean?" Sigmund asked.

"Just go back and remember where and how that movement started, and now look how fast it has spread. It is everywhere."

"I know from my nephew that they have even infiltrated the students association," said Jacob.

"I did not know the students had an association," said Abraham.

"Yes, they created it in the summer of 1919. I know because one of my nephews took a very active part in it," said Jacob. "And what better breeding ground to disseminate their program," he concluded.

The ladies were listening intently to the conversation going on around them and Sara interrupted the silence that ensued. "Abraham," she said, turning to her husband, "why don't you tell them what you are planning?"

Sigmund gave her a surprised look. "Well, I…" Abraham stammered, "I was going to discuss it with Sigmund, but it is kind of nice to have two opinions and Jacob has very good judgment," he said.

"If you will excuse us," Sigmund said to the ladies, "we will adjourn to the library."

The ladies went into the living room. "Are you going to tell us what this is all about, Sara?" Viviane asked.

"I am sure we will hear about it in due course," said Helene, and changed the subject.

Sigmund poured after dinner drinks and they all made themselves comfortable in the big leather chairs. "This room is so cosy," said Jacob, who had never seen it before.

"I love the sound of the water," Abraham remarked.

"It really is very soothing," said Sigmund, "but Abraham, you were going to tell us something."

"Yes, well, I did not want to upset the ladies too much and I really appreciated your tact about not having me discuss this topic in front of them," said Abraham gratefully, "but personally, I do not see things getting any better. Quite the contrary, I expect them to get a lot worse. I am not talking about the economic side, but the political and social situation. These Nazis are extreme rightist. They want a greater Germany and they do not want Jews, nor do they want foreigners, and should they ever come to power, they will make our lives miserable. We are already taking the blame for a lot of what is happening. Mr Rathenau is a very good example; he was a Jew and was murdered. And he was only the first since I can assure you he won't be the last, this is just the beginning."

"I think you are exaggerating," said Jacob. "President Ebert is a good man and has shown leadership."

"I agree with you," said Abraham, "but he will not be here forever. Believe me, the parties are so fractioned, he is already having a hard time trying to keep the coalition together and getting them to agree. May I also remind you that unity is strength and when the unity is lost or starts to crumble, it is the turning point where others take advantage."

"You are so right," said Sigmund, "but do tell us, what are you thinking about doing?"

"Well, even though I am a getting on in years, for I am a couple of years older than both of you…just a little reminder," he said, with a slight smile, "I am thinking of packing up and leaving."

"Leaving Germany for good?" Jacob asked.

"Where would you go?" Sigmund wanted to know.

"Yes," said Abraham, "but hear me out. Richard, one of my friends with whom I went to school, has a cousin who lives in Colombia, South America. They have always been very close, for they are practically the same age and neither of them had brothers or sisters. Even though they live on two different continents nowadays, they see quite a lot of each other, for Emanuel, that is his name, does quite a bit of business in Europe and has been spending a lot of time here recently."

"Have you met him?" asked Sigmund.

"No, I have not, but let me get on with my story. There are apparently quite a few Germans living in the country, but strangely enough, there is no brewery, can you believe it? So he is thinking of starting one and he is looking for business partners."

"And you are considering being one of them," Sigmund said.

"I am indeed," replied Abraham.

"South America? That is really far away, it must be 100 years behind Europe, at least, and you are telling us that you are considering moving there, giving up all you have here? I can assure you, the quality of life you find over there will—" but Abraham interrupted Jacob.

"The term 'quality of life' is very subjective. You can have all the culture and progress you want but if you cannot enjoy it all in peace, if you are forever worried about what is going to happen next, what quality of life is that?"

"I guess you are right," said Jacob. They were all silent for a minute.

"How much money would you have to invest in this project?" Sigmund asked.

"Basically, I would have to put in all I have, but I do think that if the business is successful, I can at least double it, and who can go wrong, producing and selling beer?"

"When do you have to decide?" Jacob wanted to know.

"I can take my time, but the longer I wait, the more the currency will lose its value unless a miracle happens and someone comes to our rescue before Germany goes completely broke."

"It is very tempting," said Sigmund, "from the economic and even political point of view. If I were just starting out, I would not hesitate one minute, but at my age, it could turn out to be quite an adventure."

"How does Sara feel about it?" Jacob asked.

"On the one hand she is worried about my health, all this stress and uncertainty is not good for me, but on the other, the thought of leaving the family and who knows if ever seeing them again, weighs very heavily on her. So, she is torn between the devil and the deep blue see. The children would, of course, come with us and they would have no problem whatsoever, young people are so adaptable. It would also give them a second language, for they speak Spanish in Colombia and it would surely broaden their horizon."

"What about university and schools?" Sigmund asked.

"I understand they have a number of foreign schools and the country is like the rest of South America, predominantly catholic so the Jesuits have a university there. I forgot to mention, we would of course be living in the capital city Bogotá."

"Is it not the third highest city in the world?" asked Jacob.

"It is at 2650 metres above sea level, on a plateau surrounded by the Andes Mountains."

"Aren't you worried about the altitude affecting you?" asked Sigmund.

"I am not," replied Abraham, "because the human body is so wonderful it can adapt to everything. It will probably take time, but I am sure it will not be a problem."

"It is a tough decision and you have to look at it from all angles," said Sigmund.

"You are absolutely right, which is why I first have to meet Emanuel and see if there is a chemistry between us, then take it from there."

"If we can be of any help to you…" Jacob began to say.

"I know I can count on both of you for good advice," said Abraham, then he looked at his watch. "I had not realised it was so late, we really must be leaving." So, they re-joined their wives in the living room.

"And…?" Sara asked, turning to her husband. "Were they surprised?"

"Very, but it is late and we do not need to get into it all over again. It is time we were on our way," he said, helping her on with her coat. They thanked their hosts for a wonderful evening and, promising to keep in touch, headed home.

"I take it Sara talked to you all about their possible plans?" said Sigmund.

"She sure did. What is your opinion?"

"My advice to Abraham was not to rush into anything. I got the impression he himself does not know what he wants."

"So, what do you think he will decide?"

"I do not have a clue, time will tell," replied Sigmund, and he kissed his wife good night.

The car door had barely slammed shut when Sara began eagerly questioning her husband. Were they surprised, did they think it a good idea? Are they going to consider investing in it? Abraham, who was used to his wife rambling on and on, had learned over time to tune it out and found himself deep in his own thoughts. Sigmund and Jacob were right. It was not a decision to be taken lightly, for once it was taken, there would surely be no backing out and South America, Colombia lay at the other end of the world. He was sure, however, that if he wanted peace and stability, he would have to look for it elsewhere, since it was not about to return to Germany during his lifetime.

He turned to Sara, who was almost yelling at him. "Abraham, is everything all right? I've asked you several questions since we got into the car and now we are home and you haven't even acknowledged my presence."

"I am sorry, Sara I guess my hearing is not what it used to be. Yes, Sigmund and Jacob were very impressed but said it was no easy decision. I should never have mentioned my conversation with Richard to you for all I have done is cause you worry and anxiety. Why don't you have faith in me now like you had in the past? If it is meant for us to leave, it will happen. Let us forget about the whole thing for the time being and get some rest. I think we both need it," he said, locking the car door, and Sara nodded her head in assent then followed her husband into the house.

Chapter 15

Peter was very busy with his job performing the duties of three men. The economic situation affected the hotel business as well and due to the political uncertainties and skyrocketing prices, people now thought twice before taking their families on expensive vacations. Companies also reduced their executive's business travel to a bare minimum, creating havoc among the tourism industry. Peter was lucky, due to his long-term relationship with the Frankfurter Hof, which went all the way back to his father, he had not been laid off, although he was forced to do the job of two other people. God only knew how long he could count on his job, for they started out by laying off the employees who had been with the hotel for a year or less and now they were looking at all those who had contracts of less than five years.

He let out a big sigh, as he continued to look through all the papers on his desk. Life was not getting any easier. On the contrary, the more one worked the less money he ended up with at the end of the month. "No, this is not right," he said out loud. "I end up with the same amount of money but it buys far less than it bought the month before." Martha looked tired and her health was not at all good. That unwanted pregnancy had been a huge mistake, but Helmut was so adorable and sweet and patient. Now that he was actually walking, it made it a lot easier on his mother for she no longer had to carry him, but now had to run after him instead.

The older children tried hard to help out but with school and other chores, it was not easy for them, either. Peter looked forward to coming home after work every evening and playing with Helmut before his mother put him to bed. He would squeal with delight when his father kicked the bright red ball over to him and would walk as fast as his little legs could carry him to get it then, looking his father straight in the eye, he would give it a kick, trying hard to keep his balance, which most of the time he lost, landing with a big thump on the floor.

He never cried when this happened, instead he would crawl to the nearest table or wall and, supporting himself on it, would stand up again. Peter watched him out of the corner of his eye and sometimes felt sorry for him then come to his rescue, especially when Martha was looking on for she would say, "Poor little one. Don't just sit there and watch, Peter, go help him," and he would inevitably end up doing as he was told.

He ran into Max once, but having discussed the issue with Martha and not at all convinced it was the right answer, he put it on the back burner. His father wasn't very encouraging, either, when he approached him on the subject who told him under no uncertain terms that if one were to rely on a party, one should rely on the conservative, well established one. His father had been an officer in the Prussian army and was a firm believer that no good would come out of any change. He despised the Republic and blamed it for all the chaos, his only wish was for the return of the Emperor. It was pointless for Peter to argue with him, for no matter what he said, he would never listen to reason or try at least to understand what was going on.

A knock on the door interrupted his thoughts. "Come in," he said out loud, wondering who it might be. It was Max, looking handsome as ever. "I haven't seen you in quite some time, so I decided to check in with you. How is life?"

Peter was taken completely by surprise, Max being the last person he had expected to see. "Life is good, Max," he replied. "My family is healthy, we have food and work; what else could one ask for nowadays?"

"I am glad to hear that," said Max. "You wouldn't believe how fast the party is growing, people are joining by the dozens every day."

"And I am happy for you," replied Peter, feeling slightly uneasy.

"You are going to become one of us, aren't you?" Max asked, looking him directly in the eye. Peter did not like his expression; there was something cold and cruel about it.

"I have had no time to think about it—" replied Peter.

"I have," Max said without letting Peter finish his sentence. "If I were you, I would give it a little thought," he said in a warning tone. "Now, if you will excuse me," and without another word, he let himself out and slammed the door behind him.

Peter stared at the closed door. "Well, those surely are some manners," he said and picking up some papers on his desk, decided to put Max out of his mind. However, try as he might, he was unable to shake off the unease that swept over him.

It was late when he finally got home. Martha was finishing ironing his shirts, the older children were at their grandparents and Helmut was sound asleep. He opened up a bottle of beer and pulled out a chair.

"You look exhausted," she said, running her hand through his hair.

"I am," he said, "what a day it has been. Did Helmut behave himself?" he asked.

"Oh yes, he was as good as gold. Now that he has learned to walk, everything is so much easier. He is becoming so independent and you would not believe how sociable he is. We went for a walk in the park and ran into Helene."

"The Jewish lady?" Peter asked.

"Yes, that is who I am talking about," she replied. "She was taking little Freddy for a walk as well and you should have seen the two of them together, they were laughing and holding hands. They are the same age, Helmut may be just a few days older than Freddy, but they both started walking the same day. It was such a happy sight. I wish you could have seen them. Helmut had his ball with him and you should have seen them playing with it. It is amazing how little children can get on. Peter, you are not listening," she said, shaking his arm.

"I am, I am, I heard every word you said, but I just remembered something." While Martha was talking, his mind wandered back to the morning scene with Max.

"Something is troubling you," said Martha, who knew her husband well.

"You are right," he replied, and as he ate his dinner, he told her about it.

"What are you going to do?"

"I do not know. His whole attitude was so threatening, but I will not let myself be intimidated by it," he said, trying to sound convincing.

"I have given it a lot of thought," said Martha. "I know so many nice Jewish people, just look at the Rosenthal's who live in the building next door, they could not be nicer. And Helene, she always stops to talk when she sees me, how could anyone join a party that so easily discriminates between Germans and foreigners and has the nerve to say that the Jews are not German, even though they were born and raised in this country. No, Peter, I have always stood up for what is right and what Max and his party are teaching is wrong. I hope you will not succumb to them, for I can tell they are putting a lot of pressure on you. For my part, I do not want to have anything to do with them and I can assure you, I will never ever become one of them. Their teachings are wrong and they collide with my whole upbringing."

Peter listened without interrupting. He knew Martha was right and knew her well enough to know that she would remain true to herself, regardless of the circumstances.

It had been quite some time since Helene ran into Martha and she was amazed at how much Martha had aged since she last saw her. She could tell that something was troubling her but dared not ask as they enjoyed watching the children play, commenting on how very different they were. Freddy was outgoing and used to having his way whereas Helmut was very shy but, once the ice was broken, his real temperament came through and did he ever have one. They were laughing in no time and playing hide-and-seek behind their mother's backs.

Martha gave Freddy a bright red ball and both children were soon running after it. "They are going to be exhausted by the time they get home," said Helene, laughing.

"Nothing wrong with that," Martha replied. "Helmut will take a nice long afternoon nap, and I will be able to get all my chores done."

Helene wondered what they might be then realised that not only could Martha not afford a maid, but also remembered her mentioning she had a job as janitor in the building. *No wonder she looks so tired,* thought Helene. "I guess I had better be getting back," said Martha. "It won't be long before the older children come home from school and they will want something to eat."

"I am sure it is quite a handful," said Helene.

"It sure is. If it is not one, it is the other, and then of course there is Peter, my husband, so I practically have no time for myself," said Martha, then continued. "Do not misunderstand me, Helene, I am not complaining, because such is life."

Helene did not reply. It took some coaxing to get the children to quit playing and when they finally did as they were told, they made their way back in silence. Each had to carry their offspring halfway home because they were so worn out. "I look forward to our next encounter," said Helene. "Freddy has no friends his age."

"Neither has Helmut," replied Martha, "but they had so much fun, maybe we can repeat it sometime."

"Maybe," replied Helene noncommittally. They said goodbye in front of Helene's house and the little boys waved at each other.

"I have had quite a morning," said Helene, turning Freddy over to Anna.

"Anything wrong?" asked Nellie.

"Everything is fine," replied Helene. "Aren't you home early?" she asked.

"I am. A demonstration was scheduled for later on today so some of us thought it in our best interest to come home."

"I see," replied Helene.

Nellie gave Freddy a kiss as Anna walked past her and noted with a smile that he was almost asleep. "That is not surprising," replied Helene, then told Nellie about her encounter with Martha and Helmut. Nellie followed her into the sewing room.

"This is such a cosy room," said Nellie, sitting down on the love seat.

"I feel extremely privileged, Nellie," said Helene.

"I think we all are very lucky, we are probably the luckiest people in the world," replied Nellie. "But what has prompted you to admit it?" Nellie wanted to know.

Helene told her about Martha and her not being able to afford any help whatsoever, of having a job on the side, as if all her chores were not enough.

"Yes," said Nellie, "it is so unfair, some have so much and others—"

Helene interrupted her, "Sigmund, is that you?" she called out, hearing footsteps on the stairs.

"Yes, dear, I am home."

Nellie and Helene looked at each other in surprise. "They are expecting trouble in town, so I decided to give everyone the afternoon off. I take it you are home for the same reason?" he asked, turning to Nellie.

"You are right," she replied.

"I will be right back," he said. When he returned he sat down beside Helene. "Whatever happened to Freddy? He seems to have passed out."

Nellie answered for her. "Daddy, we were just talking about how lucky, or privileged some of us are and how unfair life can be."

"What exactly are you talking about?" Helene then told him about Martha. "Yes," said Sigmund. "That is life. Yet it is so unfortunate, with the economic situation the way it is, people cannot make ends meet with the salaries they earn. Their money is worth less every day although the cost of living remains unchanged. If this continues, Germany will be broke."

"Is this all due to the reparations?" Nellie asked.

"It is. You sure are well informed," replied Sigmund in surprise.

"It could not be otherwise since it has been widely publicised. Some students have even made it their banner, saying that the government should be brought down because of them while others are saying that Germany should be for Germans. There are even some who have the nerve to tell some of the foreign students that they should go back to where they came from, arguing that they were not entitled to be here and are taking up the place that rightfully belonged to a German."

Sigmund and Helene listened in silence, then he said, "Everyone has a right to get an education, regardless of where they are from."

"I know Daddy, the atmosphere is not always the best, and there are some weird looking characters, especially those who are promoting this new party."

"What do they do?" Helene asked.

"Well, if you are standing in a group, some stranger will sneak his way into it and at some point interrupt the conversation by asking if anyone has heard of this party and of course nobody has, so someone will say, 'Tell us about it' and he won't have to be told twice. Once he has finished his description, he will turn to each one in the group asking where one comes from and what religion one professes and he will end his exposition by suggesting one consider joining it, for the Party is the only alternative and that it is the only way of bringing about the change the country so badly needs."

"Have you joined?" asked Sigmund.

"Why Daddy, I would never join, and besides, I am not interested in politics," replied Nellie.

"What about your friends?" Helene asked.

"One of them has, but then, he does not come from my background and he really is just an acquaintance."

"I do not have a good opinion of that new party. They are rightist and populist but they will never come to power, of that I am certain," said Sigmund.

"How about some lunch?" Helene asked.

"That is music to my ears," answered Nellie.

"Come to think of it, I am hungry," said Sigmund, and Helene left them to go see about it.

"I am glad you do not have to go to work this afternoon," said Nellie.

"It has been a long time since I've taken an afternoon off," Sigmund said. "Maybe you and I can have a little time together if you don't have other plans."

"I haven't, Daddy, and as a matter of fact, I have a couple of things I would like to discuss with you."

"I have some things on my mind as well, so we can have a little tête-à-tête down in the library," said Sigmund.

Nellie did not reply for just then they heard Helene announcing that lunch is served. Helene was in a festive mood and she thoroughly enjoyed having her husband home, even if he did spend most of his time in his sanctuary, as she had taken to calling the library, since just knowing he was around gave her a sense of togetherness she did not have otherwise. They just finished their main course when Anna came in with Freddy. He was learning to speak and as soon as he saw his father, he let go of her hand and went towards him saying, "Apa, Apa," all the way.

"It is not 'Apa' Freddy, it is 'Papa'," said Sigmund, picking him up and setting him on his lap. Freddy graced everyone with a smile. "You sure are growing up fast. I cannot believe we have already celebrated your second birthday."

"Neither can I," replied his proud mother. Freddy became restless on his father's lap so Sigmund set him down. Without uttering a word, he left the room.

"That is odd, I wonder where he has gone to," said Nellie.

"I do not know, but I am sure he will be back." Sure enough, he returned before long, having gone to find his ball. It did not take Sigmund long to understand what Freddy wanted. "If you will excuse me," he said to the ladies, "Freddy and I are going to play football." And, taking the little hand in his, led his son out of the room.

"What a proud father he is," said Nellie.

"He is indeed," replied Helene. "Have you got any plans for this afternoon?"

"I do. I have some reading to do and I have to work on an assignment as well. What about you?"

"I think I will take a nap," replied Helene and got up from the table.

Nellie just sat down at her desk when her father came in. "Helene is asleep, do you want to join me in the library?" he asked. Nellie put down her book and followed him down the stairs.

He sat in the chair behind his desk and Nellie made herself comfortable in the big leather chair across from him. "What do you want to discuss with me, Nellie?"

She stared at her father, let out a big sigh, then said, "You may not be aware of everything that is going on in our student world Dad, but there are some things taking place that are very disturbing to a few of us." Nellie paused.

"Do go on," said Sigmund.

"Well, apparently the students organised themselves into a Union in the summer of 1919 that they called the Hochschulring Deutscher Art and just lately this organisation, which represents 110000 students, has forced the national student association to accept Austrian and Sudetenland student unions as members, ones who explicitly exclude non-Aryan members." Sigmund looked at Nellie in surprise. "You did not know this, did you?" she asked.

"No, I did not, but then I did know that Jews had been banned from certain student societies before the First World War, so it does not come to me as a surprise."

"What *is* surprising is that they accepted the Austrian and Sudetenland unions who have just one thing in common: They do not like Jews and maybe that is the reasoning behind it."

"That may well be," Sigmund said thoughtfully.

"Daddy, there is still something I need to tell you. Some of my friends in the lectures have been told by strangers lately that they have no business being there."

"What do they say?" Sigmund inquired.

"Well," said Nellie, "they tell them they know they are Jewish and that Jews do not belong to the 'Volk' and they are taking up places rightfully belonging to the Germans. With inflation steadily on the rise, some cities are unable to provide the funding they used to and the lecture halls are crowded, that basically there are too many of us studying the same careers and that we will take away their jobs."

"How do you feel about it all?"

"I am not happy with the entire situation. I feel very uneasy and sometimes a lot of anguish. I also try to be brave and not to let it bother me. But what bothers me the most is feeling rejected. What have we done? I do not think we have taken away their places, some students are so old, some are almost thirty, what someone called 'professional students'. They go from one course to another, change universities… They are the worst, but nobody seems to mind them staying on forever. It is they who are taking away the places from someone who would like to get on and meet his or her goals. It is just so unfair," she finished.

"I understand what you are saying and I know it is not easy, so many things have changed in this country in such a short time, but if you ask me, I do not believe it can get any worse, it can only get better. You have to be tough, Nellie, it is so very important for you to get a good education. I have told you this often and I know I am repeating myself, but that what you have learned can never be taken away from you. You can have a big fortune today and it may all be taken from you tomorrow, but your education, your knowledge, this will be with you till the day you die."

"I know, Daddy."

"One last thing. Those few people who make you feel rejected, who are so poor in spirit that they are not even worthy of your feelings, remember…it takes two to play ping pong."

"You are so right, Daddy, I will not let myself become a part of it."

"One word of caution, Nellie, do choose your friends carefully. Use your judgment and do not take everyone at face value. Remember, what you see is not always what you get."

"Do not worry, as you may have noticed, I am very picky. But Daddy, you said you had something you wanted to talk to me about. What is it?"

"We have just discussed it."

"Oh," said Nellie, "I guess you just wanted to know how I was getting on."

"You have hit the nail on the head," replied Sigmund.

Nellie looked at her watch. "I had better go do some work," she said, getting up. "Thanks Dad, you are always so helpful."

"Just remember, you can always come to me," he replied, then got up and stood by the pond watching his goldfish. He was far more concerned than he let on to Nellie, but as he had told her, it was of utmost importance to him that she get an education and she would just have to stick it out. She only had two more years, and they would go by very fast, giving her all the support he possibly could.

He went back to his desk and said out loud, 'What a beautiful room' as he opened his briefcase, having brought back some work from the office. If he went through it now, he would be able to enjoy a nice evening with Helene.

"Sigmund," she said. He looked up startled and Helene came into the room.

"I was just thinking of you," he said, smiling.

"A penny for your thoughts," she replied.

"I have some work to do, but how about going out for dinner tonight? It has been quite some time."

"It has indeed," she said.

"We could go to that little Italian restaurant within walking distance," he suggested.

"What a good idea," she replied, taking her leave and barely hearing him say he would book a table for seven thirty.

They had a lovely, quiet dinner. Sigmund told her about his conversation with Nellie. "Things sure have changed," he said with some bitterness.

"They have indeed," answered Helene. "But we do have to make an effort and try and see the brighter things in life."

"You are so right, and we have been so blessed," replied Sigmund.

"I had a long conversation with my mother today," said Helene. "How is she?"

"She is doing well, busy as usual, but she did mention that one of her friends has decided to leave Germany for good and the family in Brussels has asked Mother if she would consider moving there."

"Has she?"

"No, she has not," replied Helene.

"Why would she want to leave, anyway? Life is not that unbearable here and although many things have changed, and if she is worried about the Nazi movement coming to power, I can assure you that that will never happen."

Helene looked at him with surprise. "How can you be so sure?"

"Trust me, I know it will never happen."

Helene had never doubted her husband, she loved him with all her heart, but this time she was not so sure he was right.

That movement, as he called it, was creeping into all the spheres of their daily life.

Chapter 16

Time would prove Sigmund right in the short term. On 23 November 1923, Hitler tried to overthrow the government in Bavaria. It would become known as the Hitler Putsch, or Uprising. At the time, the movement had 55000 members and was known for its rough ways with opponents and the spectacular intensity of its public meetings. But his Uprising did not bear the results he had hoped for and instead of marching into Berlin, he was caught and jailed. He and the other leaders stood trial for high treason in February 1924, sentenced to five years, and sent to the Landsberg prison where he wrote his book *Mein Kampf.*

Hitler's failed uprising was talked about everywhere and Sigmund was overjoyed with the news about his incarceration. "See how right I was," he told Helene, "you did not believe me at the time but see, this is the end of him."

"Yes," said Helene, "you were right, as usual. But why do you say he is finished? He will serve his time and he will then be free to go back to his movement."

"Oh no, he won't," replied her husband, "remember, he is an Austrian citizen and the Germans will surely deport him, just you watch. Then we will be rid of this big troublemaker for good."

Helene just nodded her assent. Her husband was so wise, she gave him a loving look and said, "Sigmund, whatever doubts I may have, I have put them aside, for you always know best."

"Thank you. You can trust me. I am beginning to see the light at the end of the tunnel."

The Chancellor, Gustav Stresemann, was prepared to take a pragmatic and tough line extricating the country from economic collapse. He made the most out of presidential support and imposed the necessary cuts in government expenditure, introducing very strict budgetary controls. The devalued currency was replaced with the Rentenmark, which was given equal value to the pre-war gold Reichsmark. The new currency was based on land values. In other words, the German people mortgaged their entire personal resources as coverage for the new mark. It was a very important point in convincing the Allies that Germany deserved their support. Things had changed in Europe as well; there was a more moderate government in France who were prepared to pull the French troops out of the Ruhr.

The first Labour government in Britain, under Ramsay McDonald, saw it as his main role to restore harmony in Europe and thus, a package of proposals was drawn up with the aim of restoring normality to Germany. It would become known as the Dawes Plan and entailed the evacuation of the Ruhr, a phasing of reparation payments according to an index of prosperity, and the provisions of loans by the United States. Germany decided to share control over the payments with seven foreign representatives in one central bank of issue and an American financier was appointed as the Agent General of Reparations Payments. With the loans, the government was able to finance industrial expansion and a variety of public works schemes like sport stadiums, swimming pools, huge flat blocks and opera houses. Those employed by the state received an increase in wages. The population was happy, there was work and food and the future looked brighter with every passing day.

Nowadays, Helene saw quite a lot of Martha, for both children attended the same nursery school and they inevitably encountered each other. The children would walk together and their mothers chatted while keeping an eye on them. "You won't believe Martha's change," said Helene one day over lunch to Sigmund, "she looks so much younger, she smiles more and she is like a different person. I wonder what has caused it."

"Why," said Sigmund, "has it not crossed your mind perhaps that she no longer has to worry about her husband losing his job?"

"I had not thought about that," replied Helene. "To think that such worries can make people age so much."

"They sure can, and allow me to point out to you that we have never had to worry about our next meal, or the money to pay the rent like most people. We are very fortunate and believe me, I never take it for granted," said Sigmund.

"I could not agree with you more," replied Helene. "I am so aware of it that I count my blessings every day. As a matter of fact, we both should, for who knows what the future might have in store for us?"

"Thank you for a lovely lunch," said Sigmund, folding his napkin and sliding it into its ring. "I must be going. Abraham rang me this morning and said he would drop by sometime this afternoon."

"Is he still thinking about leaving?"

"I do not know," replied Sigmund, and kissed her good bye. She walked with him to the door and watched him drive off.

He was so dear to her, even though they had been married several years, she was still very much in love with him. Helene *did* long to have another child, though, since Freddy was growing up fast and the house was so quiet while he was at nursery school. Not only that, but it would be so nice to have a little girl to cuddle. She shared her longing with Sigmund but he was not at all receptive to it. He told her bluntly that they were very lucky to have one boy and one girl and anyway, who would want to bring a child into a world with so much turmoil and uncertainty as theirs? It would not be at all fair to the child, and that had put an end to their discussion. But…life had changed: the economic chaos seemed to be over and it was starting to look as though the good old days were back to stay. Helene decided to bide her time and would bring the issue up again later, with the certainty that he would have no justified reason to oppose it.

Sigmund was just about to look at some papers when his secretary announced his visitor. "I hope I am not too early," said Abraham.

"No, not at all, not at all, old friend, I am delighted to see you," replied Sigmund.

"So am I," said Abraham, sitting down in the chair facing Sigmund's desk.

"I hope you haven't come to tell me you are leaving," said Sigmund teasingly.

"No, and you will be the first to know. I have placed it all on the back burner for the time being. It would be a shame for us to leave just when it looks as if the Chancellor is going to succeed in establishing law and order," said Abraham.

"That Chancellor of ours is a tough and very smart man. He has been so very successful in dealing with the Allies and we are no longer a bankrupt nation. And, with all that money flowing in from the Americans, we will be able to rebuild the country in no time," replied Sigmund.

"Not only that, but with Mr Hitler behind bars and the unemployment rate falling steadily, it will surely be the end of that party since it was all the unemployed who had nothing better to do than to attend those meetings and let themselves be brainwashed," Abraham added. "And if that does not finish them, Hitler's deportation surely will. The sooner they send him back to Austria the better off will be."

"I could not agree with you more. Have you met Emmanuel?" Sigmund asked.

"Believe it or not, I haven't. He was supposed to come some time ago but something unforeseen came up and he had to cancel his trip. I think I mentioned to you at the dinner we had at your home, or maybe it was after that, I can't remember, the fact is I am still waiting to meet him," said Abraham.

"It is probably just as well because when we last spoke you were pretty keen on leaving and you had practically given up on the country solving its problems."

"I know, I know. But Sigmund, business is better than it has ever been and I must say I am very optimistic about the future. If only the parties could form a strong and stable coalition and stop bickering amongst themselves so that we can have a strong and stable government, then everyone would come to terms with the Republic and those who blame it for all their misfortunes will have been proven wrong."

"That is wishful thinking, I believe," said Sigmund. "I do not see that happening, but at least it seems as if we have entered an era of prosperity."

"Let's hope it lasts," replied Abraham. "Anyway, Sara and I are having a small dinner party at our house next Saturday. I hope you and Helene can join us."

"We will be happy to," replied Sigmund.

"You will get to meet Richard and his wife."

"I look forward to it."

Abraham stood up and said, "I know you are busy and I have to get to the bank before it closes." Sigmund walked him to the door and said goodbye.

"How odd," said Sigmund out loud, sitting down behind his desk. "I thought he had a very special issue he wanted to discuss with me. Oh, well, he did have to go to the bank, which is just around the corner and it was probably very convenient for him to drop by on his way. And he is lonely."

When he got home that evening, Helene brought up the subject of Abraham. As usual, Sigmund was very protective of his friend but he did mention how much he had changed. "You know, Helene, Abraham always radiated peace, there was always a serenity around him even while we were growing up. If you did not know the answer, or if you were at odds with yourself, you would go and find Abraham. He not only knew the answers, but no matter what the situation, he never lost control and was always down to earth. I do not know how to describe it to you."

"Would you say," Helene began, but Sigmund stopped her with a wave of his hand.

"I know…he exuded a self-assurance that radiated onto the rest of us, which is the thing I find he has lost. He was like a lost soul in the office today and it was not what he said but rather as if he had lost his way."

"What you mean?" Helene asked. "Is it that he was at odds with himself?"

"Yes, dear, that is exactly what I was trying to express. He seems happy, yet he has the same misgivings we all have and hopes that this turn-around will last, but he does not trust it and he has to make a decision. Emmanuel not showing up when he said he was doesn't help matters."

"It sure doesn't. He needs to speak to him and find out what the situation in Colombia is really like, and what his offer really entails. Not only that, but Sara is probably nagging at him as well."

"I wish I could help him," said Sigmund.

"I am afraid you can only lend a sympathetic ear and be there for him, there is nothing else you can do," replied Helene.

"I am afraid I have to agree with you," replied her husband. A long silence ensued. *Shall I tell him or shall I keep it to myself?* Helene thought to herself. *Tell him, tell him,* her inner voice became louder. *No, you have to tell him, you must tell him.* She tried to ignore it but she could no longer. "Sigmund, I am worried about Nellie."

"Nellie? Why, Helene? What is wrong?"

"Well, she has gotten some strange phone calls and does not come home at her usual time."

"That is not surprising," replied her father, "the street cars are not running as on time as they were."

"No," said Helene, "there is something else. I think she is dating someone."

"What is wrong with that?"

"Don't misunderstand me, Sigmund, there is definitely nothing wrong with that, but it is—"

"Please do not worry, Helene, I know my daughter. You are probably seeing ghosts where there are none, but I will have a word with her in due time. Besides, it is late and I have an important meeting tomorrow morning."

"OK, Sigmund, but don't say I didn't warn you." He ignored her comment.

Helene's intuition was right, Nellie was dating someone. His name was Andreas and it had all happened so suddenly. She was exiting the lecture hall on a very bleak and cold winter day when someone at her side addressed her, saying, "You don't look as if you had slept through the lecture." She turned her head towards the voice in surprise and gazed into a very handsome face.

"No, I did not. But I fought against it. It was such a boring subject," said Nellie, "and the professor just rambled on and on, never once changing his tone of voice."

"By the time it was over, everyone was absolutely sedated," added the stranger.

"That is exactly the way I am feeling right now," said Nellie.

"In that case, a cup of coffee might be a good idea. Would you care to join me?" the stranger asked.

"Sure," she replied. "But I do not even know your name."

"I have observed you so often in the lecture hall, I forgot that we have never met. My name is Andreas. And I know yours, it's Nellie," he said, as they headed towards the small coffee shop across the street.

He had no trouble finding them a table and as they made their way towards it, people greeted him. "You must be very popular," she remarked. Andreas blushed.

"I have been a student for the past six years and spend my time here in between classes, what about you?" he asked.

"I usually go to the library. It is very quiet there and I manage to get a lot done so that when I get home I have very little or no studying to do at all and I can devote my time to my other interests," replied Nellie.

Just then, a young man stopped to talk to him. Nellie could not hear what they were saying but a few minutes later, Andreas excused himself, saying he had something important he must attend to. "I will see you around," he said, and Nellie noticed that they left together.

She finished her coffee then headed for the library, sitting down at her usual place and taking out her books. A long assignment was due at the beginning of the following week and she really wanted to get it finished so that she could enjoy the weekend. But every time she tried to write something, Andreas' face would loom up in front of her and try as she might, was unable to get him out of her mind until finally giving up. "At least I tried," she told herself, gathering her books, then made her way quietly towards the door. Her inner voice told her she had wasted an hour of her time, then heard herself say that she had no choice. She closed the door gently and was about to turn the corner when the face loomed up in front of her. Not again! It can't be…but it was for real this time and she knew it when his voice addressed her.

"Nellie, I had a hunch I would find you around here," said Andreas. "Are you leaving?"

"Yes, the day has been long enough," she replied.

"I will escort you home," said Andreas.

"You don't have to do that," she said blushing, then added, "I do not live within walking distance."

"In that case, I will escort you to the tramway stop."

"Really, Andreas…" she did not finish her sentence.

"It will be my pleasure," he said.

"How was your afternoon?" Nellie inquired.

"Actually, it was very nice. I had one interesting lecture then I attended a meeting with some friends, one of whom was the young man you saw while we were having coffee."

"Oh, here is my tramway. Have a nice evening," she said, as she got on the tram.

"I am sure I'll see you tomorrow," replied Andreas and he stood waving until the streetcar disappeared from sight.

Nellie was in a daze. She had never been courted before and she was enjoying every minute of it. What a gentleman he is, and he sure is handsome. Those blue eyes! I do not think I have ever seen bluer eyes than his; they are the colour of the sky on a clear summer day. Nobody was in sight when she got home so she went straight to her room and lay down on her bed, going through the day's events. It seemed all so unreal and yet it had not been a dream. "I must have dozed off," she said, glancing around her. The room was in total darkness and she could hear Anna talking to Freddy. She turned on the light and got up. It was time for dinner, and she overheard her father saying: "She may be in her room."

"Hi Daddy," she said, as he came in.

"Have you been home long?"

"Oh yes, I just lay down on the bed and fell asleep."

"You must have been very tired," he replied.

"I guess I was," said Nellie, giving him a hug.

"Dinner is served."

"I will be right down. First I have to kiss Freddy good night since I have not seen him all day."

Freddy was in bed and looked up as his sister came in. He gave her a warm smile. "Nellie, Nellie," he repeated. She sat down next to him and asked how his day had been. He told her in a sad tone of voice that Helmut had not gone to nursery school, but Anna said he might be sick.

"What about the other children?" Nellie asked.

"All of them were there, except for Helmut."

"I know, you told me. But I'm sure he will be back tomorrow."

"Do you really think so?" he asked in an eager tone of voice.

"I don't see why not."

Freddy yawned and so his sister said good night and kissed him on both cheeks but he did not answer for he was already asleep.

Her parents were seated at the table when she entered the dining room. "I am sorry I am late," she said, excusing herself.

"That's all right, I guess Freddy was still awake," said Helene.

"He was and had Helmut on his mind," said Nellie. "I gather it is the first time his friend has been out sick."

"I think it is," replied Helene.

"The boys are very close and a lovely friendship is developing between them," said Sigmund.

Nellie excused herself as soon as dinner was over saying she had a lot of work to do. Sigmund looked at his wife and asked her if she would like to join him in the study. "I have a couple of hours of work to do as well," he said.

"I have some chores I need to tend to but I will come down once I have finished them." But then, she changed her mind, saying she was tired and had a long day so she undressed and went to bed with a book. She loved reading in bed.

When Sigmund finally came upstairs, it was very late.

Noticing Nellie's light was still on, he knocked gently on her door. "I'm surprised you're still awake," he said.

"I was able to concentrate and have now finished my project," she replied.

"Did anything special happen today?" Sigmund asked.

Nellie blushed and thought…what was he hinting at? "No, Daddy, why do you ask?"

"I was just wondering. Good night," he then said and kissed her on the forehead. "Just remember, you can always count on me."

Nellie woke up the next morning with Andreas on her mind. Would she see him? Indeed, when she arrived, there he was at the tramway stop. "Hi," she said to him, then: "The tram is about to leave."

"I am not going anywhere; I was just waiting for you." Nellie blushed then they walked side by side into the building. He asked her what time her first free hour was and she told him. "It coincides with mine, shall we go for coffee?" he asked. She agreed and he said he would meet her in front of the library.

He really wants to spend time with me, she thought as she headed for class. True to his word, Andreas was there waiting for her. "How was it?"

"It was not as boring as yesterday's lecture," she replied. "At least I did not have to fight to stay awake. What about you?"

"The professor did not show up so I have been sitting across the street ever since I left you."

"You could have come in later," she said.

"I could have, had I known, but then I would not have been there to walk you from the stop," he said smiling.

She did not answer. Nellie was taught not to pry into other people's lives so she just listened to what others had to say. Andreas, on the other hand, wanted to know all about her, but she was very shy about talking about herself and always managed to change the topic of conversation. A routine slowly developed between them: Andreas would walk her to and from the tramway stop and they would spend their free time together. Her visits to the library were becoming further and further apart and her work was pilling up on her. "You only live once," she would say to try and calm her conscience. "Life is made up of other things besides studying." She was becoming very reserved at home, going straight to her room and trying to make up for the time she had wasted.

She still made time for Freddy, though, but when she lay awake in bed, she would think of the relationship that was growing between Andreas and herself. There were a lot of unanswered questions. Who was he? Why was he so popular? What were all those meetings with his friends about? And how come she was never invited? He never spoke about himself; all she knew of him was that he came from a working class family. His father had been a soldier during the war, who could neither accept Germany's defeat nor the end of the military. Andreas once mentioned that someday in the near future, Germany would again be powerful and free of all foreign influences. Just what he meant by 'foreign influences' she didn't know and made a mental note to ask him on their next encounter. However, when she did, he just avoided the issue, saying he would explain it to her some other time.

He asked her questions about herself and her family, especially her father, but she was very careful not to divulge too much information. Lately, he insisted several times on seeing her home, but she always declined and although she was very much attracted to him, somehow she felt that something was not exactly right. Trying as hard as she might, she could not put her finger on it but she had nobody to discuss Andreas with, either. Her intuition told her she should forget about him and put an end to the relationship, but every time she made up her mind to do so, he would do or say something to weaken her resolve, being more charming than ever. One day, he surprised her with a box of her favourite chocolates. "How did you know I love these?"

"I just knew," he replied. "I have seen you buy them."

"Oh," said Nellie, "but I—"

"Don't tackle your little brain trying to find the answer. I just happen to know they are your favourite." She made no further comment but as she rode home that evening, the unanswered question lingered on her mind. How could he possibly have known? She hadn't bought chocolates when they were together, could it be possible he was spying on her? A shudder ran down her spine. Why would he do so? Who was he, anyway? She tried hard to find out more about him, but to no avail. He never introduced her to any of his friends, either, so she had no way of finding out.

That evening at home in the quietness of her room, she sat down and took a sheet of paper and drew a line down the middle of it. On one side of the line, she wrote the word positive and the word negative on the other. Oma taught her years ago that whenever she was in doubt about something, she should sit down quietly and make a balance. If carried out in an honest and objective fashion, this little exercise could give her the answer. She only reverted to it once many years ago, but it had helped her make the right decision. She came to a negative conclusion, realising that she was not learning anything from this young man and all he seemed interested in was getting information from her. Not only that, but she was neglecting her studies and had not been back to the library in a while, for he always talked her into joining him in the coffee room. Also, she was coming home later and later and she could see the unspoken questions in Helene's eyes.

She asked herself why she hung out with him. "Because he is the only young man who has ever paid attention to me," she said out loud. Then she heard her inner voice say, *Nellie, that is not a good enough reason and I will not have anything more to do with him,* she resolved. The next morning, much to her relief, there was no sign of Andreas at the tramway stop so she went to class and in her free hour went to the library. She wondered if they would run into each other but the day went by without her even catching a glimpse of him.

She got home early and Helene was about to leave when Nellie opened the door. "Why, Nellie, are you back on your old schedule?" she exclaimed.

Nellie was taken aback. "What do you mean?"

"It is not important, it's just that it seems to me you have been coming home later every day." Helene did not wait for an answer and said, "I will not be long, I just have to run an errand. See you later!" And she was gone.

The nerve, thought Nellie. "It is none of her business what time I get home," she mumbled under her breath.

What she had no way of knowing was that just as Andreas was walking towards the tramway stop to meet her, one of his friends caught up with him. "The boss wants to see you right away."

"What can be so urgent this early in the morning?" Andreas asked.

"I do not know, but he is not in a very good frame of mind, so if I were you, I would not make him wait."

"All right," said Andreas, "where is he?"

"He is in the coffee room, waiting for you."

"Thanks," said Andreas, and retraced his steps. He did not even have time to take off his coat for as soon as the boss saw him make his entrance, he stood up, grabbed his coat and took Andreas by the arm and ushered him out onto the street. One look at him told Andreas that he was in a very foul mood indeed.

"You have been seeing this Jewish bitch for more than three months and you have nothing to report?" the boss demanded. "That is unbelievable. Have you fallen in love with her so that you have forgotten your duty to the party, to the fatherland?"

"Not at all, you are wrong. How could I put anything before my duty to my fatherland?" Andreas exclaimed.

"Then what is it? You better have a good story if I am to believe what you are saying," said the boss, jerking on his arm.

"Calm down and I'll explain," Andreas said, trying hard to keep his cool.

"OK, you have two minutes," replied the boss, looking at his watch.

"I have tried everything, but she does not give out any information whatsoever. I wanted to walk her home, thinking I would get invited in but she will not hear of it, so I can only walk her to the tramway hoping that someday she will have a change of heart. She is very naïve but she is also extremely clever. She ignores or changes the subject when I get personal. One day, I asked her about her relatives and she told me bluntly that it was none of my business."

The boss was thoughtful. "I did not make her out to be so intelligent and since I didn't think, to the best of my knowledge, that she's never been courted by anyone, I thought she would have fallen head over heels in love with you and gone out of her way to please you. I see I was mistaken."

"You sure were, for she is as cold as they come," said Andreas.

"I hate giving up on her," said the boss. "She could have been a great source of information, but enough time has been wasted already."

"I have someone else lined up who might be more cooperative and hopefully she won't be as boring as Nellie, for she has no spark whatsoever," added Andreas.

The boss made no comment and Andreas knew better than to break the silence. When he finally spoke, he said, "Well, that takes care of it, you will no longer see Nellie and you are to forget about her. In time, you will be informed of your next mission." Then he left without saying another word.

Andreas was beside himself with joy, he was free of Nellie. But a sudden thought made him shudder, what would the consequences of his failure be? He had failed, even though he could not be blamed for it, he had let the movement down and he knew it had eyes and ears everywhere, which meant nothing went unnoticed or unpunished.

It was Saturday, the night of Abraham and Sara's dinner. Helene had taken a lot of care dressing and she looked, in Sigmund's words, absolutely gorgeous. She was in an excellent mood and somewhat excited. "You seem to be really looking forward to seeing our friends," Sigmund said matter-of-factly.

"I am," she answered, smiling. I wonder what he would say were he to know the real reason, but he will find out soon enough, she thought to herself happily. She was sure the timing was absolutely right and that she would have no trouble convincing him into granting her most ardent wish.

Nellie was home and her father had invited her to come with them but she had declined, saying she had other plans. Helene overheard the last part of the conversation and raised one eyebrow in surprise. She was careful to keep her tongue in check and just said, "Whatever you do, I hope you have a good time." Nellie gave her one of her looks and kissed her father good-bye. Freddy, who should have already been asleep, overheard his parents say they were leaving and started crying.

"I will tend to him," said Nellie, heading for his room. Helene was on the verge of turning back to check on the child but Sigmund took her arm and led her out to the car assuring her he will be just fine.

"Helene, is everything all right between you and Nellie?"

"What an odd question, Sigmund, what should be wrong between us?" she asked.

"I just feel there is a little tension building up between you," he said, "but it might just be my imagination."

"I am sure you are just seeing things," Helene replied and changed the subject. Sigmund was not at all convinced Helene was telling the truth, for he had heard Nellie's tone of voice and seen Helene's expression.

"They will just have to resolve their problems between them," he mumbled.

"What did you say?" He turned to her. "Did you say something, dear? You were mumbling and I did not understand what you said."

"You must be hearing voices," replied Sigmund, laughing, "for I have not even opened my mouth."

"I guess I am," said Helene, joining in the laughter.

They were the last to arrive. Abraham introduced Richard and his wife to the newcomers. Sigmund looked around and Abraham said, "No," reading his mind, "Emanuel did not make it."

"That is a shame, a real shame it is," said Richard, joining in the conversation. "I have not seen that cousin of mine for quite some time and he keeps letting me down."

"I have heard the story," said Sigmund, "but I am sure that someday he will honour us with his presence. Have you ever been to Colombia?" Sigmund asked.

"No," replied Richard, "but it has not been for lack of invitation. The opportunity has just not arisen, but maybe someday."

"I strongly believe that the good times are here to stay, so why go somewhere unknown?" said Abraham.

"I know exactly how you feel. Germany has so much to offer and it is such a vast country. Once I have travelled through all of Germany, I will set my eyes on other parts of the world," said Richard.

Sara was delighted to see Helene and asked immediately about little Freddy. "He must be feeling pretty lonely," she said, "there is such a big age gap between him and Nellie," and, turning to Richard's wife, gave her the background.

"I do not think he is. He goes to nursery school every morning and he plays with Helmut who is practically an only child as well and lives not far from us," said Helene.

"Have you not thought of having another?" Richard's wife, Miriam, asked.

"It is too early for me to think about changing diapers and giving bottles again," replied Helene, trying hard to smile but thinking her very impertinent, one did not ask those questions, especially not of a stranger. Sara came to her rescue.

"We have all been very blessed with healthy children."

Sigmund took a liking to Richard immediately and could see why Abraham spoke so highly of him. He had a wonderful sense of humour and one could tell that nothing made him happier than being there for others. He was a born giver. But just as much as he liked Richard, he took an immediate dislike to his wife and wondered how he could have fallen in love with her. They were so different, being rude, calculating and very self-centred. It was such a contrast, confirming the rule that opposites attract.

After dinner, the men retired to the library. Abraham brought up the question of whether the Nazi party would survive and Sigmund said again he was sure this was the end of it. Richard, on the other hand, had serious doubts and pointed out that the movement had continued recruiting people and infiltrating the different organisations. "They are so very sly and clever," he said. "They will do anything to get information. I was flabbergasted when my nephew, who goes to college, mentioned to me one day that a Jewish girl called Nellie was being courted by the university's ringleader."

Sigmund went pale. He could hear Helene's warning and remembered his answer. Abraham gave him a look, but he kept his thoughts wisely to himself.

"What information do they want?" Sigmund asked whilst trying to keep his voice under control.

"They want to know everything, from bank accounts and relationships to who your friends are."

"What do they use the information for?" Abraham asked.

"I do not know exactly, for I am not one of them, but it may be so they can set you up, blackmail you, so on. Even though Mr Hitler is in jail, the movement is trying to survive without him."

"I do hope you are wrong," said Abraham.

"I hope so, too, for the sake of our country," Richard added. Sigmund's brain was working like mad. He could not believe what he just heard. It had to be someone else, it could not be his own daughter, but he had only one way of finding out and that was to confront her. He was eager to get home and learn the truth, but by leaving right then and there, he would only arouse suspicion. He saw the look on Abraham's face and knew he was asking himself the same question. Then Abraham suggested they re-join the ladies.

"Richard, darling, I have been wondering how much longer you were going to be. I am so tired and really looking forward to my bed, do you think you could take me home?" Abraham and Sigmund exchanged glances. Poor Richard, he sure carried a heavy cross. But it was the break Sigmund had been waiting for. Signalling to Helene with his eyes, they, too, said their good byes. No sooner had the car door slammed shut that he turned to her and said, "I should have listened to you and not said you were seeing ghosts."

"What are you talking about?" she asked. He then told her what he'd heard. "What are you going to do?"

"I am going to have a talk with my beloved daughter and find out, but I am pretty sure that she is the person he mentioned."

"My conversation with him will have to wait for another time," thought Helene, unhappily.

"You have not said a word," her husband remarked.

"What can I say? Just don't be too hard on her. But I did warn you," Helene added.

He parked the car and did not wait to help Helene out but instead stomped up the stairs and into Nellie's room. She was sitting at her desk and looked up in surprise when she saw her father. It was not like him to just come in without knocking. "Why, Daddy, is anything wrong?"

"You will have to tell me, for I do not know," he said, trying to control his anger.

"I can tell you are angry," she said.

"You just listen to me and answer my question," her father commanded as he paced the room. "Have you been dating anyone?"

Taking a deep breath, she fought back her tears. She had never seen her father this mad before and it scared her. She could not understand his anger. "I have not been dating anyone, but yes, there is somebody who is very attracted to me, who has been spending all his free time with me." She could no longer control herself and burst into tears.

Her father, who could not bear to see a woman cry, placed his arm gently around her shoulders. "Calm down, calm, down, there is no reason to get so upset. Let's discuss this quietly, why don't you tell me all about it?" He sat down by her side on the bed and when her sobs finally subsided, she was able to find her voice.

"Daddy I promise I have done nothing wrong."

"I know, I know," said her father, "but let's talk about it." This helped her regain her confidence and so she poured her heart out to him. She was even more surprised than he had been at discovering who Andreas really was.

"I knew there was something wrong somewhere, but I just could not put my finger on it." Sigmund was very relieved to hear that she had not given out any information and that she resolved not to see him again. "Daddy, whatever I did, I did it unknowingly. I would never, ever have anything to do with somebody who hates foreigners and Jews." Sigmund believed she had been misled.

"I am very proud of you," he said gently. Nellie looked at him in surprise.

"Why?" she asked.

"Because you kept your head and did not become the instrument he wanted to make of you."

"Daddy, I don't think we need to worry. I know who he is now and I will avoid him."

"Besides, the semester will be over in a couple of weeks," her father added. Nellie yawned. "I know you are tired, let's get some sleep," said Sigmund, kissing her goodnight. She tossed and turned. To think that she could have been so easily misled.

Helene was still awake. "How did it go?"

"Just as I thought, it is our Nellie. Those bastards have no scruples whatsoever. I am proud of her, though, she did not lose her head and realised that something was not kosher then decided to have nothing more to do with him."

"That girl has a pretty good head on her shoulders, I must say," said Helene.

"I just wonder if Nellie could not finish her education somewhere else," said Sigmund.

"I am sure she could. Paris or Brussels could be an alternative," said Helene.

"You forget she is not very fluent in French and would have to first brush up on the language, but we will sort that out in due course," said Sigmund. Helene was half-asleep when he crawled into bed.

Chapter 17

Nellie was a little apprehensive about going to class the following morning. The boring lecture was on her schedule and she was not sure she wanted to go to it, for fear of running into Andreas. However, her sense of duty got the best of her and she went. She need not have worried, as Andreas was nowhere to be seen because, and she could not have known this, the boss made it quite clear to him that he was to give up his studies immediately and stay very much away from the university and the surrounding area.

Andreas still didn't know what his next mission would be and he was not at all happy with the way things had developed. He felt he had lost the boss's trust and dared not ask any questions, for who was he to question his superiors anyway? As Nellie looked back on her relationship with Andreas, she realised how much she enjoyed being courted, even though it was for the wrong reasons. Perhaps someday, a handsome prince charming will come into her life and she would become his princess.

The semester came to an end, much to everyone's relief. Her parents were not planning on going anywhere since business was booming and Sigmund was extremely busy. As he pointed out one evening over dinner, he better take advantage of the good times since he was not sure how long they might last and Helene agreed with him.

"Nellie," he said, turning to her, "you are on holiday, though. You do not have to sit at home with us."

"What would you like to do?" Helene asked her.

"I have not given the matter much thought, after all, classes just ended last week."

"What about going to Paris, you could improve your French and it is such a nice city. Or Switzerland?" asked her father. "I like the idea of going to Switzerland, to Basel."

"Well, that settles it, I will see to the travel arrangements," said Sigmund.

"What is the rush?" Nellie wanted to know.

"You are getting me wrong, child, I am not sending you away. I just think that with the weather as nice as it is, and having finished your classes and gotten your grades, what point is there staying around here when you can go and discover something new and have a good time as well. By the way, I spoke to Franz last week, and it was he who actually suggested you spend some time with them. The girls are going to be thrilled when they hear the news," said Sigmund.

Franz and Elizabeth had been very good friends of Sigmund and Alice's, having met through Nellie's mother and remaining friends ever since. They lived in a house on the outskirts of Basel and their two daughters were about Nellie's age and had met once or twice. A while back, Franz had some business to tend to and brought his family along, a long time before Helene came into their lives. The girls had gotten along very well and when either Sigmund or Franz talked on the phone, they would put the girls on so that they could keep in touch. What Sigmund did not tell Nellie was that he wanted her out of the city as soon as possible should this Nazi have second thoughts. This way, he would have no way of finding her.

He told Franz the story and was absolutely flabbergasted. "What lack of scruples! Then again, what else could you expect from such lumpen. Why don't you suggest to Nellie that she come and spend a few days with us? Here she will be safe and free, and I am sure she will have a wonderful time."

"I have no doubts about it," said Sigmund. "I will suggest it to her and keep you posted." Sigmund went about making the necessary travel arrangements and a couple of days later, Nellie arrived at the Basel train station. Both girls and their mother were there to meet her.

Life sure is full of surprises, said Christina, the older of the two sisters. "You're telling me!" exclaimed Nellie, laughing. "Who would have thought a week ago that all three of us would meet here today?"

"Yes," said Elizabeth. "That is what is so wonderful about life, it is forever in motion and if you're flexible and open to the opportunities and able to take them as they come, life is never dull or boring—it is always exciting."

The driver took the luggage and they followed him to the car.

"What a beautiful city this is," said Nellie, admiringly.

"It is the river that makes it special," Olivia said.

"I like cities that have a river flowing through them, but I think the hills give this city its character," Elizabeth added. "We will give you a tour tomorrow. There is a lot to see here and, of course, there is also the countryside, which is so beautiful. You will catch a glimpse of it on our way home for we live just on the outskirts."

The car drove up a long driveway and came to a halt in front of a mansion that stood in the middle of a garden, so huge it could have been a park. "Come, Nellie, we are home."

"What a beautiful place this is," said Nellie, very much impressed. The front door opened up into a big hallway and a circular stone staircase led up to the second floor. *This must be what a palace looks like,* thought Nellie. Her room was very big and furnished beautifully in pastel colours. The bay window looked over the park and one could see the hills in the background.

"You can unpack later, Nellie, let us show you the house," said the sisters. They gave her the grand tour, each room was different from the other, but all tastefully decorated. Nellie walked around in a daze, she had been in very beautiful homes but this one was really outstanding.

Elizabeth was sitting in the living room when they came in. "I love your home," said Nellie admiringly.

"Thank you, we have put a lot of love and effort into it and there are some pieces of furniture that have been in the family for years, so there are a lot of memories here as well. Each piece has a story behind it and, in my opinion, that is what gives a home its character."

"As well as the people who live in it," added Christina.

"I was not excluding you girls," said their mother with a smile. Soon the house was ringing with voices and happy laughter, and Nellie ended up spending almost two months with them. There was so much to do and to see, and they were busy from morning till night. Christina and Olivia introduced her to all their friends, who took an immediate liking to her. She loved the city; it was so much smaller than Frankfurt and so easy to get around. There was never a dull moment.

They also spent a lot of time outdoors in the countryside. On the weekends, Franz and Elizabeth would take them on long drives to different cities and villages and sometimes they would spend the night. They went to no end of trouble to show her the country they loved so much. She could understand why, for not only was it beautiful but it had so much to offer: the snow-capped mountains, glaciers, many different lakes, wonderful forests. On her last weekend, they surprised her with a trip to Gstaad, the town she had heard so much about.

What a romantic place it was, surrounded on all sides by very tall mountains. They spent the night at the Palace Hotel where her parents had met and the following morning they took a stroll to the tennis courts. No one was playing. "This is where it all began," said Franz.

"I guess circumstances never repeat themselves," said Nellie.

"I am sure somewhere there is someone waiting for you and you will surely encounter him someday," said Elizabeth.

"How will she know he is the right one?" Christina asked.

"She will know in her heart," replied her mother.

They drove back to Basel late in the afternoon as the sun was setting. The mountains reflected a myriad of different colours and a stillness lay in the air. "This is the magic of higher elevations," said Franz, drawing their attention to it.

Nellie was sad. What a wonderful holiday, she'd felt carefree and happy and what a lot of nice people she met. As she said a tearful goodbye, she promised to keep in touch and they all promised to come visit. Now, as the train pulled into the station, she was again confronted with reality and knew there were some decisions she had to make.

The whole family was there to meet her and she was amazed at how much Freddy had grown. He ran towards her with his little arms outstretched and she bent down to pick him up. "You are getting so heavy, soon I will no longer be able to carry you," she said, setting him down.

"I am so glad you had such a good time," said her father.

"It was absolutely wonderful, but now it is back to real life again."

"When do classes begin?" Helene asked.

"A week from Monday," replied Nellie.

"That just gives you enough time to get ready," said Sigmund.

Nellie did not reply. She had some issues she wanted to discuss with him but they would have to wait until a later date.

Nellie could not help noticing that her stepmother looked tired and her face was drawn, but she refrained from commenting on it. Helene was trying to come to terms with Sigmund's decision after finally having had the long, postponed conversation with him. Much to her disappointment, he had refused to give in to her. She begged and pleaded but to no avail and although he listened to all her arguments, it had been useless. "I know it's very hard for you to accept, Helene," he'd said gently. "However, one of these days you will be grateful to me for not having given in to you. You do not realise it now, but the twenty years between us is a lot. I am in good health and I feel much younger than I am, but remember what happened to Paul, he was in the prime of life and he went just like that and did not live to see the nephew he so longed for. What guarantee have we got that I won't run his same fate?" asked Sigmund.

"We have none," replied Helene.

"So if that were to happen and I were to give in to you, you would be left with two little children to care for. Can you imagine what a burden it would be to you? It would not be fair to the child either." Helene looked at him with her eyes brimming with tears. "Let us be thankful for what we have, let's give the children we have the best of everything and be there for them and," he said, taking her in his arms, "we can enjoy our time together and you can devote a little more time to me." He pulled her a little closer to him. "Don't be sad. Just look at the positive sides I have pointed out to you."

"I know," said Helene, "it is just that I wanted a little girl so badly."

"You have a grown up step daughter who could become a daughter to you if you would allow her to get close, and with that, a complicity could develop between you. I have never spoken to Nellie about this but I know she is very lonely she has no close friends."

Helene interrupted him. "You are right Sigmund, but you are forgetting something."

"And that is?" he asked, intrigued.

"Nellie is not my flesh and blood." She saw the hurt in his eyes and immediately regretted what she said. "I did not mean to hurt you, she is the daughter of the man I adore and that makes her very special, but she cannot replace the baby you refuse me. However, in time I will come to terms with your decision." Sigmund saw no point in pursuing the issue further and, giving her a long drawn out kiss on the lips, went down to the solace of his books.

Now that Nellie was back, she was happy to be home although she was not looking forward to the start of the semester and she wished that something different would come up. But what? She asked herself that question many a time. Her father would never consent to her quitting her studies and yet it was her life and she felt it concerned her so much that she and she alone could make the decision. Was she not an individual? Her father could give advice and council, but he could not live her life for her.

She had been so happy and carefree, but since her return, a cloud of dread hung over her head until finally deciding, for her own peace of mind, to take the bull by the horns and face her father to discuss the issue with him. She knew he would be disappointed but she told herself that it was her happiness that was at stake. The timing would have to be just right and she did not have to wait for long.

It was Friday and it had been raining all day. Nellie had no desire whatsoever to go out and was in her room making a drawing when she heard the front door close and Sigmund call out: "Hi everyone, I am home." She could tell by the sound of his voice that he was in excellent spirits and indeed came upstairs whistling happily. He stuck his head in the door. "Hi Daddy," she said looking up, "you are home early."

"Where is everybody?"

"Helene is out having tea with some friends but she should be back shortly and Freddy is over at Helmut's."

"So that just leaves the two of us," he said, stroking her head.

"Yes," replied Nellie and then, summoning all her courage, continued in a low voice. "Daddy, I have an issue to discuss with you, perhaps now would be a good time?"

"Sure, why don't you ask Anna to serve us some tea in the library and I will be down in a minute."

Nellie did as she was told then said out loud, "Well, at least I can get it over with." Nobody heard her.

They settled themselves into the comfortable leather couch. Nellie poured the tea and served them both a slice of apple pie.

"Well," said Sigmund, "I can't wait to hear what is on your mind."

She took a big gulp of tea, cleared her throat and said in a small voice, "Daddy, Switzerland was an eye opener for me." He wanted to know what she meant and so she asked him to allow her to explain. "While I was in Basel, I felt free. I was my own person and everyone accepted me. I was not made to feel guilty, I was not insecure and I discovered what it means to feel not rejected."

"Nellie, I do not understand what you are talking about," said Sigmund.

"I dread going back to school. The environment will rob me of this newly found freedom. I am not wanted there and I do not want to go back," she said in a very firm voice.

"You know how much getting and education means to me," he said, trying hard to keep calm, for they had been over this before.

"I know, but I also think that being happy with oneself is also very important. I am not happy there and I was certainly not happy being used by a Nazi…"

Sigmund interrupted her. "I know, I know," he said

Nellie got a grip on herself. "I have an alternative." Sigmund was all ears. "I know that one can learn a great deal from books, but I also believe that practical

160

experience is just as valuable, if not more, so what would you say if I were to take on an apprenticeship?" she asked in an eager voice.

"Your arguments are convincing," said Sigmund, "but where are you thinking of doing it?"

"I do not know yet. I am looking around and want to find it on my own, but I also need your consent."

After a long silence in which Sigmund weighed her suggestion, he finally spoke. "You have my consent. Please do not hesitate to come to me if you have trouble finding a job. My business friends would be all too happy to oblige."

"Daddy, I just told you I want to find the job myself," said Nellie, and Sigmund said he understood. Then they heard steps on the staircase. "I guess Helene is home, we better get ready for dinner." They both stood up and Nellie said, "Daddy? You are not too disappointed, are you?"

"No, I'm not. Everything always works out for the best," he replied.

"I'm so lucky. I have the most understanding father in the whole wide world," Nellie said, hugging him. She felt so relieved, the cloud had finally lifted. What she hadn't told her father was that she already had two offers, one of which sounded extremely interesting and she would now schedule an interview as soon as possible.

Before falling asleep, Sigmund told Helene of Nellie's intentions. She listened to him in silence and when he finished, she spoke. "It is a shame she will not be finishing her schooling after all the time that she has invested in it but I can very well put myself in her place and, having fallen in love with Andreas as she most certainly has, and bearing in mind that it was her first love...so unfortunate, so very unfortunate..." she repeated, then continued angrily, "that she should have been so deceived and misled, ten horses couldn't drag me back there either," and with that ended her answer.

Sigmund looked at her in surprise. "There is no reason for you to get so upset," he said gently.

"You are wrong. I am not upset; it is just the unfairness of it all. Why Nellie? Why not somebody else?"

"I understand your feelings but—"

Helene did not let him finish the sentence, "If you want my opinion, I definitely think she is much better off finding a job where she can grow and excel and I am sure she will find one."

"I really like the fact that she wants to do it on her own," Sigmund added.

"Your daughter is growing up and becoming her own person," said Helene.

Sigmund took her in his arms and kissed her. "Thank you."

"For what?"

"For caring about Nellie," Sigmund said, as she lay in his arms.

Then her thoughts drifted back in time to when she just turned thirteen and had fallen in love with the handsomest boy in her class. She was so proud and thrilled with all his attentions only to discover at a later date that he had been flirting with her just to make the girl he *really* liked jealous. It worked and so, after a couple of weeks, he completely ignored her, never caring about the hurt he had inflicted on her. Through Nellie, she had relived the whole episode and much to her surprise, she could still feel the wrath she had felt at the time.

Before going to bed, Nellie reread the two offers she had received. She was happy she'd gone ahead and not wasted any time. With her father's consent, she would surprise him by getting a job in no time whatsoever and spent the whole weekend thinking about her new project. When Monday morning finally arrived, she dressed with care and as she did, felt a surge of excitement. If everything turned out as she wished, she would soon be financially independent. Not that she had ever had to worry about money, quite the contrary. She had a very generous allowance and with few exceptions, her father had always fulfilled her whims, but it was not the same as earning her own money. She was fully aware that she was about to open the door to adulthood.

Just as Sigmund was about to leave, he remembered Nellie had mentioned her plans to him the night before. He retraced his steps and ran into her on the staircase. "Why, Daddy," exclaimed Nellie in surprise, "I thought you had left."

"How could I leave without wishing you luck?"

"Thanks, Dad," she replied.

"By the way, you are quite appropriately dressed for the occasion," said Sigmund. "Should you require anything, just drop by the office as I will be in all day."

"I will if I am in the neighbourhood."

"What time is your first appointment? I could drop you off." Nellie blushed, "I haven't got one."

"You haven't what…? Well, all the more reason to get to where you are going early," said her father.

"No, Daddy, it's OK, I have it all figured out. Besides, I have not yet had my breakfast and I would only hold you up."

"Well, in that case, have it your way and good luck again. I have a feeling you might need it." Nellie smiled. "See you later," said her father, blowing her a kiss.

Eating her breakfast in a hurry, she was soon on her way and would go to both companies and, although she did not have an interview scheduled, it might not be a waste of time. She decided to try her luck first at the company she liked best. They were looking for a trainee to work in their import and export division and it really sounded very interesting. As she rode the tramway car, she suddenly felt apprehensive… What if they could not see her, what if they had found somebody else in the meantime, what if she did not qualify? *Stop worrying,* she told herself, *it will happen if it is meant to and if it does not work out, it just means that I will have to spend more time looking and…if worst comes to worst, I could use my father's influence.* "No, you won't," she scolded herself, then repeated under her breath: "I will do it on my own, even if it takes me all year."

She got to her first destination in no time and was soon standing in front of a building in the heart of the financial centre. Gathering her courage, she pushed open the door then walked up a flight of stairs to the first floor, following the signs to suite 150. She knocked and waited for what seemed an eternity when all of a sudden, the door flew open and a young lady asked her very politely to step inside.

She did not appear much older than Nellie. "What can I do for you?" Nellie looked in her bag and took out the letter she had received then handed it to her. The receptionist read it and asked:

"Do you have an appointment?"

"No, I thought it best to just come by."

"Take a seat," said the receptionist, "and I will see if Mrs Müller, our head of the personnel department, can see you."

"Thanks," said Nellie, sitting down on the edge of the chair. She looked around and her eyes fell on the morning newspaper lying on the table in front of her. She picked it up, started reading the headlines and was about half way through the social column when she heard the friendly receptionist beckoning to her.

"Mrs Müller will see you now."

Nellie stood up and followed her down the hallway and into a very cheerful office. Mrs Müller, who must have been in her late forties, stood up immediately. Nellie introduced herself. "I am so glad you are here. I have interviewed several candidates but have found none that fulfilled my expectations." Nellie shot her a questioning glance. Mrs Müller offered her a seat on the other side of the desk and without wasting time, proceeded to question her. She wanted to know everything, her background, schooling, interests. Nellie answered her questions as best as she could. "Do you have any work experience?"

"Oh, yes," replied Nellie, and went on to explain about having helped out in her father's business. Mrs Müller was not only impressed with Nellie's knowledge but also with her personality, thinking how well she would fit in with the team. One question lingered in the back of her mind and after a moment's hesitation, decided to ask it.

"Why have you not gone to work for your father?" Nellie gave her the reason. Mrs Müller was silent for what seemed a long time. Nellie took a deep breath and tried to relax even though her thoughts were racing. Mrs Müller's voice brought her back to reality. "The job is yours if you want it," she announced. "Your working hours will be Monday to Friday, from eight to twelve and from two to six. Trainees do not get paid much, as you know, but you will learn everything there is to know about exports and imports and international trade."

Nellie was overwhelmed she had the job and, beaming, stood up across from Mrs Müller. "I will do my utmost best," she said. Mrs Müller smiled for the first time.

"I'm sure you will. Now, come, let me introduce you to your colleagues." The office was just a couple of doors down the hall and Mrs Müller knocked before opening the door. It was a nice bright room and there were two desks, one was occupied by a lady in her late twenties who looked up, startled. "Good morning, Bettina, may I introduce you to our new trainee?" And without waiting for an answer, introduced them.

Bettina gave her a warm smile, "Welcome," she said.

Nellie took an immediate liking to her. "Oh," exclaimed Mrs Müller, turning to Nellie. "I'm sorry, I'm so absent minded but I am assuming you can start work immediately?"

"Sure," replied Nellie.

"Good," said Bettina, "because I could use some help, there is so much going on."

"If you will excuse me, I will draw up the contract for you to sign," said Mrs Müller, heading for the door.

"Come have a seat," said Bettina. As Nellie sat down behind the empty desk, she felt a surge of excitement, having succeeded in finding a job.

Bettina interrupted her thoughts. "Nellie, I will explain everything to you as we go along and please, if you do not understand something, do not hesitate to ask. I was once a trainee as well and I feel a great joy in being able to give back something of what I have received."

"Thank you," replied Nellie. "How long have you been working here?" Bettina told her that she had been with the company for as long as she could remember and really enjoyed her work. For the past couple of years, there had not been much going on, so everybody had helped out where needed, but now with the economy booming, there was a lot more work than usual and they were understaffed. She had not minded working overtime now and then but it had gotten out of hand lately and she was grateful to have Nellie to share her work with.

"Let's get started," she said, then asked Nellie if she knew how to file, giving her at least two months' worth of papers. "I know it is quite a stack, but I kept putting it off and it just kept on growing," she said, laughing. "Once you have organised it all, it will make our life much easier." Nellie set about her work, grateful for all the many hours she'd spent in her father's office doing the same thing.

Mrs Müller returned with the contract and Nellie read it carefully, mindful of her father's words: Never sign anything without having read it and don't ignore the fine print. Satisfied with the contents, she put her signature on it. Her very first work contract was now signed and she felt very proud of herself.

Time seemed to fly by. She had lunch with Bettina at a coffee shop close by and the more she spoke with her, the better she liked her. She was so down to earth and yet, there was something very spiritual about her. The day came to an end sooner than she expected and they left together. "I will see you tomorrow," said Bettina, running to catch the tramway car.

Nellie could hardly wait to get home and tell everyone the news. After letting herself in and walking into the hallway, she caught a glimpse of Sigmund. "Daddy!"

"How did it go, Nellie? I have been thinking of you all day," he said.

"It went well, very well indeed. Come on, let's join Helene in the living room." Nellie sat down with Freddy by her side and poured out her story. Sigmund's eyes beamed with pride as he listened.

"I am very happy everything worked out so well," said Helene. Freddy did not quite understand what was going on but he gave her a wet kiss on the cheek anyway.

Chapter 18

On 23 December 1924, Hitler was released from prison and
Bavaria's Minister President, Heinrich Held, reluctantly accepted Hitler's
fake promises of doing nothing illegal, therefore deciding not to deport him back
to Austria. The Austrian Chancellor was all too happy not to have to readmit a
notorious agitator who he also felt forfeited Austrian citizenship by serving in
the German army during the war.

Sigmund could not believe his ears when he heard the news over the radio.
How could anyone in his right mind not deport such an agitator? Why let him
stay in Germany? He was a proven troublemaker and nothing good would come
of it, to simply set him free and just forbid him to speak in public was outrageous.
A couple of days later, Abraham dropped by Sigmund's office. Looking up in
surprise as his secretary announced his visitor, it was not like his friend to pay
him a call without an appointment. "Show him in, please," said Sigmund,
realising that his secretary was staring at him waiting for an answer.

"There is no need," Abraham said from the doorway.

"Come in, come in, have a seat."

"You are surprised at seeing me, aren't you?"

"I am indeed, for it is not like you to drop by. Has anything happened?"
Sigmund asked in a concerned voice.

"Oh, yes, lots has happened," replied Abraham. "Haven't you heard the
news? Is it not outrageous? The mere thought of it makes me sick."

Sigmund sat down behind his desk and looked at Abraham who seemed to
have aged overnight. "What are you talking about?"

"I can't believe you have not heard. I am talking about Hitler being released
from prison and not being deported. How blind can some people be?"

"Yes, it is pretty bad and I was very upset by it myself," said Sigmund, but
Abraham carried on and ignored the interruption.

"That party was disintegrating into different factions and were fighting each
other, now you shall see, he will consolidate his grip on it again and it will only
become stronger." He paused to catch his breath.

"There is one good thing about it all," said Sigmund.

"And that is?"

"He has been banned from speaking in public, with the exception of
Thuringia where a handful of Nazi deputies ruled the roost under conditions of a
political stalemate."

"Don't fool yourself," said Abraham. "He will find a way of making himself heard everywhere." Sigmund looked pensive. It was not long before Abraham broke the silence. "Business was going so well and I was beginning to believe we had reached a turning point. I saw a ray of hope for the country again… Now this."

"Life has to go on, regardless," said Sigmund.

"You are right," replied Abraham. "Life does have to go on, but I am only asking myself if I've made the right choice."

"You can still have a change of heart."

"Yes, Sigmund, I guess it is not too late, but this time I will be wiser," he said, getting up. "I am sorry I have taken up your time, I just needed to let off steam, I guess."

"That's all right," said Sigmund, walking him to the door, then followed him with his eyes until he turned the corner. Sigmund went back to his office but try as he might, he could not get Abraham out of his mind. In all the years he had known him, he had never seen him so upset.

After leaving Sigmund, Abraham went by the bank to withdraw some money. As he was waiting to be served, his investment advisor saw him and came up to him. "Why, Abraham," he said, "how nice to see you. It has been quite some time."

"It really has," replied Abraham, "but then, time just seems to fly by."

"I am free right now," said Mr Moritz, which was his advisor's name. "Can I do anything for you?"

Abraham thought for a minute. "Yes, actually, could you get me a statement of my investments?" Mr Moritz said he would be back in just a moment and Abraham was just leaving the till when Mr Moritz returned and handed him his statement.

"Anything else I can do for you?"

Abraham glanced at the total written on the sheet and, turning to Mr Moritz, said, "I do not think so. I will study this and should I have any queries, I will get back to you."

"Feel free to do so anytime," replied Mr Moritz, taking his leave.

Abraham walked out of the bank in a daze. The total on the statement seemed right, he would take a closer look at it later, but at the moment he had other, more important matters on his mind. "Am I seeing ghosts?" he asked himself. "Why was Sigmund not at all upset? Maybe it is just me, I am growing old." He looked at his watch and saw it was just turning five. Since it was too early for Sara to be home, she was playing bridge with some friends and never got back before 6pm, he said out loud: "I will take a stroll through the botanical gardens and then head home."

A passer-by turned around to stare at him and giggled to himself, "Just some lunatic speaking to himself." Yes, nowadays there were quite a few of them around.

Abraham admired the flowers and trees and sat down on a bench to enjoy his surroundings. He took the statement out of his pocket and glanced at it. His investments had increased by three percent. Something positive for a change, he thought bitterly. The light was fading and he looked at the time: it was almost six o'clock. How time flies, he thought, then put the paper he held in his hands back in his pocket and made his way to the exit. Once on the street, he hailed a cab and arrived home just as Sara was unlocking the front door.

"Why, Abraham," she said happily, "you could not have timed it better."

"Did you have a good game," he asked, helping her off with her coat.

"Oh, yes, it was a very nice afternoon. And how was yours?"

"It was OK. I ran some errands then enjoyed the botanical gardens. There is something so peaceful about them."

"Dinner will be ready shortly," said Sara, heading for the kitchen. Abraham went to his study and looked at the messages the maid had written neatly out for him on his writing pad. Nothing special, he thought, until one name caught his eye: Richard. He looked again. Richard had called and left word he had something urgent to tell him and to please get in touch with him as soon as possible.

Abraham was just picking up the phone when he heard Sara call from the hallway: dinner is served. He knew how much she hated having to repeat herself so, laying the phone back on its cradle, he went to join his wife. The call would have to wait until dinner was over.

"Where are the girls?" he asked, noticing the table was set only for two.

"Oh," said Sara, "they are attending a function with some friends."

"Having meals together is becoming harder and harder," said Abraham, grumpily.

"You do have to realise that they are grown and have their own friends and activities."

"Yes, but you make it sound as if they were so old and independent. They've only just turned 18." Johanna and Alexandra were twins and they were always together. The maid came in just then and set the soup terrine on the table. Sara took his plate and served him, then herself. Abraham gave her a smile. "Forgive me, dear. I guess I am a little on edge."

"What about?"

He told her of the phone call he had postponed till after dinner then she said, "I just wonder what he has on his mind. It might be—"

"I don't hope," interrupted her husband, "but it might well be that Emmanuel has finally put in an appearance, in which case he could not have timed it better."

"I can tell you are still toying with the idea, aren't you?" she asked, then, without waiting for an answer, "You know, you do not make my life very easy. One day you are happy, the next you have doubts, it is very hard for me and I do not think you realise it, but you are very inconsistent."

Abraham put down his spoon and gave her what she called the look of death. How she hated that look, it made her feel so insecure, so small. I will stand my ground, she thought, calming herself.

"Don't you understand, woman? How often do I have to explain it to you? We have gone over this time and time again but you either do not listen, or you just want to exasperate me. It is because of the circumstances, what is going on in this country politically, and I only want to do what is best for you, the girls and myself. Ever since…"

"Abraham," said Sara in a firm tone of voice, "I understand, I know, but I dread this uncertainty. Why don't you just make a decision once and for all?" There was also desperation in her voice.

Abraham looked at her in the eye and said, "Rest assured, Sara, if I can ever meet with Emanuel, I will." Sara did not say anything more. She knew her husband well enough.

Just as they finished dessert, the girls came in. "Hi Dad, hi Mom," they said in chorus, going from one to the other and kissing each one on the forehead. "I sure don't get to see much of you lately," said their father.

"Your social calendar must be well booked."

"But, Daddy," said Johanna, looking questioningly at her mother who merely shrugged her shoulders. Her father did not wait for an answer.

"I regret having to leave you, but I have important business to attend to." And, giving Alexandra, who was standing by his chair, a pat on the head, he left the room.

"Have you girls eaten?" their mother asked.

"We have indeed and very well, but what is wrong with Daddy? He sure seems to be in a foul mood."

"Oh, girls, don't let it bother you, it's just the usual," replied their mother then changed the subject. "Tell me, how was the function?"

"It was great," replied Alexandra.

"We sure did enjoy ourselves," Johanna added. Alexandra started to tell her all about it but stopped in the middle of the sentence, realising her mother was not paying any attention to her account. Sara could not help but wonder about the outcome of Abraham's telephone conversation.

"Mother," said Alexandra, "you are not listening." She had to repeat her statement twice until it finally registered with Sara.

"I am so sorry, girls. You are absolutely right, I was just thinking of the business your father is trying to take care of."

"Is it very important?" Johanna asked.

"It must be pretty vital," interrupted Alexandra, "since he could hardly wait to leave the table, leaving mother to wonder so much about what is going on that she could not even lend an attentive ear."

"Girls, girls, your father is just worried about the future and he wants to do the best for us."

"Same old story," said Johanna. "Nothing ever seems to change in this household."

"I am tired," said Alexandra and Johanna agreed and so they kissed their mother on the cheek.

"I am sorry," Sara said.

"Nothing to be sorry about," replied Alexandra, "we understand."

Sara watched them go, but made no move to follow them and instead served herself another cup of tea and sat staring into space.

"I hope they resolve the matter soon, whatever it is," said Johanna to her sister. "Otherwise life is going to become quite impossible in this household."

"Oh, well," replied Alexandra, "nothing we haven't dealt with before."

Abraham was talking excitedly to Richard over the phone. "Are you sure he is coming? Is he serious this time?"

"Listen to me, Abraham, and I will repeat it for you: I got his phone call early this afternoon, he said he will be here the day after tomorrow."

"But what if he changes his mind again?"

"Be assured, he won't. There is too much at stake on this trip for him, he will be here."

"OK," said Abraham, "you can count on me, I will be at your house as planned and I must add, I am very much looking forward to meeting him. I just hope he does not let us down for the fifth time."

"He won't," replied Richard. "Have a great evening and I will see you soon." Abraham wished him good night as well then stood, lost in thought next to his desk. There is a lot at stake for him on this trip… I wonder what Richard meant by that.

"What is the news?" Sara asked from the doorway.

"Emmanuel is definitely coming and I am to meet with him at Richard's home in two days' time."

"Is it definite?"

"Richard assures me that this time we will not be let down."

"I am glad," said Sara, stifling a yawn.

Abraham came toward her, turned out the light and, taking her arm, guided her up the stairs. Sara lay in bed going over the evening's events and Abraham's last thought before he dropped off to sleep was, "I hope I won't be disappointed."

Chapter 19

Abraham left for work late the next morning. From time to time, his thoughts wandered back to his telephone conversation with Richard. He had not heard anything more from him, which was a good sign and meant Emmanuel had not changed his mind and was coming. For the past few days, he had been in a better mood than usual and if everything went the way he hoped…but he dare not think about it for fear of being disappointed. Then, just as he was getting ready for bed, the phone rang. "Oh no," said Sara, "I hope it is not Richard."

Abraham made a dash for it with a sinking heart. It *was* Richard. "I am just calling to confirm our meeting tomorrow."

Abraham let out a sigh of relief. "What time do you want us to meet?"

"How about 6 pm?"

"That is fine. I will be there on time." Then Richard wished him good night and hung up.

"I am so relieved he did not call to cancel," said Sara, who had overheard the conversation.

"So am I. And we shall see what tomorrow has in store for us," he said, kissing her goodnight.

At six o'clock sharp, Abraham rang the doorbell and Richard opened the door.

"Good evening," said Abraham.

"Come in, come in, Emmanuel can't wait to meet you."

"Well, he sure has taken his time."

"I am sorry," said a voice in the background. "It could not be helped."

Abraham turned around to face the stranger. "I am so glad I can finally put a face to your name," said Abraham, smiling.

"And I to yours! I have heard so much about you," replied Emmanuel, shaking his hand.

"Let us go into the study," said Richard, who then led the way.

They made themselves comfortable. Abraham asked Emmanuel if he had had a good trip and he said it had been uneventful but very long. "It has been quite some time since I've been to Germany and even though my stay will be short, I intend to make the most of it."

"Let's get down to business," said Richard. Emmanuel turned to Abraham.

"I do not know how much Richard has told you, but if you will allow me, I would like to begin by introducing myself. I was born in Germany and, after finishing college, I took a sabbatical year off to travel the world."

"Well, what a great idea," Abraham interjected.

Emmanuel smiled and continued.

"It was, but I did not get to see much of it, for I chose to start with South America. The first country I visited was Brazil, and what a great country it is. Then, after seeing the south of the country, I headed north and ended up in Manaus, which is a port on the Amazon and where the river flows into the sea. The river in itself is huge, like an ocean, in fact it's so wide, you cannot see the other shore. It was here that I ran into two Colombians by chance in a restaurant who, after travelling like me through Brazil, were headed home.

Our meeting was quite unusual. I was enjoying a beer at the bar when they walked in. The bartender knew them and greeted them warmly. As he served them their beers, I noticed their gaze fall on me and I heard the bartender utter the word 'stranger' in Portuguese. Shortly thereafter, they came up to me and, in excellent English, asked me where I was from. That was the beginning of a long conversation and as the evening wore on, we discovered we had a lot in common.

They were of European descent and had been all over Europe but were winding up their journey in Brazil after having travelled through South America. They told me the most unbelievable stories about their trip. I, in turn, shared my Brazilian experiences with them and my thoughts on what a great country it was, not to mention that the women were dazzlingly beautiful. Juan Carlos and Enrique both smiled at my enthusiasm. "Emmanuel," they said, almost in one voice, "you have yet to see the best of South America. Come to Colombia with us, we will show you our country and you will not be disappointed, we can assure you."

Needless to say, by this time we had already downed quite a few beers and I heard myself say, 'Why not,' who cares about seeing Argentina anyway. I turned to my new friends and said, "I will come with you."

The next afternoon, we took a hydroplane from Manaus to Barranquilla, the city where they lived. True to their word, we travelled all over the country and I fell in love with it and its people. A few weeks after settling down in Barranquilla, I was introduced to a lovely girl at one of the parties they had for me. It was love at first sight; she was not only gorgeous but also very intelligent and came from Bogotá, the capital. It did not take me long to move there so I could be close to her and find a job. I have lived there ever since."

"What happened to the girl?" Abraham asked.

"She is my wife," replied Emmanuel. "I do not see a lot of Juan Carlos and Enrique, but we have kept in touch during all these years."

"What a great story,"

Then Richard added, "You just never know where you'll end up."

"What kind of job did you find and did you speak Spanish?" Abraham wanted to know.

"No, I did not, but I took some private lessons and then of course Elsa spoke very little English so I was forced to speak to her in Spanish. As far as work, jobs were, or I might say are, plentiful. I found a lot of different occupations, which even included teaching English. Now that you know a little about me, allow me to lay out my idea to you."

He explained: "Bogotá is a very international city and even though the German colony is the second largest, no one has thought of putting up a brewery. Beer is a luxury since it's imported, which makes it accessible only to a few, making the market potential huge. Unfortunately, I cannot finance this project alone so I am looking for people who would be willing to invest." Emmanuel looked at Richard, "I trust you mentioned this to Abraham?"

"Oh, yes," replied Abraham, "he did, and I must say, I might be very interested, depending on the amount of money I would be required to put down."

"We can look at the figures some other time," said Emmanuel looking at his watch.

Abraham looked at his, too. "I had not realised it was so late, I better be going."

"Could we meet tomorrow?" Emmanuel asked. "I will put some figures together for you and we could discuss what I have in mind."

"That is a very good idea," replied Abraham.

"May I suggest we meet at my office after lunch?" They all agreed.

Sara was reading in bed when Abraham got home. "What is he like?" she asked Abraham as soon as he walked into the bedroom.

"Who are you talking about?"

"Emmanuel, of course."

"He is very nice and seems to have a good head on his shoulders. I do not think he is a dreamer, but I will find out tomorrow." Then he kissed his wife goodnight and turned out the light.

"You sure are not in a talkative mood," said Sara in a disappointed tone of voice.

"No, I am not. I have had a long day and I am very tired." Sara did not reply.

Abraham was up bright and early the next morning, with so many things on his mind he barely acknowledged his wife's presence. Sara asked the same question twice without obtaining an answer and now realised she was standing by the door.

"I am sorry," he said, picking up his briefcase.

"Will you be home for lunch?"

"No, I don't think so, don't expect me as I am meeting with Emmanuel and Richard. Just expect me when you see me." He kissed her absent-mindedly and was gone. When he arrived at the office, he found nothing but problems. His secretary, who was his right hand, had called in sick just when he needed her the most and the young lady who was assigned to replace her was not much help. She tried his patience, for he had to repeat everything twice and three times and she made no end of mistakes. To make matters worse, everyone seemed to be running late. "It is one of those days," he said to himself, trying to keep his temper in check.

His replacement secretary breathed a sigh of relief when he said good-bye to her and told her he would not be back in the afternoon. One of her colleagues, who had been with the business for years, walked up to her. "You sure have had a rough time," she said.

"You can say that again. He was not pleased with anything I did."

"Yes," said Eleanor, "I do not know what has gotten into him lately but he sure is becoming very grumpy and impatient, he never used to be this way."

"It must be his age," replied the secretary.

Eleanor gave her a look and went back to her desk.

Abraham arrived at Richards's office right on time and joined the others in the small conference room. Richard told his secretary not to disturb them. Emmanuel opened his briefcase and handed each of them some sheets of paper. Abraham glanced at them briefly. They were the plans for the building, the quotes from a German company for the machinery and a timetable. Abraham was impressed. Emmanuel did not waste any time and gave a detailed explanation about what he had in mind. After answering a couple of questions, he handed out a sheet with the financial information. According to the figures, they would be able to borrow half of the cost from a local bank at a very good interest rate and the rest would have to be put up by private investors. Abraham looked at the figures once more. The amount required represented all his savings.

How wise would it be to put all his eggs in one basket? He had always tried to diversify, but in this case, it would not be possible. It was a risk but then, everything in life nowadays was becoming a risk so who cares? "Who will run the company?" he heard himself ask.

"I will," replied Emmanuel, "but I cannot do it by myself." He paused. "Abraham, would you consider helping me manage it if you were to decide to invest in it?" No answer. Emmanuel raised the tone of his voice. "Abraham, would you be willing to come to Colombia?"

Abraham sighed. "Yes, I believe I would. I have a wife and two daughters, whom I would have to consult, but I am no longer tied to this country," he added.

Emmanuel could not help but hear the bitterness in his voice.

"You've had it," he said.

"Yes," Abraham replied, "I have. When they refused to deport Hitler, my cup was filled and I am ready to leave and try my luck elsewhere. I personally see no change for the better here, quite the contrary, things are only going to get worse, but nobody seems to care."

"Let's not talk politics right now and instead go back to where we left off," Richard suggested.

They discussed the project at length and Abraham realised he would have to rely solely on Emmanuel's knowledge of the country and of the market. They were about to end their discussion when Abraham asked Emmanuel, "Do you think you could put up a quarter of the money?"

"I don't know yet, why are you asking?"

"Someone just crossed my mind who might be interested and would be a very good partner," said Abraham.

"I trust your judgment, so feel free to discuss the venture with him."

Richard, who had not uttered one word, said, "Well, gentlemen, it is now in your hands. For my part, I have neither the money to invest nor the desire to seek out other horizons." And with that statement, the meeting broke up.

It was Sigmund who Abraham had in mind. The monetary factor would not be an issue, of this he was certain since he not only possessed an excellent business sense but had the vision and leadership this new venture would require. But was he ready to turn his back on Germany and try his luck elsewhere? Abraham was not so sure. He was so deep in thought that he arrived home before he knew it, just in time for dinner. "Daddy is home," he heard Alexandra call out to her mother.

"What? Home already?"

"Am I too early?" he asked, entering the kitchen.

"Not at all, and the girls have nothing planned for tonight."

"How nice, it will be just like in the old days," said Abraham with a twinkle in his eye.

"Oh, come on Daddy," said Johanna. Alexandra, who had overheard the sentence, interrupted her sister.

"I hadn't realised how much you miss us," she said laughing.

Abraham left to wash up before dinner. "He sure seems to be in a good mood," said Johanna.

"I guess his meeting went well," said Sara.

"What meeting?" Alexandra asked. Just then, Abraham called from the dining room.

"Isn't anybody going to join me?"

"We are coming, we are coming," they answered in unison.

Long after the girls had gone to bed, Sara and Abraham sat in the living room talking. Abraham briefed her on the afternoon's events. Sara could tell that he liked the idea. "Have you made a decision?"

"Woman," he exclaimed, "this is not a decision one makes in five minutes, a lot is at stake and besides, there are you and the girls to think about."

Sara could not resist saying: "I thought you were going to decide on your own what was best for all of us," she said.

Abraham gave her that look of death and stomped out of the room then went to sit in his favourite chair in the study. There he sat, staring into space. He went over and over again in his mind the conversation he'd had with Emmanuel. He would never entrust someone with such a huge amount of money, at the very least, he would have to be on the board of directors to oversee things, but then again, that was not a problem since Emmanuel asked him outright to be part of the management. It also meant a new start and wasn't this the opportunity he had been looking for? He was so fed up with political uncertainty and this was the chance of a lifetime, yet he could not make up his mind. It is not an easy decision, he said to himself. He let out a yawn. I will ring Sigmund tomorrow morning, first thing, and set up a meeting to discuss it with him. With that thought in his mind, he got up, turned out the light and headed upstairs. The house was in darkness and everyone was in bed. Sara stirred in her sleep as he climbed in next to her. He stroked her head gently and whispered into her ear: "I just want the best for all of us." She gave him a sweet smile before rolling over onto her side.

Chapter 20

Sigmund had been extremely busy of late. He meant to call Abraham several times after their last meeting but with one thing or the other, it always slipped his mind. A feeling of guilt crept over him upon hearing Abraham's voice on the line. "Abraham, I have been meaning to ring you," he said.

"Don't worry, Sigmund, I know how hectic life is, but I do have a matter of utmost importance I would like to discuss with you. Do you think you could manage to—"

Sigmund did not let him finish. "Why sure, old friend, anytime. Why don't you and Sara come over for dinner tomorrow night?"

"Thank you," replied Abraham, "but I would rather discuss this matter with you over a dinner drink and not bring Sara along, if that is all right with you."

"That is fine with me," answered Sigmund, frowning.

"I look forward to seeing you," said Abraham, and hung up.

That's odd, but a knock on his door interrupted his thoughts. "Come in," he called, and the door opened and in walked Nellie. "Why, Nellie, this sure is a nice surprise."

"I got off work early and I thought it might be nice if we could go for coffee and cake together." Sigmund looked at his watch and at the papers cluttering his desk.

"Give me ten minutes." Nellie sat down on the chair facing him and watched him put everything away. Her father was so organised, how she wished she could be like him. He made a couple of calls and, after giving his secretary some instructions, went to get his hat and coat. "I am ready, let's go."

They went to the café just around the corner and found a table right away. Being that time of day, there were not many people in it. They placed their order and looked at each other. "You know, Daddy, we should do this more often."

"I guess we should, but it has never crossed my mind," replied her father. "Are you enjoying your job as much as you were in the beginning?"

"I have learned so much, Daddy and not once have I regretted my decision. This is so much more exciting than reading textbooks. I am now dealing with the clients directly and it is amazing how many different people I get to meet. Depending on what country we export to, the regulations are all different so I have to learn about them. And then, of course, I try to learn a little about the country itself."

"What countries are you doing the most business with?"

"You won't believe it, Daddy, because they are so far away, but we have been dealing mostly with two South American countries. Colombia and Brazil are our two most important customers and you know, except for Brazil where Portuguese is the country's language, all the rest speak Spanish. I sure would love to go there someday, it all sounds so exotic and it must be so different from Europe. Daddy, can you imagine living in a country where there are no seasons?"

Sigmund thought for a minute. "I have never thought about it but no, Nellie, I can't imagine having the same weather all year around and the hours of light being the same year in year out," replied her father.

"I can't imagine it either," said Nellie, "but I have been told that in Colombia, there is only a dry and a rainy season and apparently come 6 pm the sun just sets. It gets dark immediately, there is no dusk and the sun just disappears."

"It sure sounds amazing," her father remarked. "I trust you know the reason for it?"

"I sure do! It is because it is so close to the equator," she replied.

"Tell me, child, where have you gotten all your information?"

"Oh, Dad, I just ask questions. And then, I must admit I have gone to the library and read up on the countries that have appealed to me."

"That is wonderful, Nellie. I must say, I succeeded very well in transmitting to you the love of learning and books. I hope, for your sake, that someday you might get a chance to visit all these countries."

"I would love to. But wouldn't you like to see something more of the world than just Germany, Daddy?"

"Maybe someday, but for the time being, there is too much happening here for me to even consider taking a holiday. Anyway, we should be leaving," said Sigmund, "we are the last ones."

Nellie took the last bite of her cake. "You are right, Daddy, I am sure it has been a long day for employees as well." He asked the server for the check who was back in a flash. They paid and left.

Freddy was still up when they got home. He had grown into a cute and handsome little boy with his mother's features but his father's temperament. "Daddy's home, Mama, and he got here first."

"First? Why, what do you mean?"

"Nellie is usually the first to come home," he replied.

Nellie smiled. "Oh, Freddy, you are so funny."

"I am here," she called out. He started laughing upon hearing her voice and ran down the stairs. She met him halfway and took him in her arms. "You are growing up so fast, little one."

Sigmund watched and he felt very blessed that his two offspring should be so close. Helene linked her arm through his, so absorbed in his thoughts that he had not heard her. "We are so lucky," she whispered into his ear, as they watched both Nellie and Freddy disappear from sight.

"They will always be friends and they will always be able to rely on each other," said Sigmund. She turned to face him and saw that faraway look in his eyes, one that came into them when something was troubling him. Over the years, she had learned to ignore it, to mind her own business as he would certainly share whatever it was with her eventually. She did not have long to wait. "Helene," he said, sitting down next to her on the couch in the living room. "Abraham is coming over for a drink after dinner tomorrow night."

"Without Sara?"

"Yes, he said he had something he needed to discuss."

"It must be pretty important."

"I am worried about him. It really is not like him to turn down a dinner invitation."

"That is odd," Helene remarked. "But then, I am sure it must have something to do with business and will probably be drawn out so he wants to take his time and be on his own."

"You are probably right, as usual. But the last time I saw him, he was so stressed out, he was not his usual self. How I wish sometimes I could devote more time to my friends and family, but the business is taking up all of my time and there is nothing I can do about it. With the economy being what it is right now, it would be foolish not to take advantage of it for it surely is not going to last forever," he said.

"Don't feel bad," Helene said in an understanding tone of voice. "I certainly do not feel neglected and who knows, maybe someday you will have so much time on your hands that you will be able to make up for it."

"Yes," replied Sigmund, "maybe someday. If and when that day comes, let's hope it won't be too late."

"Late? What do you mean? It can never be too late."

"Life is strange, Helene, and it usually does not turn out as one might wish. Anyway, how was your day?" he asked, changing the subject.

A few nights later, Abraham was just finishing his dinner when he looked at the time. "I had better be on my way," he said, pushing his chair back from the table. Sara shot him a questioning look. "Have you forgotten?" Sara shrugged her shoulders.

"It really is not important," she said.

He called out just before closing the door behind him, "I will be at Sigmund's should you need me," and left. Sara was a little puzzled when he mentioned it to her, but now, sipping her tea, she suddenly realised it probably had something to do with Emmanuel. How she wished he had remained a ghost, blaming him for her husband's ill temper and swinging moods. She let out a sigh.

"I'm sure it's Abraham at the door. I will get it," said Sigmund. "You can set your watch by him, always on time." After taking his raincoat, he led his friend into the library.

"I love this room," Abraham commented, as he walked over to the fishpond.

"It is the best room in the house," said Sigmund. "Well, Emmanuel has finally put in an appearance."

"Who are you talking about?" asked Sigmund.

"Some months ago, Sara and I had a dinner party—" Abraham began but Sigmund interrupted him.

"Oh yes, I remember now, Richard's relative who lives somewhere in South America."

"Yes, that is who I am talking about."

"What is he like?"

"He is very nice and seems to have a good head on his shoulders. He wants to set up a brewery in Colombia and is looking for people to invest in it."

"I see," said Sigmund, "and you are considering doing so."

Abraham sat back in his chair. "Yes, I am, but there are a lot more issues here than meet the eye."

"This might be the opportunity you have been waiting for, after all, you have made it quite clear that this country is going down the drain and that you are worried sick the Nazis are going to take over. You could leave and settle somewhere in South America and you would have an occupation. It is the perfect scenario."

"It also means placing all my life savings into one basket."

"Nothing wrong with that if it is going to give you peace of mind," said Sigmund, "but let us discuss this matter in depth."

Abraham handed him the detailed business plan Emmanuel had drawn up and Sigmund studied it. "Can you grow your grains or do they have to be imported?" Sigmund asked.

"No way, the soil is apparently so rich that anything and everything will grow."

"What surprises me is that if the market potential is what he claims it to be, nobody has taken advantage of it already," said Sigmund.

"Well, I guess it might be because all the equipment has to be imported from Germany and it is not an inexpensive proposition."

"Have you got any idea what it would cost?"

"Yes, just take a look at this, it is a formal quote," said Abraham, handing him the sheets of paper.

Sigmund looked at the letterhead. "I have heard of this company, it is very well known."

"And these are the architectural plans for the building," Abraham said while handing them to him.

"It looks very good on paper and seems very well planned. Do they have good architects and engineers in the country?"

"They must have. A Colombian drew up the plans and Emmanuel knows everyone there."

"I am a little curious and I do not remember your telling me how he ended up in Colombia." Abraham then proceeded to tell him the story. "One thing in his favour is that he knows the mentality very well." Abraham interjected that he would also be investing in it. "Then I assume he has done the research and studied all the risks."

"I am sure he has."

"Are you thinking of going in as equal partners?" Sigmund wanted to know.

"That is why I have come to see you. I asked him that same question and he did not give me a clear answer. I really do not know but would you be interested, Sigmund?"

Sigmund looked at him in surprise. "What an idea, Abraham, you know I have a very successful business and it is a lot of money to invest in such a faraway country."

"Sigmund, my friend, you still cannot see the dangers that are befalling our country, can you? I have tried by all means I possess to make you aware of them, but you are like the blind man who cannot see," said Abraham sadly.

"I don't understand you, Abraham, if you see them so clearly why are you having doubts? I, on the other hand, have never considered leaving Germany. I am aware of the changes that the country is going through, I do not like them but I am not worried to the point that I no longer have a life and making myself sick and everyone around me miserable."

Abraham turned red in the face. "That is quite a statement, Sigmund."

"You may not like what you have just heard, but it is the truth. You have changed, you have lost your zest for life and you have become very bitter, which radiates out onto the people around you. Take this opportunity since you may never have another one. You have the money, don't worry about putting all your savings into this project; that is the price for getting back your peace of mind. In my eyes, it is well worth it."

Sigmund stood up and poured Abraham another glass of cognac, taking a big sip. Sigmund looked at him in silence, reproaching himself for being so hard on his old friend but just as he was going to apologise, Abraham spoke. "You are right about everything you said, criticising me for not being consistent and," he sighed, "you are absolutely right."

"Have you discussed the matter with Sara?"

"I have and we have agreed that whatever decision I make will be in all our best interest." He stood up. "Sara will be wondering what has kept me so long."

"You told her your whereabouts, I trust," said Sigmund.

"Yes, but nevertheless I should be leaving." They left the library and the house was quiet, the clock striking 2 am interrupted the silence.

"You will never hail a cab at this hour," said Sigmund. "I will drive you home." Abraham protested to no avail. "I hope you make the right choice," said Sigmund, parking the car in front of Abraham's house.

"I thank you for your time," said Abraham getting out. "I will keep you posted as to what I decide."

Helene heard Sigmund leave. "No wonder he did not want to come with Sara," she said, as he walked in.

"Yes, it sure has been a very long evening and night as well. I just hope he takes the advice I gave him." She did not reply, she was sound asleep.

Sigmund lay in bed tossing and turning, unable to shut off his brain as it went over the conversation again and again. Maybe his friend was right, maybe he should consider leaving and going to Colombia, and with that thought, he fell into a deep and restless sleep. He dreamt of a faraway country, of people he could not communicate with, and of leaving everything behind he had known up until then and felt a deep pain, like a stab in the chest. It woke him up. He sat up in bed and looked around him, the pain subsiding as soon as he realised it had only been a dream. No, he could never leave and now, finally at peace, he went into a deep and restful sleep.

Sara was sleeping soundly when Abraham got home. He undressed without turning on the light in order not to disturb her but just as he was getting into bed, she called his name. "Have you made a decision?"

"Go back to sleep, dear, we can discuss it all in the morning."

She took his hand in hers and said, "Abraham, please answer my question."

"Yes," he replied squeezing her hand back, "I have made up my mind. We are leaving." Sara turned her face away so that he could not see the tears running down her cheeks.

Richard looked up from his paper when he heard someone knocking at the door. Who could it be, he wondered as he walked towards it. "Hello, Abraham, what a surprise."

"I called several times but got no answer."

"Do come in," said Richard and Abraham followed him into the study.

"I don't have much time, but could you please ask Emmanuel to meet me around noon today? He can ring me at my office. I will be there all morning."

"Certainly," said Richard. "Are you sure you do not want to speak to him now? I can see if he is awake." Abraham hesitated. "I will go upstairs and if he is up, I will give him your message, that way you will not have to wait for an answer." Abraham nodded his head in agreement.

Emmanuel lay in bed wide awake, wondering who the visitor was. "Abraham is here," said Richard, as he approached the bed.

"Abraham? He must have something very urgent on his mind to come over at such an early hour," said Emmanuel.

"He said he rang several times but could not get through."

"So what is it?" he asked impatiently. Richard gave him the message. "Tell him that's fine," and, giving his cousin a happy smile, added, "I have a feeling I have found a partner." Richard did not reply.

"I caught him just as he was getting out of bed," said Richard. "He will meet you at his office at noon." Abraham thanked him and went on his way.

Whistling to himself as he walked down the street, he thought about how he had made up his mind and, if everything worked out the way he hoped, he and his family would be starting a new life in South America. Sigmund was absolutely right. What good is all the money if I don't have peace of mind?

No more alienating everyone around him with his moods, and his relationship with Sara was bound to improve now that all the uncertainties had been dealt with. It had been a long time since he had felt so happy. He spent the morning in the office dealing with the usual, every now and then checking the time, for he did not want to be late.

Richard had given Emmanuel the use of one of his offices and he was now in one, sitting behind the desk. Papers were scattered everywhere. He thought about cleaning up the mess up before Abraham arrived but just then, there was a knock on the door. Abraham went straight to the point and Emmanuel was overjoyed with the news. He was sorry to hear that he had not succeeded in convincing Sigmund but on the other hand, as he wisely pointed out, the fewer the partners, the easier one could deal with them.

"The ideal partnership," he said laughing, "is one where there is only one and that is oneself." Abraham joined in the laughter that soon died down as they went on to serious matters. Emmanuel went over the initial figures one more time. They would both invest the same amount and Emmanuel would visit the factory providing the equipment and try and get a better deal before returning to Colombia. "You and your family will need a visa for Colombia that I will apply for when I return, but do bear in mind, Abraham, the pace is a good deal slower than it is here."

"How long do you think it will take?"

"It might be a good year, if not a little longer. But in the meantime, we have a lot to do. I have to see about getting the financing from the banks, buying the lot, starting the construction and everything else and you—" Emmanuel was unable to finish his sentence.

"And I," interrupted Abraham, "have to liquidate my business and prepare my family for a big change."

"I hope for the better," said Emmanuel.

"Undoubtedly," replied Abraham, and they shook hands.

Emmanuel left that same evening to meet with the provider the following morning and managed to fly out that same night to Bogotá. His trip had been a success, his dream was about to become a reality and he could not have hoped for a better partner, of that he was absolutely certain.

Chapter 21

The news of Hitler's release from prison was also cause for many celebrations. Andreas was overjoyed with the good tidings. He and his gang partied until the early morning hours. Following his expulsion from the university, he lived through hell and Nellie, that little Jewish bitch, was the cause of his downfall. Each time he ran into his friends, they teased him and cracked jokes about how a little Jewish girl had outwitted him. He could feel the hatred rising in him whenever he thought of her and had vowed to himself not to forget her until he had taken revenge, and how sweet his revenge would be.

Yes, she would pay for all the pain and scorn he had to endure. He had been demoted within the movement as well, how he hated being treated like a second-class member, to say the least, he who had such a high opinion of himself, doing everything he could to redeem himself. Volunteering for everything without the slightest hesitation, he devoted all his spare time to learning more about the movement. After reading *Mein Kampf*, he identified himself with it so much, he felt as if the author and he had known each other since childhood. Hitler became his hero.

The room at his parent's house was under the roof and beautifully decorated. One Saturday morning, he surprised his parents by removing everything and giving it all away to a neighbour who happened to be walking by. All he kept were his bed, night table, a chair and a military trunk. He satisfied his neighbour's curiosity by telling him that he was only redecorating, which in truth he was. He hung the Nazi flag on the wall, from which it could clearly be seen from the hallway, and on the other two walls constructed several posters that made crude fun of communists and foreigners. At the entrance to his room, he hung a huge swastika and from the arms of the ceiling lamp, he hung two pairs of handcuffs. On top of the trunk, he laid two pistols and several boxes of ammunition. His favourite book, now his bible, lay by his bedside. When he finished, he lay down on his bed and admired his work. Feeling very satisfied with himself, he got up, put on his leather jacket and made his way to the bar down the street.

His mother Helga was preparing dinner when she heard the front door slam shut. "I guess Andreas has gone out," she said aloud. The cat, who was sleeping on the floor by the fire, stretched, opened one eye, scratched his left ear and, giving his mistress a dirty look, went back to sleep.

Helga took her time washing up and drying her hands. She had offered Andreas some advice on the decorating, but he told her in no uncertain terms to mind her own business and get and stay out of his way. She did as she was told but now, knowing him gone, her curiosity got the better of her and she made her way up the stairs.

Letting out a cry of horror as she opened the door, her knees gave way under her and she held on to the door handle for support. "I would never have guessed he was a member of the movement," she said to no one. "How little I know about my own child," she added, bitterly slamming the door behind her. She did not say a word to her husband about her son's affiliation for she did not want to hear him say in a voice filled with pride, "One of the few defending the interests of the fatherland."

Andreas's enthusiasm and commitment to the party did not go unnoticed and one evening, as he was having his beer at his usual bar, a total stranger walked up to him. After exchanging a few words with the bartender, whom the stranger seemed to know very well indeed, and ordering his beer, he turned to Andreas. "How are you tonight, my friend?"

Andreas looked up startled, wondering to whom the stranger was speaking, but there was nobody else in sight. "Yes, it is you I am talking to."

"I don't think we have met," replied Andreas.

"No, we have not met face to face, but I do know a lot about you," said the stranger. Andreas looked at him in surprise. "I admire your zeal and ambition, your love for the fatherland, and your commitment to the movement." Andreas blushed. "There is no need for you to feel embarrassed, it is the truth. You may have guessed by now that I am a high ranking member of the movement."

"But I failed miserably on my last mission," said Andreas under his breath.

"I know, but that's all in the past. You are exactly the kind of person the party needs and I have come to ask you to become one of us." Andreas tried to interrupt. "And invite you to join the SA (Storm Detachment)."

Andreas opened his eyes wide; a member of the SA, the paramilitary branch of the movement?

"Yes," said the stranger. Andreas was beside himself with joy and shook hands with the stranger.

"I would be more than delighted," he said.

"I know you will give your best," the stranger said, and with a nod of his head disappeared from sight.

Andreas stood at the bar in a daze. The bartender interrupted his thoughts, "That's quite a promotion, I should say," serving him a beer on the house.

In no time whatsoever, Andreas found himself surrounded by both familiar and unfamiliar faces with everyone speaking at once. When he recognised some of the cronies who had made fun of him, he walked up to them and said, "So chaps, what happened? You're all so quiet, what happened to the jokes?" he asked, as he shook his fist in one of their faces.

"They are a thing of the past," replied the spokesman, taking a step back.

"Good, should any of you dare ever make fun of me again, I hope you know what to expect," he said, taking his leave.

He walked home with his head held high and soon became the leader of the movement in his neighbourhood, making a point of calling a meeting every week in which he not only gave out the assignments for the following one, but indoctrinated them. He was more feared than respected and on the weekends, and whenever they had time, the group would ride out into the country on their motorcycles, terrorising the peasants who ignored their presence. Whenever possible, they would insult any foreigners they encountered and attacking them physically became a popular pastime.

One day, as Andreas waited for the tramway car downtown, he thought he caught sight of Nellie. His heart skipped a beat and he stared in surprise, doubting his eyes, then ran after her but she was nowhere in sight. "I am so obsessed with her that my mind is playing tricks on me," he scolded himself, then made a point of going to that same stop every day at different hours. He strolled down the main and side streets but there was no sign of her. After a week of chasing a ghost, he resolved to give up on his way home, it was all a big waste of time and he had accomplished nothing.

That night, he tossed and turned in his bed, Nellie was haunting him in his sleep. She would beckon to him and as soon as he was close enough to touch her, she would then disappear. He felt so frustrated and helpless and woke up with this very present feeling. He looked at the time. "Why, it's not even seven o'clock." And he lay back in bed and closed his eyes. It was useless; he could not get her out of his mind. "How I wish I could get my hands on you," he said out loud, picking up one of his boots and hurling it against the wall.

Then he sat down on the floor and drew a huge picture of Nellie just as he remembered her carrying her books under her arm. Beneath it, he wrote in bold letters:

JUST YOU WAIT, JEWISH BITCH, ONE DAY WE WILL BE SQUARE AND GERMANY WILL BE FREE FROM ALL YOU DIRTY JEWS.

He looked at the poster over and over again, corrected a detail here and there, and in a much better frame of mind, lay down on his bed and fell into a deep sleep.

It was mid-afternoon when he woke up. His gaze drifted to the poster he had drawn and a thought flashed through his mind. He would take it to the meeting that evening. Passing it around, he asked everyone several times for their opinion but they knew better than to comment on it. "Come on guys, speak up," he said impatiently. One could not only tell by the sound of his voice, but by the look of death he gave them, that he was getting very angry. "Have you all lost your balls that you cannot answer my question?"

All of a sudden from the back of the room, somebody broke the silence saying, "I have balls."

"Come forward," said Andreas harshly, "and speak up." The man did as he was told. He was a newcomer and this was the second meeting he attended. "How much longer do I have to wait?" Andreas asked impatiently. Everyone was gazing intently at the poor, inexperienced guy and some were nudging each other, trying hard not to laugh.

"What a fool to get himself into such a predicament, serves him right for trying to be a smart ass," said someone under his breath.

Andreas was yelling now at the top of his lungs, shaking his fist. "Maybe if I give you a couple of beatings, you'll find your tongue."

"I think the drawing is very good, even though I do not know the character. Why don't you hang it at a tramway car stop? Your brilliant work will not go unnoticed and it sure will scare the hell out of all those bloody Jews," he said in a quivering voice.

The silence that followed could be cut with a knife then, all of a sudden, everyone was talking at once. "What a great idea," said Andreas, taking the newcomer's arm. "Let's not waste any time and get on with it." They all made a dash for the door, singing and laughing and following Andreas into the heart of the city. Once the poster was hung, they all scribbled obscenities on it then headed for the nearest bar where they celebrated their geniality way into the night.

Nellie had taken a couple of days leave from the office. She had not taken a vacation in more than a year and felt slightly tired. Sigmund offered to pay for a trip to Basel so that she could visit her friends, but she declined, saying she had a couple of things to tend to and, more importantly, she wanted to spend a little time with Freddy whom she did not see enough of. She really enjoyed her free time sleeping in and doing all those activities for which she no longer had time and thought how nice it was not being on a schedule. She devoted her time to Freddy and got to know his friend Helmut. "Such a nice kid," she commented to Helene one day. Her stepmother agreed and remarked that it was a shame that their time together was coming to an end.

"What do you mean?"

"Helmut's parents cannot afford to send him to the same school Freddy will be going to."

"I see," said Nellie. "Does Freddy know?"

"I have not told him but he will find out soon enough."

"It is not as if he were moving away from the neighbourhood, so they can still play together after school is out," Nellie commented.

"Speaking of school," said Helene, "I hope you haven't forgotten it is Freddy's first day next Monday."

"How could I forget, with Freddy reminding me daily?"

Monday morning came and Freddy was beside himself with excitement. The first day of school was a very important day in a child's life and parents, relatives and the school made quite an occasion of it. Everyone was dressed festively and Freddy looked so cute in his short pants, long sleeved shirt and red cardigan. Red really suited him well. His mother combed his hair once more, straightened his shirt collar, and they were on their way. In his arm, he proudly held a huge cone filled to the brim with candies and other goodies, which he would later share with his classmates.

They walked the three blocks to the school in silence. After going across the stone courtyard where some parents were gathered in small groups eagerly exchanging their holiday's experiences, they filed into the gymnasium, which had been nicely decorated for the occasion. The newcomers sat down with their parents until their names were called out, then went to join their teachers and new classmates. The choir sung, the school director gave a speech (which he held short to everyone's relief). Some of the older classes put on a funny play and everyone laughed heartily. Helene looked around but didn't recognise anybody. Nellie sat by her father's side and saw him glance at his watch several times. *He must be getting pretty bored,* she thought. But she enjoyed herself, hardly able to remember her first day of school, it seemed so long ago.

The children followed their teachers to the classrooms. Freddy looked around him, there were mostly boys in his class and just a couple of girls, but no sign of Helmut. However, he had no time to dwell on it for he heard his name called out and was told to take a seat in the last row and to introduce himself to the class like the others had done before him. Once the introductions were over with, they were allowed to exchange their candies and in no time at all, the sound of children's voices and laughter filled the room. Freddy forgot about his friend. Their parents joined them shortly thereafter and, admiring their classroom, wanted to be shown where their offspring would be sitting.

Refreshments were handed out, which allowed the adults to socialise. Sigmund and Helene introduced themselves to the teacher and then, taking Freddy by the hand, the family took their leave. Freddy rubbed his eyes with his hands. It had been a long morning and he was very quiet on his way home. He looked somewhat troubled but nobody paid any attention to it. No sooner had Sigmund opened the front door that Freddy disappeared up the stairs. "That little guy sure is in a hurry," he observed, laughing to Helene.

"He may be in a hurry to get to the bathroom!" replied Nellie.

Helene was thoughtful. After looking in the kitchen and making sure lunch was ready, she slipped upstairs quietly and glanced into Freddy's room. He was lying on his bed, sobbing as if his heart would break. She sat down by his side and gently stroked his hair. "It will be all right," she said soothingly, "do you want to tell me what has brought the tears on?"

Freddy sat up and she put her arms around him, hugging him to her as the weeping slowly subsided. "Helmut was not in school," he said between sobs.

"Oh, little one," she said, "Helmut is just going to a different school, but you can still see him. Let's wash your hands and face and as soon as you have finished your lunch, why don't you go over to his house?"

Freddy gave her a teary smile, "I think I'll do just that, thank you, Mama," he said, hugging her.

Sigmund and Nellie were halfway through their meal when Helene walked in to the dining room. "We went ahead without you, I really need to get to the office," said Sigmund.

"Did you put Freddy to bed?" Nellie asked.

"No, he was very upset about Helmut," she replied.

"But I'm not any longer," Freddy announced. "Nellie, will you walk over to my friend's with me?"

"Sure, as soon as we've finished our lunch."

Helene walked Sigmund to the door. "I know you don't like seeing your son so upset, but part of Freddy's growing up is realising that his path will not always go in the same direction as that of his friends. It is something he has to find out for himself and nobody can fend off the pain that goes with it," said Sigmund. Helene gave her husband a hug and thought how understanding he is, as she watched him walk down the driveway.

Once Freddy had changed into more comfortable clothes, he and Nellie got on their way. "You know," said Nellie, "I really think it is a very good thing you and Helmut are not in the same school."

Freddy looked surprised. "Why?"

"Well, you will both make other friends and you will have a lot more to talk about and share, don't you think?"

Freddy thought for a minute. "You're so right! I can meet his friends and I can introduce him to mine and we will have more children to play with and have a lot more to talk about."

"I think this situation has taught us a lesson," said Nellie. "What lesson?"

"That everything always works out for the best."

Chapter 22

Nellie was eager to get back to work. The couple of days off had done her the world of good and she accomplished all she had set out to do. Most important of all, she had gotten a lot closer to her little brother. There was the normal hustle and bustle at the tramway stop, but it seemed as if more people than usual were heading downtown and it took her some time to realise that the train was running late, which explained it all.

She glanced impatiently at her watch. *No use fretting over what I can't change,* she thought, then sat down on the bench and took out her book. More and more people were gathering at the stop and still no sign of it. "This is ridiculous," she said out loud, and put her book back in her bag, stood up and walked resolutely to the taxi stand across the way. It was empty but one pulled up as she got to it.

"You made a wise choice," said the driver. "There has been a serious accident and no one knows when that line will be running again."

"I hope it won't take all day," said Nellie. She arrived at the office an hour late. Everyone glanced up from what they were doing when she walked in and Bettina greeted her with a big smile.

"You look well rested," she remarked.

Nellie sat down behind her desk and began to go through all the papers that had piled up during her short absence. Her colleague was unable to concentrate, she kept looking up from her work and glancing at Nellie who was so taken up by what she was doing she was totally unaware of what was going on around her and of her friend's inner turmoil. "I am going to get some coffee, would you like me to bring you a cup?" she asked.

Startled, Nellie looked up. "Sure," she replied, and went back to the papers. Her Brazilian client had placed an order and, having taken care of them from the very first stages, she would be able to see it through. Excited about her success, she wanted to tell Bettina about it when she remembered she'd gone to get them some coffee. It then suddenly dawned on her that she had been gone a long time.

It was not the coffee, but the entire office staff who were holding Bettina up. She was being questioned from all sides. How did she take it? Did she make any comments? Is it really her? Does she know who did it? When she was finally able to make herself heard above the din, she told them they had better ask Nellie herself, she was the only one who knew the answers and, excusing herself, made her way back to her office.

"The line at the coffee place must have been very long," said Nellie, as Bettina set her coffee cup down on her desk. Without waiting for an answer, she said, "I am so thrilled that our Brazilian client placed the order." But there was no answer. "Bettina, is something wrong?"

"What? Why?"

"I just told you something but you seem not to have heard," said Nellie.

"I am sorry, you were saying?" Nellie repeated her comment.

"That was good work on your part," Bettina replied absentmindedly.

The day went by fast. Nellie spent the break at her desk catching up. Normally, she would have gone for lunch with Bettina, but she was acting so peculiar and had not asked her to join her, she just left and said she would be back later.

Bettina skipped her meal and went for a long walk instead. She finally came to terms with herself and decided it would be in Nellie's best interest, as well as her own, not to say anything. It might be an excuse for taking the easiest way out and maybe she was behaving like a coward, but then, shouldn't she think about herself, unable to predict Nellie's reaction? After all, she was an Aryan and very much committed to the party. Her decision had set her mind at peace and now she was back at work in a much better frame of mind.

Nellie sensed her change of mood as soon as she returned and thought she was back to her old self. The afternoon went by fast. Nellie debated whether to take a cab home or to try her luck with the public transportation and chose the latter. As she left the office, she did not notice all the questioning looks that followed her, nor was she aware of the comments being made behind her back.

Just when she was about to cross the main boulevard, she saw her tram leave. Now she would have to wait 20 minutes for the next one, but at least she knew it was up and running. As she made her way to the bench, a poster caught her eye she had not noticed it before. Taking a closer look, she thought the face looked like her own, but…it couldn't be. She read the inscription and obscenities written on it and felt herself turn pale. Looking at the face again, there was no doubt it was her, and she began to shake. All of a sudden, her legs gave way under her, everything went black and she fainted. When she regained consciousness, an elderly lady was kneeling by her side, stroking her head. It had not taken her long to put two and two together. Nellie looked at her in a daze.

"Everything will be fine," the lady said, giving Nellie her arm and helping her to her feet. "I will walk you to the taxi stand and see you home."

"You are so kind," said Nellie, her eyes brimming with tears. They got into the cab together and Nellie gave the driver her address. During the short ride, the lady told Nellie about her Jewish circle of friends and how it hurt her to see the way Jews and foreigners were being abused and how ashamed she felt at the powerlessness of the government to deal with this growing movement.

Nellie was very touched by her compassionate heart and invited her in to meet her family but excused herself, saying she had to get home and would not hear of Nellie paying for her share.

Nellie bade her farewell, saying she would never forget her kind deed, and let herself into the house, feeling as if she were entering an oasis of peace. Safe and sheltered, she slowly made her way upstairs and once in her room, she lay down on her bed and closed her eyes. The poster with her face stared back at her and the tears she had been holding back began to flow freely, her body shaking with each sob. Who could hate her so much to cause her all this pain, she asked herself time and time again.

Sigmund came home early and in a very good mood. It had been quite some time since he had invited his family out to dinner and just before leaving the office, he asked his secretary to reserve a table for them at that quaint Italian restaurant within walking distance from his home and that they all liked so much. The house was in complete silence, as he crossed the hallway towards the stairs. But what was that sound? He stood still, listening intently. He could not place his finger on it at first, for the sound would subside then remerge. However, it did not take him long to identify it; someone was sobbing and it was coming from upstairs.

He dashed up the steps and again stood still. He wondered what Freddy was so upset about then realised that the sobs were coming from Nellie's room. "How strange, it's not at all like her to lose control of herself," he thought, then took a couple of giant strides. Not bothering to knock on the door, he just flung it open and gazed into a picture of sheer distress. His child lay on her side, hiding her face in the pillow she clutched to her. "Nellie, Nellie, what is wrong?" he asked as he sat down beside her, taking her hand in his. "What has brought this on?"

Nellie turned her teary face towards him and opened her mouth to speak but the sound of her sobbing only increased. He just sat there, looking down at her and stroking her head, repeating over and over that everything will be fine. He tried his best to appear calm and patient, as well as to hide his anguish, sensing something was very wrong indeed. What he had no way of knowing just then was that they had arrived at a turning point in their lives. Nellie clung to her father's hand for dear life and gradually the sobbing subsided, even though the tears continued to flow.

Sigmund heard Helene come home who saw his briefcase by the front door and went looking for him. She started to walk into Nellie's room but Sigmund shook his head and put his finger to his lips so she turned on her heels and headed for the kitchen. "Just what we need, a crisis," she said out loud.

Nellie slowly sat up in bed and, still holding her father's hand, began pouring out her story. Sigmund was flabbergasted and could hardly believe what he was hearing. His temper flared up and he fought to keep it in check, forcing himself to stay calm.

"I have no enemies, I don't know who can hate me so much and I have never hurt anyone," she said in a broken voice.

"Those people have absolutely no heart or feelings, Nellie, they are the worst kind of lumpen that exist," he said harshly.

"I will have to resign from my job," she said, her eyes brimming with tears.

"Oh, no you won't," he said firmly.

"How on earth will I ever face my colleagues, all those people who have seen the poster?"

"Nellie, one does not run away, you have to face all challenges of life. You have done nothing wrong and have absolutely no reason to go into hiding. Go back to work as usual with your head held high. You have a responsibility to not only see that Brazilian deal through but hopefully many others," he said in a firm tone of voice.

"I just don't think I can do it," said Nellie.

"You will do it, child. Don't you see? Can't you understand that by changing your way of life, you will just be giving in to them and they will have succeeded in taking over your life and freedom of choice? Is that what you want?"

Nellie thought for a minute. "No, Daddy, I want to be in charge of my destiny."

"If that is what you want, then do as I say," he replied impatiently.

"I will go to work as usual and try to ignore what happened today," said Nellie, putting on a brave face.

"That's my girl… You have to be strong if you are going to get ahead in life," he said and added, more to himself than to her, "I just wish I knew who was behind this, not that it would do much good." He looked at his watch. "I know you are probably not hungry, but I am sure Helene and Freddy are and they are probably waiting for us, so let's clean up and go down for dinner." Nellie did as she was asked.

Sigmund suddenly remembered the dinner reservation and went looking for Helene, finding her in the kitchen and giving the meal her last touches. She looked up in surprise, for her husband very rarely set foot in that part of the house. "I just remembered I made a dinner reservation for us all at the Italian restaurant."

"How nice," she said, surprised. "Any special reason?"

"None at all, but we had better be leaving."

"I will ask Anna to put everything in the refrigerator." Even though they were late, the table was waiting for them. Freddy kept them entertained with his stories from school and the anecdotes about Helmut and his friends. It was not until they were in bed that Sigmund shared the day's events with his wife. "I take it Nellie will have to find something else to occupy her time with," said Helene.

"No, she will go on with her life as usual."

Helene shot him a surprised look. "Why, Sigmund—" she began her sentence but he did not wait for her to end it.

"Listen to me," he said in a voice full of determination, explaining her the reasoning behind it. Helene understood immediately.

"You are so wise," she said admiringly.

"It is not a matter of being wise, Helene, it is common sense. None of us can allow ourselves to be intimidated. If we allow them to succeed, we will be placing a noose around our necks and it will only be a matter of time before we are completely at their mercy."

A long silence ensued and Helene broke it, saying offhandedly, "It won't be easy for Nellie to confront all those people in the tramway who have probably identified her with the poster's picture."

"You were reading my mind. I think I'll drive her to work, that will make it a little easier for her," said Sigmund. Helene nodded in agreement.

They had just switched off the light when Helene broke the silence. "I think I know who could well be behind it," she said, and not waiting for her husband to answer uttered one name: "Andreas."

"You are certainly right," said Sigmund. "He is doing it out of spite."

He drove Nellie to work the next morning and on the way, she told her father that she really had nothing to worry about, for she had realised as she lay in bed that everyone had surely seen the poster the day before and since no one commented on it yesterday, nobody would today. Sigmund debated for a minute whether to tell her who he thought lay behind the whole matter but decided against it. It would only trouble her.

Chapter 23

Abraham's time in his homeland was running out. He and his family would be leaving in a little more than a month and it had been without argument that Sara and the girls agreed to his decision. Seeing his determination and being given a deadline, they had no choice but to prepare for the move. Now, as the time for their departure drew closer, they were actually looking forward to it. Emmanuel had been most helpful. Even though he returned to Europe on a very short trip with a very tight schedule, he had taken the time to show them pictures of their destination. The girls were very much impressed by what they saw and by his vivid descriptions, talking excitedly about all they would undertake once they arrived at their destination. Everyone was throwing farewell parties for them. "You don't realise how many friends and acquaintances you have until you either die and everyone turns up at the funeral, or you move away," said Abraham to Sara, as they were leaving for yet another dinner. Sara nodded her head in agreement.

After greeting their host, Abraham made his way over to where Sigmund was standing, alone with a whiskey glass in his hand. They greeted each other warmly. "It won't be long before you will be leaving," said Sigmund sadly.

"Yes, time is going so fast and I still have a lot to do, but I have also accomplished a great deal. The business, as you surely are aware of, has been sold, much to my relief."

"Did you get the price you were asking?"

"Not really, but considering it was a cash deal, I did not fair too badly."

"There is nothing better than cash in hand," replied Sigmund, absentmindedly.

"You seem to have something on your mind," said Abraham, who knew his friend well.

"As a matter of fact, I do." And Sigmund related to his friend the latest event.

Abraham listened attentively and he could not believe his ears. "Poor child," he said. "It must have been terrible for her, what a dreadful experience. Do you know who might be behind it?"

"I sure do," said Sigmund and uttered the name, "Andreas."

"It rings a bell," said his friend.

"The professional student Nazi recruiter who was dating Nellie."

"I remember now, but why would he do such a thing?"

"Out of spite and hate."

"So what has Nellie being doing since she quit her job?"

"You are wrong," said Sigmund. "She would have not gone back to work had I not pointed out to her that by doing so, she would have allowed them to scare her away. She agreed with me and went to work, as usual, the following day. I am sure it was not easy for her, but none of her colleagues mentioned the poster and eventually it disappeared from sight."

"Sara and the girls argued and flung tantrums about having to leave," said Abraham.

Sigmund interrupted him, "You are very happy with your decision."

"I am," replied Abraham, "and after listening to Nellie's ordeal…even more so. I am afraid I am going to be right, after all. This Andreas is just an example of what they are capable of, mark my words, Sigmund, and we are sitting on a bomb, biding its time to explode. Won't you change your mind?"

"What about?"

"Leaving."

Sigmund gave his friend a cold look. "Abraham, we have gone over this time and time again. I can't leave. I do not want to leave. And I cannot turn my back on my fatherland. I simply will not run away."

"You are and have always been free to make your choices, but what future does Nellie have here? If you do not want to leave then let her come with us," he said passionately.

Sigmund stared at his friend in disbelief. "Why, Abraham, what an idea? Send my only daughter away to some far off land?"

Abraham lay his hand gently on his friend's shoulder and asked gently, "What future has she got here? She has shown a lot of courage on more than one occasion, but she must be very frightened."

"She has to face up to the risks that life brings with it, just like everyone else, the mere fact of being alive entails risks, which one cannot escape, even if one runs off to Timbuktu," said Sigmund in an abrupt tone of voice.

"Why don't you just give this possibility some thought? Even though you seem not to want to admit it, I get the impression you are a little concerned."

Sigmund interrupted him impatiently: "I will sleep on your suggestion."

"Remember…time is running out," said Abraham. "And if she is to come with us, a great deal of paperwork must be done."

"I am aware," replied Sigmund, and they went to join their wives.

Helene was in deep conversation with one of her friends she had not seen for a long time and barely acknowledged her husband's presence. It was just as well, for Abraham's suggestion still rang in his ears. He could hardly wait to get home to the privacy of his study to think, but the evening just seemed to drag on forever. Everyone was enjoying themselves and nobody seemed to want to leave. Helene was having such a good time, so he would be patient.

Several of his friends came up to him and made small talk, one of them remarked that perhaps they would all have to follow in Abraham's footsteps someday in the near future. Everyone shot him a surprised look, but just as Sigmund was about to open his mouth, he saw the first guests take their leave. This was the moment he had been waiting for so he walked up to Helene and, putting his arm around her, waited for her to finish her sentence and said, looking at his watch and in a very determined voice, "Sorry dear, it is now time for us to go home."

He was tempted to share his conversation with Abraham with her, but decided otherwise. This was an issue that really only concerned Nellie and himself. True, Helene was her stepmother and cared a lot about her, but she did not have the bond the two of them shared. If he allowed her to leave, it would mean relinquishing the past, for she was the only link to his one and only true love and knew this was one issue he would have to face with himself. He walked Helene to their room, kissed her goodnight and said he would come to bed later. "Don't stay up too long," his wife said sweetly, "it's already late." Without bothering to answer, he headed downstairs to his sanctuary.

He stared at his goldfish for a long time. They were so happy and content and he recalled how often in the past he had wished he could turn into one, just for a couple of hours, swimming around leaving all his worries behind and shutting off his brain. His thoughts went back to his conversation with Abraham. Since making his decision, he was a changed person and nobody knew better than Sigmund how difficult it had been for him. He was happy and, most importantly, had found his way and a new purpose in life.

Sigmund could still see the look of disbelief that crossed his face when he told him that Nellie returned to work the following morning as if nothing had occurred. Was he too hard on her, too strict? Had it happened to one of his friend's daughters, they would not have gone back, for in Sigmund's eyes, Abraham was overprotective and spoiled his offspring to death. He would have seen to it that they were safely tucked away. "One can't hide from life," Sigmund said out loud, then he sat down behind his desk and put his face in his hands. There is really no good reason for me not to accept Abraham's offer. He is right, she does not have much of a future here, perhaps none at all if the politicians don't succeed in curbing this extreme right wing movement.

I am being selfish, he thought, *and I can't bear to see her leave. But this is the chance of a lifetime for her and she will get to see at least one of the countries she has read about. It is also for her safety since one thing is certain: Andreas is not going to give up and God only knows the things he is capable of. I must let her go.*

He looked at the picture of her on his desk and his eyes filled with tears but he resolved to discuss it with her in the morning. What if she were to reject the idea? "Wishful thinking, Sigmund," he said, scolding himself. She is far too smart to pass up this opportunity. He felt both sad and relieved as he turned out the light and made his way to his room, knowing deep inside him that he had made the right decision. He was at peace.

On the way home, Abraham told Sara about Nellie and his offer. "She is such a lovely young girl, she will be a nice addition to our family," said Sara.

"I am going to book a place for her on the ship, regardless. I can always cancel it," said Abraham.

"What about her visa?"

"I am sure Emanuel will be able to arrange something. We do not want to get the girls excited, so let's not say anything to them about it until Sigmund gets back to us," said Abraham. His wife nodded her head in assent.

The following morning, Sigmund knocked on Nellie's door before going down for breakfast. She looked up in surprise as he walked in. "Good morning," she said, and when he closed the door behind him, he saw that she was already dressed and tidying up her room.

"I just came to ask you if you would like to meet me at my office after you finish work today," he said.

"Sure, Daddy, is there any special reason?"

"None, whatsoever, I just thought it would give us a little time together and you would not have to take the tramway car back. Speaking of public transportation, if you get ready, I will be all too happy to drop you off."

"No, Daddy, I will meet you at the office, but thank you for asking, you know all too well how much I dislike having to rush in the morning, it really puts me under a lot of stress."

"Have it your way," replied Sigmund, "but I have to hurry, I have a lot going on this morning. See you this evening." He waved to her from the door.

Nellie was puzzled. She knew her father well enough to know he had an issue he wanted to raise with her, but what could it be? She hadn't antagonised Helene and had been on her best behaviour, she had nothing to feel guilty about. She would find out soon enough.

"An unexpected visitor," Sigmund said, as Abraham appeared in the office and interrupting Sigmund's busy schedule.

"I won't take up much of your time," he said, as the receptionist ushered him in. He pulled out a chair nevertheless and sat down.

"What has brought you here?"

"I just wanted to follow up on my invitation to Nellie. Sara is absolutely delighted at the prospect of having her with us, the girls have not been told as yet, but I have succeeded in booking a cabin for her on the ship. I am waiting for an answer from Emanuel concerning her entry visa and I was just wondering if she has a valid passport."

"You sure are keen on having her join you," said Sigmund. "The decision is in her hands. I will ask her what she thinks this evening and if that is what she wants, she will leave with you."

"Will you not reconsider your decision?"

"You know the answer to that," replied Sigmund. "Once and for all, the answer is NO. I will not leave and please do not bring up the subject again."

"What if things get really bad?"

"Then I would have to reconsider, but at this stage, I do not see it happening," replied Sigmund irritably. Abraham stood up. "I will ring you with an answer," Sigmund said, escorting his friend to the door.

Abraham went on his way feeling very pleased indeed. He was sure of the outcome, but he also hoped his friend would be less stubborn and would try to see things in his light, but now he was sure that that would not happen in his lifetime and mentally resolved never to bring it up again.

Sigmund did not have one free minute. His time was taken up with meetings and solving problems and he had been so busy that not once did he glance at the time. Now, back in his office, he suddenly remembered that Nellie was supposed to meet him. He looked at his watch. She should have been here by now. Maybe she was unable to leave on time, and without giving it another thought, he went back to cleaning up his desk until he heard footsteps outside his door. He opened it, then let out a sigh of relief only to realise his imagination was playing tricks on him. He returned to what he was doing but his eyes kept going back and forth to his watch. As time went by, he felt a growing uneasiness. Where could she be? Why was she not here by now? What if she had run into Andreas? He started to break out into a sweat and tried to calm his mind. He considered phoning her office but decided against it, not wanting people to make fun of his daughter by saying she had such a protective father that she had no life of her own.

No, he would wait. He was sure she would show up. As he sat behind his desk unable to concentrate, he realised he had not assessed the situation correctly and was getting a glimpse of what it meant to live in fear, fear that something would happen to his beloved daughter. It was a dreadful feeling, one he certainly did not care to live with. He now understood the full meaning of Abraham's offer, why had he been so blind? Why had he not perceived the danger? Could it be possible that he was making a mistake by not listening to his friend?

He was pondering all these questions when all of a sudden, the door flew open and Nellie walked in. Sigmund stood up in a flash and let out a huge sigh of relief. She was only an hour late. "Sorry, Daddy, just as I was leaving, I got an overseas call from one of my clients. He was in a very talkative mood," she said. "I kept looking at the time but he kept asking me for more and more information."

"No big deal, child," he replied, "those things are to be expected when one holds such an important position," he said with a twinkle in his eye, not about to share his anguish with her. "Considering that we are running late, I will call Helene and tell her we will not be home for dinner and you and I can go to your favourite restaurant. We should have no trouble getting a table," he said.

Nellie gave him a huge smile. She had not expected her father to be so understanding, for she knew how much he stressed punctuality. When Sigmund hung up the phone, he said to Nellie, "Helene is just so flexible and considerate, I appreciate that quality in her so much." What he did not know was that she had cooked his favourite dinner and was looking forward to a quiet evening at home. They had not seen much of each other lately and had shared no intimacy, for their free time had been taken up by the many social engagements they had attended lately. He probably did not miss their time together as much as she did and had it been otherwise, he would have made a point of spending their first free evening in weeks with her. But she was neither as flexible nor understanding as her husband believed, it was just a matter of being practical. No amount of nagging or arguing would change his mind, quite the contrary, it would only create a rift between them and it was simply not worth it. She sat down to dinner with Freddy, who, with his incessant and funny stories, kept her very much entertained and any disillusionment receded into the background and she was soon laughing with him.

The walk to the restaurant led them past Nellie's office and the tramway stop. Taking Nellie by the arm, he impulsively led her to the stop. She looked at him in surprise, for he had shown no desire whatsoever to take a look at what at haunted her sleep for so many endless nights. "This is all that is left of it," said Nellie, pointing her finger to where the poster had hung. A shudder ran down his spine and he looked around to see if somebody was watching. Seeing nobody, he walked up to the site and did not utter a word. But then, she took his arm and pulled him away and had he looked into her face just then, he would have seen the bitter hurt in her eyes. He would never know how much she resented him for not having taken the time himself to see what she had faced. Now that he decided on the spur of the moment to do so, it was too late. Sigmund was filled with remorse for his selfishness and admiration for her courage.

The restaurant was well attended but, just as he had predicted, they did not have to wait to be seated and were given a table in a corner. Sigmund kept the conversation light while Nellie sat back and tried to relax. She just finished eating her dessert when Sigmund asked out of the blue, "Tell me, Nellie, how would you like to go to Colombia?"

She looked at him in disbelief but was too surprised to answer. Thinking she had not heard, he repeated his question. "I would love to," she replied excitedly. "Are we going for a holiday? Have you changed your mind about travelling to far away countries? When are we leaving?"

"Not so fast, child, let me answer one question at a time." He ordered a cognac and, as he sipped it, he told her about Abraham's invitation. "Well, there's got to be a reason behind it, Daddy, do you know what it is?"

He did not answer immediately. "I might as well tell you," he said when he finally spoke. "I firmly believe this guy Andreas is the author of the poster prank."

Nellie opened her eyes wide. "Andreas? I had completely forgotten about him. But what could he possibly have for a motive?" she asked in an unsteady voice.

"Nellie, no man likes to be outwitted by a woman and you hurt his pride and ego. I mentioned the incident to Abraham…"

"And he invited me to come with them," she said, finishing her father's sentence. "How long would I be leaving for?"

"I would say a year, hopefully by that time the government will have put all these shadowy figures behind bars, which would then undermine the movement, and you will have learned Spanish and seen a little more of the world. You did once tell me it was your dream."

"Daddy, I am under the impression that you are sending me away. Are you worried about my safety?"

"No, not really, and I am not sending you away either, you have to make up your own mind and I will go along with whatever you decide. However, I must warn you, should you decide to accept, there is a lot of paperwork involved and there is not all that much time left."

"It is a wonderful opportunity and is very tempting, it would be like a dream come true. When are they leaving?"

"I believe in three weeks." Sigmund asked for the check.

"Thank you for a lovely dinner," said Nellie.

"I realise you have a lot to think about, but I hope you will be able to get some sleep," said Sigmund.

Neither one of them spoke, as they walked back to where the car was parked. Nellie tossed and turned all night, but by dawn, she had made up her mind. Once in bed, Sigmund mentioned to Helene the reason behind his dinner with Nellie. She was so surprised that she sat up and exclaimed, "It's the chance of a lifetime!"

"It sure is."

"Is she going to accept?"

"My guess is as good as yours but we will find out in due course."

As soon as Nellie arrived at work the following morning, she went straight to Mrs Müller's office and handed in her resignation. After reading it, she set the sheet of paper on her desk, turned to Nellie and said coldly, "It's about time you tried your luck somewhere else." Without waiting for an answer, Mrs Müller ordered Nellie to go to her office and pick up her belongings and would meet her there with her paycheck.

Nellie did as she was told. There was no sign of Bettina, which was just as well, and she had just finished storing the few mementos she kept on her desk in her purse when Mrs Müller walked in and handed her the check, wished her good luck and turned on her heels, marching out the door. Nellie looked around one last time; it had been her first job she had learned a great deal, certainly enjoying her work. But now, she now had something much more exciting to look forward to.

Over dinner that evening, she told her parents what she had decided and that she already quit her job. Sigmund said, surprised, "You sure did not waste any time."

Laughing, she said, "Why, Daddy, you, yourself told me there was no time to waste."

"There sure isn't," replied Sigmund, "and if you will excuse me, I shall give Abraham a ring and inform him that you will be joining them."

The next few weeks were very hectic. Nellie spent as much time as she could with Freddy since she would really miss him but she shared her knowledge about Colombia and her images about travelling around South America with him. Before she even realised it, the day of her departure was upon her and everyone went to the train station to see her off. Abraham and his family were there waiting for her. After a tearful goodbye and a few last minute hugs, and lots of promises to write frequently, she joined the others on the train that would take them to Rotterdam where they would board the ship.

Sigmund drove home with a heavy heart. He had not only parted with his daughter, but he bid his oldest friend farewell, fully aware that he would never see him again. Helene was saddened by Nellie's departure, and although she had not always been easy to get along with, they had some good times together. Freddy did not hide his tears. He hung on to her as she kissed him good-bye until Helene gently pulled him away and in the car, finally broke the silence by saying, "I can hardly wait for her return to hear all about her adventures."

"And you will have a lot of your own to share with her," replied Sigmund. If only he knew all the things the future had in store for them.

Chapter 24

All of them felt the emptiness that Nellie's departure left, but as expected, it was short lived. Freddy spent more and more time with his friend, Helmut, who had turned into a fine lad and so very full of life. He was mature for his age, and it was not at all surprising since he did have three elder siblings to groom him in the art of survival. Freddy admired Helmut very much, one might even say he was a little envious as well. His mother was too busy to keep tabs on him, which allowed him to enjoy a lot more freedom then Helene would ever dream of giving *her* son, and he always had someone to do things with.

Freddy doubted very much that his friend had ever, or would ever, experience the loneliness he sometimes felt. Growing up as an only child was no easy task, and Sigmund and Helene forgot this all too often, demanding he sometimes behave like an adult. So, whenever he and Helmut were together, they played pranks on each other that inevitably ended with one or the other in trouble. Like the time they hung a bucket half-full of water over the kitchen doorway and hid behind the door, waiting for the maid to appear. They heard the sound of footsteps, and making a big effort to control their excited giggles, let go of the rope without looking at their victim. The bucket made a deafening noise as it crashed to the floor, followed by a piercing shriek of surprise. The two boys looked at each other in disbelief, for the voice was not the maid's but Helene's.

Helmut, trying his hardest to suppress the laughter, followed the outline of his neck with a finger, signalling to Freddy (who had gone pale) that they would probably get their throats cut for this one. The timing could not have been worse, for Sigmund, unbeknownst to them, was home and had witnessed it all. He allowed himself a smile, remembering how many years ago, he had done the same thing, but as soon as he made sure his wife was unharmed, commanded his son to come to him.

Even though he called only Freddy to him, Helmut did not leave his friend's side. Not only had his parents drilled into him that you had to take responsibility for your actions, they also taught him the meaning of loyalty. Sigmund sent Helmut home after instructing him to apologise to Helene, then scolded Freddy, telling him he could forget about spending the following weekend with Helmut at his grandparent's farm outside Frankfurt. This was quite a blow to him, for he had been looking forward to his first weekend away from his parents for the past month.

"But, Daddy," he pleaded.

Sigmund was implacable. "No, Freddy, I will not give in this time. Your actions have proven to me that you are not mature enough. Just imagine the consequences if that bucket had fallen on your mother's head. You have shown no common sense whatsoever."

Freddy did not utter a word, for it was useless, once his father made up his mind, there was no changing it and since that little episode, he and Helmut were on their best behaviour. The trip to the farm had been postponed, not on Freddy's account, but because his grandmother had fallen ill with a very bad cold.

He loved going over to play at his friend's house. There, he was always made to feel welcome and at home. Martha had a special place for him in her heart, perhaps due to the fact that she had watched him grow up, sometimes referring to him as her fifth child, and never treating him as a guest. Everyone at his friend's house was so easy going, and yet they all radiated so much warmth.

As he grew older and was able to make comparisons, he realised that his friend's family did not have the same monetary means as his. There was no maid to prepare dinner or serve them and they all had to pitch in and help. It was amazing how a family could unite around the preparation of a meal. They all took turns preparing the salad, cutting onions and setting the table. The highlight of one of the dinners had been when Freddy was given the chore of chopping the onions. He had never held one in his hand, so Helmut very patiently went about explaining how it had to be done. Freddy had no sooner begun to cut the first one that his eyes began to smart and soon the tears were running down his cheeks. Helmut burst into laughter and soon everyone else joined in. Their giggles only increased when Freddy turned on his friend and said, "You could have at least warned me!"

To which, Helmut replied, "How on earth was I to know you've never held an onion in your hands?"

From that day onwards, any time Helmut showed his friend something new, Freddy would invariably ask: "Strings attached?" And Helmut would answer negatively, which soon became a standard joke between them. Sometimes, they would do their homework together, for even though they attended different schools, they were in the same grade.

Helene was none too happy about the turn this friendship was taking. It had been fine when Freddy only saw Helmut occasionally, but as she once told Sigmund, "If something is not done soon, it won't be long before Helmut moves in with us."

Sigmund looked at her in surprise. "Why, Helene, I do not see that happening, they are just good friends, nothing wrong with that," he replied.

"I don't agree with you," she said, trying hard to keep her temper in check.

"Sending him to a private school has defeated the purpose. The idea behind it was for him to associate with children who share his background, but he completely ignores his classmates and hangs around at Helmut's."

"That is not so. The main reason was the quality of the education, and in fact, it was you who brought that to my attention. Helene, I think you are just using this as a pretext; the core of the issue is that you dislike Helmut." Helene tried to deny it, but Sigmund cut her short. "I think he is a nice kid with good values and even though he his sometimes full of mischief, Freddy needs someone like him in his life, one who can make up for the things he lacks."

"Like what?" Helene asked impatiently.

"Like brothers and sisters."

"You are to blame for that. I would have loved a big family," she replied, losing her temper.

"Now dear, let us not get into it," said Sigmund. "We had that discussion years ago and it is a closed issue."

Helene stormed out of the room. "She will get over it," he said to himself, and went back to what he was doing. He was right, because she had no choice, but the bitterness would always be there, tucked away inside her.

The long awaited weekend finally arrived. Freddy packed his bag according to Helmut's instructions and took a hurried leave from his parents, trying hard to cut all the dos, but mostly don'ts, short walking down the street with his head held high. Helmut's father accompanied them to the train station and had just purchased their tickets when the train pulled in. Peter took his leave after reminding Helmut to give his grandfather a hand. *They're going to have a wonderful time,* he thought, watching the train disappear around a bend, reminiscing about the first time he had invited a classmate to come along. The property had been in the family's hands for four generations. Helmut let Freddy have the window seat so he could see out and they chatted excitedly, planning the next two days. It was autumn, the leaves were turning and all the different colours sparkled in the sunlight.

"Nature is so beautiful," said Freddy.

"It gets better the further north we go," said Helmut. It was a two-hour train ride and when they arrived at their destination, both grandparents were at the station to meet them.

"We finally get to meet you, young man," said Helmut's grandmother. "I feel as if I already know you, I have heard so much about you."

"Come on, Grandma, you can give him a hug, he's part of the family," said Helmut proudly, and she did as she was told.

Grandpa shook hands with him. "Let us be on our way," he said, leading them out to the street. "As you've probably noticed, this is a very small village with a very big train station," he said, turning to Freddy.

"We have to go to the city to do our shopping, for there is nothing here," said Grandma, "but it is so quiet and peaceful."

"Nowhere in the world will you sleep better than here," said Helmut.

"We have to take the bus, then we will have to walk the rest of the way," said Grandma. Freddy looked at her in surprise but did not say anything. When they got to the bus stop, they saw it fade away in the distance.

"We just missed it," said Helmut.

"Never mind, the next one will be here in twenty minutes," said Grandma. Then she inquired about everyone and politely asked Freddy about his family. Twenty minutes passed and no sign of the bus.

Grandfather started grumbling. "Everything in this country seems to be falling apart, not even the busses can be on time these days. It won't be long before the trains will also be running late."

Grandma, who heard this comment for the umpteenth time, completely ignored him.

Freddy's curiosity was aroused. "What makes you think so?"

"It is a sign of the times," Grandpa replied. "When the Emperor was in charge, there was only one boss and everything worked like clockwork, but nowadays, you have undoubtedly heard the saying too many cooks—"

"Ruin the soup," Freddy finished the sentence.

"Yes, sir," said Grandpa, "and that is exactly the case." He would have elaborated more, it being one of his favourite topics of conversation, if the bus had not arrived just then.

It was a very pretty ride over rolling hills and through some thick woods. They got off at the last stop. Helmut pointed to a narrow, winding road that led up a hill. "That is Bunny Hill."

"Bunny Hill," repeated Freddy, surprised, "what an odd name."

"It was named many years ago after all the rabbits that lived on it."

"I assume there are none left," said Freddy.

"Are you kidding? There are still quite a few around and they aren't shy at all," said Helmut. "But come on, let's follow the others."

Grandma and Grandpa had gone on ahead.

"It sure does look like a long walk," said Freddy, who was very much taken aback by the fact that Helmut's grandparents did not own a car.

"It is not as far as it looks," he said. "We'll be home when we reach the top and you will be able to see the house once we are halfway there."

Freddy took his time, letting his gaze take everything in. "Come on lazy bum, hurry up," Helmut chided.

"I am coming," replied his friend, accelerating his pace. After a good half hour, the house came into sight, standing alone and looking down towards the valley.

"All the land you see around here belongs to us," said Helmut proudly. His friend was overwhelmed.

"Where are the rabbits?" Freddy wanted to know.

"They are everywhere; you just have to be on the lookout for them. There's no way you can miss them. You see that clearing over there?" Helmut asked, stopping and pointing to the right of the road.

"Yes, I see it."

"Well, at dusk you will see deer. There is a big herd of them and they all gather there, evening after evening."

"I can't wait," said Freddy.

Helmut looked at his watch then up at the sky. When they reached the house, Grandma was waiting for them with a big jug full of apple juice. "It's made from home-grown apples," she said, serving Freddy first.

He took a big sip. "It is delicious," he said, "and it tastes so different from the one my mother buys."

Grandma replenished his glass and watched him drink it with an amused look on her face, saying to herself more than the children, "Watching him discover a whole different world will be quite an experience."

"Grandma, did you say something?" Helmut asked.

"No, I was just thinking out loud. Why don't you show your friend the house?" she suggested.

Freddy didn't quite know what to expect. Although he had driven through small and quaint villages with his father before, he'd never been to a farm or set foot in a farmhouse. The house was big and comfortable and very cosy. In the living room, Freddy's attention was drawn to a very old furnace made of cast iron.

"What is this for?" Freddy asked, standing in front of it.

"That," said Helmut, "is for heating and it is very old. It has a story behind it, just like everything else in this house, but Grandma would be more then delighted to fill you in on all the history if you are interested. Not only does she know it better than I do, but this property, including the house, has been in her family for generations. I think it goes back two hundred years. With time, each member of the family who owned it made the necessary changes. This is the original part of the house, all the rest has been added on with time," said Helmut, looking out the window. "Let's hurry, the sun is setting."

"Oh, yes, I nearly forgot," said Freddy, and they both walked outside quickly and stood facing the clearing. Sure enough, two deer were happily grazing. The setting sun reflected on the leaves of the trees around it, making everything glow and come to life. As the sunset, the clouds of dusk intensified in colour. More deer came into the clearing. "It is magical," said Freddy.

"I told you," replied his friend. "This is a magical place."

They stood and watched until it got too cold for them, then went indoors to seek the warmth of the fire. Soon after dinner, the boys were ready to go to bed. Freddy loved Helmut's room, thinking it was the best in the house, and he told him so. Facing east, it was a corner room with windows that overlooked another smaller clearing so if you woke up early enough, you could see the sunrise without having to leave your bed. Freddy made a mental note of it, having never seen the sunrise, much less from his bed.

His room at home was lovely and overlooked the garden, but this one sure had a much better view, he thought before falling into a deep sleep. He dreamt of deer and rabbits and apple trees with branches bending over with the weight of the bright red fruit. The first rays of sunlight woke him up and he looked over at Helmut who was half-awake. "Stand by the window and you can watch the sky change colour as the sun rises," he said. Freddy got out of bed in a flash. "You do not have to rush," said Helmut, "the sun takes its time rising into the sky."

"I do not want to miss out on anything," replied Freddy, opening up the window wide. He stood there looking out and breathing the pine-scented air. "This is so very different from being in the city."

"It sure is," replied his friend as he stood beside him. They watched the sky and clouds turn light pink as the colour reflected onto the fields and trees, tinting them a more intense green. Freddy looked on in fascination. The sound of a mooing cow in the distance broke the silence.

"Come on, get your shoes on. If we hurry, we'll get to the barn in time to see them being milked." Indeed, they arrived just as a farm hand was walking in with his milking stool under his arm. Helmut answered Freddy's unspoken question. There were eight of them and were all standing in one line, feeding in the trough.

"They look so tame and friendly," said Freddy, who had never seen one so close up before.

"They are," replied Helmut, patting one gently on the head. "This is my favourite. Her name is Flora. I watched her being born. When she was a little calf, I would tease her by holding out my finger to her and she would suckle on it, mistaking it for a tit."

His friend ruffled up his nose. "I would not care to try," he said.

"Then I will spare you the experience," said Helmut.

They watched the process for a while and were about to leave when Grandpa arrived. "You are up early, did you sleep well?" he inquired, addressing his guest.

"Very well indeed," replied Freddy.

"I have to show him everything! There is no time to sleep or be lazy around here," said Helmut.

"In that case," said Grandpa, "I could use some help. Would you mind shuffling the hay for me?" he asked. "You can show your friend how to do it and between the two of you, it won't take too long." He then handed each one a pitchfork.

"One more thing you are going to learn," said Helmut, leading the way.

"Doesn't anyone eat breakfast around here?" asked Freddy.

"We do, if we can find the time for it. Can you wait until we have finished our chores?"

"I guess I will survive," said Freddy grinning. "Let's give pitching hay a try."

The field where it dried was quite a ways from the house. On their walk, they encountered several rabbits, much to Freddy's delight, who jumped away, startled, when they were barely upon them. They also stopped to watch a hawk fly over, saw it dive and in no time at all, it was flying over them again, a mouse dangling between its claws. "Everyone is having a nice meal except us," said Freddy wishfully.

"Our turn will come," replied Helmut. "The more we linger, the longer we will have to wait. So come on and let's get on with it." And before long, they were standing in front of a mountain of hay.

"It will take us all day to shuffle this. So much for breakfast, it will be dinner before we are finished," said Freddy.

Helmut did not reply, instead he showed his friend how to do it and they worked in silence. About an hour into it, Helmut heard a piercing shriek. "Are you all right?" he called out, dropping his fork and rushing over to where he had left his friend, but there was no answer. He quickened his pace and was almost upon him when he heard him reply in a very small voice:

"I am still alive."

It was a sight to behold. His pitchfork lay on the ground and he was leaning over, holding his side. "I told you to watch what you were doing and take your time," said Helmut. Just then, his eye fell on a stain that was spreading out on the side of Freddy's shirt. "You are bleeding," he said in a frightened tone. "Come on, Grandma will know what to do." Helmut took Freddy by the arm and, leaning on his friend, they walked quickly to the house. By now, Freddy had turned pale and was holding on to his side for dear life. Grandma, who was just taking a loaf of freshly baked bread out of the oven, looked up in surprise as they entered the kitchen.

"Freddy is bleeding," said Helmut anxiously, pointing his finger at the spot. She walked towards him and lifted up his shirt. The bleeding had stopped.

"Looks as if the pitchfork mistook you for hay," she said, laughing. "You will live." And she walked over to a cabinet and took a small bottle of antiseptic out of it, poured some onto a ball of cotton and cleaned the small wound. Freddy winced with pain.

"It burns," he said.

"Not for long," replied Helmut. Once she finished, she bade the boys to stay and have their breakfast. The mere mention of food was music to Freddy's ears and he soon forgot his injury. The boys ate everything that was set in front of them without saying a word, helped Grandma wash the dishes afterwards, then left to resume their chores.

"You must have been famished," said Helmut. "I have never seen you put away so much food in one sitting."

"I was not only starving, but everything was delicious. I have never tasted a better sausage or a better ham, to say nothing of the bread fresh out of the oven. Don't you miss all this when you are in the city? If I had the grandparents and house you have, I would not waste one minute away from here."

"Well, you can come with me as often as you like," said Helmut. "But my parents love the city. They like coming out here every so often, too, but while you see the glamorous part of it, there is a lot of hard work involved. There is never any free time, the animals need constant attention and in the long run, one loses all one's freedom. No Freddy, I would never trade in my city life for this one," said Helmut. "But let's get this job over with, so we can go and have some fun."

Freddy looked at him. "What do you mean?"

"Trust me, there are better things to see and do than standing on a pile of hay." Just then, Grandpa came over to check on how they were doing and decided another hay mountain needed to be tended to. Once he was out of earshot, Helmut vented his frustration on his friend. "That is what life is really like around here,

209

no free time whatsoever…do this, do that, do the other and you cannot complain, for if you do not do as you are told, you are bound to get yourself into a lot of trouble." Freddy made no comment and they eventually finished, just as the sun was setting. "So much for all the plans we made," said Helmut, placing the pitchforks back where they belonged.

"There is still tomorrow," said Freddy, stifling a yarn. Before entering the house, they stood and looked over at the clearing. A couple of deer were grazing. "I think this is my favourite part of the farm, besides the kitchen and my bed," said Freddy.

The boys were very tired. Freddy was having a hard time trying not to fall asleep over his dinner and halfway through, Grandma excused them from the table. They did not wait to be told twice. Freddy managed to get undressed and brush his teeth before falling into a deep sleep as soon as his head touched the pillow.

In the early morning hours, he heard a couple of roosters crow in the distance. Startled, he sat up in bed, thinking he had missed the sunrise, but the room was in darkness. *That rooster must be an early riser,* he thought to himself and, turning over on his side, went back to sleep. When he woke up, the room was flooded in light. He looked over at Helmut's bed. Noticing it was empty, he looked at his watch. It was past ten in the morning. "Oh, no, how could I have overslept on my last day here!" he spoke out angrily.

Just then, Helmut entered the room. "Sleeping beauty has finally woken up," he said grinning.

"Why did you let me sleep?" Freddy asked.

"I tried to wake you but it was no use, you were knocked out. But don't be distressed, we still have a lot of time before the train leaves and Grandpa has not said anything about needing help so we will be able to walk down to the stream and I can teach you how to fish." Indeed, they accomplished everything they set out to do and it was not long before they were back at the train station. Grandma gave each one of the boys a hug and told Freddy he was more than welcome to return whenever he chose.

Sigmund and Helene were at the station to meet them. They took Helmut home and listened to Freddy's incessant chatter about all he had done and seen. When his parents were finally able to get a word in, they told him they had received a letter from Nellie.

It was the first news they'd had from her in four months. She was happy and doing well and they said they've left it in his room for him to read.

Chapter 25

Freddy was very eager to read his sister's letter. He ran up the stairs and, dropping his bag by his desk, picked up the envelope. He stared down at the handwriting for a long time and finally opened it, taking out several sheets of paper.

"Dear all," she began, but he had to interrupt his reading, for the letters suddenly turned into a blur as his eyes filled with tears.

He spoke out loud, "I miss your laughter and I miss your smile, little sister." Then, wiping his tears away, he sat down on the bed and began to read anew.

After very long train ride, they arrived in Rotterdam. A young, good-looking cabdriver drove them from the station to their hotel near the port. She had her own room and from her window, she could see the ships in the distance. There were quite a few of them and she tried to guess which would be the one they would be leaving Europe on.

A wave of excitement overcame her. She was about to start on a journey of discovery. The next morning, after a leisurely breakfast, they all went for a long walk, taking advantage of an exceptionally beautiful day. Rotterdam is renowned for its bad weather, as was common knowledge. She very much enjoyed looking at all the shop windows lining the street, but had not seen anything that screamed 'take me' at her. After a light lunch that consisted mainly of fish, they returned to the hotel to pick up their belongings. The long awaited moment had arrived. Abraham pointed out their ship to them as the cab came to a halt in front of the passenger terminal. A crew member led them to what would be their home for the next four weeks after they showed him their passports and relevant documents. She had mixed emotions, as she walked up the gangway. The excitement was still present, but it was overshadowed a little by the realisation that what had been a dream was now becoming fact.

Thousands of kilometres would lie between her and her family. She wiped a tear from her eye and, looking around, noticed the tears running down Sara's cheek. She discretely looked away. The steward showed them to their cabins and before he left, informed them that dinner would be served in the restaurant at seven in the evening. She was very much impressed by what she saw. Her cabin was small compared to the bedroom she had at home, of course, but it had everything she might need and it even had an en-suite bathroom. There was a small, round window that in ship language is known as a porthole.

Following Helene's advice, she'd packed a small bag with only the clothing she would need during the journey and was now more than grateful she had heeded it, for there was absolutely no room for her to have arranged everything she brought. She left her big suitcase where it had been placed on a luggage rack and stored the bag she had just unpacked underneath her bunk.

Looking around her, she thought that it was really more like a cubbyhole than anything else, but at least she had it all to herself. Her thoughts were interrupted by a knock on the door. It was Sara. She put on a heavy jacket and followed the others onto the main deck. The ship was about to set sail and from the railing, she looked on as the crew untied the lines and the ship slowly came alive, gradually moving away from the dock. They stood close together and watched, fascinated, as the port disappeared from sight in the rays of the fading sun. Their first meal on board was excellent. A ship, she wrote, was like a floating home, but everything was built on a much smaller scale. It had been a long, exciting day and they all retired right after dinner. She had brought several books along and took one to bed with her but with the slow rocking motion of the ship she soon fell asleep.

All of a sudden, she woke up and found herself grasping onto the side of her bunk. The rocking motion had given way to a vigorous sway and she felt as if her stomach were filled with butterflies. Wanting to find out the reason for this change, she kneeled on her bunk and, holding on to the frame of the porthole, looked out. The sun was just rising and the colour of the water was almost black. Filled with awe, she watched as a huge swell heaved the ship up and then, as the water mass receded, fall with a loud groaning sound. They had left the sheltered waters and she would have continued to look out had her stomach not felt queasy, as if hundreds of butterflies were flying in it. She lay down again and closed her eyes and just as she was drifting off to sleep, there was a loud knock on her door. She got up slowly and, trying to keep her balance by holding onto whatever she could find, made it to the door and opened it.

Sara was standing, pale faced and dressed in her bathrobe. "I just came to check on you. The girls are all seasick and I'm not doing too well myself," she said.

Nellie told her she felt a little funny but once she got back into bed, she would be fine. Sara reminded her that her cabin was just across the hallway and should she need anything not to hesitate to knock on her door. Nellie thanked her saying she would and headed back to her bunk. She was seasick and there was nothing she could do about it, hoping it would go away with time but her wish did not come true, it stayed with her for the most part of the journey. The only time she had some respite was when the ship was in port and she was able to eat normally, keeping the food down. Luckily for her, it called at several ports.

The worst time was during the Atlantic crossing, the weather had been dreadful. They seemed to hit one storm after another and no matter how hard you strained your eyes, there was absolutely no land as far as you could see. One day, the captain announced over the microphone that some dolphins were following the ship, but Nellie just felt too ill to leave her cabin. What a respite it had been when the ship finally docked early in the morning in Barranquilla, Colombia, their port of destination. They disembarked right after breakfast and she felt no regrets about leaving the ship.

What a relief it had been to feel the solid ground beneath her feet, even though she felt the swaying motion of the ship for several more days. The heat was unbearable, not to mention the humidity. And there were mosquitos everywhere. A car and driver had been waiting to take them to their hotel, a beautiful old colonial building in the centre of town, and no sooner had the three girls left their belongings in their rooms, they had set out to explore what the entire hotel had to offer.

The building was surrounded by a huge garden lined with the tallest palm trees they had ever seen. After coming across the swimming pool, they immediately ran back to their rooms and changed into their bathing suits. The water was chilly but in that heat, it felt so refreshing. Not feeling cold when getting out of the pool was a newly discovered luxury. They spent three wonderful days there relaxing, swimming, eating and sleeping. In other words, recovering. They had taken a couple of walks around the hotel's neighbourhood but the heat inevitably drove them back to the pool for a refreshing dip.

The journey that had followed was like nothing she ever dreamed of. They were escorted to the port on the Magdalena River where they boarded a big steamboat that would take them up river to the city of Honda. They were the only foreigners on board. At first, she felt completely isolated due to the language barrier but everyone was so friendly towards them that she soon began using her hands and eyes to communicate with her fellow passengers. There was one girl her age in particular to whom she had taken an immediate liking. After returning her smile several times, the stranger walked up to her one morning and pointing her finger at herself and said, "Maria."

Nellie understood and, imitating her, said, "Nellie," then introduced her in this same manner to the other members of her group.

Since the depth of the river was so unpredictable, they could only travel during the day and were therefore forced to tie up close to shore for the night, just before the sun set, leaving the following morning with the first rays of light to get the most out of the day. As soon as dinner was over, one of the crew would invariably bring out his guitar and Maria would sing and sway to the music, releasing all the passion that was pent up inside her. They watched, fascinated, as her whole being seemed to radiate a joy of life and her big, coal coloured eyes sparkled with mischief.

The scenery was so completely different from what she had ever seen before. The water was a murky brown and as they travelled up river, the vegetation became greener and greener and much more abundant. The valley narrowed and the Andes Mountains stood up even taller against the sky. She spotted a woman washing laundry on the riverbank while children played by her side or splashed water on one another. The air was filled with different, unknown smells and sounds. The birds broke the silence of dawn with their shrieks as they left their nests, the parrots being the loudest, of course.

Everything would have been just perfect had it not been for the mosquitoes. They were not only everywhere, but they were eating her alive and the itching was driving her out of her mind. Maria came to her rescue, showing her how to use lemon to take away the sting. Nellie had been somewhat sceptical, but to her relief, it worked. From that day onwards, she never went anywhere without a piece of lemon in her pocket and Maria saw to it that she was well provided. The excitement of the first days began to wane and one day seemed to drag into the next. They were all getting bored and irritable and could hardly wait to leave the boat that held them captive. The scenery changed with every passing day.

One day, she overheard Sara say to Abraham in a very frustrated tone of voice, "There is only so much of this I can take, life is made out of other things as well." Nellie didn't hear his reply but she could not have agreed with her more. On the morning of the seventh day, they finally saw the city of Honda loom up in the distance and stood on the bow of the boat, watching the shoreline come closer and closer. Maria, who was standing next to Nellie, pointed out to her where she lived and told her that this was the end of her journey as well. She had been in Barranquilla visiting her grandparents and now she had to get back and help her mother tend the store.

Someone was waiting for them when the boat docked and after tending to their luggage, escorted them to the only hotel in town. It was just a plain, simple building, lacking all the amenities of the previous one, but at least the rooms were clean. Maria walked with them halfway then told them she would come and get them in the late afternoon to show them around before taking them to her home for dinner.

Their escort handed Abraham an envelope. Once in the privacy of his room, he opened it and it was as he surmised: a short note from Emanuel. In it, he outlined their itinerary and started out by saying it would not be long now before they reached their destination, but the strenuous part of their journey lay ahead of them. They were to spend two nights here in Honda gathering their strength and on the third day, they would leave for Bogotá, their destination, by mule. Abraham let out a gasp. This was something completely unexpected.

After arriving at the hotel, Nellie and the others took a long nap. The heat was exhausting and the wind that blew from the fan hanging from the ceiling over her bed had no impact on the temperature whatsoever, but at least it kept the mosquitoes away.

As agreed earlier, they all met in Sara's room and it was then that Abraham shared the information he had received.

"You are surely not serious about us continuing our journey riding on a mule," Sara asked, incredulous. Nobody seemed to be listening to her, for the girls immediately voiced their approval saying what a wonderful adventure the whole trip was turning out to be. When Sara was finally able to make herself heard, she asked about the luggage.

"What about it?" Abraham asked, rhetorically. "A mule will carry that as well." The girls roared with laughter, imagining what a mule would look like with their entire luggage loaded on its back.

Someone knocked at the door and it was Maria. After offering her something to drink, they followed her out of the hotel. It was late afternoon and it had cooled down quite substantially. After a short walk along narrow cobblestone streets lined with colourfully painted houses, they reached the town square. The main park, which faced the church, was planted with beautiful old trees that provided a lot of shade. Some elderly people were sitting on the benches beneath them, enjoying the evening. They walked into the church, which was very big and extremely ornate. Everything that sparkled was made of gold.

Maria showed them a plaque that bore the date the church was built. It was very old indeed and had been built under Spanish rule. They then retraced their steps and walked up a steep street to Maria's house, walking past the little store, which was unfortunately closed, for Nellie and the others would have loved to have taken a peak at it.

Maria's mother, a small, stately and proud looking lady, greeted them at the door and made them feel immediately at ease. She ushered them into the living room and even though it was sparsely furnished, there was a warm and cosy feeling to it, which was probably due to the many plants that were scattered everywhere. Once they quenched their thirst, Maria and her mother proudly gave them a tour of their home. Sara commented on the crocheted bedspreads. Maria's mother's face lit up; some she had made herself and some had been done by her grandmother. She walked over to a wooden trunk, opened it and took out a hand crocheted tablecloth. Mother and daughter held it out so that their guests could admire it. It was a work of art.

It was customary for girls to have a dowry and they usually started working on it at the age of fifteen. Maria's great-grandmother had made what they were admiring and when her mother got married, it was given to her as a very special gift. One day, it would be passed down to Maria and added to *her* dowry. Then they showed them pictures of their family and some of the many trips they had taken. No, they had never been abroad but then, Colombia was such a big country with so much waiting to be discovered.

It was amazing how well all of them were able to communicate having learned more than a couple of words of Spanish, which they were now being able to put to good use. Dinner was very interesting, for they were served a variety of Colombian dishes. All in all, it was a lovely evening and upon saying their goodbyes they were able to make Maria and her mother understand how much they appreciated their hospitality. Maria replied by saying that hospitality was deeply engraved in the Colombian culture.

Two days later, they were on their way. What a sight it was to see them sitting on top of mules. She did not go into detail of their trip, but wrote that suffice to say that after the first day, she could hardly sit. After three days, they arrived in Bogotá where Emmanuel and his family were eagerly awaiting them.

Comfortably settled in their home, they would all be lodging with them until Abraham and Sara found a suitable house, with Emmanuel's help. Nellie ended the letter by saying she hoped everyone was well and happy and promised to give them an update soon.

Freddy put down the missive and looked around his room, lost in thought. He really envied his sister. Then he heard his mother's voice calling him and looked at the time, then went to wash up before dinner. At the table, the conversation revolved around Nellie's letter. Sigmund was happy to know she had arrived safely at her destination and Freddy hinted how much he wished he could have gone in her place.

"Who knows," said his father, "life might have an adventure in store for you as well." That night in bed, Sigmund confessed to Helene how glad he was not to have let himself be convinced by Abraham, looking around him and feeling very happy at being surrounded by all the modern comforts money could buy.

Chapter 26

As soon as classes were over the following day, Freddy went to find Helmut, eager to share the contents of Nellie's letter with him.

"To think that we have to go to school while others are able to have so much fun," said his friend wishfully.

"I know," said Freddy, "life is just not fair."

"It sure is not," said Martha, overhearing the conversation. "But part of growing up is learning to cope with it," she added as an afterthought.

Helmut walked over to her, "Is anything wrong, Mama?" He could tell by her tone of voice that something was troubling her. Martha looked in Freddy's direction and, after hesitating for a minute, said, "I am troubled and sad. The owner of the building at the corner of Schwindstreet—"

"You mean the tall grey building?" asked Helmut.

"Yes, that one," replied Martha. "She and her husband are Jewish and they are absolutely lovely but they are leaving for America. The janitor walked out on them as soon as he got wind of it and now they have asked us to take their place."

"What is wrong with that? We can stay here."

"No, you do not understand. We are definitely going to have to move in there, for they do not know when or if they will ever be back. It saddens me to see so many of our nice Jewish neighbours leaving, it is as though they were all losing faith in our country, and maybe rightly so."

"Well," said Freddy, "we will probably be the exception to the rule for we have no plans of going anywhere. Just last night at dinner, my parents were saying how happy they were to be right here."

"I am glad to hear you say that," said Martha.

"So when are we moving?" asked Helmut.

"In about two weeks' time. The new family who will be taking over our duties will be moving in about then," said Martha.

Freddy was thoughtful. "How much further is your new home going to be from my house?"

"It's not that far, it may take you three minutes longer, but we will still be in the same neighbourhood," replied Helmut.

Freddy let out a sigh of relief. "In that case, nothing has changed," he said.

"You are mistaken," replied Martha. "The flat is a lot smaller than this one."

"Which means," Freddy said with a grin then, turning to Helmut, "you will be spending a lot more time at my house where there is room galore."

"I don't think Helene would approve," said Martha under her breath, but her comment went unheard.

Freddy spent the weekend helping his friend go through his things and pack. It did not take them long, for Helmut did not have much. Freddy was shocked to see how meagre his friend's possessions were compared to his. He no sooner walked into his room that he opened the door to his wardrobe, looked inside and felt himself blush with shame. There was not a single empty drawer or shelf. "I hope we never have to move," he told his mother, "for it would take me at least a month to pack."

"I do not think that is an issue," replied Helene, "but you might want to go through everything one day and get rid of the things you no longer use or play with."

"One of these days," said Freddy, then he turned on his heels avoiding any further comments. Someday, he would take the time out to go through all his clothes and would pass them on to Helmut. He was sure that Martha would be able to alter them to fit.

Helmut hated the cramped space and depressing darkness of his new home and just as Freddy had foreseen, he spent more and more time at his friend's. Helene tolerated it, for when she discussed the issue with Sigmund he very wisely said he would rather have the house full of children than have them playing on the street. Life was good to them and everyone seemed to have settled into their own little routines. Helene kept busy and was very contented, to say the least.

Sigmund missed Nellie but kept his feelings very much to himself. Business was thriving and she certainly would have been able to help out had she been around. Once in a while, in the silence of his office, his thoughts would turn to her and he would question himself now and again for sending her away. Setting everything up in such a way that she had been unable to refuse, send her away he had, regardless of the motives, but he was also sure after a year she would be ready to come home. Nevertheless, he could not brush away one nagging thought in the back of his mind: What if she were to meet someone, fall in love and decide to settle there? Not only is she beautiful, but she is also so full of life.

His thoughts drifted back to when she was a little girl. Suddenly, he saw her grandmother's face smiling at him and could almost hear her say how proud her mother would have been of her had she lived to see her grow up. Yes, Alice would have been very proud indeed and she would have provided her with the tools that would have enabled her to grow and evolve, becoming a better human being. It would have also meant her leaving the nest and being exposed to the unknown world. Yes, she would not have begrudged her absence for she had always been very much aware of what an enriching experience travelling and seeing the world constituted.

He'd acted in her best interest as well as his own, for it had given him peace of mind. However, he hoped that if she were to meet somebody, it would occur here since he did not relish or envisage going through the hardships of that long journey she so vividly described. Just reading about it had been a nightmare. He was certainly not getting any younger and he was definitely too old to ride on a mule.

On the political scene, not much had changed. The parties continued to base their decisions on their own personal gains instead of what was best for the young republic and it became increasingly difficult for the Chancellor to build a coalition and for it to get its proposals accepted by Parliament.

Everything came to an abrupt change with the onset of the depression in 1929. The Americans asked for the immediate repayment of their loans but the money had been invested in long-term projects and was therefore not readily accessible. This led to huge job cuts and the number of unemployed rose steadily. American share prices plunged as people got out of the stock market. The Nazi Party and extremists did not waste time turning these new circumstances in their favour. People were going hungry and the cities and countryside were becoming unsafe. The welfare system had been designed to cover a certain number of jobless but the number of unemployed overstretched its means and was soon very much in debt.

The only way out was to raise taxes and reduce the benefits of the unemployed, but the opposition would not hear of it and this brought on a political crisis that could have been solved if then Chancellor Müller had been allowed to invoke the emergency decree the way Chancellor Ebert had done during the hyperinflation. President Hindenburg was adamant. This brought about the collective resignation of the Cabinet in March 1930. Hindenburg chose Heinrich Brunnig to head another government and a package of financial austerity measures was proposed, but voted down. It had been implemented by Presidential emergency decree and when Parliament protested, it was dissolved.

The Nazis made good use of this situation. They put up shelters for the homeless and soup kitchens for the hungry, thus luring them into their ranks. They reaped what they had sown in the elections of July of 1930 and their number of representatives increased to 107 and, defying a ban that had been imposed on the SA (Storm Detachment), their delegates appeared in Parliament dressed in their brown shirts. While Parliament was in session, some of their members smashed the windows of Jewish homes in the surrounding neighbourhood. The Prussian police came out in force to gain control of the situation. Sigmund could not believe what was happening, he who had so much faith in his country. Seated behind his desk in the silence of his office, mulling over the latest events, David's farewell words came to his mind from so many years ago in the bar of the Frankfurter Hof. "Good luck to you," he had said. "Who knows? You might need it more than me."

David and Lina were the first to leave and after many years, Abraham and Sara followed suit. "Is my faith in, and love for my fatherland so strong that it has not allowed me to see the signs the others saw?" he asked himself out loud. He remembered Abraham asking him bluntly the last time he had tried to persuade him to join him in his new enterprise whether he was blind to everything that was going on around him. Then he remembered how angry he got and how he ordered him to never bring up the subject again. Now it looked as if he'd made his choice and, by the looks of it, chosen wrongly.

It was not too late, he thought, and he could still change his course, yet the mere thought revolted him. He looked at his watch. "About time I left," he said out loud and, grabbing his hat and coat, headed home.

Helene met him at the door and although she greeted him with her usual smile, he could tell something was wrong. He kissed her and noticed her eyes were red. Hugging her close, he asked, "Have you been crying?" She nodded her head, unable to speak while trying to control her sobs. Something must be very amiss, thought Sigmund, for he had only seen his wife weep on very rare occasions. "Is it Freddy?" he asked, worried. She shook her head.

Finally getting a grip on herself, she spoke in a small, quivering voice. "It is mother. She has decided to leave Germany and go to Belgium where she has family. She says the hatred against us Jews and foreigners is only going to get worse and why should we impose ourselves on a country that does not want us. You know how she is. There is no stopping her once she has made up her mind."

The news took Sigmund by surprise. "Has she set a date?"

"Yes," replied Helene, "she is spending next weekend with us and taking the train on Monday. You must be hungry," she said. "I will go see about dinner."

Sigmund walked slowly up the stairs. He did not relish spending the weekend with his mother-in-law whom he did not see much of anyway, but her decision came as a big shock to him, even though she was one of these people who had no trouble packing a bag on short notice and taking a trip somewhere. He asked himself if she might be reading more into the situation than he was. By the time he came down to dinner, Helene was her normal self.

She spoke about getting the guest room ready and her husband knew without a shadow of a doubt that their home would be immaculate and ready to pass inspection, and inspected it would be, down to the last little detail. Even though his mother-in-law complained daily about how poor her eyesight was, nothing went unnoticed and her observations and remarks were anything but pleasant.

Sigmund shook his head. Helene was watching him out of the corner of her eye and asked teasingly, "Are you having a little disagreement with yourself?" Aware that he sometimes spoke to himself out loud.

"I was, in fact. I was just saying to myself how lucky I am not to be in your shoes when inspection time comes around." Helene started to smile and then, realising what he was implying, lost her temper.

"I know you are not happy at the prospect of my mother's visit," she said.

"Not at all," answered Sigmund, "quite the contrary. I am looking forward to having a long conversation with her, maybe she will open my eyes to what it would appear I am unable to see."

Helene could tell by the tone of his voice that he genuinely meant it and immediately changed her attitude. "Are you worried? Or are you doubting the wisdom of your decision?"

"I don't know what to think," replied her husband impatiently. "Let us drop the subject."

His mother-in-law came and left and everything went just as he had foreseen. He brought up the subject of her departure but she merely said she was going into a self-imposed exile, following the Emperor's footsteps, and when he tried to get to the root of her decision, she just stated that she saw no reason whatsoever for being where she was not welcome. She was free, after all, and freedom was an undeniable right to each and every individual, she was just making use of it before it was too late.

"What do you mean by too late?" Sigmund wanted to know. "Well, one never knows. Don't forget their latest actions: shattered windows and absolute disrespect for Parliament. These little episodes have proven to me that when it comes to them achieving their goals, whatever those might be, there will be no stopping them."

Freddy had walked into the room just then and much to her relief the conversation took another turn. Sigmund decided not to pursue the conversation any further, but resolved to keep his eyes and ears open. He took time off from the office to drive his mother-in-law to the train station and Helene bade her a teary farewell and promised to come and visit as soon as she was settled. On their way home, Sigmund interrupted her thoughts saying, "There is no need to be so sad, you still have your sisters around." She nodded her head in agreement. *But for how long,* she wondered.

Under Chancellor Brunnig's government, which lasted two years, Parliament convened for shorter and shorter periods of time, resorting more and more to presidential emergency decrees. The government could be defined as being suspended between authoritarianisms and a parliamentary democracy, very much questioned at first. As time wore on, people accepted it as normal. The Chancellor became more and more dependent on President Hindenburg who, at his advanced age, just wanted to be left alone with his army comrades in his country estate.

What really became a wakeup call for Sigmund was when the Nazis entered the state governments between the years of 1930 and 1932 in Anhalt, Brunswick, the state that had conferred German nationality on Hitler. According to the news, Mecklenburg, Oldenburg and Thuringia not only turned their sessions into a mockery of the system, but also refused their salaries and went after the communists, as well as everyone who did not agree with or fit into their concept. It was amazing how fast life had changed. More and more people were seen standing on the street corners doing nothing or sitting in the parks. Cars were broken into and there were many street brawls, most of them incited by the Nazis. People no longer had the means to buy new clothes, and they walked around in frayed clothing.

This whole state of affairs had one positive outcome and that was in April 1931 President Hoover pushed through a moratorium on the reparations and the servicing of the Inter-Allied debt. The motive behind it being, not only was a collapse of the German economy detrimental to the American interests, but to the European economy as well.

Sigmund's business also reflected the economic downturn, even though orders were still coming in, but at a slower pace. He gave his employees the choice between salary cuts or layoffs. They all chose to hold onto their jobs, even if it meant working for less money.

Freddy's life went on as usual, even though he got a first-hand glimpse through Helmut of what was going on. He would sometimes mention to him a conversation he'd overheard between his parents. Stress was running high at home and his parents were very much concerned about the security of their jobs. Martha knew her job as janitor of the building was not at risk but she still worried about Peter's paycheck, for there was no way they could live on hers alone.

The children were spending more and more time at Bunny Hill where they were properly fed with the produce from the farm, having plenty of fresh milk to drink. They would return to the city with bags full of potatoes and vegetables. Helmut was badly in need of a pair of shoes but when he asked his mother for money to replace them, she told him point blank that he would have to make them last, for there was no money to spare on luxury items. "You can go barefoot, but none of us can go without food," she exclaimed bitterly. "The days of plenty are gone for good." Helmut shrugged his shoulders and left the room.

One night at dinner, Freddy said Helmut's parents had a terrible row and that Martha was so angry, she almost walked out on them. Helene glanced at Sigmund, wondering if everything that went on in *their* household was discussed in Helmut's home.

Apparently, Peter told Martha he had changed his mind about joining the Nazis and Martha said that in her view, nothing had changed, on the contrary. Peter went on to explain that they were the only party that really cared about the people, not only were they feeding them and housing them, they were also insisting that all foreigners and Jews leave since they were taking the jobs away that rightly belonged to the Germans, as well as banning the communists. If they were all dealt with, the crisis would be averted and they would see prosperity again.

Martha screamed that she would rather starve than be married to a Nazi. Helmut told Freddy he did not understand why his mother had gotten so upset. If his father became a Nazi and Hitler became chancellor, all their problems would be solved and they would have jobs and salaries and his parents could afford to buy him the pair of shoes he so badly needed. Freddy ended his account saying he felt both sad and guilty. Sad because he could tell his friend was really suffering, he was so sensitive and took everything so much to heart, and guilty because he had so much. Unlike Helmut, he not only had one pair but several pairs of shoes, and always came home to find a huge meal waiting for him.

Sigmund and Helene exchanged glances. "Why do you think Martha does not like the Nazis?" asked his father.

Freddy thought for a minute. "Because they don't like us Jews," he said, biting his lip and looking his father in the eye.

"Why, Daddy, that means they don't like us either because we are Jewish, in a way, aren't we? If Peter were to join the Party, he would probably forbid

Helmut to—" he did not finish his sentence, overwhelmed by the magnitude of what he had just unveiled.

"Yes," said Sigmund.

Then Helene joined in the conversation. "Martha has a number of Jewish friends, as well. Freddy, let me get one thing straight, we are all Jewish and we acknowledge it with pride. The fact that you and your mother belong to the Christian faith does not mean a thing. Do you understand what I am saying?"

Freddy nodded his head. "Daddy, Grandma felt intimidated and left. Are we also going to have to leave?" Sigmund and Helene looked at each other.

"I do not know, Freddy, I hope not, but only time will tell."

"Do not worry your little head about it, just enjoy every day," she said, as they left the table.

Freddy headed for his room and lay on his bed looking around him. "I sure hope Peter listens to Martha so that Helmut and I may continue to be friends." With this thought on his mind, he drifted off into a fitful sleep.

Helene joined her husband in his study. He looked up from his work as she walked in. "Poor Freddy, I hope he does not take it too much to heart," said Helene.

"It is life and we cannot spare him from the realities of it," replied Sigmund.

"Indeed we may be forced to leave one day, but where would we go?" she asked. Sigmund thought for a moment. His mind went blank.

"Let's not discuss the issue any further. But bear in mind, Helene, the day Mr Hitler becomes chancellor, we will be on our way," he said in a very determined tone of voice.

Chapter 27

Nellie was sitting at her desk, writing in her diary. As she wrote the date, she realised that on this very day four years ago, she left Germany with the intention of returning in a year's time. She set down her pen and went into a daze. "It does not feel that long," she said out loud. The first couple of months had been awkward for all of them and even though Emmanuel and his wife went out of their way to make them feel at home, it had not been easy.

It wasn't about the amount of space, for the house was huge and not only had she had her own room, but she needn't worry about a thing for there were servants ready to satisfy any need. Everything was so different, so unexpected. The first thing she had to come to terms with was the lack of transition between day and night. The sun simply set every single day at six in the evening, there being no dusk and then there was the language barrier. She, who was so outgoing, had a hard time communicating, for even though she had become quite good at using her hands and eyes to make herself understood when she could not find the proper word, she sometimes felt very frustrated with herself.

It took Sara and Abraham three months to find the right house for them and it was about time, for everyone was getting on each other's nerves. The house was surrounded by a huge garden, which brought back memories of her home in Frankfurt. It was also quite centrally located. One of the highlights of living in the tropics was the flora. There were so many different species of plants, some of which she had never seen before, most of them blossoming all year round. It had been a journey of discovery, not only of her surroundings but herself as well.

The lack of seasons got to her at first but she could sense them and at the beginning of spring, she was much more aware of the birds chirping. Emmanuel hired a Spanish teacher for them and she took daily lessons, amazed at how fast she learned. Of course, the knowledge of French had come in very handy, as both languages were very similar. And she had been very homesick at first, she missed her home and most of all she regretted not having spent more time with her father, for it was he who she pined for the most. But she promised herself to make up for it upon her return. She looked forward to seeing her brother and sharing her experiences with him and she even missed Helene. Yes, she had resented her, but recalling a conversation she'd had with Sigmund a long time ago, she felt very grateful to her. For unbeknown to her, she had given Nellie the freedom to live her life without having the burden of her father. How right Sigmund was when he had told her he was entitled to a life of his own as well and had not sacrificed his happiness for her.

A friend of Emmanuel's had offered her a job and she had taken it with the understanding that it would only be for a year. "Life is so unpredictable," she said to herself, if she had only known. When the time had come for her to return, she wrote her father and told him she would like to postpone her trip for a couple of months, suggesting they come visit and then they could all go back together. Sigmund's reply had been adamant and the thought brought a smile to her lips. He had written, 'Ten horses couldn't drag me on that adventure, not to mention the idea of riding on a mule'. He had, however, consented to her staying for six more months. Just before that time was to elapse, he wrote her, suggesting she extend her stay. There was no cause for alarm but due to the economic situation in Germany, he considered she might be better off where she was. Nellie was overjoyed. A knock on the door brought her out of her daze. It was Sara, holding a letter in her hand. "It has been some time," Nellie said, taking the letter from her.

"It has indeed," said Sara, heading out the door.

She sat down on her bed and opened it carefully. It was from her father and she read avidly. He wrote about Helene, Freddy and the business, bringing her up to date. A couple of issues he mentioned made her laugh out loud but then, as she read on, the light tone changed into one of worry and she began to frown.

He wrote of the political uncertainties, how President Hindenburg had gotten rid of Chancellor Müller and chose someone by the name of von Papen to replace him. He had been military attaché to Washington in 1914 and was caught trying to sabotage the Canadian Pacific Railway through which American arms were being sent to First World War Allies and was therefore declared persona non grata. 'Can you believe it? Giving such an important post to someone with such a background. Just one more example of how fast people forget, even though it made headlines in all the major newspapers at the time and had caused quite a scandal.'

The Chancellor, contrary to all the others before him, had recently taken to announcing his policies over the radio rather than in Parliament, so the news was filled a lot of the time with his boring monologues that inevitably ended in criticism of the parliamentary system. The Nazis made no secret of their intention to intern communists and social democrat opponents in concentration camps. Sigmund became therefore quite concerned when the Nazis won 230 seats in Parliament; that constituted a major victory for them in the elections on 30 July 1932. Due to a vote of no confidence, called by the communist 512 to 42, Chancellor von Papen's cabinet was dissolved. New elections were called on 6 November 1932 and the Nazis suffered a huge defeat. Their seats were reduced to 196 and also lost 35% of the votes in the communal elections in Thuringia, which were held in December of that same year.

Sigmund, along with many others, breathed a sigh of relief at the outcome. The liberal newspaper wasted no time proclaiming that mass propaganda had lost all its appeal and the Nazis were finished as a party and would never come to power. Their joy was short lived because the influential industrialists, afraid of the Communist Party gaining the upper hand, began to support them.

Her father wrote that he was very concerned with everything going on and was seriously considering leaving Germany. Nellie let out a gasp. "Leave Germany…" she repeated out loud and returned to her reading. He was thinking of moving to Paris, but he asked her not to worry her little head about it, everything would turn out for the best, then ended the letter saying how relieved he was knowing her safe and happy. She reread the letter one more time and when she finished, she returned the sheets of paper carefully back into the envelope and put it away in the top desk drawer with the others.

She saved all her father's letters. On the days when she felt homesick and lonely, she found a lot of comfort in them. Suddenly, she realised the implications of what she had just read. She might never see her home in Frankfurt again. A chill ran down her spine. Her thoughts were interrupted by a knock on the door. It was Abraham.

"I am just leaving for the office and thought you might like a ride," he said.

"I had not realised it was so late," said Nellie, looking at her watch.

"I will wait for you downstairs," replied Abraham.

She combed her hair, washed the tears from her face, grabbed her purse and ran downstairs. He was already in the car waiting for her.

"Did you receive good news from home?" he asked. She thought about it, then decided to share the contents of the letter with him. "It is too bad your father did not listen to me. I insisted several times he join me in this venture, in fact the last time I mentioned it to him, he angrily forbade me to bring up the subject again. I tried to open his eyes but I was unable to get my message across to him. Why Paris? Why does he not come here?"

Nellie gave him the reasons her father had stated and Abraham was silent. "Each one to his liking," he said, ending the conversation. Nellie thanked him for the ride and walked into her office, then immersed herself in her work and soon forgot all about the letter.

Sigmund felt both sad and relieved after writing his daughter. Things could have been different had he listened to Abraham, but now it was too late, even though he toyed with the idea of going to Colombia. It would be so good to see his daughter again and the family would be reunited. He weighed the pros and cons but his heart could not be persuaded to leave Europe. He lay in bed, unable to sleep, tossing and turning and trying to stop thinking about the future and the decision he must reach. However, no sooner did he close his eyes, that voice would take over the stillness, the one that haunted him night and day, repeating the question like a mantra he had no answer to and invading every corner of his mind.

He sat up abruptly. Helene, who was asleep at his side, mumbled something that sounded like, "Can't you keep still?"

"How lucky she is," he said out loud, getting up and looking for his slippers in the dark. He knocked something off his night table that made a loud noise when it reached the floor.

"What is going on? It is impossible to sleep here if you keep this up. I am going to have to move to Nellie's room," she said angrily.

"Why? What are you talking about?" Sigmund asked, turning on the light and retrieving the paperweight that had caused the disturbance. "All you have done is sleep. I do not know what you are complaining about."

He was heading for the door when she looked up. "Where are you going? It's only two in the morning."

"To my study. I surely do not want to feel guilty for depriving you of your beauty sleep," he answered sarcastically.

"Why, Sigmund, is anything wrong?" she asked.

He looked at her in disbelief and then, trying to keep his voice calm, asked, "Are you living in your own little world, not wanting to admit that the Germany we used to know is dying? We are going to have to leave and I do not know where to. That is the question that has taken away my peace," he said bitterly.

Helene looked at him wide-eyed. "I had not realised anything was troubling you, why don't you come back to bed and we can discuss it? Maybe together we can come up with an answer," she suggested sweetly.

He stood uncertainly by the door then made up his mind to go back and lay down beside her.

"What are our options?" she asked, eager to end the forthcoming discussion as soon as possible so she could go back to sleep.

"I wrote Nellie describing the political situation and sharing my fears with her. In order not to upset her by letting on I had no idea whatsoever where I wanted to move to, I told her I was considering moving to Paris."

"Why Paris?" interrupted Helene, "Why not Brussels? We have relatives there, after all," she said, "and I would like nothing more than to live in the same city as my mother. I miss her so much and I would very much like to enjoy her company while I can. I am so very fortunate she is still alive," she added.

Sigmund looked at the ceiling in desperation, trying to conceal his anger then said, "I will never even consider living in that city, why, what a drab, boring place. And don't forget, it has the worst weather of all Europe. No, Helene, you are free to go and visit your mother as often as you like and if you want to settle there it is your choice, but as for me, I am still too full of life to go into seclusion there."

"You? Full of life? All you do is work and all you think about is work. You are not even aware of all this city has to offer. I really do not see why it would matter much to you."

"Helene, that is not fair," he snapped angrily. "I would like to go to the Opera and the Theatre more often and in fact we have gone, but if you want to have all the amenities you are used to, something has to be curtailed and in this case, it is our pleasures. You seem to forget I have to attend to the business that gives us our livelihood," he finished. Helene was about to say something but decided to keep it to herself. She was dozing off when Sigmund finally broke the silence. "We were going to look at the different options and instead we have ended up, as usual, arguing over things that are irrelevant considering the importance of the decision we, or I, have to take. We are tired, I suggest we let the subject rest and try to get some sleep and maybe tomorrow we can tackle it again. Who knows, we might come up with an answer," he said, taking her in his arms and kissing her good night. "And by the way," he whispered into her ear, "I did not mean it seriously when I said you could go live with your mother."

Helene smiled. "I know," she said softly. "You can't live without me."

The next day, Sigmund went to the office as usual, but as soon as he walked in, everyone sensed that the boss was in no good frame of mind. He addressed his secretary harshly and made her retype a letter to one of his providers three times after he found fault with everything. Finally, exasperated with himself, he put on his hat and coat, slammed the door to his office and, without uttering a word, headed for the street.

It was a clear winter day and the sun was shining. Even though it was very cold, it was the kind of weather that invited one to go for a stroll. He walked aimlessly through the streets until he came to a newspaper stand. Le Figaro, the French newspaper, caught his eye, so he took a copy, glanced at it and said to himself, "This might give me the answer."

The saleslady shot him a look of disgust as he paid for it, muttering between her teeth, "Another stubborn foreigner." Sigmund gave her a dirty look, took his change and left clutching his paper tightly underneath his arm. He quickened his pace and hailed a passing cab back to his office, feeling a surge of impatience and curiosity.

His secretary looked up as he walked in. "I have some urgent phone messages for you," she said.

He waved his hand to silence her, "Later, later, I do not want to be disturbed," he said emphatically, then opened the door to his office and closed it in her face.

"Well, it will all have to wait till later. I do not understand what has gotten into him," she said.

"I would not lose one minute sleep over it," said her colleague.

"You are right, I should not let it trouble me," and without pursuing the matter further, she turned her attention back to her work.

Once seated comfortably in his chair, Sigmund spread the paper on the desk and went straight to the classified section. When he was a child, his parents insisted on the importance of languages and had hired a private teacher to give him French lessons. He no longer spoke it fluently now, for he never had the opportunity to practice it. The property section took up several pages. He scanned through it and as far as he could tell, the prices were not astronomical. Finding a place to live would not be a problem. Having found the answer, he quickly glanced through the other sections.

A headline in the cultural section caught his eye. It was an announcement of the opening of an exhibition by an artist named Picasso that was being promoted by a woman called Gertrude Stein explaining how she had discovered his works. With interest, he read on, the last paragraph having quite an impact on him. It narrated how Paris had become a Mecca for foreigners who were forced to leave their country of origin for various reasons, bringing with them their heritage and thus enriching the arts while contributing to the excitement of this vibrant city that never slept.

He looked at the time. "I had better get back to work," he said out loud and put the newspaper in his briefcase then rang for his secretary. He greeted her with a smile as she walked in. His mood had changed for whatever unknown reason and her boss was his old self again. She gave him his messages and some correspondence for him to sign and he dealt with everything he had pending, leaving the office earlier than usual.

Helene had had a feeling Sigmund would be home early and was therefore not at all surprised to see him. "Where is everyone?" he asked.

"Freddy is over at Helmut's and today is the maid's day off," she replied.

"How nice, we have the house to ourselves," he said, taking her in his arms. He then let go of her and said, "I won't be long, I am just going to wash my hands and leave my briefcase in the study."

When he returned, Helene was setting the coffee table in the living room. She brought in a fresh pot of coffee and an apple cake she had baked that morning and served Sigmund then herself. They ate in silence, enjoying each other's company. She broke the silence saying, "I have given the matter some thought." Her husband gave her a questioning look but did not interrupt her. "I was thinking of the conversation we had in the early morning hours and I just want you to know that I will follow you wherever you go. I know you have only our best interest in mind." Sigmund took her hand in his. "Just do what you have to do," she said.

"In that case, Helene, I will make a trip to Paris to find us somewhere to live and I am sure it will not take me very long for according to the classified section of Le Figaro, everything is available."

"When will you leave?"

"As soon as I can make the time," he replied. He felt as if a big load had been taken off his shoulders and he was finally free to follow his heart. "Thank you, Helene," he said, squeezing her hand tightly.

"What for?"

"For trusting me," he replied, smiling. That night, he slept like a baby but Helene woke up several times, wondering what the future in Paris would have in store. Sigmund woke up the next day feeling very well rested indeed. It was a wonderful new sensation. It must have been ages since he felt this invigorated, he said to the image in the mirror, having not realised until now how stressed out he had been.

Now, with his mind at ease and having found the path he was to follow, he felt light-headed and happy. He would go to Paris as soon as possible and in the meantime, he would discreetly put his business up for sale. While he got dressed, he spoke to Helene, who was still in bed.

"I did not sleep too well," she said, answering his question. "I tossed and turned."

"I, on the other hand, had a very repairing sleep and now I am ready to take on the world," said Sigmund.

"Are we going to tell Freddy about our plans?"

"No way, he will know in due course, no need to burden him with our worries, besides, we do not want word to get out that we are leaving. If Mr Hitler comes to power, he is going to make it very difficult for people to travel and we sure do not want to cause any suspicion. To the outside world, we have to continue to be the happy contented family for whom there is only one place and that is Germany, Germany above everything else." Helene nodded then got out of bed and followed him downstairs. They ate their breakfast in silence. Freddy had already left, just his empty plate stared them in their faces.

As usual, Helene walked her husband to the front door. "I may not be home early," he said, kissing her good bye.

She felt tired and drained and went back to bed. "I will sleep for an hour," she thought and set the alarm clock, but try as she might, sleep would not come. Her mind leapt from one thought to another and she could not take it off the forth-coming events. She finally gave up in frustration and walked around her home, looking at all their beautiful furniture. She then opened her wardrobes and admired all her clothes. It is going to take me a week at least to get everything packed. She hoped something would happen to change her husband's plans.

Sigmund left for Paris a couple of days later. Helene insisted on going to the train station to see him off but he would not hear of it, arguing it was a waste of her time and he wanted to avoid attracting attention. He was just one more businessman headed for a meeting in another city. Once he found his seat, he stowed his small suitcase on the luggage rack above his head and set his briefcase down by his side then watched as the train rolled slowly out of the station. As it picked up speed, his mind seemed to do so as well, besieging him with questions to which he ignored the answers. He had bought himself a map of the city and studied it in detail, outlining the residential neighbourhoods he was interested in according to the prices set forth in the real estate pages of Le Figaro.

Helene had made just one request and that was their home should be within walking distance from a school. He did not dare take the map out for fear of attracting attention, but he had a mental picture of it and went over it one more time. How he wished Helene could have come with him so they could decide together, but discretion was of the utmost essence. Alice's brother had moved to Paris before the war and even though he had given him his address and phone number, he had lost all contact with him after Mrs Winters' death. Now he regretted not having kept in touch. However, he did make a point of going through his old address books, which he refused to throw out for one never knew when they might become handy, and found it. He then carefully copied it onto a piece of paper, which he placed in his wallet. As he was unable to find that particular street on the map, Sigmund was led to believe that Paul lived on the outskirts. Would he call him? He was not sure, since so many years had passed and it would surely awaken memories that had long been put to rest. The train's motion made him sleepy, he fought against it for a while and eventually gave up and dozed off. The train made several short stops along the way and he would wake up, startled, look at his watch and, realising he had not yet reached his destination, doze off again. The train stopped just before reaching the Swiss border and the German and Swiss customs and police agents came on board.

The Germans were extremely meticulous, looking at everyone's travel documents and asking questions about the purpose of their trip, giving the passenger seated across from Sigmund an extremely rough time as well as being extremely rude to him. Sigmund was beside himself with rage, who did they think they were? His temper flared as he watched one of the officers grab the passenger by the arm and drag him off the train. Reaping the benefits of the showdown, when Sigmund's turn came, they barely looked at his travel documents. He let out a sigh of relief as the train slowly went into motion and knew right then and there he would never return to Germany. It saddened him, but he had just witnessed what was in store for those who waited too long to leave. Helene would have no problem since it was the men they were after.

In contrast, the Swiss officers were very polite. The train slowed down and they were entering the Basel train station. Sigmund gathered up his belongings and got off, then looked around and saw his friend Franz Kahn coming towards him. They hugged each other briefly, delighted to see each other. Franz escorted him to the car where they were to conduct their business.

"Are you sure you cannot spend the night?"

"No way," replied Sigmund, and in just a few words described the scene he had witnessed.

"How lucky you are, Sigmund," he said.

"I am fully aware of it. I also realise that there is no going back. I am on a one way ticket," he answered sadly. "You do understand that time is running out, don't you?"

"I sure do," replied Franz, "but there is nothing to be worried about." He opened his briefcase and handed Sigmund some bank forms. Sigmund signed the papers, authorising the transfer of all his assets over to his friend for safekeeping. "The account has been opened and everything is ready. As soon as I leave you, I will hand the papers over and the transaction will be done immediately."

They walked back to the station, as the train to Paris was just coming in. "I will phone you to make sure all is well," Sigmund said as he embarked the train. Franz watched it leave and began to feel sorry for his friend; he was so attached to his country and Franz was sure he would never come to terms with being an expatriate.

The signing of the documents had taken a lot out of him, leaving him tired and drained. He'd devoted many hours finding the best way to protect his fortune, for he was sure beyond any doubt that the Nazis would appropriate themselves of anything they could lay their hands on and the last thing he wished to see was them reaping the benefits of his and his family's hard work. His wealth belonged to his children and he had a duty to safeguard it for them.

Out of all his friends, Franz was the only one he could trust whole-heartedly. Used to having complete control of it, on paper it was no longer his. He was as poor as a church mouse. So many changes in such a short period of time. "That is life," he thought, not realising he had spoken the words out loud and everybody was staring at him. He could feel the train slowing down and he glanced at his watch. A few more minutes before it would come to a complete stop at its final destination. He felt a tingle of excitement at the thought of the unknown and wondered what the future had in store for him here. He would soon find out.

Chapter 28

He took his time gathering his belongings and, as an afterthought, took a slip of paper out of his wallet and placed it in his coat pocket. Like all mayor trains stations, murky figures found shelter in them and there was nothing wrong with being prudent. He slowly made his way to the exit, trying to avoid being knocked down by those who were running to catch their trains. While he waited in line for a cab, he took in his surroundings. The buildings were nice but looked dirty and run down. The street did not look too clean, either. Everybody is blind to it however, for this is Paris.

When his turn finally came, he gave the cab driver the address who in turn shook his head and said with a sneer, "Do not understand." Sigmund gave him a look and handed the paper over to him. The driver glanced at it, shook his head and said, "I have been waiting here for a couple of hours only to pick up a fair that wants to be dropped off three blocks down the road? Monsieur, you don't understand?" Sigmund shook his head. "I have been standing in line for a long time and now all I will get is 10 francs for the run."

Sigmund nodded and said in poor French, "That is the risk you take, Monsieur, when you go for the easy jobs, thinking only about the big money. Let's go."

The driver mumbled something about…these foreigners…and set the car in motion. It was a very short ride indeed and he pulled up in front of a small, two-story house on a very narrow street. A small sign by the entrance read 'Pension'. Sigmund asked the driver to wait and this time he received a very polite reply, "Monsieur, do take your time." *How nice and polite they can become when they smell money,* he thought, walking towards the door.

There was a write-up on this bed and breakfast in Le Figaro and he had cut it out but was unable to make a reservation due to the circumstances, however, with luck they might have a vacancy. He knocked on the door and waited. Just as he was about to knock again, the door swung open.

"Monsieur, you wish?" asked the stunning young lady standing in the doorway. Sigmund stated his business. Luck was with him and he was given the last room. She walked him to a small but cosy room on the ground floor. Before returning to her desk, she informed him that the bathroom was at the end of the hallway. *Oh well,* he thought, *it could be worse.* He walked out onto the street and paid the driver who looked very disappointed indeed when he realised that his passenger no longer required his services.

Sigmund returned to his room and while he was unpacking, he realised how tired he was. He decided to forego dinner, for he did not relish having to go out and look for a restaurant, and went straight to bed. He was asleep in no time but slept fitfully. He missed his bed and having to go for a midnight stroll down the corridor to the toilet made him realise how spoiled he was. He did not feel at all rested when he woke up for he had tossed and turned all night. A good hot bath will put me in shape, he thought as he got out of bed, then headed to the bathroom.

To his disappointment, it was occupied and a male voice was singing at the top of his lungs. He was about to knock on the door but thought better of it and headed back to his room. He picked up the copy of Le Figaro lying by his door and, without even looking at the headlines, went straight to the property section. He found several ads that appealed to him and, after marking their location on the map, headed back down the hallway. Nothing had changed. Sigmund knocked on the door and waited. No answer. He pounded on it with his fist. Finally, the singing stopped. "One cannot even take a bath without being disturbed! I will be out in a minute," the voice called. Sigmund waited, his impatience growing. Finally, the door swung open to reveal a nice looking couple. She cast her eyes down as she walked past him, her companion gave him a mock of a bow. "All yours, Your Highness," he said and, taking the girl by the waist, led her down the corridor.

Sigmund stared after them in disbelief and thought, *France was really living up to its reputation.* He bathed and dressed in a hurry and without even waiting for breakfast, which was included in the price of his room, left. Now he was more determined than ever to find a home.

He took a cab to the address that was his first choice and, as he had done so many years ago in Frankfurt, walked the neighbourhood to get a feel for it. He did not forget Helene's one request and made sure there was a school close by. He was not at all disappointed with what he saw, but he would have to make the rounds before making up his mind. He spent all day going from one to the next, taking notes on his pad about all he had seen so he could later compare them and come to a decision. It slowly became clear to him that he would probably be spending about a week at his bed and breakfast, for there was no point in seeing a real estate agent until he had decided on what part of the city they should reside.

The city really lived up to its name. The architecture was beautiful. On nearly every street corner, there were posters announcing various forth-coming events. He could tell that in contrast to his home city, this was one that never slept. His path led him towards the Champ de Mars and Les Invalides. He glanced at the time and made up his mind: he would visit Napoleon's tomb. After purchasing an entry ticket, he eagerly made his way to the entrance. Standing by the tomb then walking around it, the purpose of his trip was forgotten and he found himself going back in time, remembering everything Napoleon had accomplished. The code of law he had created was still actual.

Sigmund stood deep in thought, transported to another time. They had something in common, they were both soldiers who had been able to serve their

234

countries, but one had not been stigmatised by his blood and had been able to climb the ladder of success even though he had later fallen into disgrace and exiled to the island of Elba. His own military career, on the other hand, had been restricted from the very beginning to that of officer in the Prussian military. He would have loved to have been promoted to colonel or general, but he had accepted his fate and became a very successful businessman instead.

"No," he said to himself, "I have no regrets." And besides, brooding over the past was just a waste of time, he had a mission to accomplish and he had better get on with it. He glanced at the sarcophagus once more and left, but his pensive mood stayed with him throughout the rest of the day. Deep in thought, he walked for an hour until he reached his destination.

He liked this neighbourhood best of all, it was a little removed from the city centre but there were beautiful villas surrounded by large gardens. It was very classy and the equivalent to their neighbourhood in Frankfurt. That was probably the reason he felt so drawn to it. "I would love to live here," he said to himself, and walked all around, stopping here and there to admire a tree or a villa, keeping an eye out for a sign that read 'for rent'. The more he saw of it, the better he liked it, but he was almost sure a villa here would be way out of his budget. A real estate agent would have the answer but it was too late to see one. "If I hadn't made that stop, I would not have to wait to find out," he said in reproach. Then, "Never mind, I will seek one out first thing in the morning."

He caught the eye of a passing cab and hailed it, asking the driver to drop him off at the Champs Elysees. He walked down the avenue admiring its layout as he looked for a restaurant and realised he had not eaten all day. Luckily, he found a quaint little Bistro and because of the time of day he did not have to wait to be seated, given a table by the window from which he could watch the comings and goings of the crowd outside.

What a diversity of people, he thought. "People from all over the world are here." Some were rushing to get somewhere, some were strolling along; it was like a never-ending fashion show. Some outfits were quite elaborate while others were very simple, but all of them were unique and different. He would have to return with Helene, she would fully enjoy it. The waiter interrupted his thoughts as he placed his order on the table. Like everything else, the meal was no exception and also lived up to the reputation of the French cuisine.

Feeling rested, he decided to walk back to his lodgings, window-shopping along the way. He did not have a shadow of a doubt that Helene would soon feel very much at home here and realised it was the second time he thought about her that evening. "I must be missing her." Recognising that their separations had been very short and far between. How he wished they could have made this trip together, but it was out of the question, brushing the other thoughts out of his mind. "Circumstances, circumstances," he repeated to himself angrily.

The stunning young girl from the day before greeted him as he walked into the hotel and inquired in a soft voice if he'd had a nice day. "I sure did," he replied politely, taking the key from her, and bade her a good night. He got himself ready for bed and fell asleep as soon as his head touched the pillow.

Helene missed her husband more than she cared to admit. When Freddy came home from school, she explained to him that his father had gone on a business trip. Freddy looked at her in surprise, "Daddy never mentioned a word about it."

"Yes," replied his mother, "it was all very sudden."

"When will he be back?" Helene told him Sigmund had not given her a date, all he had said was he would be back as soon as possible.

The days dragged on and still no word from Sigmund. Helene began to worry about her husband and Freddy's questions about his father's whereabouts became more insistent. She had to mind her tongue in order not to give away their plans and she felt bad about not confiding in her own son, but the stakes were too high. Just one indiscretion and…no, she did not dare think about the consequences.

A couple of weeks later when she least expected it, the phone rang. It was Franz. He told her that their common friend was well and that his mission had been successful. She thanked him and as she set the phone back on its cradle, she noticed her hand was shaking. *This is it,* she thought, *there is no going back.* It was now up to her to carry out plan B. Freddy had become used to his father's absence and refrained from asking his mother the question as to his whereabouts. The last time he did, she almost broke down in tears and he felt very embarrassed indeed.

School was over for the week and he was in excellent spirits, thinking about all the things he had to look forward to for the following two days. He whistled one of his favourite tunes, as he let himself into the house. Helene looked up from what she was doing when she heard her son's voice calling, "Mama, Mama, where are you?" She was about to call out to him when he walked into her sewing room, oblivious to all the papers lying on the floor.

"How was school?" she asked absent-mindedly.

"Not bad, not bad at all, now that the day is over. But, boy did they give us enough homework to make up for the free time."

"Oh, well," said his mother, waving her hand. "Are you hungry?"

"Yes, I could do with some food, but…is everything all right, Mama?" Freddy asked after looking at her closely. Something in her tone of voice did not sound quite right.

"Should something be wrong?" she asked cynically.

Freddy ignored the question and left the room saying he was going to wash his hands. He could feel the tension in the air. I will eat then go and do my homework so it is out of the way. I will also be out of her way and free to enjoy my spare time. They ate their lunch in silence but he noticed that his mother only played with the food on her plate. He was about to comment on it but decided wisely to keep his observations to himself.

"I had better continue what I was doing," said Helene, folding her napkin and placing it back in its ring. Freddy stood up and followed her up the stairs. He was inclined to go find Helmut but remembered he was still at school. Thus, unable to find any other distractions, he sat down at his desk to do what he had set out to do.

Helene went through all her papers and tried her best to keep her emotions in check. How was she to break the news to Freddy? How would he react to it? Would he understand her not confiding in him from the very beginning? Or would it create an issue between them? How she wished his father were here, having this conversation. Sigmund told her quite clearly when she mentioned the subject that Freddy was not only intelligent but kept up with what was happening in the world as well. Had she forgotten that he read the paper every day before leaving for school? No, how could she forget when she was awoken every morning by the noise of the front door closing after her son retrieved the paper so he could glance over it while eating his breakfast?

"Don't be afraid," he had said, placing his arm around her shoulders, "I know you will not only find the right words, but Freddy will also understand. Although he is only twelve, he is very mature for his age and he will realise that it is the only choice we have." His words echoed in her ears as she tried to summon enough courage to face him.

Freddy had just finished his homework and was placing his books back in his school bag when his mother came in and walked over to where he was standing. Freddy looked at her in surprise, for it was not like her to come in without knocking. "Why, Mama…" he did not finish his sentence for Helene took him gently by the arm and pushed him into the chair.

"I have something very important to discuss with you, my son," she said, standing next to him. Freddy looked at her.

"If that is the case, Mama, let me first find you a place to sit," he said, rising.

"Don't bother bringing that big bulky chair over," said his mother, "we can just as well sit on the bed, it might even be more comfortable."

"Are you sure?" Helene did not answer; she only walked over to the bed and, after arranging the pillows, sat down on it. Freddy followed suit. The silence that ensued could have been cut with a knife. Helene tried hard to keep a steady voice when she finally spoke.

"You realise, Freddy, how much your father and I love you, and you, more than anyone should know that if it were in our power, we would spare you from all the hardships that life brings with it. Unfortunately, this is not always possible. Today we are confronted with a situation that is not in our hands to change. We can either accept it and be doomed, or we can try and flee from it and begin a new life elsewhere. Your father has wisely made the choice. We are to go and join him."

"Why, Mama, that's wonderful news! A few days without school!" exclaimed Freddy.

"No, son, you do not understand, it is not a couple of days. We are to leave and never return."

"Never to come back?"

"Yes," replied Helene, hugging him to her so he could not see her eyes swelling with tears.

"What about my friends, Fritz my little parakeet? Everything I own is here, I have known no other place and I—"

Helene silenced him by placing her finger on his lips. "Freddy, you keep abreast with the news, you know what is going on in the world, you are certainly aware that there are some children and some adults who do not want to have anything to do with us."

"Yes, Mama," and he proceeded to describe a scene to her he witnessed at school several days ago. A senior student screamed at the top of his lungs 'All Jews are pigs'. A teacher, who was standing nearby, walked over to him but instead of reprimanding him, gave him a pat on the back. Some of his classmates surrounded him, clenched their fists in the air and started chanting 'Jews are pigs' until another teacher who overheard them asked them to shut up, restoring some kind of order. Freddy and his friends had watched from a distance and felt very scared.

"When did this happen?"

Freddy thought for a minute. "It was the day Daddy left."

"I see," replied his mother. "Why didn't you tell me about it?"

"I really wanted to discuss it with him."

Suddenly, everything became clear to her. "Freddy, we do not have much time. I want you to sort out your things, just lay them on the bed and I will pack them for you, but I want you to bear in mind that we cannot take much, so please…"

"I understand, Mama," replied Freddy, trying hard to be brave. "When do we leave?"

"We will be leaving early tomorrow morning."

"Are we going by train?"

"No, we are being driven." She omitted mentioning that Franz was sending his car and driver to pick them up.

"Can I say good-bye to my friends?"

"No, Freddy, nobody must catch wind of what we are planning."

"Can't I say farewell to Helmut?"

"No," replied his mother firmly, "and should he come around, I will tell him you are not home."

"But what about the maid?"

"I have given her the weekend off and by the time she returns, we will be well into our journey." She pulled her son close to her then stood up and as she walked towards the door said, "Come on, let's get started, we both have a lot to do." Sigmund had been right once more. Freddy hadn't prodded her with questions, or maybe she had not given him time to do so, and it had been much easier than she envisioned. But it was not over yet, she reminded herself.

Freddy sat down on his bed and looked around his room. Two of his classmates had not returned after the Christmas break and he had been led to believe that they just had gone to other schools. Now he understood and was about to follow in their footsteps. He sorted out his clothes as his mother had asked and went through his books and personal belongings. It grieved him to leave practically everything behind, but he consoled himself with the thought that he would have a whole new wardrobe. He had been told he couldn't take

238

much, to keep it to a minimum, so he placed the books that were dearest to him on the bed.

He glanced over at Fritz. His mother had given it to him to make up for the loss of Gretchen, who had died of old age. He had wanted a German Shepard but Helene had her fill of four legged animals in the house and issued him an ultimatum: a goldfish, a bird or, if he really wanted to please her, none at all. He found his father's goldfish boring so, having no other choice, decided on this beautiful pale blue-feathered parakeet and had never regretted it. He had no trouble finding a name for him, either, it was Fritz from the very start. Now, standing by the window with Fritz perched on his finger, he confided the news to him and as he spoke, he broke down in tears.

Freddy took no notice of his mother until she was standing beside him. "Mama, we are not leaving him behind, are we? He is part of the family, you know."

Helene took a deep breath. "He has to stay here, unfortunately."

"But why Mama, why?"

"Freddy, now don't be unreasonable. The cage is too big and he is used to his surroundings, and besides, I am sure the maid will take good care of him."

"I do not want to leave, either," replied Freddy.

"None of us want to, child, but you've just gotten a taste of what is in the cards for us Jews at school and you can trust me, one day in the near future, not only will we be verbally abused but physically attacked and those around will look the other way." The conviction in her voice ruled out any further discussion. Freddy wiped his tears away, put Fritz back in his cage and placed it on the table where it belonged. He helped his mother pack without uttering another word.

Just before going to bed, they carried their bags downstairs and placed them by the main door. Helene woke him up long before dawn and urged him to get dressed as fast as he could. As soon as they were ready, they got into the awaiting car and drove off. Neither one of them looked back and were well on their way to Basel when day broke.

Helmut had spent the night at one of his friend's houses. Life at home was becoming unbearable and his parents did nothing else but quarrel whenever they were together. He had to go home, though, because the friend and his parents were spending the day out in the country with some acquaintances and, much to his disappointment, he was not asked to join them, even though he had dropped a couple of hints. So reluctantly and with some misgivings, he made his way home. His father had surely received his paycheck the day before, and it was more than likely he would have spent most of the night out with his friends.

His father had become ever so popular since he changed jobs and with it his whole outlook on life as well. He was no longer the contented man whose foremost priority was his family and his work and he would have had more drinks than he could carry as well. Nothing infuriated his mother more than having to care for a drunk.

He arrived home in the middle of a terrible argument and rushed into his room, dropped his bag and fled. *Why do they insist on living together?* he

239

wondered. Quite a few of his friend's parents had separated and from talking to them, he knew that having to make a choice between one or the other was no easy task, but then if one could live in peace and harmony, it was well worth the price. Arriving at his destination, he decided to ask Freddy his opinion. He knocked on the front door. No answer. He knocked again. No answer. He knocked a third time. No answer. "They must have all gone out," he resolved, then turned on his heels and left. When he arrived home, the storm had passed.

He spent the rest of the day in his room reading and sleeping and staying out of everyone's way. It was not until late afternoon the next day that he went looking for Freddy again. The curtains were drawn and the house looked pretty much as it had the day before. "I do hope they are back," he said out loud. He knocked. The maid flung the door open. "Is Freddy home?" he asked impatiently.

"No, he is not in, they have all gone."

"What do you mean?" asked Helmut, bewildered.

"Everyone has left."

"I do not understand," he said.

"Well," replied the maid, "they have gone, vanished into thin air."

"Is Fritz gone as well?"

"No, they left him behind."

"Well, if you do not mind, I will care for him until my friend returns."

"One less thing for me to worry about. Go fetch him," she replied indifferently.

Helmut did not wait to be told twice and took the steps two at a time then ran into Freddy's room. It was a mess and everything was scattered all over. They must have left in a big hurry. He looked for a note, a hint left for him by his friend, but found nothing so he grabbed the cage and raced down the stairs, tears flowing freely down his cheeks. He felt a deep sorrow. Not only was his family life shattered but he lost his chum as well. Perhaps someday they would meet again, he consoled himself, trying hard to put on a brave front and be positive. He nodded his head at the maid who was standing by the open door talking to a man wearing a brown shirt and heard the man call out to him, "Come back, I need some information." But Helmut did not look back, instead he quickened his pace.

Much to his relief, no one was home and he was spared the explanations, for the time being. He set the birdcage on his desk and opened the door. Fritz shyly stuck his head out and when Helmut held his finger out to him, he climbed eagerly on to it. "Well, I guess there is just you and me left," and the bird spread his wings as if voicing his assent.

The following morning, Helmut headed off to school as usual. He made a little detour, however, and walked past Freddy's house. From what he could see, nothing had changed, but then he did not walk all the way up to the house. Suddenly, he had company; the guy who had been speaking to the maid was walking beside him.

"I called out to you yesterday," he said, "why did you ignore me?"

"I did not hear you, I am a little deaf," replied Helmut.

"Where is your friend? Where did the family go?"

"I do not know," replied Helmut, "I was just as surprised as the maid."

"Don't lie to me," said the stranger harshly. "I do not want to beat the truth out of you."

"Even if you did, I could not give you any information for I do not have any."

The stranger shook his head in anger. "Dirty Jews," he muttered to himself, as he turned on his heels and left. Helmut noticed he was trembling. He wondered if Sigmund had known they were after him. It was a very close call and he shuddered. All of a sudden, his sadness turned to joy…wherever his friend might be, at least he was safe.

<u>Part II – Paris</u>

Chapter 29

Freddy fell asleep almost instantly. Helene looked out the window, taking in every little detail for the last time. It was still dark. Under the light of the street lamps, she could barely make out the outline of the houses and buildings she had grown to love. She felt both sad and relieved. Their departure went as planned and Freddy cooperated fully. His father would be very proud of him. She missed Sigmund, but each turn in the road brought her closer to him. "Tomorrow, or the day after, we will be reunited," she thought happily. "But do not get your hopes up too high," she scolded herself. "There is still the border."

In the note Franz had sent with the driver, he mentioned they would be taking a small detour in order to avoid the main road and, with any luck, the border crossing at that particular point would be unmanned by the Germans. Her eyes felt heavy; she closed them to rest and was soon asleep.

Sigmund looked anxiously at the time. They should be at the border by now. He paced the floor. He was not the only one. Franz kept checking his watch and looking out the window. There was no way of knowing if they had left on time or what problems they might have encountered. "Patience, patience, patience," he repeated to himself, and was just about to call Sigmund when the phone rang. He rushed to it and smiled happily. They were safe, they'd pulled it off. No one had been at the border on the German side to stop them, and he rang Sigmund with the news.

"Yes, I understand. Do not worry, I will have her call you as soon as they arrive," he promised.

Sigmund was beside himself with joy. He walked through his new home, looking at everything and stopping to arrange a little thing here and little thing there. It would not be long now before they were together again; with the exception of Nellie. How he missed her and longed to see her. Hopefully, if all went well, she might come home the coming year but he did not allow his mind to dwell on the subject, for today was a joyful day, his family was safe and out of harm's way.

As they drove up the driveway toward the house, Helene was overwhelmed by the beautiful setting and view. She remembered Nellie's description of it: a palace surrounded by a park, and it could not have been more accurate. Franz and Elizabeth were at the door waiting to welcome their guests. "We finally get to meet," Elizabeth said warmly, shaking hands with Helene. "And you are no stranger to us, Freddy, for when your sister stayed with us some years ago, she told us all about you. Have you heard from her lately?"

"We received a letter from her some weeks ago. She is happy and doing well," replied Helene.

"We can pursue the conversation later," said Franz. "Sigmund is impatiently awaiting your phone call, Helene." He led them into his study, dialled the number, then handed her the phone. He quietly left the room.

Sigmund answered on the first ring and his tone of voice reflected the happiness he felt. "I am relieved everything went so well," he said. When Helene praised Freddy, he replied, "I told you, but you always worry so much."

"I can't wait to see you," said Helene.

"Well, it won't be long now, just one more day. I will be at the station to meet you and to take you to our new home."

"Do tell me about it."

"No, Helene, I want you to see it for yourself. But I did see to it that Freddy's school is close by." He then told her where he would meet them and asked to speak to his son.

"Mama and I faired very well, considering the circumstances," said Freddy. "I just wish I could have brought Fritz with me, but there was no room."

"We will buy another one."

"Are you sure they sell them in Paris?" Freddy asked in an excited tone of voice.

"I think so. I do not know why we would not find one. Paris is known for being a shopper's paradise, among other things, and for importing products from all over the world. People say, and I have been told, that if you cannot find something in this city, it is because it does not exist."

"It sounds as if there is a lot to see and do," said Freddy.

"Oh, yes," replied his father. "I can't wait to show you both around."

Freddy handed the phone back to his mother and Sigmund told her he was sure they would all be very happy here. She was about to hang up when Franz entered the room and Helene handed the phone over to him. He took a paper from his desk and scribbled something on it. Sigmund was delighted to hear that they would be arriving in the late afternoon. He described the meeting point just in case Helene had not quite understood and Franz wrote it down in his neat, easy to read handwriting and gave it to Helene. "Just in case you have any doubts," he said.

She smiled and thanked him. "That's Sigmund, he always thinks of everything." Elisabeth showed them to their rooms, which were side by side. Helene had the same room Nellie had once slept in and she remembered her mentioning the beautiful trees. The fact that there were no other buildings around made everything seem vast and peaceful. As she stood by the window, a bird flew past. *How easily one forgets the beauty of nature when one lives in the city,* she mused.

They had an early night as they were all tired and had to rise early. The next morning, Franz drove them to the train station and after promising them a visit in Paris, left them comfortably seated in their compartment. The last leg of their journey was about to begin and after looking out at the passing scenery for a while, Helene took out her papers and magazines. Freddy was already immersed in a book.

The trip took forever as the train stopped at every station, or so it seemed. Helene dozed off a couple of times only to be awakened by Freddy asking if they were almost at their destination. "We still have a long way to go," she replied.

"This journey is taking forever," said Freddy, impatiently. "Not only is this a very slow train, but with all the stops it makes…and Mama, I looked Paris up on the map and it really is not that far. We could have driven, maybe it would have been faster," he ended impatiently.

"It probably would have, but it would not have been as convenient," replied Helene. "Freddy, when one is looking forward to something or someone, time just seems to stand still and then when it becomes a reality, the joy and expectation vanishes at the speed of light."

"I know, Mama. It is like when you are looking forward to a nice big slice of chocolate cake. Once it is set before you and you eat the first bite, you no longer enjoy the second one as much, as if you'd never craved it."

"That is a very good example," replied Helene. "Sounds like you might be getting a little hungry if you are thinking about food." Then she opened a bag and took out a neatly wrapped package. "Maybe this will help," she said, handing it to him.

He opened it carefully. "Mama!"

"I know it is your favourite and I saved some for you, hoping it would ease the pain of this drawn out journey."

Freddy laughed. "I actually have nothing to complain about. I was able to see things Nellie shared with me and I am very much looking forward to Paris. Papa has promised to replace Fritz and I am sure I will make new friends. Papa also said he would show us around."

"Well, it won't be long now, just a couple more hours," said his mother.

The long wait at home had become unbearable to Sigmund and so he headed to the station, arriving there with time to spare. Standing at the meeting place they had agreed on, he gazed impatiently down the empty track. Nothing. Suddenly in the distance, he saw the lights of the approaching train. Here they come. He made his way slowly toward the platform and saw them as soon as they got off the train. He waved. Freddy was the first to see him and waved back. They quickened their pace. Sigmund gave them a big hug and then, taking Helene by the arm, and with his son walking head held high by his side, led them out on to the street.

Freddy was amazed at how busy the station was and commented on it. His father explained that this was the only station in Paris from where trains departed to all corners of the country and that at this time of day it was busier than ever, for a lot of people commuted from the little towns surrounding the capital.

They had a long wait for a cab and Sigmund was becoming impatient. "This queue is so long, we should take the metro," he mused out loud.

"Are you referring to the underground?" asked Helene.

"Yes," he replied, but then if we took it, you would not see anything. Helene agreed with him and they decided to leave the metro for another occasion. While waiting, they vividly described all they had been through. When their turn finally came, they got into a rundown looking cab. Helene arched an eyebrow and Sigmund understood the meaning immediately. He shrugged his shoulders and then said, "Do not forget, this is Paris."

They left the heart of the city and were soon in what looked like a very nice residential, upscale neighbourhood. *I could live here,* she thought, and was about to say something when the cab pulled up in front of one of the houses she had been admiring.

"Welcome home," said Sigmund, opening the front door. He showed them around. The house had a similar layout to their home in Frankfurt but on a smaller scale. Both Freddy and Helene liked what they saw.

"You have gone to a lot of trouble," said Helene.

"Yes," admitted Sigmund, "it was not easy finding what I had in mind."

"I am sure we will all be happy here," said Helene.

"It reminds me a lot of the home we just left," said Freddy.

"Well," replied his father, beaming, "that was the idea. Come, Freddy, let me show you to your room."

They took the stairs two at a time. His window looked out onto the garden. "I remember how much you enjoyed watching and listening to the birds," said his father.

"Thank you, Papa." Just then, Freddy looked over at his desk and saw the cage. He walked towards it. "Papa!" he exclaimed excitedly. "I know it's not Fritz but I am sure you will become good friends."

"You have thought of everything," said Helene, admiringly.

"I tried. I want all of us to be happy here since we are starting a new life. Come, let me show you our bedroom." On the way, he stopped to show her the sewing room.

"It is amazing how fast you were able to furnish it."

"It took time and a lot of prodding, but I only chose the basics. You still have to put in your personal touches to make it really home," he said.

The master bedroom was a very good size as well, even though it was a little smaller than the last one, but it faced south and had big windows. "It is a very cheerful room," said Helene. "Why, Sigmund," she said, noticing the vase of red roses on her night table. "I did not know—"

He did not let her finish her sentence. "There are some qualities of mine you have not yet discovered," he said. "I do have to keep them hidden to protect myself." She laughed and he pulled her into his arms and whispered in her ear, "I have missed you so much. I hope we will never have to be separated again."

"I hope so, too," said Helene.

"But," said Sigmund. "We were not far from each other, for we were both working towards the same goal and I am very proud of both you and Freddy. You have proven to me that you can be strong, which comforts me for should I no longer be one day, I know that you will get on with your life," said Sigmund.

Just then, Freddy walked into the room. "And you, Freddy," said his father, turning to him, "have shown me that you are not only very mature for your age but that you can stand your ground."

Freddy beamed with pleasure. "Papa, could I have some writing paper and a pen?"

"Don't you want to unpack first?" his mother asked.

"I have done so already and since I was not allowed to say good-bye to my friends, I would like to write at least Helmut a note. You do not mind if I invite him to come visit, do you Mama?"

"Not at all, not at all," replied Helene. Sigmund handed him what he had requested.

"Thanks, Papa."

"We will be leaving to go for dinner in half an hour, that should give you plenty of time."

"I won't make you wait."

Sigmund took them to a bistro located on the main avenue. As they walked along, he explained that their neighbourhood was called Passy and was well connected to the centre of Paris by two tramlines and of course the Metro. Then, turning to Freddy and pointing at a two-story building, he said, "This is your school."

"It is even closer than the one in Frankfurt," Freddy remarked.

"I have already enrolled you and you will start on Monday."

"Is it a German school?"

"Why, Freddy, of course not," replied his mother. "It's a French public school so everything is taught in French."

"And will I manage?" he asked.

"I have already found someone who will give you lessons. As a matter of fact, I have scheduled your first lesson for tomorrow afternoon and I am sure you will be speaking it fluently in no time. I have also arranged for Mr Bernard to teach us as well," said Sigmund.

Helene nodded her head and inquired how he had heard about him. The real estate agent recommended him. "There are a lot of foreigners living in this part of town, it is supposed to be quite international," said Sigmund.

Helene liked the bistro. It was small and quaint and so conveniently located. They were given a table by the window and just as her husband had foreseen, she fully enjoyed watching the comings and goings, commenting on how well people dressed.

"Just wait until I take you to the Champs Elysee, this is nothing in comparison," said Sigmund.

Before going to bed, Freddy asked his father if he would mail his letter for him. "We'll do it together on our way into town tomorrow and I will show you the post office since I am sure you will be paying it quite a few visits." Freddy nodded, and as he lay in bed, he went over the events of the last couple of days in his mind. Frankfurt seemed so far away and yet they had only been gone two days. *One sure can get a lot done in one day if one chooses to,* was his last thought before drifting off to sleep.

In contrast, Helmut's days had been long and boring. He refrained from walking past Freddy's house, the encounter frightened him and his gut feeling told him to keep away. His friend vanished from the face of the earth leaving no address or phone number and it was very hard for him to assimilate. How could someone simply disappear? He discussed the issue with his mother, who had not been the least surprised. So many of the Jewish families who had been their neighbours for years and years went abroad.

"If I were in their shoes and had their money, I would have left a long time ago. How I wish we could also move somewhere else," she complained bitterly. "These Nazis are only creating havoc, not only for the foreigners and Jews but for us as well. Ever since your father joined the Party, he is never home and it's intruding indirectly on our family life. Nothing is more important than serving the Party and attending their never-ending meetings." Helmut listened to her patiently, though he'd heard all this before.

"Maybe if we ever hear from Freddy we might be able to go join him," said Helmut.

"Join them? Are you out of your mind, child? They have probably gone to America. We barely have enough to eat and here you are talking about travelling. Wake up and look around you, Helmut. Stop behaving and dreaming as if you were in the same league as your well-to-do friends, for you are not. To get it straight, we do not belong among the elite of this country, we are the working class…yes, the ones who suffer when prices go up, who depend on a salary, the ones living in fear of losing their jobs. And let me tell you, Helmut," Martha said vehemently, "you will never hear from that rich friend of yours ever again, mark my words."

Helmut shrugged his shoulders and held his tongue, no use getting in to a discussion with his mother about Freddy. He sneaked away as soon as he could and went to his room. He felt sad. His mother had changed so much in the last couple of years. Nothing pleased her any more. The last time they were out on the farm visiting the grandparents, he overheard them say that she was turning old and bitter. He had turned to his mother for a word of comfort and was told off instead. Vivid recollections of when things had been otherwise came back to him, the times when she had been sweet and loving and listened patiently, pointing out the positive side of things. Now there was only anger and resentment in her.

He was certain his father was mostly to blame and Helmut wished he could do something about it, but his hands were tied. He started despising his father and had a lot of trouble hiding it, therefore avoiding him as much as possible. In the serenity of his room, he got out his writing pad and began a letter to his friend. His mother was wrong, one day he would hear from Freddy and in the meantime, he would save it until he received an address. He wrote about his sadness, his loneliness, about how Fritz had given him a ray of hope that his chum would someday be back, even if it were only to pick up his pet. He also mentioned the stranger who questioned him about Freddy's family whereabouts. He reread what he'd written and felt as if he was now relieved of a very big burden. The comfort and understanding he looked for in his mother that had been denied him he now found in the solace of writing. Paper could not talk back and hurt him. He resolved from now on to keep a kind of diary in which he wrote down whatever he felt he needed to share, thus withdrawing from his family even more.

One day upon returning home from school, he found a postmarked envelope on his desk and wondered whom could it be from as he had given up on Freddy a long time ago. He picked it up and looked at the stamps, then turned the envelope around and looked for a return address, of which there was none. *That is strange,* he thought, and tore it open. He took out a neatly folded sheet of paper, recognising the handwriting immediately.

He read avidly:

Dear Helmut,
Sorry I was unable to say good-bye to you. I hope you are doing well. I am living in Paris and I hope you will come and visit soon. I have started school, which is absolutely no fun whatsoever, everything is taught in French and I have had to take private lessons so there has not been much time for play. The school is within walking distance from our home and I have just made one friend. His name is Georges and not only is he very nice, but also very helpful to me. Paris is a great city, there is so much to do and see. I hope you will come soon, how about next weekend? By the way, my address is Villa Eugene Manuel Nr. 7 Rue Eugene Manuel,
Paris, France

Helmut took out his phone book and jotted down the address. The letter ended with Freddy asking him to please give kind regards to his parents and grandparents and, as an afterthought, asked whether he had been out to Bunny Hill recently. He was placing the letter back in its envelope when Martha walked into his room, unannounced.

"Who wrote you?" she inquired. "Surely not that rich kid."

"Yes, Mama, I told you I would hear from him and you were wrong, they did not move to America but to Paris. It is not that far and Freddy has written asking me to come visit."

"Why Paris?" Martha mused. "They must have family there."

"I do not know," replied Helmut. "But maybe I could—" His mother did not let him finish the sentence.

"No, Helmut, and don't start getting all kind of ideas in your head, you're going nowhere, do you understand?"

Her son gazed at her quietly. He knew from experience that it was no use pleading with her. The core of the issue was money and there was no way he could get around it. "I understand," he said. His mother walked out of the room without uttering a word and Helmut went to his desk and looked for the letter he had started some time back. He reread it, then added the latest developments.

Hitler had become Chancellor and everything changed. Both boys and girls were forced to join different leagues, or the Hitler Youth Organisation. Their free time was no longer theirs to dispose of. They were obliged to attend meetings that lasted forever as well as being forced to march in parades and sing patriotic songs at the top of their lungs for hours on end. Nothing was more important in life than the fatherland, and one had to devote oneself completely to it.

They were also sent out into the countryside. Freddy was lucky if his only problem was having to learn another language. The grownups were all complaining about a disruptive family life, about their children becoming raucous and disrespectful of what all family values stood for. It was not unusual for a couple of them to come home with broken bones or totally exhausted on any given weekend. Parents were losing their authority and the state seemed to have taken over. Helmut ended his letter by saying that at least he had a reason for being away from home, that if life at home had been unpleasant before, it had now become unbearable. Then he thanked his friend for the kind invitation, hoping he would understand that, for the time being, a trip to Paris was out of the question.

Chapter 30

Mr Bernard turned out to be a very dedicated teacher. Not only was he passionate about his work, but also anything that had to do with France. To put it mildly, France should be the axis around which the whole world revolved and French, not English, should have been the universal language.

He arrived right on time that Thursday afternoon, for he hated being late and wasting other people's time, well aware of the meaning of time and making it clear to his pupils from the very beginning. Unpunctuality was something he would not tolerate and as a consequence, he had no second thoughts about dropping a couple of gifted students who broke the golden rule, saying that life was too short for one to be annoyed and mortified and no amount of money was worth it.

Freddy listened, unable to take his eyes off his big moustache having never seen one quite like it. The ends, which were very long, curled up almost to his nostrils and when Mr Bernard smiled, his mouth formed one line all the way to his ears. Freddy, completely distracted by it, was no longer listening. His teacher cleared his throat loudly. Freddy looked up startled. "Now that I have your full attention again, young man, I want you to understand that even though I am fluent in German, that language is banned from this room. You are here to learn French and that is the language that will prevail at all times. Have I made myself clear?" Without waiting for a reply, he took a book with drawings out of his bag and with the tip of his pencil pointed out the different everyday items and said their names out loud. He had his student repeat each word several times until he pronounced them perfectly.

Some words were easy for Freddy, but some like frog, grenouille in French, was very hard for him and Mr Bernard sometimes had trouble keeping a straight face, just listening to the pronunciation and watching Freddy's expression. Once he had enough vocabulary, he proceeded to write them down for him. "Study this for the next lesson and copy it several times so that you learn the spelling," he said, bringing the lesson to an end.

Freddy was eager to learn. He worried about going to school on Monday and not understanding a word that was spoken, so as soon as his lesson was over, he asked his father if he could have one every day. Sigmund agreed without hesitation and Freddy really applied himself, not only taking his daily lesson but also forcing himself to read Le Figaro, even though he had to look up most of the words. Once he finished reading an article, which took him quite some time, he felt very proud of his accomplishment.

"Something good always comes out of something bad," Sigmund said to Helene who was sitting in the study with him. "Look at Freddy, he has matured so much."

"Yes," replied his wife. "And is he ever keen on learning the language now that he realises how valuable it is."

"What about you Helene, how do you feel?"

"I am contented, what else could I want? I have you and Freddy around me, nothing much has changed in that sense. I am adapting to the new environment and certainly, Mr Bernard with his lessons is adding his grain of salt. And you, Sigmund? Have you regretted your decision?"

Sigmund took his time answering the questions. He finally said, "No, I have not regretted my decision, how could I? After all, I had no choice. It has not been easy, but I am trying hard to adapt. Helene, you must understand, while my time was very much taken up finding us a place to live, I had a purpose. But now that everything seems to be falling into place, you yourself said that you are finding yourself with a lot of time on your hands, and so am I. I always thought that the day I no longer had to go to work I'd be able to do all those things I so often complained about not doing for lack of time, like devoting myself to reading and taking care of my investments, basically catching up. But somehow, now that I have the freedom, I find there is something lacking. I am no longer challenged," said Sigmund. "Do not worry, though, I know that eventually I, too, will find my way."

Helene made no comment but Sigmund's disclosure came as no surprise to her. She had been observing him and even though she consoled herself with the thought that time would take care of it all, deep down inside her she knew her husband would never come to terms with this new life. The circumstances had forced him into making a decision but his heart was still in Frankfurt. The knowledge saddened her and she, therefore, did not allow it to surface very often.

Freddy came home in high spirits from his first day at school. Everyone was very interested in this new addition to the class and he had been the centre of attention. Even though he could not make himself completely understood, the vocabulary Mr Bernard had taught him came in very handy and his classmates helped fill in the words he did not know.

The class itself was mixed and really small, all in all there were twenty students, more boys than girls. The teacher introduced him and he received a very warm welcome. A different atmosphere from that in his former school prevailed here, everyone was friendly and easy-going. Even the teachers he was introduced to had shown a genuine interest in him, asking him personal questions. "In this school, each subject is taught by a different teacher with one responsible for the whole class," Freddy explained.

"That is a change," said Helene.

"In Germany, all subjects are taught by the same teacher with the exception of sports."

"Tell us about your classmates, what are they like?"

Freddy thought for a minute. "I guess they are all French, with the exception of Georges." They spent the breaks together and in one of them, he confided to Freddy that his father had lived in Hamburg at some stage of his life and one of his ancestors way back was German. Nothing gave his father greater pleasure than being able to speak that guttural sounding tongue. He was sure that as soon as he told him about his new classmate, he would urge him to invite him over so that they might converse in his favourite language.

"What about Georges, does he speak German?" Sigmund asked.

"I am almost sure he does not speak it. He has a little knowledge of it, for when I would say a word in German, he would translate it into French."

"Yes," Helene began, "it is such a shame that once people migrate to another country, they usually choose to forget their native tongue. So many people could be bilingual, but instead they want to become part of that new culture and, surely not wanting to draw attention to themselves, allow themselves to be absorbed into the new society by acquiring sometimes a whole new identity."

"Well, that will not be our case," said Sigmund resolutely. "We will continue to speak German amongst ourselves. And I will make sure none of us ever forgets their background."

Georges was the youngest of a family of eleven and being the youngest, he was also quite spoiled. His father was a jeweller and silversmith and had continued with the family tradition. His own father had schooled him in every aspect, seeing to it that he make an apprenticeship, as well as studying German, in Hamburg where he spent six months. When his mentor passed away, he inherited the business, which was not only well regarded by the elite of the city but the provider for the most renowned stores. The quality of his work and his innovative designs had opened many a door to him, allowing him to give his family an upscale way a life in which money had never been an issue. He hoped that his youngest son would someday follow in his footsteps.

Yet, the depression had also taken its toll on France. People were watching their pennies and luxury items were no longer the top priority for the wealthy. With the rising unemployment rate and threat of fiscal collapse, the masses became more and more depressed and desperate, venting their rage and frustration at the state by staging a series of marches and strikes, each more menacing than the preceding one.

The more than twenty newspapers of different trends that circulated at the time had two things in common: their opposition to the government and their pervasive anti-Semitism, which had been enhanced by the appearance of *Mein Kampf*, published in French. There was no control or censorship on the news, which meant that anyone who had the means could control and influence it just by either funding or purchasing a newspaper and, needless to say, they were in abundance.

The political unrest taking place did not contribute to Sigmund finding his peace. On the contrary, it was like viewing a movie for a second time. The destitution of the right wing mayor of Paris in January 1934 caused a violent demonstration that vented its fury against the Assembly and the then Prime

Minister Daladier who was forced to resign. He was replaced by Gaston Doumergue who had been retired from public life and had therefore few enemies who could oppose him. With this move, some calm was restored.

Freddy and Georges soon became close friends. They not only walked to school together but spent most of their breaks together as well. Roland was another classmate who hung out with them. They liked him because, in contrast to them, he was quiet and subdued and yet his wonderful sense of humour always made them laugh.

Freddy adjusted to his new surroundings in no time and was happier than he had ever been. He missed his friends, especially Helmut with whom he corresponded regularly, but he found in Georges someone who shared his same interests. He had less leisure time than he'd had in Frankfurt, for he still had to take French lessons, but after a month of private tutoring, Sigmund enrolled him in the Berlitz School of Languages, which was a lot cheaper.

Mr Bernard was sorry to lose his gifted student. When first meeting the family, he hoped they would the ones who really valued his ability as a teacher as well as finding the stability he sought in his career, thinking these foreigners would be his source of income for a long time to come. However, this wishful thinking was shattered in a matter of seconds when, after just a month of daily lessons, Sigmund informed him that his services were no longer required.

Mr Bernard was stunned by the news, "But Monsieur," he said when he finally found his voice. "Even though your son has come a long way in such a short time, he still cannot hold his own."

"I am fully aware of it," replied Sigmund.

"If that is so, why have you made this decision?"

The silence that ensued could have been cut with a knife. Sigmund was not used to having his decisions questioned and he fought to control his flaring temper. "My son will continue his lessons at Berlitz," he replied icily.

"I should have known this was going to happen, that school is taking our livelihood away from us. There is no way I can compete with their prices. You do realise that you are paying for a completely different product, don't you? He will never find the personalised tutoring he's had with me and his progress will be hampered by those in the class who are not as gifted as he is."

"I am fully aware of it. But the issue has been resolved and there is nothing more to discuss," Sigmund said, showing him to the door.

Mr Bernard shook hands with him gracefully and said, "But should you not be satisfied, feel free to contact me. I harbour no ill feelings," he said, and without waiting for an answer or looking back, went on his way. He walked at a fast pace, seething with rage and frustration, but his mood gradually changed. Berlitz, or any other school of languages, would not have had second thoughts about hiring him, but he did not want to give up being his own boss and therefore his freedom. "One can't have one's cake and eat it, too," he mused. However, if things did not change in the near future, he might be forced to reconsider.

The daily price hikes were reflected in his living expenses and it had gotten to the point where he was barely earning enough to cover them. His only hope rested among the growing numbers of foreigners who were streaming into the country, that there would be a couple who appreciated his product and would turn their backs on Berlitz. His students were usually referred to him by word of mouth but it had been some time since he'd had a referral and as much as he disliked the idea of taking money out of his savings, he decided the time had come to advertise his services.

A few weeks later, Helene was glancing through the classified section of Le Figaro when she stumbled upon the ad. Pointing it out to Sigmund, she said, "He really was a very good teacher, there is not one at Berlitz who—"

Her husband snapped at her. "And his rates were equally outstanding."

Helene glanced at him in surprise. "Is something troubling you?" she asked sweetly.

"My call to Franz has gone unanswered, again!"

"I am sure everything is fine, maybe something unforeseen happened," said Helene.

"Maybe," replied Sigmund. "But I doubt it." And without another word, he devoted his attention, or so it seemed, to his reading. He couldn't concentrate, unable to get Franz out of his mind. "I just hope my gut feeling is wrong," he spoke out loud.

"What did you say?" Helene asked, looking up from the newspaper.

"Nothing, Helene, nothing, just let me be," he said irritably.

His wife shook her head. She didn't want to admit it herself, but she found it very strange that Franz and his family had shown absolutely no sign of life. He promised to visit them in Paris, but he hadn't rung once to find out how they were doing. She thought she knew the reason and hoped vehemently she was wrong.

A couple of weeks later, Georges invited his new friend home. They went there directly after school and on the way, Georges gave Freddy a short description of each family member. "Here we are," said Georges, stopping in front of an impressive cast iron gate. He rang the bell and one of his sisters came running down the steps to open it. "This is Liza," he said, introducing them.

"I thought I was never going to meet you," she said to Freddy.

"One has to be patient, that I know, and you prove it to me more and more that this is not one of your virtues," said her brother teasingly.

She gave him one of her looks and said, "You might be in for a surprise someday, but come on, let's join the others."

They followed her into the house through the living and dining rooms and into the kitchen. Freddy could not believe his eyes. The rooms were huge. Georges leaned down to kiss his mother who was sitting in a chair near the kitchen table. She seemed very frail. His friend introduced them but when she looked up, Freddy noticed her eyes were closed. He thought that was strange but he decided to mind his manners and not ask any questions.

She sent them off to clean up before sitting down to eat. Once they were out of earshot, his friend told him that his mother was blind, forgetting to mention it when describing his family. According to his father, she'd had the most beautiful blue eyes in the world, they were the colour of a cloudless sky and changed according to her moods. Those eyes that had so bewitched him had fallen prey to glaucoma. His father spent enormous amounts of money taking her to several specialists but none could restore her eyesight.

"All this happened before my time," said Georges.

"It must have been a very difficult time for your mother, as well as the rest of the family."

"I'm sure it was, but it surely brought them closer and none of us allows mother to feel she is a liability to any of us. She may be blind but she can recognise our footsteps and does not need to be told who is entering the room. It really is quite amazing when you think how one sense, like hearing in this case, can become more developed to take over some of the other functions."

Georges showed Freddy briefly his room. It was about three times the size of that of his. "You can almost play football in here," he said admiringly.

"Not quite," then he heard his sister's voice calling. "We're coming!" he screamed back. "We better hurry. Dad's probably just come back and is waiting."

They rushed down the stairs and into the kitchen just in time to overhear Georges' father say, "I wonder what's keeping Georges and his friend so long."

"Here we are," said Georges, and introduced Freddy, who greeted him in German. Georges' father gave Freddy a huge smile and in fluent German asked him to have a seat beside him, taking an immediate liking to him. He asked him about his family and his life in Germany and they both got so absorbed in their conversation that they forgot about everybody else. Georges' father delighted in sharing some of the experiences he had when he lived in Hamburg and told a few anecdotes that were so funny that Freddy had trouble keeping a straight face, once he even burst out laughing. Their conversation was interrupted when the maid began clearing the dishes and Georges managed to get a word in before his friend had to reply to another one of his father's questions.

Georges' mother turned her face towards her husband, sensing that both Freddy and Georges were becoming impatient. She cleared her throat several times before catching her husband's attention and Georges' father finally got the hint. "I hope I have not bored you too much with my stories," he said. "It is just so nice having somebody who can speak the language I learned to love so much. And please, Freddy, please feel free to come over anytime. I would be quite honoured if you were to consider me as one of your friends."

"It is I who consider it an honour, sir," he said. "And you can count on it, I shall return."

Georges' father took his hand in his and said while shaking it, "Your parents must be very proud of you, you are a fine young man indeed."

Freddy blushed to the roots of his hair but the meeting marked the beginning of a friendship that would permit both parties not only to reminisce over past times but also discuss history, for both shared that same passion.

Freddy wasn't aware of how much he missed being able to speak in his mother tongue or how much effort went into his speaking that foreign language. He did become more fluent in it, although he still had to search for words and translate them from one language to the other, which was at times very frustrating.

Once dismissed, they went up to Georges' room. "It has been a long time since I've seen my father so communicative," said his son. "Your visit has done him a world of good since he lives for his work and is a loner."

"My father used to be the same way," said Freddy. "But ever since we moved to Paris, he seems to have lost interest in his books and in life in general, time hangs heavily on his hands and it is so unlike him to be idle."

Georges could sense his friend's sadness and worry. "You have not been here long, you know, for you it is easier since you have school to attend to so, like it or not, you have had to adapt. I am sure that if you give him time, you will see a change in him for the better."

"I hope you are right," replied Freddy. "Speaking of parents, I think I should be heading home now." Georges walked him to the door and on their way, they stopped by the living room to say goodbye to his mother.

"Do come back anytime," she said, shaking his hand. She was so petite and frail and yet her grip was so firm and strong. Freddy was happy, whistling on his way home, totally unprepared for the upheaval he encountered as soon as he let himself in.

Chapter 31

"We are broke, Helene," he heard his father say. "Broke, broke, all the hard earned money my father left and I worked so hard to increase and preserve is gone, gone, and not a penny left."

"But Sigmund, not all of it has vanished…"

"Helene, don't you understand?"

Freddy took a deep breath and stood in the doorway, trying to grasp the meaning of the words he was hearing. "We are no longer rich, we are poor." Freddy walked to his room, set his bag of books down on the desk and stood by the window looking out on to the garden. If everything has been lost, and we have no money, we will not be able to keep this house and we will have to move. But how had it happened? He remembered his father mentioning several times that he was unable to contact Franz. Did his friend betray him? Did he make off with their money and break his father's trust? He wondered.

He heard footsteps on the stairs and his mother's voice saying, "Freddy should have been home by now."

"I am home, Mama," he said, coming towards her. "I got back some time ago."

"So, you know," said Helene, her voice quivering.

Freddy cast his eyes down. "Yes, Mama, you and Papa were practically screaming at each other when I walked in."

"I might as well tell you, no use keeping it from you, we are as poor as church mice. No, that may be a little exaggeration, but Papa's investments, the ones he had given to Franz to manage for him, are not even worth the paper they are written on." Freddy could not make heads or tails out of what she was saying. His mother took no notice of it and rattled on. "Our fortune invested in bonds is worthless."

"Helene, that is enough," said Sigmund. "I will explain the situation to Freddy," he said.

"Go right ahead, I guess you believe I will not do you justice," she snapped.

"Mama," said Freddy. "Why don't we leave this discussion for later? I have a lot of homework to do and I would like to get it done before dinner," he said, hoping that by then his parents would have calmed down.

"I think that is an excellent idea," said his father. "When you have finished, come down to the study. I will be there reading."

Freddy sat down at his desk, forcing himself to concentrate. When he finally finished his work, he let out a big sigh. The house was quiet and to his relief, there were no further outbursts of anger.

Sigmund was sitting behind his desk staring into space when his son walked in. "All done?" he asked. Freddy nodded his head and pulled out the chair opposite his father's desk. Sigmund went straight to the point. "I heard your mother say we were as poor as church mice and that is not true," he said. "The truth is that the money I loaned to the different entities has been lost and these bonds made up most of my portfolio. Yes," he repeated more for his benefit than for that of his listener, "I invested in high yield bonds, which also are high risk, looking for a good return on the money, for we needed the income to live on. I have no one other than myself and Franz to blame. As you know, I have been trying to reach him and when I finally did some days ago, I asked him to sell the bonds and wire out the money. Today he rang to tell me that my holdings were worthless and there was no cash to be wired out. As you can imagine, I was speechless and could not believe it. When I finally found my voice to ask the reason for this, he said that everyone has defaulted on their payments due to the depression. In other words, everyone went bust."

"Why do you blame Franz?"

"Because had I been able to speak to him earlier, as you know I have been chasing after him for the past two months, I could have instructed him sooner. And maybe—"

"Papa, I do not believe that would have made a difference." Sigmund looked at him thoughtfully.

"You know, I broke the golden rule and I hope you learn from this, Freddy, for it will be up to you someday to remake the family fortune and I know you will succeed. I doubt I will live long enough to see it, though. Now, coming back to the present, I did set some of the money I received when I sold the business aside. It is not much, but it will allow us to lead a modest life. We will of course have to move, for we can no longer afford the rent, but we will find something in this same neighbourhood so you will not have to change schools or give up your friends."

"Thanks, Papa, and I will see what I can do to help out."

"That is not necessary," replied his father. "Just study hard and think twice before you spend your allowance as you will be receiving the same sum."

"Thanks, Papa, that is very generous of you."

"I hope you learn from my mistakes," said his father, putting an end to the conversation.

That night as Freddy lay in bed, he thought of different ways he might be able to earn some money to help out. Life sure does change in minutes and his had certainly undergone a lot of changes. Frankfurt... Paris... His family had been well to do and now they were poor. His thoughts went back to Helmut. He had not given up hope that he would come visit someday but Helmut's latest letter had not sounded too cheerful, either. His life had not changed that much in comparison. His parents were still together his father had to give up drinking due

261

to the circumstances, which had taken some of the sting out of his parent's relationship. But, like all his former classmates, he was obliged to join the Hitler Youth Organisation and every minute of his life was scheduled for him, from the time he woke up until he went to bed. Freddy dropped off to sleep feeling very blessed indeed. They might be poor, but he was free, free to do as he pleased in his spare time.

That was probably worth far more than all the money in the world.

Neither Helene nor Sigmund could fall asleep. They tossed and turned in bed, each ignoring the other for fear of unleashing yet another argument. Sigmund was very hard on himself. It was his entire fault. Greed…greed…greed… How often had his father, God bless him, drilled into him 'the higher the reward, the higher the risk'? But that was not the only reason, it was the whole economic downturn and some had just taken advantage of the situation and defaulted on their debts, plainly ignoring the commitments they had made, leaving a lot of people in misery. He was one of the lucky ones, at least he had not placed all his eggs in the same basket and even if he had lost the money he had invested in bonds, it had not ended up in Hitler's arcs. He repeated this thought out loud.

"That is a nice consolation," said Helene. "What about Franz?"

"What about him? There is nothing he can do now. I was keeping an eye on those bonds, but it was too late. At least we did not lose it all. I still have some shares which are worth practically nothing or very little right now but might increase in value if the world economy picks up."

"So, being practical," said Helene, "what have we got?"

"We are not as poor as church mice as you told Freddy," he answered with a sneer. "But Freddy really impressed me tonight, I have to say. He acted so mature, listening calmly to what I had to tell him and then saying he would try to find a job to help out with his expenses."

Helene did not answer and when he looked over at her, he saw that she was fast asleep. Watching her, he felt a wave of tenderness overcome him. *She has been a very good wife and mother and we have lived through so much together,* he thought. *And despite the age difference, which was now becoming more evident, we are still very much in love with each other, which explains why we continue to look in the same direction. For was that not what love was all about?* He leaned over her, gently kissed her forehead and, feeling at peace with himself, fell asleep.

The next morning, he woke up early, his dream fresh in his mind. He had dreamed of Nellie. Even though he knew from her letters she was happy and well, he missed her. In his dream, he decided to travel to Colombia to see her but something came up that obliged him to change his plans every time. With each postponement, his yearning for her grew until it became almost unbearable. He wondered if it was meant for him to leave this life without ever seeing his daughter. Was it a premonition? He did not allow his mind to dwell on it for long, it was too painful and there were some matters that required his immediate attention, like finding a less expensive place to live.

Freddy was eating breakfast and reading the classified section of the newspaper when his father walked in. "You are up early son, any special reason?"

"No, no, I just wanted to share something with you," said Freddy, then told him about Helmut's situation.

"You are so right, Freddy, money is just a tool that allows one to live a more comfortable life, but as you have just said, it cannot buy it all. Freedom of movement, freedom of expression and thought can never be bought. The world is changing, Freddy. I have been following what is going on in Germany very closely, times are uncertain and civil liberties are being threatened. We ran away from the dangers Germany was posing on us but I sometimes ask myself if the Nazis will not try to recover all the territory that Germany not only lost during the war but was forced to give up. Time will tell. At least we are safe for now. France has not only been good to us but to so many who are in the same situation." Freddy looked at his watch. "You had better hurry," he heard his father say, as he rushed out of the room.

Sigmund sat at the table lost in thought. Had he made the right decision by not following Abraham to Colombia? The thought pained him, for as time went by, he realised more and more that he had indeed made the wrong choice. *One has to be practical,* he chided himself, *what's done is done and there is no going back...* Or was there? Perhaps there might have been, but now, with his economic situation being what it was, he shook his head and reached for the newspaper then scanned through the news, as usual, before looking at the rental section.

There were quite a few properties listed that might be suitable. After making the appointments, he sat down and wrote his landlord, advising him that the lease agreement would not be renewed and was sealing the envelope when Helene walked in. "Don't you think he might come down with the rent knowing he has such good tenants?"

"I doubt it, however it is worth a try, even though there are few properties of this quality out there and the demand is rising daily with the influx of foreigners seeking refuge," he said, walking towards the phone. But he received the reply he expected. He was indeed sorry to lose them, but no, it was the only income he had and he had to live on it, as Sigmund was surely aware with the cost of living rising practically daily, there was no way he could lower the rent. He said he hoped they would find something suitable for less money, but the only thing he could do was release them from the lease as soon as they found something.

"Well, that is at least something," said Helene.

"Yes, it only proves what I said before, that he is not doing us a favour and as a good businessman he will undoubtedly raise the rent, knowing he won't have any trouble finding a tenant. But I must be leaving. I do not want to be late."

"I am coming with you," said Helene. "I will just get my purse." She was back in no time and, seeing the look of surprise on her husband's face, she said, taking his arm, "We are a team. You know it really does not matter much where we live as long as we can all be together."

"I agree with you," said Sigmund, "but there is always one that is absent and I miss her so much." He was about to share his dream with her but changed his mind; it did not feel like the right time.

The agent was expecting them. Since they were looking at properties in just one neighbourhood, they only had to deal with one agency. The properties were all within walking distance of each other but they did not waste time looking at the first one for it was a ground floor flat. Sigmund showed his impatience, as he had been quite specific about his requirements. The agent said he had only three properties that might be suitable and they chose the third one. It was the best they had seen, even though, as Helene would later describe it to Freddy, it was dark and overlooked an inner courtyard, but it was just a block away from Freddy's school and the rent was within Sigmund's price range. It was also available immediately.

Helene felt a huge knot in her throat as she waited for the lease to be drawn up. It seemed to her as if she were on a downhill spiral. The flat they had just taken was dark, the bedrooms were small, the kitchen was old. At least the reception was a normal size and Sigmund did have a study where he could enjoy his books, even though it was a lot smaller than the one he had now. There was no sewing room or place she could call her own. Sigmund watched her out of the corner of his eye and knew exactly what was going on in her little head, then silently took her hand in his. She felt her eyes fill with tears, which frustrated her even more because she wanted to be strong, and she did not want her husband to know how much the whole situation hurt her, but it was all in vain. He could read her like an open book.

The agent interrupted their thoughts. The lease is ready. Sigmund reviewed it, they signed it and would be able to move into their new home in two weeks' time. They walked out the door without saying a word to each other then stopped for coffee and cake along the way.

"It is not what it is, it is what one makes of it," said Helene, breaking the silence. "And I intend to make the nicest home we have ever had out of it."

Sigmund smiled, reassured. "I am sure you will succeed and we will all help."

When Freddy arrived home from school, he found both his parents in the process of sorting out their clothes. "We have found a new home," said his mother. "It is just around the corner from your school."

"That is wonderful. I will be able to sleep a little longer. What is it like?"

"You will see for yourself. It is certainly not the nicest flat but I will endeavour to make it the happiest home we have ever had," said Helene.

"So when are we moving?"

"Exactly two weeks from today, which should give us ample time. I thought you might want to see it so I made an appointment with the agent. If you are ready, we can leave now," said Sigmund.

"How thoughtful of you, Dad, I'll be ready in two minutes."

Helene watched them leave. What would Freddy's reaction be? She'd felt sad and sorry for herself at first, then she suddenly realised she had to be strong and supportive to her husband, not a burden. Ever since leaving Frankfurt, he received blow after blow. Paris was not what he had dreamed of and now with the economic worries and his longing for Nellie… He had aged so much, so fast.

Adele, Helene's youngest sister, who had finally left Germany and moved to Paris, was shocked when she saw him.

"Is Sigmund sick?" she asked when she was able to have a moment alone with her sister.

"No, not to my knowledge, he has not complained about anything ailing him, but maybe it is time for him to have a check-up," said Helene.

That conversation had taken place a few weeks before and she made a mental note to bring up the subject, but it completely slipped her mind and she would now make a point of saying something to him as soon as he returned.

The agent was standing outside waiting for them when they arrived. Freddy followed his father up the two flights of stairs without saying a word. As soon as the agent opened the door, Freddy's worse fears were confirmed. The flat did not face the street but onto an inner courtyard, making it very dark.

"Do you like it?" Sigmund asked.

"Yes, Dad, it's fine. I spend most of my time in school anyway. Mama is going to make new curtains so once it has all our personal belongings, it should be very cosy."

"All it needs is some colour and warmth," said the agent. On their way home, they walked past Freddy's school, which was just around the corner. "This is fantastic, Dad," he exclaimed. "It's almost as if I were living at school. I can probably get up half an hour later than I do now."

"And?" Helene asked. "What did you think of our new home?"

"It will be very nice once you add your personal touch to it, but the best thing about it is that I do not have to get up so early," he said happily.

Later on that evening, Helene brought up the subject of her husband's health. There was no reason for him to go see a doctor, he said, but Helene insisted, saying he had not had a check-up since they left Frankfurt. Sigmund was adamant, he was fine and had never felt better. There was nothing for her to worry about.

When Freddy was at the neighbourhood grocery store buying some sweets, he noticed a help wanted sign that read: Delivery boy with bicycle required. He got a bike after Aunt Adele had given him the money for one on his last birthday. Trying hard to conceal his excitement, he asked to speak to the manager. Unfortunately, he had already left for the day but the person he was talking to introduced himself as his assistant and told him they were looking for someone who could work from four to six in the evening, five days a week as well as Saturday mornings. He could not tell him what the pay was but if he was interested, he could fill out an application form. Freddy did so immediately and decided he would not say a word to his parents until he had the job.

The next day, he could hardly wait for school to be over to hear the outcome. The owner interviewed him personally and asked if he could start work that very day. Freddy was thrilled to death: His very first job! He did not think twice and told his boss he would be back with his bicycle in half an hour.

His parents were having coffee with a slice of freshly baked cake that his mother had made. "You are just in time," said Sigmund.

"I can't stop. I have to leave right this minute."

"What's the hurry?" Helene asked. "You just walked in."

Freddy told them why and Sigmund said, "Well, you did not waste any time, son. I am proud of you. But are you sure this will not interfere with your schoolwork?"

"No, Papa, I have it all figured out."

"Freddy," Sigmund interrupted him. "Your education is far more important to us than any millions you might earn."

"I know, Papa, trust me, I know that I can spare the time." Then he gave them each a kiss and left.

"Brings back memories of Nellie when she found her first job," said Sigmund, talking to Helene.

"Freddy is growing up," she said. "All these circumstances are helping to make a man out of him and that is very important."

"God only knows what the future has in store for us," said Sigmund. He then added grimly: "Especially for you and him, for one of these days I will be gone and there will be just the two of you, and Nellie of course. Freddy will have to look after you."

"Oh, Sigmund, that day is really in the very distant future."

"I hope it is, but one never knows." Noticing she was about to say something, he cut her short. "Helene, let's not discuss this any further. I was only stating the obvious, that is all."

Freddy was pleased with the way things had turned out. His employer accepted his terms and he would work every day from five to eight in the evenings and Saturday mornings. When he returned to the shop, his deliveries were waiting for him. He placed the bags in the basket on the front of his bicycle and, after taking note of the address, set off. His boss watched him leave. The new delivery lad was not only smart but had lots of charm, which would surely captivate most of his clientele made up of mainly elderly ladies. Due to the difficult times they were facing, maids were a luxury very few could afford and thus they came to rely on their groceries being delivered. He smiled, thinking that it would not surprise him if he did not get a few more clients, and he was not disappointed. Freddy's polite and friendly reputation soon spread and with it came new customers.

For his part, Freddy enjoyed his job. The ladies were nice and friendly and tipped him generously. One evening, something happened that was going to open a whole new world to him. It was his last delivery and his client was an elderly gentleman who, for some unknown reason, had taken a special interest in him. He always asked him about school, listening attentively, making a point of following up on the conversation the next time he saw him. That evening, he asked Freddy to come in and place the packages in the kitchen. "What a day it has been," said Freddy, rubbing his hands. "I am glad it is over. The weather is changing."

"I can tell you are cold. May I offer you a nice cup of hot chocolate?" the elderly man asked.

"Sure," said Freddy.

"Please, do sit down," he said, pulling out a chair for him.

Freddy did as he was told and soon a cup of hot chocolate topped with whipped cream was set down in front of him. "I am glad you are not in a rush as I have something I would like to show you, but I have not wanted to intrude on your time."

Freddy was about to reply but Mr Beraud, for that was the gentleman's name, held up a pair of tweezers with a piece of paper dangling from its tip and from his pocket he pulled out a magnifying glass. "This is a very rare stamp," he said. "Look at it through the glass to see those wonderful colours and the inscription on it."

"Yes," said Freddy, who had never taken any notice of stamps before, always thinking of them as pieces of paper one glued on an envelope to show that the postage had been paid.

"This is my hobby. I am a collector and have been collecting stamps for a great many years. One can collect by themes, by countries, etc. When I began, I decided I would specialise on just France."

"And have you?" Freddy asked.

"I did for a while, but now I have begun collecting stamps from all over Europe. It is really quite fascinating, there is so much involved. Would you like to view my album?"

"I sure would! I have never seen one."

Mr Beraud left the room to get it then returned with what looked like a leather bound book. His host took a lot of pride in showing it to him, pointing out the most important stamps. "Look, these here are new editions and these—look at the date on them. The older they are the more valuable they become. That's because there is only a limited edition printed and they soon become scarce. I mean by this that you can no longer find them at the post office, so you can only buy them from other collectors."

"How do you get in touch with them?"

"That is a good question. In 1849, when the first French stamps appeared, people began collecting them and schoolboys and others would meet in the gardens of the Palais Royale to swap them. This was the beginning of the first stamp market. People met there regularly on Thursdays and Saturdays and sometimes there were up to 400 people. The Imperial Guards finally got fed up because there were so many complaints about thefts and so they were barred from the gardens."

"Where did they go?" Freddy asked, fascinated with the story.

"They went to the Luxembourg Gardens, but they were soon barred from there as well. In 1887, a rich landowner who was a passionate stamp collector gave the city of Paris a stretch of land with the condition that a stamp market be allowed there. It was called the Carre Marigny, just off the Champs Elysees, and this brings me to the reason for this conversation. You are an intelligent, reliable and honest young man and it is hard for me to get out and move around in the crowds. So, I was wondering if you would be kind enough to go there and buy some stamps for me. I will, of course, pay you for your time."

"I will be more than happy, sir, but it will have to be on Saturday afternoon. After I finish work, I will come by and pick up the list, if that is all right with you. But now you must excuse me for I do have to get some homework done," said Freddy, taking his leave.

"I will be expecting you," replied Mr Beraud, walking Freddy to the door.

His parents were already having dinner when he walked in. "Aren't we a little late?" his father asked. Freddy apologised and told them the reason. "Sounds very interesting, young man, at the rate you are going, it won't be long before you become the neighbourhood's courier," said Sigmund.

"I do not know about that Papa, but I am looking forward to seeing this market for myself."

As soon as he finished work on Saturday, he went to Mr Beraud's who handed him the list, some money and warned him of pickpockets. Freddy did not know what to expect and was overwhelmed by the amount of people. The dealers had their stands lining the walkway and although Freddy was in no hurry, he was pushed forward by the crowd. Mr Beraud had given him a name and a stall number and soon he found it and handed the dealer the list. While he waited, he looked around. When the dealer handed him the envelope with the stamps he asked for, Freddy asked him which was the most valuable stamp he had. He thought for a moment and showed him a very beautiful stamp bearing the date 1896. "What makes it so valuable?" asked Freddy.

"Well, it's the age on one hand and the colours on the other. There are very few stamps that have the colour green in them."

Freddy thought for a minute. He had received his pay for the week that morning and made the dealer an offer. "It's yours. I know you will be back for more," he said, placing the stamp in an envelope then handing it to him. "And take good care of it; it can only increase in value."

Freddy whistled happily on his way to the metro. It had been quite an afternoon. He stopped at Mr Beraud's who was keen on hearing Freddy's impression who immediately showed him the stamp he bought for himself. "That is a very rare and old one," he said admiringly. "Would you consider selling it?" Freddy thought for a moment then quoted him a price. Mr Beraud did not argue and gave him the money.

Chapter 32

While Freddy's life revolved around going to school, finding a way of earning a little extra money and adjusting to a more modest lifestyle, his friend Helmut was having to deal with issues he had never dreamed would come his way. With Hitler's rise to power, the Hitler Youth Movement had been founded. Belonging to it was voluntary but his father insisted Helmut join and he had obeyed against his better judgement. There was no time for leisure and any free time he had was taken up by either homework, which was usually a couple of hours' worth, or the Movement's activities, which were never-ending. The organisers had quite an imagination and they always came up with something new; if it weren't marching, it was learning a new song, or listening to the Party's philosophy for hours on end.

Upon President Hindenburg's death, Hitler had not only proclaimed himself president, but retained the title of chancellor as well. "At this rate, he might well become the Holy Trinity," whispered one of his friends, hearing the news over the radio.

Helmut shook his head, giggling, and looked around before speaking then said, "I am sure he will have no trouble adding a third title in the future." His friend made signs for him to mind his words and when Helmut looked around, he saw they were being observed by a small group of older students. One had to mind one's tongue these days, for any unfavourable remark overheard by the wrong person about the Führer could be reported and there were all kinds of methods of punishment to deal with this grave offense.

So much had changed and yet he was still better off than most of his Jewish friends and their families. They really were in big trouble. Fingers were being pointed at them, they were called dirty names and some of his classmates totally refused to have anything to do with them. Nowadays, most of his teachers ignored his fellow Jewish students. It had not been apparent at first, but as time went on, it became very obvious. The students were surprised at first and accepted it as part of their fate. Regardless, they still attended classes, kept to themselves and tried to maintain a low profile.

There was one exception and that was Mr Meier. He was in total disagreement with the Jews being discriminated against and he went out of his way to make them part of his classes. He was warned several times about his behaviour and one day, he did not show up for class. It was rumoured that one of the students denounced him and after being beaten up, they sent him to jail. Nobody heard anything about him since.

Just when one thought the situation could not get any worse for them, the Nuremberg Racial Laws came into effect. These laws redefined German citizenship and set about regulations for the protection of German blood and German honour. German citizenship could only belong to a German National or kindred blood. All Jews were defined as being not of German blood and it was forbidden for them to fly the German flag. The government made sure everyone was aware of these laws by broadcasting them over the radio. One could not tune into a radio station without hearing about them, making the headlines of the newspapers for several days and weeks. People were incited to denounce anyone who had anything to do with a Jew or any Jew who did not comply with the law.

Even though Helmut understood the words, he could not fully comprehend their meaning. He finally understood what they meant when he went to see his dentist. After ringing the doorbell, he walked up the stairs to the second floor. The door was open so he went in. The secretary was sitting behind her desk as usual. Nothing seemed out of the ordinary except that the waiting room was empty. She looked up at him sadly. "Is the doctor not in?" he asked.

"Yes, he's in."

"Good, my appointment is for five o'clock, is he on time?"

She looked at him, unable to speak. Just then the doctor appeared. "Why, Helmut, how nice to see you," Doctor Rott shook his hand.

"Are you ready for me?"

Dr Rott let out a deep sigh. He had known Helmut as a baby when his mother brought him with her, not having anyone to take care of him. He watched him grow up and develop into the fine young man he had become. "Is anything wrong?" Helmut asked.

Dr Rott cleared his throat. "I am so sorry, Helmut, but I am afraid you are going to have to go somewhere else. Under the new laws, I am not allowed to take care of Germans. I can only look after my own people."

Helmut did not utter a word; he just looked at him in disbelief until finally the words came and said, "I am so very sorry. I had not realised."

"I know," said Doctor Rott. "You have now understood the meaning."

Helmut shook hands with the doctor and his secretary and headed home with a heavy heart. He thought of Freddy and thanked God he was safe and did not have to face all this hardship. Did his father have a premonition or was it just fate? He would never know the answer. His mother shot him a concerned look as he took off his coat.

"Have you seen a ghost?" she asked. "You are as pale as a sheet."

"No," replied Helmut. "But I have now finally understood."

"What have you understood?"

"I will tell you over dinner." And he told his story. Peter blushed crimson red with embarrassment, for even though he was a member of the Nazi Party, it did not mean he agreed with everything it did. Quite the contrary, he had become more and more disappointed with it as time went by. The lies, the lack of credibility, but more than that, the cruelty with which they treated others was something that went completely against his values. He had been taught to be compassionate and humble, to honour and respect the Catholic Church, not to persecute and criticise all it stood for. Last but not least, he was taught to respect others, by not doing unto others what one did not wish others do unto one.

He watched one of his friends almost beaten to death because he criticised Hitler in a public place. Someone overheard the remark and took his friend Johan by the collar and flung him onto the stone floor. Had it not been for the fast reaction of his friends, he would not have survived the flogging. It happened some time ago, but the image was still engraved vividly in his mind. He turned to Helmut and said, "I have to set something straight, not only are they no longer German, but they can no longer work in their professions."

"So, if I understand correctly, this means that a lawyer can no longer represent his clients, an architect can no longer build a house and a doctor can no longer practice medicine."

"That is correct," replied Peter. "And if they do not heed the ban, they can be denounced. As citizens, we are obliged to denounce anyone who breaks the law."

"So how are they going to earn their living?"

"Well, Helmut, as you and I well know, the Jews are mostly very wealthy and I am sure they have a nice little nest egg saved up so they will not go hungry, trust me. And those who don't, well, they will just have to look for jobs like sweeping the streets and driving garbage trucks."

"Why this discrimination? Is not everyone born free and equal?"

"Germany, Helmut, belongs to the Germans. Jews are not Germans, they take our jobs, they take everything from us, they have no reason for being here, and if they choose to live here, they have to abide by the rules and trust me, nobody is keeping them here," said Peter.

"It is all so sad," said Martha. "I never thought I would live to see this."

"We have to go with the flow," said Peter. "So for God's sake, don't try and go against it, for you will get us all into very big trouble. Now, if you will excuse me, I have had enough of this conversation," and he pushed back his chair and left.

"Freddy is Jewish," said Helmut. "How lucky he is not to be here."

"He and many others," replied Martha.

"Hopefully, a lot more will be able to leave. You do not agree with Papa's political views, do you?" asked Helmut.

"No, I don't, just like I have not seen eye to eye with him on a lot of other issues," replied his mother bitterly.

"I have always been aware of that," replied Helmut, remembering the bitter fights he'd overheard. "Why do you stay with him then?"

His mother gave him a sad look. "I am a prisoner, I have no choice."

Helmut took her hand. "Mama, I will take care of you and one day, you will be free."

Martha smiled, deeply touched. "I know you will." He was her youngest and there had always been a sweetness about him, which made him very special and she fervently wished this would remain with him throughout these difficult and cruel times.

One night, Helmut was awakened by terrible screams and shouting of obscene words. He listened and found the noise coming from across the street. First, he sat up in bed then ran to the window. Yes, he was not wrong. The screams were coming from Nathan's house. Helmut stood there, petrified, for a moment and then went to his parent's room. Martha had also heard the noise. "It is Nathan," said Helmut. "I am going to go over and see."

"You are not going anywhere, young man," said his father in a stern voice. "It is none of our, or your, business."

"But he is my friend."

"I know," said Martha, feeling deeply for her son, since they had grown up together and he had taken Freddy's place in her heart. The shouting and screaming subsided. "Let's go back to bed," she said, walking Helmut to his room then tucking him in and gently closed the door behind her. Her husband was asleep, snoring as if he had not a care in the world. Martha looked at him with revulsion and muttered under her breath, "He has no heart, whatever heart he had, was taken from him a long time ago."

When Helmut walked into the neighbourhood bakery the following morning, it was abuzz with the events that had taken place the night before. Apparently, Nathan's little sister had fallen ill and was screaming with pain. Her parents took her to the hospital where, after being told under no uncertain terms that admission was for Germans only, they had had no choice but to return home with the now almost unconscious child. Nathan's father called a Jewish doctor friend who came by but one of the neighbours denounced him. The police came and took him and Nathan's father away. "And what about the girl?" somebody asked.

"Who cares?" said another.

Helmut noticed two women exchange glances, but wisely kept his opinions to himself then told his mother what he had heard. Martha dropped her head in her hands. "This is all so terrible!" she exclaimed. "You are learning the cruelties of life at such a young age," she said, taking her son's hand firmly in hers. "How I wish I could shield you from them."

"It is life, Mama, and we cannot change it."

Nathan was not at school that day but Helmut did not dare go over to his house for fear of unleashing even more trouble, and tried to catch a glimpse of him, but to no avail. The drapes were all drawn and there was not a soul around. A couple weeks later, Martha gave Helmut the good news: Nathan and his family had left. Helmut looked at her in disbelief. "And what about his sister and father?"

"They have all left," replied his mother. "How do you know?"

"I have my sources," said Martha. "I just wanted to set your mind at ease."

Helmut was overjoyed. God heard his prayers.

Life in Germany was definitely not static but was in continues turmoil instead. Things seemed to change overnight. Belonging to the Hitler Youth movement was now mandatory, and the Church Youth movement therefore lost all its influence. Helmut was now lectured on the purity of the German, so-called Aryan blood, and was introduced to a pagan cult exemplified by the slogan Blood and Soil, as well as being militarily trained. One day, as they were lining up, his classmate walked up to him and whispered in his ear, "I told you he would replace the Holy Trinity, remember?"

Helmut looked at him, slightly puzzled, then grinned and whispered: "President, Chancellor and Supreme Commander of the German Armed Forces."

Hitler had taken this title after obligatory military service was reinstated. Helmut had once complained to his father about the futility of all this and received a very harsh reply. "You should be proud being German. No amount of work or time the fatherland demands of you is excessive and you should go about it joyfully."

"You are a good example," said Helmut, unable to keep his tongue in check.

"What do you mean?"

"You've used all your influence to avoid doing your military service, which, as we both know, is compulsory."

He barely finished his sentence when his father's fits were upon him. "You bastard," he screamed in rage. "Who do you think you are?" And slapped him hard on the face.

Helmut looked at him defiantly and was about to answer something when his mother stormed in. "Let go of the boy," she said, stepping between them. Peter gave them both a dirty look and walked out of the house. Helmut had tears of rage in his eyes.

"What brought all this on?"

"He has two sets of values; one is to serve the fatherland with joy, he says, but what kind of an example is he?"

"He is no better than the rest of them," replied his mother. "But Helmut, you had better not forget, this is your father we are speaking about."

Helmut nodded his head. "How could I forget? Even if he does not behave like one, he will always be my father."

A couple of weeks after this incident, Peter left for the remilitarised zone. Helmut often wondered if his mother had her hand in it, but he wisely refrained from asking, knowing he would never be told the truth. During his absence, Martha regained some of her zest for life but it was of short duration for Peter returned after a month. "I take it you are not happy to see me," he said, after being given a cold welcome by his wife.

"I do not care one way or another," she replied, shrugging her shoulders. "Just keep out of my hair and everything will be fine."

"I will make sure I am sent somewhere as far away from you as possible," he said and, turning on his heels, disappeared into the night. He was true to his word. A week later, Martha walked into their bedroom and found him packing his bag.

"Leaving so soon?"

"Not soon enough for my taste," he replied.

"Where are you going?"

"I'm going to Austria."

"Austria?" she repeated. "What in God's name are you going to do in that country?"

"Stir up some trouble," came the reply.

Martha looked at him dumbfounded. "I do not understand," she said.

"That is just as well. I will probably be gone for a long time and you will most likely jump with joy as soon as the door closes behind me," he said sarcastically.

"I do not know about that, but at least—"

"At least what? Why don't you finish your sentence?"

"Oh, never mind, it's not even worth the effort."

Peter closed his bag and left without uttering another word, going straight to the meeting place as he was told and joining other high-ranking Party officials.

Secretly, Germany had been putting pressure on Austria to have closer links with Germany and now Austria had accepted. A couple of days after their arrival, an agreement between the two countries was signed and it was officially announced that Austria and Germany would not influence the internal policies of each other. Austria promised her policy would be based on the recognition that she was a German State. The Austrian Nazis, who were then in prison, were set free and two pro Austrian Nazis took their places in the cabinet. One was made Foreign Minister and the other Minister of the Interior with control over the police. The swastika emblem now flew from all public buildings. Austria had been annexed to Germany without the firing of a single shot.

Martha read about it in the newspapers. "No regard for human beings, no regard for borders? Nothing good is bound to come out of this," she said to herself out loud. She always wondered about her husband's position in the Party, but now her worse fears had been confirmed. He was a high-ranking official. She placed her head in her hands and asked herself what she had done to deserve such a fate, allowing her tears to flow freely. Suddenly, she dropped her hands in her lap and stood up. It was he who had denounced Nathan's father's friend, it was he... How could her husband have turned into such a monster? She would never know the answer. She felt sick to her stomach. "Dear Lord, please, please don't let him come back, please, dear Lord, keep him where he is," she prayed.

Chapter 33

True to her promise, Helene made their new home as cosy and cheerful as she possibly could. She sewed some curtains and made the colourful cushions herself, and although one could not hide the fact that the flat did not receive much light, it did have a homey feel about it.

She was in the kitchen putting away the breakfast dishes, since she had been forced to do away with the maid due to the circumstances, when she heard her husband curse loudly in no uncertain terms. Quickly setting the teapot, she was holding on the table, she ran to the study to see what the cause of his fury was. "Those pigs," he said. "Here, read this." And he thrust the morning newspaper into her hands.

Beneath the headline, *Nuremberg Racial Laws* was a sentence that read: *Nothing like the complete disinheritance of Jewish citizens has been heard of since medieval times.* Another headline caught Helene's eye and she read the article. The Jews in Bavaria had to turn in their passports and when they were returned to them, the word 'international' had been crossed out and replaced by the word 'national'. This meant their passports were no longer valid for international travel. Helene put down the paper with a pained expression.

"They are prisoners and patriots in their own country and will be murdered by their fellow countrymen," Sigmund said bitterly. "We are very blessed," said Helene.

"You can say that again. And your foolish sister, Adele, left just in time."

"I am sure she is counting her blessings today. I just can't believe this is happening," said Helene.

"Mark my words, there is worse to come," replied Sigmund.

"I am sure the Jewish community is up in arms," said Helene.

"I have no doubt about it," replied Sigmund. "But there is not much they can do. Those of us who managed to get out and seek refuge in a European country were smart, but the smartest were those who left Europe and migrated to the United States or Palestine. All those Jews who fought for Germany in the First World War, the families of those who gave their lives without hesitation for the fatherland, the prominent citizens who contributed so much in every field, their pain must be excruciating," he continued, trembling with anger.

Their conversation was interrupted by the sound of the doorbell. "I will get it," said Helene.

"Don't bother, I will go," said Sigmund, leaving the room. He returned with a huge smile on his face, holding an envelope in his hand. Helene did not need to be told…it was a letter from Nellie.

She wrote that she was well and happy and had been offered a job at the brewery as secretary, which she accepted. Now she would be earning enough money to pay the rent on a flat and had indeed found a small one bedroom, very well situated in the heart of the city. Abraham negotiated the rent for her, for he knew the owners, and just a week ago, she moved in to what she called her own little kingdom. She furnished it very simply but in good taste and every evening when she came home from work, she felt like a queen returning to her castle.

She also met a delightful young man who was Colombian and had asked her out on a date several times. She asked if there was any possibility her father would consider coming, for although she had thought about coming home, or Paris as she corrected herself, it was completely out of the question for the time being. How was Freddy doing? She recently received a letter from him telling her about his dealings in stamps and she enclosed some new editions for him, then ended the letter saying she missed them all very much but they should be happy to hear that she is well, safe and happy.

Sigmund placed the letter lovingly back into the envelope and turned his face away. Helene caught a glimpse of his tears and hugged him to her. "You miss her very much, don't you?"

"I do, Helene, and I fear I will never see her again."

"Why, Sigmund?"

"It is a premonition. I had a dream," which he then told her about.

"Dreams don't necessarily come true, you know."

"I know, Helene, but I believe I am right. Let us change the subject. Freddy will be home soon."

"I had better start preparing lunch," said Helene.

Ever so relieved to know his beloved daughter was safe, he wondered what that young Columbian man was like, then turned his attention back to the newspapers, but there was nothing but bad news.

Hitler had occupied the demilitarised zone and France reacted by sending troops to reinforce the border, but other than a little whimpering from France and Britain, nobody else raised their voices against it. Sigmund was sure that nobody outside Germany cared about the fate of the Jews. He asked himself what other policies Hitler would put into place without the international community challenging them.

Freddy was home and Sigmund could hear him talking to his mother, so he lay down the newspaper and went to join them. Freddy was very pleased with himself. Not only had he had a good day at school, but Mr Beraud recommended him highly to his friends and he was making more money off his stamp deals than he ever dreamt of.

"That is good," said Sigmund. "But tell us about your grades."

"No need to worry, Papa, trust me…you will be happy."

"I will believe it when I see it in black and white."

"Oh, come on, Sigmund, he hasn't let us down yet," said Helene.

"I am aware of that, but one never knows."

Freddy did not bother to answer. His father handed him Nellie's letter to read.

"What a shame we did not go to Colombia," he said. "We would have all been together, living in a big, beautiful house like the one Nellie lived in." But he did not get any further, for his mother shot him one of her 'that is enough' looks.

"Maybe things would have been different," said Sigmund sadly. "One makes choices and sometimes the choices one makes in good faith are not always the best," he added bitterly. "In the paper this morning, I read this quote from a famous German poet."

How easy it is to leave the fatherland,
How hard it is to find a second one.
Though it is better to leave the fatherland,
Than to be the target of hatred of the people.

"If I had known what I know today, we'd probably all be together," Sigmund lamented.

"Everything usually works out for the best," said Helene.

"These stamps are really beautiful!" Freddy exclaimed. "Maybe I can get someone interested in collecting Colombian stamps."

"I believe you are better off having your supplier close by," said his father. "From a business point of view, you do not want to be dependent on your sister and on the mail. It's just a thought."

"But someday," said Freddy, "someday."

"A lot of things can change," said Helene. "Right now lunch is served." And they all sat down to a hearty meal.

With Germany in breach of the Treaty of Versailles, her neighbours were feeling very much threatened and so increased their military capabilities. To Sigmund, it was clear and without a shadow of a doubt, at some stage this monster would have to be contained, the monster who was signing non-aggression pacts with some while breaking treaties with others, exporting agitators into neighbouring countries and looking to destabilise their governments in order to create satellite states as part of its expansion policy. But it sure did not look as if it would happen any time soon. Europe was as passive as a spectator watching the happenings on a stage.

Sigmund felt very bitter and tried to conceal his feeling, but sometimes they would surface in the remarks he made, upsetting Helene and those around him. She understood him. Her husband had been full of vitality but he'd lost everything; his business, his fortune and his friends. Yet, there were still his books and it was in these he found comfort, immersing himself in one for hours on end. Helene sometimes asked herself if it was his way of escaping the realities of life.

"I am worried about Freddy," Helene said to Sigmund one evening.

"Why? Is anything wrong with him? I have not noticed anything out of the ordinary; he is happy and very busy. You are probably seeing something," said his father.

"No, Sigmund, haven't you heard him coughing?"

"No, I have not."

"He has been coughing for the past three weeks. I have given him honey and cough drops, but it is not subsiding."

"He had better see the doctor."

"I mentioned it to him but he does not want to see one. He keeps reassuring me that it is just a cough, nothing to worry about."

"Helene, just make an appointment with the doctor for our own peace of mind. If not well-treated, a cough can turn into something serious," said Sigmund impatiently.

Helene was given an appointment for the next afternoon and that evening, not only did Freddy cough but he complained of chest pain.

"I should never have listened to you," said Helene in an anguished tone of voice. Her son had never been sick before.

"Mama, I promise you, it is nothing."

"The doctor will set our minds at ease tomorrow afternoon," said his mother.

"But Mama, I have plans."

"Well, you are going to have to cancel them," said his father.

"Your health comes first."

"Yes, Papa," he said, and he walked to his room.

Helene and Freddy returned from the doctor's visit with a heavy heart. He didn't like the sound of his cough and took samples of his sputum. Not wanting to alarm them by telling them his suspicions, he just said that Freddy had lost weight since the last time he had seen him and suggested he might want to stay home and rest for a couple of days.

"No, way, doctor, please understand, I do not feel sick and I have a lot to do."

The doctor, who knew his patient quite well, smiled then said, "Well, just go about your business as usual then until we get the results, which should be within the next couple of days." And he gave them an appointment for the following week.

Sigmund put down the book he was reading when they walked in. "I was not seeing visions," said Helene.

"It is a good thing you went, then, now all we can do is wait."

"By next week, my cough will be gone and it will all have been a waste of time and money," said Freddy. "And now, if you will excuse me, I have some deliveries to make."

"That boy," said Helene.

"The doctor said he's lost weight, which is not surprising with all the physical activity he does," replied Sigmund. "We're very lucky that he has always been in good health but then, you have always taken excellent care of us, even though we do sometimes take you for granted." Helene gave him her sweetest smile.

The doctor rang a couple of days later and said he had received the results and asked if they could come in to see him. This time, Sigmund went with them. The doctor did not beat around the bush.

"It looks like Freddy has tuberculosis."

Helene and Sigmund stared at each other in disbelief. "How can that be possible?"

"What is that?" Freddy asked.

"I have to take another sample to confirm, but the germs are there."

"Could you please elaborate?"

"It is an illness of the respiratory system, which is spread by coughing and sneezing. Mainly it affects the lungs, but it can also affect other parts of the body. It is caused by germs and one can really see them under the microscope," the doctor explained in a lecturing tone of voice, which reminded them that he was also an eminent professor at the faculty of medicine.

"How about taking a lung X-ray," asked Sigmund, "would that not be more precise?"

"No," replied the doctor, "they are more expensive and less accurate."

"So how sure are you that your diagnosis is correct?" Helene asked.

"Ninety percent," replied the doctor.

"Well, being practical, if the disease is curable, how does one treat it?" Sigmund inquired.

"It can be fully cured and actually a vaccine was developed in 1923 by a French bacteriologist, but due to all the controversy it created, it has not been introduced to the public."

"So what is our course of action?" Sigmund asked, becoming impatient with the doctor for not getting to the point.

"This young man needs to leave Paris and go someplace where he can breathe fresh mountain air. I will also prescribe some medicine for him to take."

"How long will it take for him to be completely cured?"

"Depending on the seriousness, it can take from six months to a couple of years. I will be able to give you a more precise time frame once I receive the results." Then he handed Sigmund a prescription and said as a warning, "Freddy should start taking this immediately. He must take it regularly without skipping a dose and he will need plenty of rest." They left the doctor's office in shock and before going home, they stopped at the pharmacy to have the prescription filled.

In the privacy of her room, Helene sat down and wept. When she finally calmed down, she went looking for her son. He was in his room talking to his father. She listened as Sigmund said that after they all had a good night's rest they would decide on a plan of action. Her eyes gave her away and Sigmund hastened her out of the room saying, "Freddy had some things to attend to."

As soon as his parents left him alone, he rang the grocery store to let them know that he was sick. The owner wished him a quick recovery and told him that his job would be waiting for him once he was well enough to return. "It will be hard to find a replacement for him, he is such a serious and dependable young man, I only hope he is not suffering from some severe illness," he said to one of his employees.

"All the little old ladies are going to miss him as well, he is so charming to them, to say nothing of Mr Beraud who did nothing else but sing his praises."

Freddy took the news in his stride. He did not feel sick but he was aware of the seriousness of his condition. Then his mother came in and he smiled at her reassuringly, seeing the worried look on her face. "Mama, I will get well, I promise to do everything the doctor tells me to."

Helene gave him a hug. "I have not a doubt in my mind. Here is your medicine," she said, handing him a glass of water and some pills. "I will be your nurse," she added, laughing.

"I could not wish for a nicer one," said Freddy. "What should I tell Georges? He is going to miss me at school tomorrow."

"Why don't you tell him the truth? You are sick and I am sure he has heard you coughing so he will not be surprised. You do not have to elaborate on what the doctor told you."

He rang his friend who said, "So, you've finally come to your senses and decided to stay home and take care of that cold of yours. It was high time."

Freddy laughed out loud. "You are beginning to sound like an old lady."

"I am not a lady, but I do have some experience, you know, after all, I am not an only child like you. I will keep you up to date with what we do in class," said Georges, "so you won't have that much to catch up with."

"That would be greatly appreciated," replied Freddy. Hanging up the phone he said to himself, "God only knows when I will return." The doctor had said something about fresh mountain air.

Were his parents going to follow the doctor's advice and if so, where would they send him?

Sigmund made several calls that evening. His son would have the best care money could buy. The next morning, he told Helene and Freddy the plan. They were to leave the following morning for Crans Montana in Switzerland. They both looked at him, bewildered.

"Are we not going to wait for the results?" Helene asked. "No," replied Sigmund firmly. "There is no time to waste."

"Are you coming with us?" they asked in one voice.

"No, I will stay here. Everything has been arranged."

"How long will I be away for?"

"A week will probably be adequate."

While they packed, Sigmund went to the train station to purchase the tickets. He was happy to get out of the house and be by himself. The sanatorium in Crans Montana had come to his mind when he heard Freddy's diagnosis. He and Alice visited the village one summer and had been struck by its beauty. The village owed its existence to the pure mountain air and there was not a doubt in his mind that Freddy would fully recover there. Fully aware it would cost him the last of his savings, he didn't care, his son had to have the best money could buy.

He hesitated at the ticket counter about the number of tickets to purchase but, although he would have loved to see that little village again and be at his wife's side when she left Freddy, upon hearing the price, he decided the money would be better spent on Freddy's health. As he walked home, he looked at his past. He had been able to afford every luxury, and now he had to watch very closely the little he had. Nothing had gone well for him since leaving Germany and it appeared as if Goddess Fortuna had turned her back on him. The next morning, he took his family to the train station. He held his son close to him for a long moment and then, trying hard to keep his emotions under control, watched with a heavy heart as the train slowly picked up speed and disappeared from sight.

Chapter 34

Freddy and Helene arrived at Crans Montana in the late afternoon. On the drive up the mountain, they enjoyed the fantastic views of the Rhone Valley below. The sun was setting and the lake in the distance glowed red. "What a beautiful drive," exclaimed Helene. The winding mountain road soon flattened out as they arrived at the plateau on which the village was located. Sigmund had referred to it as a village but it had since developed into a town. So many people were settled here, not only attracted by its reputation for pure, dry, dust free and low pollen content air, but by the various water and land sports its surroundings had to offer, both in summer and winter. It had developed into quite a touristy town.

"I believe I am going to like it here," said Freddy, as they drove through it. They saw a lot of quaint little restaurants and some very nice and expensive looking shops. Freddy even thought he spotted a sign that read 'buy new and used stamps'. He mentioned it to his mother excitedly. "I may be able to continue with my stamp dealings," he said.

"You might," she replied, "but remember your health comes first."

They stopped at the bed and breakfast Sigmund had reserved for her and it was just like he had described: Small, not luxurious but immaculate. The bed had a very inviting down duvet on it that was perfectly fluffed, and she was sure the pillows were also filled with down. It was just a block away from the clinic, hidden from it by very old and tall pine trees. She left her bag and they continued on their way.

They were expecting them. After registering, Freddy was shown to his room. It was small but it had everything he needed and from his window, he had a fine view of the mountains. "I hope you will not be too homesick," said the nurse. Freddy smiled. The fact that he was sick and would be staying here was just beginning to sink in. Helene helped him unpack. They had not quite finished when the doctor walked in. He introduced himself as Dr Wolf, was in his forties and had a very easy-going manner about him. He asked Freddy of his symptoms and Helene handed him the remittance letter Sigmund had picked up the day before. He read it carefully and then examined his teenage patient.

"We will get you well here, and you will be out enjoying all the outdoor sports in no time," he told him.

"Really?" Freddy asked.

"Yes, as long as you work with us. We are a team and our goal is to get you well so if you do as you are told, you will be up and running in no time."

The nurse came in and took some tests. Freddy hated needles but he now had to succumb to a blood test. He could not bear the sight of blood. "Now, don't you faint on me," said the nurse. "Just look the other way."

Freddy did as he was told and it was over in no time. She had such a steady hand that she found the vein immediately. No pocking around like the French nurses.

"You are excellent," he said, "and should they ever have to repeat the test, I hope I can count on you to do it."

The nurse felt very flattered. "Sure, just remember to ask for Vicky."

The doctor gave him some pills to take and warned him that he might feel drowsy. "You had better get into bed," said his mother, leaving the room so he could have some privacy.

"I will have some results tomorrow afternoon," said Dr Wolf. "I know how worried you must be and there is nothing worse than uncertainty."

"Yes," said Helene.

Vicky interrupted the conversation by saying there was an emergency. Helene went back into the room and found Freddy sound asleep. Then she saw the telephone on the night table and remembered she should call home. Sigmund had been waiting impatiently next to the phone and picked it up as soon as it rung. He was relieved to hear everything had gone well and that Freddy was in good hands. Helene promised to ring the next day as soon as she had some more news.

She took her scrapbook and colours out of her purse and, settling herself comfortably into the only armchair in the room, began giving the finishing touches to the painting she had started some years back but had no time to finish. It was a hobby she had taken up as a young girl. Her mother always said she was very talented. "Talents are gifts from God," she would repeat now and again, "and it is a sin not to exploit them. Just think of the many people who would love to have the ability to do it and who have unfortunately not been thus blessed."

Helene felt the tension leave her body and, not having the will to fight the drowsiness she was experiencing, surrendered to it. They were both woken up by the nurse bringing the patient his dinner. "That is our good fresh air," said the nurse. "It is what people come here for."

"I did not know I was so tired," said Helene, excusing herself. "No, Mama, I am glad you got some rest."

Helene stayed until Freddy had finished eating. He was not too hungry even though the food was very good. Helene waited until Freddy drifted off to sleep and left, walking to her lodging. One could smell the scent of the pine trees. What a romantic place this is, how she wished that Sigmund could have been at her side to share it with him. Perhaps someday…

She unpacked her bag, hung up her clothes in the wardrobe and went to bed, then rolled herself up in the duvet and was soon fast asleep. The bright rays of the sun woke her up the next morning. Freddy would surely still be sleeping. The day was so beautiful that she could not resist going for a stroll. The snow-capped mountains glowed in the sunlight and the wind seemed to caress the pine trees as they moved gracefully to and fro. A regatta was taking place on the lake and everything looked picture book perfect. She felt very blessed at being able to admire so much splendour.

Her walk took her to the centre of town. All of a sudden, she felt hungry and remembered that she'd had nothing to eat since lunch the day before. She walked into the first coffee shop she came across and ordered a big pot of tea and some rolls. She had all the time in the world. What a nice sensation it was to be on one's own, to not have anyone to take into account. That was not quite true, she had Freddy to worry about, but she did feel as if she were on a much-needed vacation. How long had it been since she had someone make up her bed for her and help with the housework? She could not remember. She made up her mind that she would make the most out of the week and return to Sigmund well rested.

She looked at the time. It sure did fly when one was having fun. After paying the check, she left and went into a bookstore she passed and looked around, buying two books she thought Freddy might enjoy then walked at a fast pace to the clinic.

Freddy was wide-awake when she came in and delighted with the reading material she'd gotten him. Freddy gave her Dr Wolf's message. She was to stop by his office as soon as she got back. A look of concern spread across her face and her heart skipped a beat. "I will be right back," she told him, then hurried out.

Vicky escorted her to his office. She did not have long to wait. The diagnosis the doctor had made in Paris was absolutely correct and there was no reason for concern, but he did want to make her aware of two things. Her son would have to stay at the clinic for at least six months and he would not only have to take the prescribed medicine, but he would not be allowed any physical activity for the time being. He was just to get plenty of rest.

"That is going to be very hard on him," said his mother. "He is so active."

"I am aware of it," replied Dr Wolf. "The other problem we are going to have to face is that with the medicine, his chest pain and cough will disappear in a couple of days and he will no longer feel he has something ailing him, which means he will want to resume a normal life, but that will not be possible for now. I just wanted you to know everything that we are facing before I give Freddy the details of his treatment."

Helene thanked him and said how very relieved she was, for it could have been a lot worse. Freddy was sitting up in bed reading but looked up as they walked in. After taking his vital signs, Dr Wolf explained the treatment to him. "Stay in bed and rest?" said Freddy.

"That is exactly what I said…for six months."

"But, what about school?"

"You will have to catch up when you return. I am sure your friend Georges will help you."

Helene took his hand in hers. "Let's think about getting well and worry about all the rest later."

Freddy felt he could no longer keep his eyes open and said to himself he would just close them for a second but soon was fast asleep.

"It is the medicine," said Dr Wolf. "As he recovers, we will decrease the dose and he will be less drowsy."

Helene wrote Freddy a note telling him she would return shortly then walked back to her room and rang Sigmund. He was very relieved to hear that the diagnosis had been the same. Did she like his doctor? "Oh, yes," replied Helene, and she said not only does she feel that he knows what he was doing, he also had Freddy's trust. In addition, she liked the fact that he made a point of keeping his patients informed and that he was accessible day and night, something that was not always the case in this day and age. Sigmund told her to see to it that she got some rest herself and was already very much looking forward to seeing her in a week's time.

"No, nothing special has happened," he said. "Adele rung to invite me to lunch, but I did not accept the invitation, as I didn't want to miss your phone call." Helene tried to insist he go but Sigmund told her she need not worry, there was plenty of food in the house. He then reminded her it was a long distance call and they should try to keep their conversations short. They agreed that they would only speak every other day. The week went by so fast and Freddy had done nothing else but sleep and eat, which made him gain a little weight.

One evening, Sigmund suggested Helene stay for another week. Helene was taken by surprise at his offer, for she was fully aware of how much he missed her and how lonely he was. "I will come home as planned," she told him. "It does not make any sense for me to extend. I would rather return once Freddy is sleeping less and is allowed to move around."

Sigmund agreed, and on the eve of her departure, she felt sad and depressed. It was the first time she would be separated from Freddy. She could now sympathise with Sigmund. How hard it must have been for him when he wished Nellie farewell and watched the train leave the station. She was standing by his side and felt sad as well, but it was not the same grief she was feeling now. "Everything one goes through is for a reason," she thought, and in the end, this would only help her be more understanding towards her husband.

Before leaving for the train station the following morning, she went to the clinic to see Freddy one more time. He was awake and anxiously awaiting her return. "Don't you worry about me, Mama," he said, "I am a big boy and in good hands. I will get well soon and be home before you know it. Doctors may think they know it all, but they are not always right."

"Knowing you," said his mother, laughing, "You are going to make it your business to prove that you can get well in less time, right?"

"Absolutely! It is a challenge," he said. "And you know how much I like to be challenged."

"Is there anything you might need me to do for you when I get home?"

"Yes," said Freddy. "On my desk, I left a list of stamps I wanted to buy. Maybe you or Papa can go to the market and purchase them for me."

285

"I will do my best to oblige," said Helene. Just then, Vicky came in and announced her cab was waiting. Helene hugged Freddy close to her and hid her face so that he could not see her tears.

"We will take very good care of him," said Vicky. "When you return, he will be well on his way to recovery." Helene blew him a kiss from the doorway and disappeared from sight.

Freddy spent the first month just eating and sleeping. Tests were taken again and the results were not at all good. They showed an inflammation of the lymph glands, which was not a good sign. His parents were very upset upon hearing the news, but Dr Wolf tried his best to put their minds at ease, saying it was nothing abnormal, quite the contrary.

For Freddy, however, the news was a setback as he had been looking forward to leaving ahead of time. Now he might be forced to stay even longer. He became apathetic and lost all interest in food. Dr Wolf did not like the course things were taking and needed someone or something to get Freddy out of the mental state he was in. Wracking his brains trying to come up with a solution, one day he caught sight of the Evangelical pastor as he walked quickly down the corridor. "I now have my answer," said Dr Wolf to himself, and hurried after him. "Have you got a minute to spare?" he asked.

"For you, Doc, always," and the doctor led him into his office and stated his case. "Leave it with me," said Father Christian, "I will think of something to get your patient out of the state he is in."

Freddy did not even bother to look up when he heard the door open. He thought it must be dinnertime again but the mere thought of food made him sick. He turned over on his side and covered his head with his duvet. "How are you doing this evening?" an unknown voice inquired. Freddy stuck his head out and thought, who could this stranger be and what could he want?

"I am Father Christian," said the stranger, coming closer to the bed. Freddy looked up and saw a man in his early thirties. He was smiling and he had a twinkle in his eyes. Freddy introduced himself and shook hands with him. "So, young man, are we feeling just a little sorry for ourselves?" he asked, laughing.

Freddy was taken aback by the question. *How dare he make such a statement,* he thought to himself. He was about to reply when Christian, not bothering to wait for an answer, continued his monologue. "You won't believe what a lovely day it has been outside. There was not a cloud in the sky and everyone who could be out was enjoying the warm weather."

"Why are you telling me this? I guess you have come to torment me but then, how could you know?" but he did not wait for an answer. "I am not allowed to go anywhere. I have to stay in bed and rest. So, whatever kind of a day it is outside is of no concern to me, one day is just the same as the next and none of them are bringing me closer to leaving this prison," Freddy said passionately.

"Why, Freddy, how can you say such a thing? I am sure that you are getting stronger and your symptoms are subsiding."

"I wish," replied Freddy. "It might be true with others, but it certainly is not the case with me. If anything, my condition has worsened," and he went on to tell him about the inflammation they had discovered.

"You have only confirmed the statement I made; you are feeling sorry for yourself and have not once thought about how lucky you are or counted your blessings." Freddy gave him a perplexed look. "See? You are doubly blessed your parents can afford this costly treatment, how many are there who can? Have you thought of that?"

Freddy was thoughtful. The pastor was right. He hadn't thought about the added expense his sickness represented and had been very selfish, only thinking about and feeling sorry for himself, never thinking of all the sacrifices and stress his parents were going through. Suddenly, he saw Christian in a different perspective. "You know, I had not thought of all the things you just mentioned."

"I know, because when one digs oneself into a hole like you have done, there is only one centre and that is oneself, everything revolves around that centre and the rest just ceases to exist," said Christian. "Why don't you tell me a little about yourself? I would like to get to know you a little better."

Freddy slowly opened himself up and told him about his life in Paris, his friends and his side job. Father Christian listened attentively. He also mentioned his stamp dealings, saying that was the one thing he missed the most. He had become quite passionate about stamps; he had even started a small collection. "There is no reason why you cannot continue dealing in and collecting them."

"Really? In fact, as we were driving through the town I thought I saw a sign on one of the stores."

"That is correct. I can get you the stamps you need and I can also deliver the stamps for you. I am sure the dealer in town would love to get his hands on the new French editions."

"That certainly will not be a problem, my mother promised to run an errand for me and, as a matter of fact, not only did I bring some new editions with me, but also some very special ones. Would you care to see them?"

Father Christian shook his head. "I really do not understand much about them but I can have a word with the dealer in town."

"Please do, and invite him to come up and see me," said Freddy enthusiastically. The pastor said he would and took his leave.

When Dr Wolf came in to check on his patient, he found him in a completely different frame of mind, sitting up in bed and looking very pleased with himself. "You seem to be doing better," said Dr Wolf.

Freddy smiled at him. "I am. I just had a visitor who unlocked several doors for me." Dr Wolf did not understand what he meant but he did not care, silently blessing Father Christian.

The next afternoon, the dealer paid him a visit and brought some stamps he thought might be of interest and Freddy showed him his. They exchanged some, not many, and he bought the rest. Freddy promised he would have a new assortment soon then hid the money he received and sat down to write his parents. As an afterthought, he told them that out of his money, he subscribed to a philatelic magazine and asked them to please remember to buy the list of stamps he had left on his desk and to mail them to him as soon as it was convenient. He ended the letter saying he would reimburse them later.

Dr Wolf was once more amazed at what the power of the mind could bring to bear on the body. Freddy appeared to be on the way to recovery and decided to allow him to go out for a walk for an hour a day. As time went by, he would gradually increase his physical activity. Freddy was overjoyed. His first destination was the stamp store.

The dealer looked at him in surprise when he saw him walk in. "I am so happy to see you up and about," he said, stretching out his hand. And a friendship developed between them.

"I had to teach my legs to walk again," said Freddy, laughing.

"I bet. How long were you bedridden for?"

"It has been so long that I have lost track."

"That is just as well."

Freddy admired his wares and looked at his album. It was very impressive, having limited himself to collecting Swiss stamps. "What I really like about this hobby is that one has so many options," said Freddy. "And they are all just as exciting." As he was leaving, his friend gave him a book, depicting all the European stamps that had been printed to date.

"This should make the time go faster," said his friend, and Freddy was thrilled with the gift.

Chapter 35

Sigmund read Freddy's letter with mixed emotions. He was relieved to hear he was on his way to recovery and finally emerging from the depressive state he was in, but he was also angry. "I can't believe he is wasting money on stamps," he said to Helene in a harassed tone of voice. "I thought I had made our economic situation quite clear to him, he has not even thought once about the extra expenses we are incurring or where the money is coming from to pay for his medical treatments."

"Sigmund, please do not be so hard on him," said Helene. "He is just a teenager."

"He may well be a teenager, but I expect him to be sensible and have some common sense and to use his brain. I do not believe that is asking too much or is it?" Helene ignored the question.

"This business of chasing after his stamps... He seems to forget sometimes that I am his father and not his butler."

Helene stared at him in silence. It had been a long time since she saw him in this bad a mood. She wondered what the real reason for his anger was, Freddy was just a scapegoat. She did not have to wait long for the answer.

"This Government is preparing yet another tax reform and there have been so many, I have lost track of the number that have been approved. One thing is certain, it will only bring us more expense and hardship. It infuriates me so much to see how the state wastes the hard-earned money of its citizens on stupid experiments. A bitterness rises within me whenever I see the damned and humiliating times we are living. I do hope Freddy will see better ones than we have," he said, turning to Helene.

"I hope so too," was all she said.

"Freddy's birthday is coming up. How would you like spending that special date with him?" he asked.

"Will you come with me?"

"No, Helene, as much as I would like to see my son, I will not incur in any more expense than I have to."

"That is not fair. Why don't you go? I am sure he would be delighted to see you."

"No, Helene, you are yearning for him and it will do you good to get away from me as well. So is it a yes or a no?"

She did not have to think twice. In the terrible frame of mind her husband was in, he was better left alone. "Thank you, Sigmund, I will go. I will not tell him anything, I will just surprise him."

"That is an excellent idea. You can stay at the same bed and breakfast you stayed at last time and see for yourself how he is coming along. I would, however, like a full report, and do ask the doctor when he thinks Freddy might be well enough to return to Paris."

Helene got the hint. Sigmund was also worried about their financial situation. "I will spend one week with him," Sigmund agreed.

The next morning, Sigmund went down to the Carree Marigny to buy the stamps Freddy had requested. It took him forever. The place was so crowded he could barely move and the crowd pushed him, a fact that did nothing to improve his temper. Quite the contrary, he cursed Freddy and his stamps several times. The crowd diminished around lunchtime and he was finally able to get close to the stand he was looking for. Fortunately, the dealer had the stamps in stock. He purchased the whole list and then headed for home.

He knew nothing would please his son more and so he would not deduct them from his allowance as he normally did, for they would be his birthday present. On the way, he changed his mind and stopped at the station to purchase Helene's ticket. He was very much tempted to buy one for himself but refrained from doing so as he knew he would only feel guilty about spending money he did not have. He wished sometimes he could be more flexible and less hard on himself but it was not in his nature.

"Hopefully, he will be in a better mood," thought Helene as she prepared a nice dinner. There was nothing more stressful in life than economic worries. Life was so unfair and uncertain. Newlyweds usually have to worry about finances; it is the normal course of life. They are just starting out, trying to save enough money to buy their own home, probably surprised by a pregnancy they had not planned, money thus turning into a centre point of their relationship. That had not been the case with them. Sigmund had been the owner of a well-established business so they had been spared all those financial worries. But one could not escape the realities of life, they catch up with one sooner rather than later, and now at their ripe age, they were having to pay dearly for the privilege they had enjoyed. "That is life and there is no evading it," alleged Helene, as she dwelled on these thoughts, only hoping that all these worries would not affect her husband's health.

He was not the youngest, turning sixty-five in the next few months, and he was becoming disillusioned with life in general. Maybe women were different. She had to admit to herself that it had not been easy to do away with all the luxuries she had become accustomed to, having learned a long time ago that it was of no use to lament over the issues that have been. Someone told her once that it was futile to constantly look in the rear view mirror, life went on and one had to look at the present and the future. Crying over bygone days only ruined the mental state by making one unhappy and depressed. Life was too short to be unhappy and one owed it to oneself to make the best out of each and every day.

The closing of the front door interrupted her thoughts.

"Helene, Helene, where are you?"

"In the kitchen!" From his tone of voice, she could tell her husband was in a better mood. She had her back turned to the kitchen door and did not see him come in. He kissed her gently on the back of the neck and when she turned around to face him, he handed her a lovely bouquet of red roses. "Why, Sigmund," she said, her eyes filling with tears, unable to remember how long it had been since he brought her flowers.

"I am sorry I have been so grumpy," he said. "I sometimes ask myself how you put up with me."

"Love, Sigmund, love changes everything."

"I guess so." He handed her the train ticket. "I bought a round trip as it came out cheaper." She looked at the dates. "You will be gone for ten days."

"That is plenty," replied Helene. "It will allow us to miss each other and we will have something special to look forward to. You know," she said looking him in his beautiful blue eyes, "you may be grumpy, but all the adversity has brought us a lot closer than we might have become had the sun always shone down on us."

"You are right, Helene, you have stood by me like a soldier and you just need to remember that I do not take it for granted. Oh, and I got Freddy his stamps. I hope he makes a big profit on them. You won't believe what I went through to get them. They will be our birthday present to him. Is dinner about ready? I am starving."

Helene laughed. "Just let me set the table," she said, and hurriedly placed the roses in a vase and set it in the centre of the table, then lit the candles on either side.

"It all looks so festive," said Sigmund, returning from washing his hands. "Is there a special occasion?"

"Yes, Sigmund, there is…we are alive and we have each other. Is that not reason enough to celebrate?"

"It sure is and we are very blessed."

Helene was bubbling with excitement when she boarded the train. She loved surprises and could barely wait to see Freddy's face when he saw her. In one of his latest letters, he had reminded them that his birthday was coming up and had asked if they had any plans. The question was left unanswered.

Wintertime was upon them and everything was covered in fresh snow. It was actually snowing hard when the train pulled into the station in Crans Montana. Helene felt her heart beat faster. She would be able to go skiing. That sport had meant everything to her but she had not been able to practice it for many years. As they drove through town, there were skiers everywhere. It was après ski time. The music was blaring, they were drinking mulled wine and everything looked so romantic. She could hardly wait to feel the cold wind on her face and listen to the sound of the skis on the snow as they cut through it. But first, she had to see about Freddy. "I am here to spend time with him," she said, chiding herself, having let herself get carried away with so many memories. She left her bag at the bed and breakfast, just as she had last time, then headed for the clinic.

Vicky was on duty and looked up in astonishment when Helene walked in. "What a surprise!" she said as she greeted Helene warmly. "Is he expecting you?"

"Not at all," Helene answered, smiling.

"He will be delighted to see you."

Freddy was sitting at his desk when his mother walked in. "Mama!" he said, beaming. "What a surprise, I was not expecting you and had already come to terms with that fact. No wonder I never got an answer to my question. I should have known."

Helene hugged him close to her. "I have missed you so much. The house is so quiet without you."

"How is Papa?"

"He is fine, his usual self."

"Grumpy?" Freddy asked.

"At times," replied his mother. "But let me take a look at you," she said, stepping away from him. "You are looking much better. I see you have gained some weight."

"Dr Wolf told me this morning that I am recovering very quickly. The tests are not one hundred percent yet but they are getting there. In other words, there is still no date, but I do not think it will be too far into the future. We will have to wait and see. Oh, and I forgot to tell you, the doctor has increased the time I can go for a walk. Now I can go for three hours total, an hour and a half in the morning and the same in the afternoon."

"That is excellent news," said Helene.

"He also said that if my recovery continues, he might allow me to go skiing."

"That would be wonderful. You have never done it, but it is such a great sport. One experiences such a sense of freedom and gets to see so much of nature than one would not see otherwise."

"You love the sport, don't you Mama?"

"I do."

"Then you should go for a couple of runs while you are here."

"We will see." Helene opened her purse and handed him a letter. "I rang Georges and he came by the house."

But Freddy was no longer paying attention, he was reading avidly. Georges wrote that he and his family were doing well and that they missed him very much and hoped he would be home soon. He was taking notes for Freddy and if he devoted some time to studying them, he was sure he would have no trouble catching up. His youngest sister sent him greetings. Freddy smiled reading that last sentence. "She has a crush on me."

"Who has?"

"Georges' youngest sister does, ever since she met me. But there is nothing more to tell, Mama."

Dr Wolf dropped by, having heard of Helene's arrival. "He looks so much better, doctor."

"He has made some fine improvement and we are well on the way, but I am afraid there is still a way to go. How long have you been outside for today?" he asked Freddy.

"I was out for three hours."

"Freddy, it would be nice if you escorted your mother back. You are staying at the bed and breakfast, aren't you?" Helene nodded.

"Can I have dinner in town with her or do I have to come right back?"

"Not tonight," said Helene. "I am a little tired."

"Well, that settles it. If you have a minute tomorrow, please drop by my office."

"I will, doctor. When is it convenient for you?"

"Anytime, I will be in the clinic all day. Just tell Vicky and she will advise me you are waiting."

"Thank you, doctor."

Freddy put on his heavy winter coat. "Come on, Mama, I have not been out at night since I got here. It will be nice to get a full view of the moon and the stars for a change."

"What do you mean?" a puzzled Helene asked.

"I just get a partial view from my window and I cannot always see the moon. The moon, as you might remember, has always fascinated me."

"I know," said his mother. "But before we go, I would like to check your wardrobe, you might have some mending for me to do."

"Oh, yes, as a matter of fact I do. I put the garments aside."

"We can take them with us," said Helene, folding them and placing them in a bag. "I will carry them, for I do not want you exerting yourself."

They took their time getting to their destination. Freddy told her about the friends he had made and mentioned that the stamp his father had bought on his behalf had doubled in price. "Did you sell it?"

"No, I have not needed the money so I am holding on to it."

They walked silently for a while, enjoying the night. The wind came up and in the darkness, they stopped to listen to it and watch the moon playing hide and seek with the clouds. "Nature can be so beautiful and yet its forces can create so much havoc," Helene mused.

"What are you thinking about?" Freddy asked.

"Like when it snows day in and day out. The beautiful white snow that looks so harmless accumulates then suddenly something triggers it into moving, unleashing an avalanche that can destroy and bury everything within its reach in no time. When one sees those forces, one realises how vulnerable and how small and insignificant man really is and yet we all seem to believe we are the greatest and nothing can defeat us. The power of nature makes us humble."

Freddy did not answer. His mother had an eye for things he himself was not aware of and he thought about how much he could learn from her. He liked her room, it was a good size and, looking out the window, realised they both had the same view of the mountains.

Helene opened the bag and took out the clothing she had to mend.

"Mama," said Freddy, "why don't you do that later? I have something to ask you."

"Go right ahead, I am listening." She noticed Freddy's face had turned red and that he was blushing to the roots of his hair. Helene could tell he was embarrassed. She waited. He cleared his throat several times.

"Mama," he finally said. "Does it look silly if I speak to a girl?"

"No, Freddy, it's the most natural thing in the world. Why?"

"I was just wondering," he said, then changed the subject and told her he had received a very sweet letter from Nellie. They talked for a while and his mother wondered if he had perhaps met a young lady. But although her curiosity was aroused, she refrained from bringing up the subject again.

Freddy soon took his leave and Helene retrieved the sewing kit she had made a point in bringing with her, knowing she would have some mending to do, and begun her chore. It was not long before she was dozing over her work. She had not realised how tired she was. Deciding she had better postpone what she was doing, she undressed and went to bed and was asleep before her head hit the pillow.

Freddy dropped by around mid-morning and was surprised to find his mother still in bed. "Are you unwell, Mama?" he asked in a concerned tone of voice.

"No, no, I'm fine. I am just a little tired. You know it is, a long train ride and Papa has not been the easiest person to get along with lately."

"Is something worrying him?" Helene hesitated then said, "Yes, he is very worried about our financial situation. The government is not helping matters, either, with yet another tax reform and let's face it, he is growing bitter and resentful and I do not know what to do about it."

Freddy thought for a minute. "It is understandable," he said. "After all he has been through and my being sick with all the added expense I am causing. I realise I am getting the best money can buy and I am very grateful," said Freddy. "I just wish I could recover faster and return to Paris to continue with my schooling and earn a little money as I was doing before."

"I appreciate it has been quite a change for you, as well, but health is the most important asset one has. One can have all the money in the world, but if one is ill, one cannot enjoy life. Life is to be enjoyed and lived to the fullest and to succeed one must first take care of oneself, like you are doing. Take my word for it," said Helene. "When you come home, you are going to see everything in a different light and you will not take everything you have for granted."

"Mama, do you think Papa might be sick?"

"That thought has crossed my mind several times as a matter of fact, when Adele saw him she found him very much aged. I have tried to persuade him to go see a doctor and have a medical check-up but he will not hear about it. There is nothing else I can do. One can take the horse to the water but one cannot make him drink."

"Papa is so stubborn." Freddy looked at the time. "We can walk back together."

"It will not take me long to get dressed."

"I had forgotten that Dr Wolf wanted to see you." Freddy sat down and looked out the window.

Dr Wolf gave Helene a very good report. He was of the opinion that if his tests continued to improve, Freddy would be able to go home for a couple of weeks in about a month, and he was going to let him exercise longer. "That is excellent news, doctor," said Helene. "My husband will be delighted."

"Please do not raise your hopes too high."

"I will keep it all in perspective," said Helene, "and by the way, does Freddy ski?"

Helene looked at him in surprise. "No, doctor, he doesn't."

"Would you mind if he learned?"

"Not at all as I am an avid skier myself."

"Well, then, that is the exercise I am going to prescribe for him," he said smiling.

Helene returned to Freddy's room and found him sitting by the window, just as she had left him. "Is anything wrong?"

"I was just thinking about Papa. I miss him." Helene told him what Dr Wolf had told her. "That is wonderful news, Mama, and also about the skiing. But I will need some clothing."

"We will have to look around and see what we can find."

In the early afternoon, Dr Wolf paid them an unexpected visit. He was carrying a package that he handed to Freddy. "My son is a little older than you are and has outgrown this. I thought it would come in handy for the exercise I am going to prescribe." Helene thought she had not understood correctly but when Freddy opened the bag, he took out a pair of ski pants and an anorak. "That is so nice of you, doctor, I cannot thank you enough," said Helene.

"This young man has been through so much, I am sure he will enjoy his new sport."

"When do I start?"

"I have it all set up so you can begin tomorrow. You will have to be down near the bunny hill at ten thirty and there is a small group going from the clinic so you will be driven down. Meet them down in the reception area at ten." Then he turned to Helene. "You are welcome to ride along." Helene thanked him, but she had just made plans and would go skiing the following day.

Freddy left the next morning with the group. The clothing the doctor had given him fit perfectly and he was thrilled. They all got skis and boots at the ski shop then headed over to the hill, chatting excitedly. An instructor was expecting them. Freddy learned fast and was soon going up and down the hill as if he had grown up on skis. After a couple of hours, he felt tired and quit, he did not want to exert himself and jeopardise his possible trip home.

He longed to see Paris and all his friends again and suddenly felt very homesick. Lost in thought, he then saw his mother's figure loom up in front of him. It could not be her, she had gone skiing for the day, but he heard her call his name and looked up, startled. It was her. "Mama!"

"You were dozing."

"What are you doing here?"

"I just got back. Did you enjoy it?" she asked.

Freddy said he did, very much, and gave her a detailed account of all he learned, then they had a bite to eat in town and Helene walked back to the clinic with him. He looked tired.

Vicky was expecting him. She took his vital signs once he was in bed and he fell asleep before she even left the room. Dr Wolf came by before leaving for the day. Freddy was half-awake. He sat up in bed when he saw who his visitor was. "I can't thank you enough, doctor, it was wonderful. Will I be able to return and go on the steep runs?" he asked.

"Sure, we just have to give it all some time."

The next morning, Vicky brought Freddy a letter and he opened it right away. It was a birthday card from Nellie. How could he forget? It arrived right on his birthday and was a very sweet card. She wished him all the best on this special day and was glad Helene was there to celebrate it with him, adding that she hoped someday in the near future, they might be able to spend some time together as well. She also included a whole series of new edition stamps.

Helene came in followed by Father Christian and Freddy introduced them. "I understand everything is going well for you, young man."

"The news is all good."

"And you are a year older, but are you a little wiser than you were yesterday?" he asked looking at him seriously.

"That I do not know," replied Freddy. "But I have learned a new sport," and proceeded to tell him all about it.

"It all has to do with attitude, as I told you some time back. When you have the right mental attitude, you can change so many things and discover so many new challenges. You are on a discovery trip and I hope you will be on it all your life." Then he handed Freddy an envelope saying, "As a token of my appreciation, I have brought you this." It contained two stamps and Freddy looked at them closely with his magnifying glass.

Knowing Father Christian, they had to have a meaning…and he found it. They were German and depicted Goethe's house in Frankfurt, the city where Freddy was born, also printed on the year he was born.

"What a lovely gift," said Freddy. "I will place them in my album."

Father Christian shook hands with Helene and left. "What a nice person he is, and he has a great sense of humour."

"He does. He also is a great psychologist and I am very indebted to him," said Freddy. "He helped me so much." He would have elaborated more, but Helene handed him his present.

"This is from both your father and myself." He smiled when he read that the stamps were worth far more than he had paid for them, considering all the hardship he went through just to get them for him.

That afternoon, he and his mother went for a walk. On the way back, they stopped at Helene's lodging, saying she had a surprise for him. Lying in the middle of the room was a pair of skis adorned with a red ribbon and a birthday card. "Those can't be for me," said Freddy.

"They are your first pair of skis."

He gave her a bear hug. "Mama, this is the best present of all." Helene's stay was coming to an end and she had written Sigmund a full report. The mail took so long that she had not heard anything from him, nor had she called. And although she missed him, she had a wonderful time, catching up with her mail and enjoying her favourite sport, not to mention having a great time with her son.

Freddy's question, asking if Sigmund were sick, was at the back of her mind the entire trip and now she was eager to get home, satisfied that Freddy was on the road to recovery. God willing, he would be back in Paris in a couple of weeks. There was nothing more she could accomplish here and she felt she was needed at home. Freddy was saddened by her departure but he also had something to look forward to for Dr Wolf had told him he could go skiing once a week.

Chapter 36

Sigmund was at the train station waiting for Helene's train to arrive. He had missed her, even though he had made good use of his time. The first thing he did was make an appointment with his doctor, not that he felt sick, he just felt so very tired. He even felt tired in the morning after a good night's rest. The doctor took some blood tests and had rung him that morning to give him the results. Nothing to worry about, he was just a little anaemic and prescribed an iron complex for him to take.

He looked impatiently at his watch; the train was late as usual. It seemed to him that he spent more time nowadays at the station than anywhere else, then walked to a newspaper stand and bought a paper. The headline caught his eye: German Capital Fails TO Obey Hitler. Sigmund read on: 'Money flows into the United States proceeds from Germany have reached another record high'. The statistics were just for the United States. The article did not mention the other financial centres like London, Zurich or Paris.

Sigmund folded the newspaper. The train had finally arrived and Helene was the first off. He admired her from where he was standing. She looked beautiful, her face had gotten some colour and she was wearing one of his favourite suits.

"Hi, gorgeous," Sigmund said, as he walked up to her. They hugged briefly then walked out of the station arm in arm. Helene told him all about Freddy's ski experience but did not mention the skis. She was sure he would have reprimanded her if she had, and it was none of his business for she had paid for them with her own money.

"So, you think Freddy will be returning soon?"

"Yes, I do."

"How soon?"

"It all depends on his recovery and if he continues the way he is, it could be in a month's time. But he will have to go back."

"I know, but it would just be so nice to have him back again." They rode the metro home.

Once there, Sigmund opened the newspaper and read it out loud. All the measures Mr Schacht, Hitler's finance minister, has taken have done nothing to stem the flow of capital out of Germany and anyone caught sending money abroad will be punished with the death penalty. Helene looked up from what she was doing.

"What? The death penalty?"

"Yes," replied Sigmund. "Before it was punished with a jail sentence of 15 to 16 years."

"They must be pretty desperate. I don't understand what is wrong with sending money abroad."

"The state needs every penny it can get its hands on to buy all the raw materials for its military industry," said Sigmund.

"So, they are rearming," said Helene.

"Undoubtedly."

"Do you think we are going to see another war?"

"I do not know if I will live to see it, but I am sure you and Freddy will."

"Why are you always so pessimistic?" Helene asked.

"What do you mean?"

"I can put two and two together. A couple of weeks ago, you told me that you did not expect to see Nellie again, now you are saying there will probably be a war but you will not be around to see it. Are you hiding something from me? Has a doctor told you that you are ill and you haven't had the courage to tell me?"

"Helene stop it," said Sigmund, laughing.

"What is so funny?" she asked angrily.

"You have such an imagination. I am fine. To set your mind at ease, I went and saw the doctor and he told me that I am a little anaemic."

Helene interrupted him. "That would account for that grey colour of yours."

"Well, it will soon disappear once my iron levels get back to normal. You have been seeing visions, as usual, but I should be used to it by now," Sigmund said and continued reading the paper.

The phone rang. It was Adele. "Have you read Le Figaro?" she asked Helene.

"No, I have had no time, I just got back."

"A plane has crashed in Bogotá. They were having some kind of a military air show and a plane went down. The presidential stand caught fire, forty people died and a hundred and fifty injured."

Helene was no longer listening, thinking how she was going to break the news to Sigmund. Had something happened to Nellie? A chill ran down her spine. Adele was screaming over the phone, "Are you still there? Are you still there?" Helene hung up the phone without saying a word then walked over to where Sigmund was sitting and saw all the colour had drained from his face. She glanced at the paper and read the headline: Deadly crash in Bogotá. He knew already, she did not have to break the news to him.

He set the paper down. "Helene, this is awful."

"I know, Adele just rang to ask if we had any news of her. What can we do?"

"We can only wait. It happened during the weekend and we have no way of knowing if she was in town or if she might have gone to Abraham's farm," said Sigmund.

"I am sure she will give some sign of life," said Helene. "All we can do is wait."

"I spend my time waiting, waiting for those papers that might change our fate to come through, waiting for Freddy to get well, and now waiting to find out if my daughter is dead or alive," he said bitterly, leaving the room.

Just then, the phone rang again. It was Adele. "Are you all right?"

"Yes, I am," replied Helene. "No, we have no news."

"The Consulate might have some information."

"Yes, I will tell Sigmund. I have to go to him," she said to Adele. "And yes, I will ring if we have any information," then hung up.

Her husband was sitting behind his desk staring into space. He wondered if his premonition had become reality.

"Why don't we send Abraham a telegram?" Helene asked.

"We could, but if they are not in town as I mentioned before and we do not get a reply it will only increase our anxiety."

"What about going to the Colombian Consulate? They might have a report," Helene suggested.

"I don't want to undertake any action yet. Somehow Nellie will notify us if she is safe," replied Sigmund. "As I said before, all we can do is be patient and wait." Then he opened a book he had on his desk and began reading, soon forgetting about Helene's presence.

It had been a very long emotional day for her so she went into her room, her bed looked so inviting. She put on her nightshirt and got under the duvet and her last thought was Nellie before she drifted off to sleep.

Sigmund could not concentrate on what he was reading. Finally, in the privacy of his study, he allowed the tears to flow. Nellie may be dead, Freddy sick, how long was his bad luck going to last? He imagined all kinds of scenarios but Helene's idea about the Consulate was not so far-fetched, they would probably have a list of the victims. He would ask Helene to go the following day, but she would have to go alone for the pain would be unbearable if her name were on it.

It was past midnight when he finally went to bed. Even though he was exhausted, he could not fall asleep. He tossed and turned. He would imagine her in a hospital more dead than alive or he visualised her in a morgue, the corpse waiting to be claimed by her relatives. He scolded himself for having these thoughts and tried to think about a happy event, such as Freddy's homecoming, but it was all in vein. He could not get Nellie off his mind. Mentally drained in the early morning hours, he finally fell asleep.

Helene woke up the next morning well rested. She looked at Sigmund and, seeing him sleeping soundly, surmising he had spent a restless night got up as quietly as she possibly could. On her night table, she found a note. It had not been there the night before. Sigmund must have placed it there before going to bed. He was so considerate, never waking her if he could help it.

The note read:

> *The Colombian Consulate might have an answer, would you mind going? Love you always, S.*

She looked at the time then dressed in a hurry. Before leaving, she wrote Sigmund a note.

Have gone to do as you have asked; hope to return with good news. Big hug, Helene.

There were quite a few people standing outside the entrance and she slowly made her way into the building. Once inside the hall, she walked over to what looked like an information desk behind which sat a beautiful young lady. Helene stated her business, trying hard to keep her voice steady. The attendant took a list a couple of pages long and handing them to her, saying the names are all in alphabetical order.

Helene went straight to the page she needed and Nellie's name was not on it. She breathed a sigh of relief, then double-checked. No, the name she was searching for was not on it. As she handed the pages back, the young lady said, "At least someone who can go home happy."

"Yes," replied Helene, "it is so sad. We have been very lucky." Then a thought flashed through her mind. "You do not happen to have a list of the people who have been taken to hospital, do you?"

"We sure do, but this one is not in alphabetical order," she said, handing it to her.

Helene moved away from the desk, making way for others. It took her thirty minutes to go through it. When she finally finished, she was satisfied that Nellie's name was not on it. She felt very blessed, but she also felt very sad for all those whose worst fears had been confirmed, whose hopes had been shattered and were now struck with grief.

Sigmund was up and dressed, waiting impatiently for Helene's return. As soon as he heard the key turn in the lock, he rushed to the front door and immediately read the answer on her face. "Thank God," he said.

"I even looked at the patient's list and the results are negative as well."

"No news is good news, as they say," said Sigmund.

"I am sure we will receive a sign of life from her at some stage," said Helene.

In the late afternoon, they received a telegram, which put an end to their agony that read:

I am safe and well, Nellie.

Sigmund read it several times. "Thank God," he exclaimed, and was about to say something else when the phone rang. It was Adele; the news is good, Nellie is safe. He thanked her for ringing and handed the phone to Helene who thanked her for her suggestion and hung up. "What suggestion?" asked Sigmund.

"The Consulate was her idea."

"Oh," said Sigmund. "I thought it had been yours."

Nellie had spent the weekend in the countryside just like Sigmund surmised. Abraham's farm was one of her favourite destinations, just an hour and half drive

301

from the city and the house was very comfortable, built in a colonial style. All the rooms converged onto an inner courtyard tiled in beautiful stone, its only decoration a large birdbath in the centre. If you got up early and made no noise, you could watch the colourful birds bathing. It was indeed a pretty sight. Being on the farm was never boring, you could go horseback riding, sun bathe, go for long walks or just relax and do nothing. She had been a little frightened by the horses at first, but Abraham insisted she take riding lessons and her fear vanished and she fully enjoyed the long rides they all went on through the beautiful countryside.

They did not even hear about the accident until arriving back in the city late Sunday night. Nellie and Abraham thought her parents would be worried about her but they had no way of getting word to them, everything was closed. They tried sending a telegram early the following morning but to their misfortune, the telegraph employees were on strike and only returned back to work in the afternoon. When Nellie complained, saying that their service was vital to the whole community, she was told that if it was so vital it should be reflected in their pay. Nellie did not reply. She was just relieved that she had been able to set her parents, and especially her father's, mind at ease.

Freddy was not at all eager to go home. The skiing was becoming a passion for him and he was out on the slopes every day, although he was still not allowed to go on the steeper runs. He complained to Dr Wolf one day, saying he was getting pretty bored going up and down that short hill and felt he would be able to master something a little more challenging, but Dr Wolf just listened and smiled.

"Let us make a compromise. If in two weeks your tests come out better than they have so far—"

Freddy interrupted him. "How much of an improvement do you need…ten, twenty percent or more?"

"About thirty percent," replied Dr Wolf. "Then I will allow you to try those runs you are dreaming about."

"Nothing less?"

"No, young man, I will not accept anything less than that. It is your health we are talking about. Once you have completely recovered, you will have a whole lifetime to enjoy all the winter sports, not only skiing. Just think how much better off you are now than you were a couple of weeks ago when you could not leave your room."

"That is a good point. I guess it is human nature to never be satisfied with what one has."

"You are becoming very wise," said the doctor, taking his leave and nearly colliding with Vicky in the doorway. She handed Freddy a letter from his father and he looked at it, feeling very guilty. It had been weeks since his mother's visit and he still had not written his father thanking him for the stamps.

Sigmund began the letter by reprimanding him for his silence. He could not believe that he, Freddy, was so busy that he did not have a minute to spare to sit down and drop his father a thank-you note. He wrote how anguished he had been about Nellie and ended the letter saying that the only thing he had to look forward to was his son's homecoming. He hoped Freddy would obey the doctor's orders and do nothing foolish to jeopardise his recovery. Freddy, feeling extremely guilty, sat down and wrote his father a long letter. He signed off saying he was very excited about the prospect of coming home and that he missed him very much. He had so many unanswered questions and was sure he would be able to answer them for him.

"He has finally written," said Sigmund to Helene, opening the letter and reading it to her. Then he turned to her and said, "He mentioned something about having some questions he needs an answer to. You do not happen to know what they might be, do you?"

Helene thought for a minute. "He did ask me something about whether he looked silly if he spoke to a girl."

"That solves the mystery," said Sigmund. "We are beginning to take notice of the opposite sex."

Chapter 37

One evening after they finished dinner and were comfortably seated in the living room, Sigmund asked Helene if she had been following the political developments in Spain. "No, I have not. Why, is there anything special going on?"

"I would say that a lot is happening."

"Would you mind enlightening me?"

"Not at all, but first I will fill you in on the historical background as it will help you understand the current situation better. In the year 1902, King Alfonso XII ascended the throne. He became increasingly despotic and in 1909, he was condemned for ordering the execution of the radical leader Ferrer Guardia in Barcelona. He also prevented liberal reforms from being introduced."

"In other words," said Helene, "he was not well liked."

"No, he was in constant conflict with the Spanish politicians and was also blamed for the Spanish defeat in the Moroccan war in 1921. His anti-democratic views encouraged someone by the name of Miguel Primo de Rivera to lead a military coup in 1923. This man promised to fight corruption and regenerate the country. In order to accomplish his goals, he suspended the constitution, established martial law and imposed a very strict system of censorship. He promised that when he came to power, he would only rule for ninety days."

"But like all politicians, he did not keep his promise," said Helene.

"That is correct. Unemployment was high as it was around the rest of Europe and he tried to reduce it by spending money on public works. In order to finance them, he introduced higher taxes on the rich. They, of course, complained, so in order to keep peace, he changed his policy and tried to raise money by public loans. This caused rapid inflation and the population became very unhappy. He also lost what military support he had and was forced to resign in January 1930."

"So, what happened to the king?"

"The king was still reigning, as you will see. A year later, Alfonso XII finally agreed to hold democratic elections and it was the first time in sixty years that the Spaniards were finally going to be allowed to vote. They voted overwhelmingly for a republic and the King was advised to go into exile in order to avoid large-scale violence."

"I take it he left."

"He did."

"It has some similarities with Germany, does it not?"

"Let me finish. A provisional government took charge and called for elections to be held in June. The Socialist Party (PSOE) and other left wing Parties won. A moderate republican by the name of Niceto Alcala Zamer became Prime Minister and he included several radical figures such as Manuel Azana, who later became Prime Minister, in his cabinet. With the support of the Socialist Party (PSOE), he attempted to introduce an agrarian reform and regional autonomy but the Courts blocked these measures, blaming the Catholic Church for Spain's backwardness. He defended the elimination of special privileges to the Church, stating that Spain had ceased to be Catholic."

"That statement must have gotten him into a lot of trouble."

"It did, but he was lucky. A failed military coup in 1932 rallied support for Azana's government and the courts approved his former Agrarian Reform Bill and the Catalan statute this time around. His modernisation program was undermined by lack of financial resources."

"You are giving me a lesson in Spanish history," said Helene. "What is the point of it all?"

"The events of the past will allow you to understand the present," said Sigmund. "Are you getting bored?"

"Not really, I just wonder what all this is leading to."

"You will soon see if you let me go on with my story."

"I promise not to interrupt anymore," said Helene stifling a yawn.

"The November 1933 elections saw the right wing CEDA party win 115 seats, whereas the Socialist Party only managed 58. The CEDA Party now formed a parliamentary alliance with the radical party and over the next two years demolished the social reforms that had been introduced by the former government. This all led to a general strike and an armed uprising in Asturias."

"That rings a bell," said Helene.

"Yes, it should, it was all over the papers. Prime Minister Azana was accused of encouraging the disturbances and jailed on a ship in the Barcelona harbour."

"He was acquitted, was he not?"

"Yes, he was," replied Sigmund, impatiently. "And he is back in politics. He was helping establish a coalition of Parties of the political left that included the Socialist Party (PSOE) the Communist Party (PCE) among others that became known as the Popular Front. The Anarchist refused to support the coalition and urged people not to vote."

"Why?"

"Because it advocated the restoring of the Catalan autonomy, amnesty for political prisoners, Agrarian reform, and an end to political blacklists and the payment of damages to the property owners who suffered during the revolt of 1934. The right wing, which has gathered strength, has formed the National Front, which includes the CEDA and the Carlist Parties. The Falange Espanola has not officially joined, it but most of its members support the aims of the National Front. In the election that was held a few months ago, the Popular Front won 263 seats of the 472. It has upset the conservatives by releasing all left wing political prisoners, has introduced Agrarian Reforms that have penalised the landed aristocracy and they have transferred right wing military leaders such as Francisco Franco, among others, to posts outside of the mainland. They have also outlawed the Falange Espanola and granted Cataluña political and administrative autonomy. A lot of capital has left Spain and the country is in an economic crisis. Workers have been striking, demanding an increase in their wages and the situation is really not good, not at all, Helene. The conservative Niceto Alcala was ousted as President a couple of weeks ago and replaced by Manuel Azana."

"I wonder how long it will take for the military to plan another coup?"

"With the experience they have, it should not be long, but this time Spain might find itself on the brink of a civil war, which might prompt other countries to become involved."

"Such as?"

Sigmund did not hesitate to answer: "Germany. It is all most unsettling."

"You are always so pessimistic."

"Just remember this conversation," said Sigmund.

"I am going to follow the developments in Spain very closely," said Helene. "We will see who is proven right."

"Time will tell," replied her husband. "And now I think it is time we got some sleep." He looked at his watch. "You have been very patient, Helene, I had not realised it was this late."

"I was not patient. I have really enjoyed the evening."

"So have I."

The next morning, Helene asked Sigmund why he thought Germany would get involved. Sigmund thought for a minute.

"Because it would widen Hitler's sphere of influence."

"I am afraid you might be right," said Helene.

"As I said last night, only time will tell," said Sigmund.

That afternoon, they received a letter from Freddy. His tests had turned out much better than even the doctor had hoped for and was now allowed to ski the more challenging runs. He also said he would be home in a few weeks, mentioning that he was thinking of buying himself a second hand typewriter so his father would no longer complain about his handwriting, "It could come in very handy and I might even be able to earn a little money with it," he added.

"That boy," Sigmund said, shaking his head. "He does not think of the consequences or of the added expenses something used can entail. I bet he has not even thought that there is something like a warranty that a used object does not have."

"I wonder what deals he has in mind," said Helene.

"Knowing him, he would probably be taking care of the correspondence for everyone at the clinic."

Sigmund's guess was not farfetched. Father Christian had given him the idea, having mentioned that he could use some help on one of his visits.

"With what?"

"The mail. I have to write all the letters myself and you won't believe how time consuming it is. If I had someone with a typewriter who would do it for me, I could devote that time to my flock."

The idea lingered in Freddy's mind. He would earn money that he could spend at his will without having to account to his father for every single penny, for not only was he required to send Sigmund a weekly list of his expenses, but if there was not as much as a penny not accounted for he was sure of receiving a rebuke in his father's next letter. With this in mind, he read the classified section of the local newspaper and was rewarded for his trouble. A couple of weeks later, he found what he was looking for, but there was only one hitch. He did not have the money. The owner told him he could pay for it in instalments, but Freddy did not feel at all at ease with the idea of owing money. He hoped that his father would see his point and help him out.

Sigmund sat down at his desk and wrote Freddy a letter. He told him how overjoyed he was with the good news, his recovery being foremost on his mind, and was very much looking forward to having his son home again. As far as the typewriter was concerned, the answer was a big 'no'. Knowing Freddy, he would be sitting for hours on end in front of it and that posture would be like poison for his body. He could consider one, once he had completely recovered, but he also reminded him that in their situation only a portable one, which could fit into a suitcase, would be adequate. He finished his letter reminding him that he had to obtain a visa for France before returning and asked him not to send his letters airmail but normal as this postage was cheaper.

Freddy was disappointed but there was nothing he could do and anyway, he was having so much fun skiing and meeting people his age that he soon forgot about it. Time went by very fast. Dr Wolf took the last tests and gave him the results a couple of days later. "You can go home, young man, but you will have to return."

"I know," said Freddy. "I will return in the winter."

"You may have to return before then but I have made a copy of your clinical history for you, please give to your doctor and he is to keep an eye on you." He handed him a big envelope. "Please take good care of it."

"I will," replied Freddy, then shook the Doctor's hand.

"When will you be leaving?"

"Tomorrow, but I have to get my visa for France."

"That should not take too long."

"No, it should not. I will spend the night in Bern and then continue on my journey."

"I am sure your parents can't wait to see you."

"I am really eager to see my father."

"Give them both my regards and take care of yourself." Dr Wolf gave Freddy a big hug. He had become attached to him and reminded him so much of his son, yet he felt so much closer to Freddy. His own son had built a wall between them that he had been unable to demolish. "By the way, I forgot to tell you that when you return, you will no longer have to stay at the clinic, you can stay at the Pension Enzian. You will be well cared for there."

"That is super news, doctor."

"Good luck," said Dr Wolf and walked out.

Freddy was packing when Father Christian walked in. "We are leaving?"

"Yes, but I will return."

"I am going to miss you."

"So will I. And maybe when I come back, I will be the proud owner of a portable typewriter and can become your private secretary," said Freddy.

"That," replied Father Christian, "would be more than welcome. What time is your train tomorrow?" Freddy gave him the time. "It will be my pleasure to see you off."

"But you have so much to do," said Freddy.

"That is no concern of yours, my friend." Freddy laughed.

Freddy was up and ready when Father Christian picked him up. It was a short drive to the station and they drove in silence. Freddy looked at the mountains and the runs he had learned to love. "Sad?" asked his friend.

"A little, but I am also looking forward to seeing my friends and being back in my own surroundings."

"There is always a bittersweet feeling about parting, the sadness of taking leave and the anticipation of what is to come."

Freddy had no trouble finding his carriage and his seat. Father Christian boarded the train with him and made sure he was comfortable. He gave his friend a big hug and asked him to please keep in touch. Freddy relaxed. He was finally on his way home.

It was snowing when the train pulled into the station. Freddy went straight to the hotel next to the station and left his things then, after asking for directions, took the streetcar to his destination and arrived half an hour before they were to close for the day. There were no people ahead of him so he was served immediately. He handed over all the required documents and was asked to take a seat. The lady called him and, handing over his passport, told him she had issued his visa but pointed out to him that it was an exception as the procedure normally took two days. Freddy thanked her for her kindness and then, taking the train schedule from his pocket, glanced at it. Just as he had foreseen, he would have to spend the night in Switzerland's capital.

The city was covered in snow and he rode the streetcar back to the station, deciding on the spur of the moment to go for a walk. He admired the narrow cobblestone streets, with their overhanging archways and old fountains. The city was a lot smaller than Paris. It felt strange to be surrounded by so many people and to hear German again. The language made him think of Frankfurt. Everyone here seemed to be hurrying to get somewhere. He came to the bear pit and admired the bears. There were two adults and two little cubs. They looked so cute standing on their hind legs. They were the city's symbol, for Bern means bear.

Suddenly feeling cold, he found a coffee shop across the road and ordered a wonderful cup of hot chocolate to warm him up. He took his time drinking it and decided he would walk back to his hotel but soon changed his mind. It was snowing hard and a very cold, northerly wind was blowing so he took the streetcar back. Feeling tired and cold he crawled underneath his duvet and was soon fast asleep. He woke up just as the sun was rising and looked at the time. He would have to hurry.

Helene was up early. She was so excited about Freddy's homecoming that she could not sleep and was ready to leave for the station long before the train was bound to arrive. "I am afraid you have got the time mixed up," said Sigmund.

"I thought it arrived at nine o'clock."

"No, Helene, that is the time it leaves Bern."

She took off her coat and laid her purse on the chair. "How come you are so calm? You have not seen your son in I cannot remember how long."

"Helene, men, as opposed to woman, do not tend to show their emotions, and in my case, I take everything in my stride. Of course I am excited and I look forward to having some father/son conversations with him, but I am a patient man. We will leave a half an hour before the train is due to arrive, which will give us ample time. I do not know about you, but I have some matters to attend to," and with these words he headed for his study.

Helene could not concentrate on anything. She went into Freddy's room half a dozen times, straightening something here, moving around something there, then she went into the kitchen and checked on the meal, all the time continually looking at her watch. It seemed as if time had stood still.

The phone rang. She ran to it thinking it might be Freddy, advising them he had missed his train, but no, that could not be possible, he was due to arrive in less than an hour. She picked up the receiver, it was Adele. "Has my nephew arrived?"

"His train is due in shortly and we will be having a late lunch, would you care to join us?" asked Helene.

"I do not know. Gerald is at the symphony, they had rehearsal all morning and although everyone knows what time it starts, its ending time is always a mystery."

"I know Freddy would be delighted to see you."

"Don't expect me, Helene. But I will see my one and only nephew some other time."

Sigmund was standing in the doorway making signs to her that it was time to leave. "I will talk to you later, Adele," said Helene, then placed the receiver back in its cradle.

"That sister of yours spends more time on the phone than anyone I know," said Sigmund.

"She is lonely, Gerald was not home and she could not make up her mind."

"Her mind up what about?"

"Joining us for lunch."

"So much for consulting me," said Sigmund.

"She is just as anxious as we are to see Freddy, and she is the only family member I have close by, after all."

"And the most boring," said Sigmund to himself.

"You did not tell me you had any plans."

"I do not," replied her husband. "I just thought it would be nice to have a quiet afternoon with no outsiders. Freddy will probably be very tired after the trip and he does need all the rest he can get. Remember, he has not yet fully recovered," said Sigmund.

"I do not think your idea of a quiet afternoon is going to take place. All his friends have rung asking about him, and I am sure Georges will be over just as soon as he can. I will take second place as usual."

"Why does it not surprise me?" Sigmund asked.

They arrived at the station a couple of minutes late. Sigmund spotted his son immediately and hurried over to him. All the emotions he had tried so hard to control emerged and he hugged his son to him. "You do not know how long I have waited for this day," said Sigmund.

"I have missed you very much as well," replied Freddy. He gave his mother a warm smile. "I can't wait to see my room again; it has been so long I have forgotten what it looks like."

"Nothing has changed, it's just as you left it," said Helene, laughing.

"Have you heard anything from Georges? Is there any mail for me?"

"If you are thinking of Helmut, he has not written, but Georges and all your friends know you are arriving today so I am sure they will all come by."

"Aunt Adele is dying to see you," said his father in a sarcastic tone of voice. "She might as well come over too."

"…Even though I believe it is pretty doubtful," Helene hastened to add.

"I hope you will make some room in your social calendar for me," said his father.

"You can have prime time," said Freddy, laughing. "I did not realise how popular I am."

"Don't allow that thought to get to your head, for regardless of one's standing, one should always remember one's roots and remain humble," said his father. *He always takes everything people say so seriously*, Freddy thought, *and he will probably never change.*

Once they got home, Freddy went straight to his room and looked around, having forgotten how big it was. Then he went through all his thing, looked lovingly at his books, then glanced briefly at his wardrobe. He had probably outgrown most of his clothes so he tried on a pair of trousers and indeed they were a couple of inches too short. Just then, his father called him. He left the room dressed as he was. Sigmund looked at him from head to toe.

"You did not gain any weight," he said, "but you are nearly as tall as I am."

Helene looked at him. "I guess I will be busy letting out hems," she said. Freddy admired the festive looking table his mother had set. "It is a special occasion," she said.

Freddy told them of all his activities, about his friends and spoke enthusiastically about Father Christian then, without thinking twice about it, brought up the subject of the typewriter and what all he had planned to accomplish with it. His parents listened, exchanging glances. "You know," said Sigmund. "I really admire you. You are always thinking up deals. I am sure you will never have trouble making money."

"Thank you, Papa. You mentioned that if and when I got one, it would have to fit into a suitcase…have you had a breakthrough?"

Helene and Sigmund exchanged glances. "No, nothing so far, no luck." Sigmund had used Freddy's illness as a pretext, but refrained from telling Helene that all prospects of leaving had been shelved due to their economic situation. The glances his parents had exchanged had not gone unnoticed. Freddy did not need to be told, he knew the truth.

They just finished their meal when the doorbell rang. "It must be Georges," said Freddy, leaving the table to answer it.

"I told you," said Helene.

"Life has returned to this home," said Sigmund. "It was so quiet while he was away." Helene nodded.

Freddy returned with Georges. "It has been a long time," said Sigmund.

"It sure has, but as of now, I think you will see a lot more of me."

"Have you had lunch?" Helene asked Georges.

"I have, thank you."

"I am just going to run over to Georges' house," said Freddy.

"My whole family is looking forward to seeing him."

"I won't be long," said Freddy and hurried off.

"It is his younger sister who is eager to see him," said Helene.

"You are mumbling, darling, what did you say?" asked Sigmund impatiently.

"His younger sister has a crush on our son."

"How do you know?"

"Freddy told me in Crans Montana."

"That is the normal course of life, is it not?" Sigmund asked irritably.

"I was looking forward to having Freddy for myself this afternoon."

"I told you at the station that—"

"Helene, you repeat yourself like a radio."

"It is more likely you will get to spend some time with him tonight," said Helene, ignoring his rude remark.

"We shall see."

She busied herself in the kitchen, thinking about how less tolerant her husband was becoming as time went by. He finished taking the supplement the doctor had given him but he had refused to go back and have another blood test. She did not see any change and even found him sound asleep in his chair a couple of times when she walked quietly into his study. It was not like him and her intuition told her something was wrong.

She heard the front door close. Freddy was home. "Did you have a nice time?"

"Yes, but Georges' mother looked even frailer than I remembered."

"We are all not getting any younger," replied Helene. "Do you find Papa very changed?"

"I find he has aged a lot and there is much bitterness in him."

"What makes you say that?"

"It comes out in his letters. Have you not noticed it as well, Mama?"

"I have, but there is nothing I can do about it. He won't go anywhere, he does not want to see anyone unless he has to and he practically lives in his study surrounded by his books."

"Maybe I can change that," said Freddy.

"I wish you would. And you might persuade him to go back and see the doctor."

"I will try."

"He wants to spend some one-on-one time with you. That is all he has talked about since he heard you were coming home."

"Was he upset because I left?"

"He was," said Helene.

"I had better go see him." Freddy found his father in the study, looking as if he had just woken up. "Had a little nap?" Freddy asked.

"When you get to be my age, you take catnaps to keep you going," said Sigmund.

"I have never heard that word before."

"It is a very short snooze, just enough to build up your energy."

"I see."

"How are your friends?"

"They are all fine. Georges' little sister has grown up so much and she is really very pretty. She gave me a big hug when I walked in and she always sends me special greetings according to Georges' letters."

"You just reminded me of something," said Sigmund. "You raised a question in one of your letters and I decided it would be best answered when we were face to face."

"What are you talking about, Papa?" Freddy was blushing, for he knew exactly what his father was referring to. Since he had been so foolish to ask the question, he would now have to sit through yet another lecture. He braced himself for a long evening.

"You asked if it looked silly if you spoke to a girl."

"Oh, yes, I remember now. I do not even know why I raised the question."

"Well, let me tell you, Freddy, that we have all had those very same thoughts at some stage or another. One has to get used to having contact with these dangerous creatures whom we cannot do without and there are several basic principles you should never forget. One, you should always let the other person see that her company is agreeable to you but that there are always others around. Two, you should never chase after the other against her will. It is not only ineffective, but it also shows a lack of dignity. Three, you should not let yourself get too impressed. Believe me, girls want a boy's company just as much as boys

312

want a girl's company. Four, you should always be yourself and take care of your appearance. If you try to be someone you are not, or if you try to show more than you have, she will soon see through you and you will only have made a fool of yourself. I have given you these principles but there are many more. In fact, one could write a book about this subject. Experience is the best teacher. But, I have to say, Freddy, it is easier to go through life with them than without them…or even against them. And one last thing, there are always more fish in the sea. Look around."

"You are very well versed on the subject," said Freddy.

"Well, I do have quite some years under my belt. Each one has to learn for himself. Have you met someone?"

Freddy hesitated. "Sort of. I met her on the ski lift. She is very beautiful and has a good sense of humour. She came up to me one day and asked about my skis."

"That is typical," said his father laughing. "They are experts at finding pretexts for starting a conversation."

"So we got to talking. She lives in Crans Montana and is, of course, Swiss. She was born there and is an excellent skier, as one would expect. While I was speaking to her, or better said she was luring me into a conversation, I noticed the boys I was with were giggling and later made funny comments. I did not know what to make of it and thought that I had really made a fool of myself."

"You did not, but boys love to tease and if she was very pretty as you say, they were probably a little jealous, wishing they had been the centre of her attention and not you."

"That is quite a logical explanation, Papa, and I appreciate the advice you have given me."

"When in doubt, just come to me," replied Sigmund. "In fact, it looks as if Nellie has met someone."

"Really? She has not mentioned anything to me," said Freddy.

"I do not know much either, she just mentioned his name and that she has been dating him for some time now."

"Where is he from?"

"If I am not mistaken, he is Colombian and I believe his name is Arturo."

"Maybe if she decides to get married, we could all go."

"Freddy, you are dreaming. Let us cross that bridge if we ever get to it," said Sigmund.

"I am glad she is happy and hopefully, I will see her again soon." His father did not reply. "Papa, I can tell you are not happy."

Sigmund looked up in surprise. "I am as happy as I will ever be. We are living in very unsettling times. Look at Germany; look at what is going on in Spain. The President Niceto Alcala has been ousted and replaced by Manuel Azana and the Spanish Army Officers are already plotting to overthrow reforms made by the popular front. Spain is not far from a civil war."

"How come you know so much?"

"You know how much I enjoy reading about history, but I also follow what is going on in the world very closely and I can add two and two together. But we can discuss Spain later. Did the doctor give you a medical report?"

"He did." And Freddy went to his room to get it.

"Are you having a nice conversation?" asked Helene.

"Yes, Mama. Papa is so wise."

Sigmund read the medical report. "It really is not too bad. I want you to recover fully, even if it costs me my last penny. Once that is accomplished, you will hopefully never encounter any further health restrictions. You will be able to hold a job and in the worst case provide for your mother."

"You are not ill, are you?" Freddy asked.

"No, I went to see the doctor recently and he found me anaemic. I have taken the medicine he prescribed and I should be fine now."

"Don't you think it might be worthwhile going back to see him just to confirm? We could go together, as I do have to take the doctor my report and he does have to check me regularly."

"That is a good idea. An excellent idea in fact, it will get your mother off my back."

"She is a little worried about you and talking about me providing for Mama makes me a little uneasy," said Freddy.

"Now you listen to me. It has nothing to do with my health. It is just a fact of life. I am several years your mother's senior. I am not going to live forever and, if there is no fatal accident, she will outlive me. Therefore, you will have to provide for her unless she were to remarry, which I believe would be most unlikely."

Freddy smiled. "I cannot imagine my mother with somebody else by her side, but the issue right now is your health."

"I hope I have made my point."

"You have, Papa."

"What are your plans while you are home?"

"I shall catch up on all I have missed at school of which Georges offered to help me. I would also like to go back to my job. The owner said he would keep it open for me."

"I have no objection, as long as the doctor approves it," said Sigmund. "By the way, how are your deals coming along?"

"You won't believe how many stamps I sold and the money I made. It is quite amazing to see how much a stamp can increase in value. Those last ones you sent me almost doubled in price."

"So you have capital to reinvest?"

"Yes, and I am very much looking forward to returning to the Carre Marigny. I have a couple of orders to fill."

"You must be tired, after all you've had a long day."

"Yes, Papa, I hate to admit it."

"Thanks for spending some time with me," said Sigmund.

"Not at all, in fact, I really want to spend more time with you, Papa. I realise I can learn a lot from you."

His father felt very flattered he also realised that his little boy had become a man.

From that day on, they both made a point of spending the evenings together. Helene sometimes joined them. She was happier than she had been for a long time, and Sigmund was becoming his old self again.

He returned for another blood test and the doctor told him to check back for the results. But when Sigmund came back from the doctor's, he told Helene exactly the same thing Freddy had once said. "I could have saved the time and money, I knew there was nothing wrong with me, but at least I bought my peace for you have nothing to nag about for the time being," he said jokingly.

"I will surely find something else," replied his wife.

These were happy times and they were a family once more. Freddy devoted time to his father and Sigmund found in him someone he could share his passion for history with also a companion. Helene went about her housework in a different frame of mind and everyone seemed at peace. Adele came over a couple of weeks later, she had spoken to Freddy on the phone several times but between one thing and another, her time had been taken up by other, more urgent matters. Sigmund went out of his way to be nice to her, complimenting her on her new hairdo, which was absolutely dreadful as he later remarked to Helene. Adele spent the afternoon with them and she told her sister later over the phone she had fully enjoyed her visit and found Sigmund looking the picture of health. Also, he had been ever so charming and was back to his old self.

Sigmund mentioned to both Freddy and Helene that the President of Spain, Niceto Alcala, had been ousted and replaced by the left wing Manuel Azana who had, until then, acted as Prime Minister. The rightists were calling for the army to take over and restore social discipline to save Spain. There were military uprisings in the country. "What did I tell you some time ago, Helene?" asked Sigmund.

"You were right, as usual."

"Right about what?" asked Freddy.

"Your father said Spain was heading for a civil war and he was right."

"But who is fighting whom?"

"The struggle is between fascists, communists and democrats," replied his father.

"Do you believe the repercussions will be felt in the rest of Europe?" Helene queried.

"Undoubtedly," replied Sigmund.

One evening a couple of weeks later, Freddy's time with his father was interrupted by an unexpected visitor. It was Georges. "This is a surprise," said Freddy.

"I have…" but he stopped, his voice breaking.

Freddy took his arm. "Sit down, take a deep breath and when you are ready you can tell us what is troubling you," said Sigmund understandingly.

"My oldest brother is leaving for Spain."

"What is he going to do there?" Freddy asked.

"His 'so-called' friends have talked him into joining the International Brigades and fighting for Spain's just cause."

"He must be out of his mind."

"We all think he is, and my mother is dreadfully upset about it. We have all tried to dissuade him but he won't listen to reason. His mind is made up and he is due to depart tomorrow morning."

Freddy was stunned. Sigmund broke the silence. "I can feel for you and your family. It is such a tragedy. So many families are going through the same ordeal. Young people full of idealism fighting for a foreign cause they do not even understand the background of. However, it is the fruit of General Franco's war propaganda."

"What do you mean?" Georges asked.

"He is receiving weapons from Portugal and asking Germany and Italy for arms. By internationalising his countries' conflict, he has given birth to a cause, which, as you can observe, has been answered by so many dreamers like your brother, for example."

"Is that not a little harsh?" Freddy asked.

"No," replied his father. "They all believe they can change the world but do not foresee the consequences, the sadness they are inflicting on their loved ones or the risks they are taking. They see themselves as saviours and their conviction is so high that no amount of reasoning will change their minds. They leave peaceful countries and jobs behind to die or be injured in the struggle against fascism."

"You are right," said Georges. "We have not succeeded in dissuading him. He might come to his senses once he is on his way, but if he does not, all one can hope for is that his life is spared." Georges felt better having shared his grief and felt he could face his family again, then took his leave, saying he wanted to reason with his brother one last time. Both Sigmund and Freddy wished him good luck.

Sigmund turned to his son. "He is wasting his time. His brother's mind is made up. So many young people of all nationalities, and by this I mean not only Europeans but from all over the world, are flocking to Spain." Freddy looked surprised. "It is all over the papers." His son blushed, for he had not held a newspaper in his hands for some time. "You want to keep yourself informed about what is happening in the world, no matter how busy you are," Sigmund continued, reprimanding his son. Indeed, Georges' attempt was fruitless. His brother left at sunrise and a deep feeling of loss crept over the household.

Hitler became involved in the Spanish conflict after meeting with Franco at the General's request and signing a deal with him. The German Luftwaffe had flown the General and his troops from Morocco back to the south of Spain where he proclaimed himself head of the opposition forces. On that September day, Walter Warheit of the German General Staff was on his way to take up his post as German Commander and Military Advisor to the General. The following month, the Advisor suggested a German Condor Legion be formed to fight in the Spanish Civil War. After some consideration in Berlin, the suggestion was accepted. Mussolini, not wanting to be left behind, contributed twenty thousand troops to the cause.

Chapter 38

Having discovered the monster her husband was, and wishing she would never have to set eyes on him again, Martha went about her daily chores joyously. She felt as if she had just been released from prison. Sure, life was not easy living and became more difficult with every passing day, for food was scarce and she had learned to improvise. However, she belonged to the privileged ones for she could still count on fresh produce from the farm at Bunny Hill. If things continued to worsen, she would probably have to consider moving out to the country. She did not want to contemplate this alternative yet, Helmut still had one year of schooling left and she really wanted him to finish. With the future looking bleak due to Hitler's expansionist policies, she felt this would probably be the only education he would receive.

She kept very much to herself and was polite to those she met on the street, but she trusted no one. Denouncing neighbours and friends had become a national sport and she thought long and hard about what drove people to turn their backs on their friends and family members. She finally came to the conclusion that it was either jealousy or a means of settling grudges.

Her own inner peace radiated onto the other family members. Helmut's grades had improved substantially, for one; he no longer lived on edge waiting for the next bitter quarrel between his parents to break out. His hell on earth, as he used to call it, had been replaced by an oasis of peace. But this contented ambiance was suddenly shattered by Peter's unexpected return.

The whole family had gathered in the kitchen and were about to sit down to dinner when he walked in. Everyone froze. "Is this the way you greet your husband and father after such a long absence?" he roared.

The colour drained form Helmut's face. *Oh, no,* he thought, *this cannot be true.*

Martha was the first to regain her composure. "Why, this sure is a surprise, I thought that I had seen the last of you when you left."

"As you can see, much to your affliction, I am alive and well and I am back among my family where I belong."

"You are wrong," replied Martha gathering all her courage. "You no longer belong here."

Peter looked at her, seething with rage. "You seem to forget that this is my house and that it is I who pay the bills. I have told you repeatedly you are free to leave, all you have to do is pack your bags, but of course you won't because you have nowhere to turn," he said. "You are my prisoner and I am your jail keeper, so don't keep staring at me with that wide-open mouth of yours, showing me all your dental work, get my dinner on the table. I have not had a bite to eat since last night."

Helmut turned red with contained rage, but his mother looked at him pleadingly to keep his mouth shut, as she set another place at the table and served her husband his dinner. He ate as if it were his last meal. "You are not going to stand around watching me like I'm on some kind of stage, sit down and eat." Everyone sat down and put food on their plates, but they could only play around with it, having lost their appetites. "Eat, I said."

"We are not hungry," said Helmut in a small voice.

"And what about you," he said, turning to Martha.

"The sight of you has taken away my appetite."

"Good, maybe by eating less, or not at all, you will lose some weight." He busied himself with his food and did not utter another word. When he finally finished, he pushed his chair back and said with a sneer, "You will not have to put up with my presence for long; I just came back for a change of clothing. I am leaving for Spain tomorrow."

Martha breathed a sigh of relief but at breakfast the following morning, Peter received a message advising him that his trip had been postponed for a week. Thankfully, she did not see much of him. He left very early and by the time he returned late at night, she was sound asleep. She went about her business as usual but there was a look of sadness on her face, and reflecting on her life, she'd had so many hopes and so many illusions that had been nothing but dreams, dreams that would never come true. Things might have been different had Peter not joined the Party. The Party was not to blame, she corrected herself, there was something evil in him that would have emerged sooner or later. The Party provided fertile ground for it and his wickedness just flourished.

Peter left a week later in the middle of the night and nobody came to see him off. The door slammed behind him and he did not bother to look back. He hated his wife and all the values she stood for and, had he not possessed such a strong character, she would have run all over him and brought his career, not only to a halt but might have even landed them all in jail as well. As far as his children were concerned, they were all grown up and independent. Only Helmut was still at home and he could not bear the sight of him, since he was not only the spitting-image of his mother and her 'baby', he was the only one who had the courage to stand up to him. In fact, he had all the qualities the Führer looked for in young people and would have been a means to enhance his own standing in the Party, but it was too late now. The respect he had not received from his family, he found within that entity. Sure, his behaviour had not always been very orthodox, but it served his cause well.

Why look back at the past he told himself, the future lay before him and it would be an exciting one, he was about to begin a new life in a distant country and if everything went according to his wishes, this was the last time he had both set foot in his home and his eyes on his family. "Good riddance," he said out loud. A drunk staggering on his way home waved at him. *That must be a good omen,* thought Peter, and smiled. He soon joined a group of dark figures, his travelling companions.

Things had taken a turn for the worse in Spain. The government was forced to leave Madrid and make the city of Valencia its headquarters. The Junta tried to cut both the road and rail links between the two cities but did not succeed. The Republicans rejoiced with the supporters they had in Britain and France when the Italian troops, who were taking part in the offensive, left their positions and fled. With the support of the Condor Legion, General Franco decided to try and capture the Basque country. He advanced slowly and with growing difficulty. Guernica, the capital of the country, was the target of the German aircraft and refugees from the surrounding countryside had found shelter in the capital. The population, which was 7,000 in normal times, increased to 10,000. A thousand Basque soldiers were stationed to the north of the town and no troops were retreating through it.

It was 26 April 1937, Monday market day. The Germans made the city their target and the German Heinkels flew low, dropping bombs near the train station and machine-gunning the area around it. The Junkers 525 followed them. They unloaded their bombs, a ton at a time, but the deadly cargo did not consist of just fifty and hundred pound bombs, it consisted of great torpedoes weighing a thousand. They tore down buildings, penetrated refuges and the people, who had been brave so far, now panicked.

An escort of the Heinkel 518, whose crew had amused itself machine-gunning the roads around the city and killing or wounding everything in the countryside, seemed to have been waiting for the inhabitants to flee. As soon as they saw them running for their lives, they dived low over them and machine-gunned everything below. They killed woman and children. Those who had kept their calm hid in ditches and leaned against tree trunks, or ran across the fields. Some of them decided to run back into the city to try and escape from the planes. But the pilots had no pity and had turned into monsters. They bombed the city for three hours. No one knows exactly how many died in the offensive. It is believed that more than 1,645 people were murdered. Amazingly enough, the crucial bridge on the road through the town and local arms factory was not hit. The bombing of Guernica caused great indignation outside of Spain and showed what one could expect from the Germans.

Peter and his companions arrived in Spain a week before the attack and were notified only a couple of hours before what their mission would be. It was then that he learned that his companion's real identity were pilots. He wondered what he was doing here, he'd never shown interest in flying or aircraft so why had he been sent here? He soon found out that he was to man one of the machine guns and cheer his comrades on. Peter felt a surge of adrenaline when the plane took off and avenged himself in every woman he killed. No longer able to control himself, he shouted with glee as they hit more and more targets, whatever sensitivity he might have once possessed was now replaced with a heart of stone. He turned into an ogre and he and his companions got carried away, turning their mission into a game.

Their plane was the last to return to the base and when they finally arrived, after circling the ruins of the city several times to rejoice over the damage they had caused, several high-ranking officers greeted them and congratulated them for having hit the most targets. The pilots pointed a finger at Peter. "He's the one who should take all the credit for it. When he came on board he said, 'we have a mission to accomplish and we will be the best' then led us on. There was no stopping him and had we not run out of ammunition, we probably would still be in the air."

"This merits a celebration," said one of the officers, leading them toward the bar. The one who seemed to be in command walked alongside Peter. He stopped just outside the entrance and spoke in a low voice. "The Führer is very proud of everything you have accomplished. As a token of appreciation, we are sending you to the Balearic Islands. You can rest and enjoy yourself, and I am sure you will not be bored. When the Battleship Deutschland arrives, you are to supervise the unloading of the military supplies it will be bringing."

Peter glowed. "When is she due in?" he asked.

"In a week, more or less," was the answer.

A week of beach, having fun with the beautiful and shy Spanish girls, eating and drinking, what a life he would lead. He thanked the officer. "Do not thank me, you have worked hard to earn it," and after a slight pause, he added, "I just wish we had more like you," he said, and led the way to the bar.

"One last question," asked Peter, taking his arm and pulling him back. "When do I leave?"

"Tomorrow you will fly with the same pilots you flew with this afternoon."

They would have spent the night in the bar and probably gotten drunk had they not had to get up very early the following morning. Peter slept fitfully. The sounds of the day before were still ringing in his ears. He got up, washed and dressed. He felt numb and so very tired. "I will have plenty of time to rest once I arrive at my destination," he reminded himself. "Some fresh air might help," he then thought, and decided to wait for the car outside. He was just closing the door behind him when it pulled up alongside the curb.

The pilots looked as if they had not slept much themselves and everyone boarded the plane without speaking a word. Peter dozed off, awakened only by the roar of the engines. He looked out the window; they were on the runway and in the air in no time. They circled for a few minutes over what remained of the town and he gazed down upon it. He wondered how many woman and children had he killed. 'Thou shall not kill, thou shall not kill.' There it was again, the little voice that had tortured him all through the night. He closed his eyes, just wanting to forget, comforted by the thought that once he arrived at his destination, Guernica, like all his other missions, would retreat into the past.

The pilots in the cockpit were wide-awake. The plane was on its course and time hung heavily on their hands. "I wonder how our passenger is faring," said the captain.

His co-pilot opened the cockpit door. "He is sound asleep. I have never met anyone as ruthless."

"There was no stopping him and as for myself, I do not know what got hold of me," said the captain.

"Nor of me," said his co-pilot. "It was as if the devil had taken over my body."

"Let's not discuss it."

"Well, at least our superiors were pleased."

"A lot of good that is going to do when we meet our Creator and have to account for our actions here on earth."

"I hope that is not going to happen any time soon."

"Frankly, I really have no time to fret about it. One has to live in the present and not worry about the future. Everything is so uncertain. We may not be alive tomorrow."

"Have you been told what our next mission will be yet?"

"No, and to tell you the truth, I do not care, I have no other choice than to obey, even if my conscience tells me otherwise."

"You have a conscience? Mine left me a long time ago."

The captain shot his co-pilot a surprised look and said, "You have probably silenced it, but I have not yet found the switch so I still have to live with mine. Maybe that is not a bad thing since it keeps me human," he added as an afterthought. His co-pilot did not reply. A whole world separated them.

The plane shook slightly as it hit the runway. Peter opened his eyes. "I have finally arrived in Paradise," he said and smiled broadly. There was someone on the tarmac to greet them and the pilots were going to get out and stretch their legs but were told to stay on board. On his way into town, Peter caught a glimpse of the plane as it rose high into the cloudless sky.

"No time for leisure," said his escort gruffly. He dropped him off in front of a small, run down cottage, saying he would find everything his heart could possibly desire inside, then turned around hastily and left.

A beautiful, olive skinned girl greeted him as he walked in and introduced herself as Anna. That was the only word Peter understood. *What a contrast to my middle-aged, unkempt wife,* he thought, as he looked at her admiringly. His intuition had not failed him and he was on his way to a wonderful new life, telling himself the past was no longer, he had left it behind and the present was all that mattered. But try as he might, the events from the last couple of days and hours refused to be banned from his mind. The vision of the bombed city and the dead and mutilated bodies followed him everywhere. He fled into her arms trying to find solace in them, only to be tortured by the vision of Martha and his children. He tried everything.

He partied with Anna until the wee morning hours and fell into bed exhausted, but no sooner did his head hit the pillow that the vision of his life unfolded before him as if on a screen. The intake of alcohol did not help his cause, if anything it made it worse, for he had to contend with the ensuing headache, and it amazed him to see how fast in life things could change. He said to himself out loud: "The roles have now switched. Martha was once my prisoner and I her jailor, now it is the other way round."

Anna had mixed feelings about him. One minute he could be so sweet and caring, the next he could turn into a lump of ice. She was also afraid of him. She understood a little German, just enough to fetch him a beer or serve him breakfast, and she was intrigued by him. But something was gnawing at him and yet she was unable to span a bridge between them. It frustrated her so. On the other hand, being practical, she thought, *Who knows what I am being protected from.*

One day, his attitude changed and nothing seemed to matter to him any longer. There was a faraway look in his eyes and he would stare into space for hours on end, not even conscious of what was happening around him. Anna tried talking to him at first but it was as if he had lost his hearing overnight. Soon realising the helplessness of the situation, she gave up on him.

But Anna was mistaken. He was aware of her presence and his surroundings, he had just lost all interest in the present and within the last couple of days had realised that the past is relentless and would not let him out of its grip. He asked himself time and again why he had become who he had become and as he sat there, gazing into space, he suddenly saw himself as a child again, surrounded by his loving and caring parents. They didn't have much money but they had solid values and had tried to pass them on to their children. All of a sudden, he heard his mother's voice.

"What has become of you, Peter? I taught you to be lenient with those who are different and you have rejected them. I taught you to be generous towards others and you have only pursued your own interests. I taught you to remain humble but fame and power have gone to your head. You have turned away from all my teachings and sold your soul to the devil." He looked up. The voice had gone and all he could hear was the roar of the waves. His mother was right.

He'd failed in every aspect, allowing himself to be seduced by power, transgressing against his own values and convictions in order to gain the power he had. He closed his eyes and ears, the mere thought brought the memory of Nathan's screams and Helmut's horror-stricken face to mind. His actions dehumanised him completely and yes, he had become a monster. Wherever he went, whatever he did, the voice repeated incessantly, "Look what has become of you." The eyes of a monster staring back at him in the mirror. He could not flee from himself and he could not silence his conscience, either, for now he was desperate and could only find release and peace in death. Yes, his only option was death; he knew he had no choice and his resolve began to take shape in his mind. He had nothing to lose, no one would miss him and he would have set an end to his misery, his conscience silenced for good.

The MS Deutschland anchored and some fisherman and their families ran down to the beach to take a look at this big, foreign ship. Peter had just boarded when, out of the clear blue sky, the Spanish Republican bombers dove down over it. A complete squadron kept on coming and they bombed the ship until there was virtually nothing left of it. The villagers fled in panic and finally the City of Guernica had been avenged.

Providence had had mercy on Peter and he died instantly. Weeks later, an SS officer knocked on Martha's door but his summons went unanswered, much to his relief. He hurriedly took an envelope out of his coat pocket and, after sliding it beneath the door, walked swiftly down the street. Martha's eyes fell on it as soon as she let herself in. She opened it with misgivings, her fingers trembling as she removed a sheet of paper that read: "We are sorry to inform you that your husband has died a hero's death." She stared at the contents in disbelief. One more example of the ruthlessness the people in power possessed. She gave Helmut the news after dinner. "Mama," he said, "do you realise what this means?"

"I am a widow," she replied.

"And you are free, free at last," was Helmut's last thought before he fell asleep, having shed no tears.

Chapter 39

The time had come for Freddy to return to Crans Montana. He whistled to himself while packing his bag. Winter was well on its way and he was sure that it would not be long before the ski season opened, having not forgotten the lovely Swiss girl he encountered on the slopes.

Marianne; she was so pretty and so much fun to be with. He really looked forward to seeing her as well as all his friends. Freddy sent Father Christian a note advising him of his arrival and he was absolutely certain that the pastor would be meeting him at the station if he did not have another engagement. He was also happy to be leaving Paris. He had seen his friends and returned to his part time job as delivery boy, much to the delight of his lady fans, and he smiled thinking of them. But he also found Paris very oppressive and missed his freedom and privacy. The continual questions about his whereabouts and well-being, among others, were making him increasingly impatient towards his parents and with every passing day, it was becoming more and more difficult for him to control his temper. But because he could sense the tension rising, he wanted to avoid an outburst at all costs.

Upon his return, Dr Wolf told him he would probably have to stay for three weeks to a month. However, if he found the job he was hoping for, he might be able to stay for the season. He opened his wardrobe door and took out a box and set the content on his bed. Unbeknownst to his parents, he had purchased a second-hand typewriter with his savings and if everything went according to plan, he would be able to support himself, thereby easing the economic burden on his father. He finished packing and joined his parents in the living room. "All packed?" asked Helene.

"Yes, I am, Mama…" The sound of the doorbell interrupted his answer. "I will get it." It was Georges, he looked pale and shaken.

"We just got word that my brother and his friends have been killed. No details. My parents are devastated."

Helene and Sigmund, overhearing the conversation, silently exchanged glances. It was just as Sigmund had predicted weeks before. They hurried to the entrance hall. "I am so sorry," said Helene. "We overheard what you were saying, but please, let us not stand here in the cold."

Freddy took his distraught friend by the arm and ushered him into the living room. "Sir," said Georges, turning to Sigmund. "The events turned out just as you predicted."

Sigmund nodded and said gently, "You did everything to prevent him from leaving but each one is the master of his destiny."

"I am going to miss you, Freddy. Do you know when you will be back?"

Sigmund replied for him saying, "As soon as possible, I hope. I am confident that Dr Wolf will find him almost fully re-established and that the fresh mountain air will work wonders."

After some more small talk, Freddy stood up and said he would walk Georges home to give the family their condolences.

Georges' mother was sitting in her wheelchair and when she heard Freddy, she lifted her head and her face lit up. "It is so terrible," she said.

"We did everything to prevent him from leaving," said Georges' father, "but to die so young…"

Freddy's heart went out to them, but no words could mitigate their pain. Georges gently pushed him out of the room. "I have tried to distract them with small talk, but to no avail. Dad received an order from a very important Parisian family for a large modern table centrepiece. I designed one and showed it to him, but he just gave it one look and shrugged his shoulders. I do not know what I am going to do after you leave."

"It is going to be very lonely here, I know," said Freddy.

"It really is too bad you can't postpone your departure."

His chum ignored the hint. "As time goes by, things will get back to normal. One can't grieve forever and life does not stand still."

"How long are you planning on being away?" his friend, changing the subject.

"A couple of weeks…"

"I can see that look in your eyes…tell me the truth."

"I would like to stay until spring."

"You must be joking."

"I am not," and he shared his plans with his friend. "I will be supporting myself, which will be a heavy load off my father's shoulders. I really believe they will both agree to it."

"I would not be so sure if I were you."

"What about that project he has for you, spending the summer in England? Are you going to shelve it?"

"Not at all, one has nothing to do with the other. I had better leave now."

Georges' sister came into the room, her eyes swollen from crying, but when she saw Freddy her face lit up. "Hello, Freddy, what a surprise! I did not know you were here."

"I will walk you to the door," said Georges.

"You are leaving already?"

"I have been here for a while," said Freddy, "and I still have to finish my packing."

"So it is true," she said, looking at her brother. "I told you I never make up stories but you just choose to believe what you want to."

"What is this about?" Freddy asked.

Georges grinned and watched his sister blush to the roots of her hair. "Oh, nothing important, girls just have a way of living in their own make-believe world."

"If you say so, I have no experience along those lines," Georges muttered under his breath just loud enough for his friend to hear.

"You do not expect me to buy that," Freddy laughed out loud and, giving his friend's sister a brotherly hug, followed him down the long corridor and out the front door to the gate.

Out of earshot, Georges whispered, "So who is she?"

Freddy looked at him in surprise. "What are you implying?"

"I am just asking who she is."

"I really have to run." They shook hands then Georges wished him good luck and followed him with his eyes until he disappeared from sight.

His sister was standing in the same spot when Georges returned. "You sure have a crush on him, don't you?"

"He is such a gentleman and I love his eyes, they give him away."

"I would stop thinking of him if I were you," said her brother. "He is Jewish you are Christian and a world lies between the two of you."

After breakfast the next morning, Freddy and his parents took the metro to the train station. The trip had become a part of their routine. Standing in the smelly, stuffy carriage, Sigmund remembered the good old days in Frankfurt when he would drive the family to and from the station, never once dreaming he would have to one day submit himself to the indignity of public transportation. He had the Nazis and Mr Hitler to thank for this, not to mention that scoundrel of a friend who had been unreachable by phone. He then heard the last part of Freddy's sentence: "It will be out next Wednesday."

"What are you talking about?"

"I was talking about the new edition of stamps."

"Stamps, stamps, stamps, nothing else interests you," replied his father bitterly.

"Now, Papa, that is not true."

Sigmund shrugged his shoulders, he was not going to get into an argument, giving vent to his frustration and becoming the centre of attention of all his fellow passengers whom he felt were doing nothing else but staring at him from behind their Le Figaro's.

They got off the train without exchanging another word, then, "I am sorry I was so harsh," he said, as he placed a hand on his son's shoulders. "I am going to miss you very much. It hurts me profoundly to part from you." Freddy could see tears in his father's eyes. This took him completely by surprise, for his father had always been a master at controlling his emotions.

"I will return, Papa," said Freddy, "and when I do, I assure you I will be completely cured."

"That is my one and only wish and once it is granted, I will be able to rest in peace."

Helene handed Freddy a bag. "I baked your favourite cake."

"Mama," Freddy started to say but she ignored the interruption.

"When you share it with your friends, you will think of home," she said.

Freddy hugged her and then his father. "Don't stay away too long, son," he whispered in his ear.

The last passengers were boarding the train. Freddy did not reply, he just picked up his suitcase, hugged his parents one last time and got on board. No sooner had the carriage door slammed shut behind him than they were on their way. He waved at his parents until he lost them from sight and went to find his seat.

The elation he'd felt during the last couple of days gave way to sadness. The rumbling of the train soon put him to sleep, but the conductor screaming 'Lausanne! End of the journey!' at the top of his lungs woke him up. His booming voice was so loud, even the dead must have heard him and, just as a graveyard came into sight, he giggled out loud at the thought of them all sitting up in their graves not knowing what was going on.

He collected his belongings and was the first one to leave the train, not having much time to make his connection, he rushed through the crowd. As fate would have it, he had to walk to the other side of the station to get to his train and arrived none too soon. He walked from carriage to carriage until finally finding an empty seat. It was a shorter trip, the time passed quickly and he enjoyed watching the scenery. There was something so peaceful and relaxing about the Swiss countryside.

Just as he had surmised, Father Christian was at the station to meet him. "Is it welcome back or welcome home?" he inquired with a twinkle in his eye.

"It is welcome home," he replied without hesitation.

"Boy, so you have come to stay."

"God willing, yes, and I have brought the typewriter. All I need is to find a job and I will be set at least until April."

"April? I thought you were coming to stay."

"I am, but I promised Georges that I would be back by April for a break," he said, not mentioning the promise he had made his father.

"Well, then let us be on our way."

It had snowed the night before and it looked like a winter wonderland. Father Christian said, "The ski stations opened last weekend."

"I will be busy with the clinic, finding work and going skiing."

"All those activities should keep you out of trouble. You have not told me where I am to drop you off," said his friend.

"Pension Enzian. I am sure mother reserved a room for me." They pulled up in front of the chalet Freddy remembered so well. "Nothing has changed."

"No, just a few more people who have moved here and a few more tourists. Enough going on for me not to be bored. I will come back and pick you up for dinner," said his friend, putting the car into gear. "We can catch up then."

His landlady gave him a warm welcome and handed him the key to his room. He thought how nice it was to be on his own, as he unlocked the door. It took him a few minutes to unpack, then he lay down on his bed and was asleep before he knew it.

Father Christian got tired of waiting in the car and let out a sigh. He disliked winter intensely and hated walking on snow. His shoes felt wet, his feet were cold for days on end and he could feel the chill already running down his spine, but he had no choice: He would have to get out and see what had happened to Freddy.

The stairs creaked as he took them two steps at a time, as was his habit. He caught a quick glimpse of the landlady following him with her eyes, blaming the creaking probably on his weight and not on the old wood. He gently opened the door. Freddy was sitting up in bed rubbing his eyes. "I must have fallen asleep," he said sheepishly. "So sorry, have you been waiting long?"

"It does not matter, get ready and let's go. I do not know about you but I am starving."

Freddy grabbed his jacket, put on his warm winter boots and led the way out the door. "It is this lovely, clean, fresh air that tires everyone out," said the landlady. "Nobody is used to breathing pure oxygen anymore and when they do, it is like an anaesthetic…it knocks them out. But then, that is what they come here for," she kept on mumbling to herself, not realising that her guests had left.

"That is what happens as people grow older," remarked Freddy, laughing. "They talk to themselves as if they were in the best of company."

"I would not laugh about it," said his friend seriously. "Who knows, maybe they are, but they are invisible to us."

"You must be kidding," said Freddy.

"No, I am serious." Suddenly, he burst out laughing.

"Thank God, I was starting to believe you had lost it." Then Freddy described the vision he had on the train and his friend found it hilarious. It was like old times, as if Freddy had never been away.

Their dinner lasted well into the evening, each one filling in the other with everything that had happened. Father Christian had been fairly busy but, as he remarked, his life was not as glamorous or as exciting as his friend's. And anyway, how could it be? Crans was not Paris, a city that never sleeps and offers everything one could dream of, subjected to one having the economic means. This small little town had the one thing that Paris could not offer, however, that which was accessible to everyone regardless of race, social or economic background: The wonderful fresh and clean air that had cured so many people suffering from respiratory disorders.

This gave the town a cosmopolitan, international feeling and, in father Christian's case, it especially allowed him to have contact with people from all over the world. He enjoyed people and was always receptive to new ideas and point of views. As he pointed out to Freddy, his constantly changing flock had contributed enormously to his own personal growth.

"One day last summer, I took a stroll down to the water mill, which is at the other end of town. I do not know if you have seen it but it is an idyllic spot. The water flows steadily and the wheel turns at the same pace day in day out. It is so peaceful. I was standing watching it and a boy and a girl were playing on the manicured lawn not too far from it. The boy was teasing her and she had her hair combed into two ponytails tied with white ribbons. As she ran, they seemed to be dancing in the wind. I looked at the children, they were so carefree and happy, then I turned my attention back to the water mill. Just like life, I thought to myself as I gazed at the constant flow of water, it flows forward and there is no turning back, what has happened has happened, and like life, it follows a direction. The children added to the colourfulness of the scene. In life, the people who surround us can have either a positive or negative effect, or no effect on us whatsoever, but life, like the flow of the water continues undeterred."

"In other words, we are only influenced if we are receptive. If we close up like a clam, all those influences will pass us by, so basically it is our choice." Freddy elaborated.

"You have chosen well and I like the person you have become.

I much prefer it to the one who left."

"Is that a compliment?"

"I am speaking from the heart."

"Thanks," said Freddy.

"What is your schedule for tomorrow?"

"I will be spending most of the day at the clinic."

"I am sure we will run into each other as I have some patients I have to spend some time with."

Freddy lay in bed, pondering his friend's words. He *had* changed. He was deeply touched by the events that had taken place in Georges' family and realised that there was far more to life than just having a good time. After his tests were taken, Freddy waited patiently for Dr Wolf who was running late, as usual. He busied himself reading a copy of the local newspaper and it was the classified section he was mainly interested in.

Vicky, Dr Wolfe's nurse, came around and told him he would not have much longer to wait.

"Are you looking for a job?" she asked.

"Why, yes," replied Freddy, "I bought myself a typewriter and am hoping—" But his words were interrupted by Dr Wolf arriving at the clinic.

"Good morning, Freddy, sorry I am late." And Freddy followed him into the consultation room without saying another word to Vicky. "You seem to be on the road to complete recovery. We will, of course, have to wait for the results of the tests, which should be in a few days, but if they are as normal as I surmise, you will be able to return home in a couple of weeks."

Freddy looked at him. "I am hoping to spend the season here and stay until April."

"Right now I do not see—"

"No, Dr Wolf, you do not understand. I love the mountains, the fresh air, the skiing and—"

"What is her name?" the doctor asked, Freddy blushed. "So there *is* a girl."

330

"Well, sort of, I have not seen her yet, but I want to find a job so I am independent."

Just then, Vicky announced the next patient. "We will continue this conversation next week when we go over the results. In the meantime, I would like you to exercise…"

Freddy ended the sentence for him. "The usual, right?"

"I am sorry I interrupted your conversation," said Vicky. "But I could no longer humour the patient."

"That's quite all right."

"So, what kind of a job are you looking for?"

"Anything."

"I heard the pharmacist is looking for a temporary delivery boy. You can tell him I told you about it, he is my boyfriend."

Freddy looked at the time and said, "I will go and find him right now."

"Good luck," she said to him.

A delivery job was not exactly what he was looking for but it would do for the time being. He pondered what Dr Wolf said about being able to go home in a couple of weeks. How was he to convince his parents, but mostly his father, about not returning till April? His father's words still rang in his ears, "Don't stay away too long, son."

Before heading into town, he stopped at his lodgings to pick up the stamps. The dealer was on the way to where he was going and it would do no harm to stop by and offer them to him. The cash would come in handy, as he still had to purchase his lift tickets and who knows, if he ran into Marianne he might invite her to dinner. That was the nice thing about having his own earned money; he owed no one an explanation. How he hated having to write down every penny he spent and his father's letters asking him to account for the one miserable penny that did not allow his accounts to balance. He brought up the issue once, asking him, "Can't you be generous and ignore it? We're not talking hundreds or thousands." His father wrote back saying that one penny here and one penny there all add up and pretty soon one was looking at a large amount of money.

Freddy had to concede that his father had a point and applied the same principles to his own accounting. The pharmacist was delighted and told Freddy he had been looking for some time but no one was really interested because it interfered with their skiing. Freddy had assumed it was just a part time job but he was wrong, it was full time. Of course he had two hours for lunch and Sundays off as well. But even if there were no deliveries, he would have to stay and hope that some work would turn up. So, he basically had to work all week and even though the pay was good, it really was not what he envisioned.

"I am sorry," he told the pharmacist. "I was hoping to get a part time job that would not only give me a little extra money but would also allow me to be out in the fresh air exercising."

The pharmacist interrupted him saying, "You *would* have the weekends."

"Yes, I realise that, but it is not enough. I am recovering from TB and my doctor's orders are—"

"I know what they are," said the pharmacist. "Come back and see me when you are fully healed." The pharmacists then turned his attention to a customer. Freddy walked down the street with his head held high.

Chapter 40

After seeing Freddy off, Sigmund and Helene slowly made their way back home, each one deep in his or her own thoughts. Sigmund was trying hard to bring his emotions under control; never letting them control him, he always controlled *them*, but this time something happened. The sadness and sense of loss overpowered him, a feeling similar to when he gazed at his beloved Alice, knowing that she was departing this life. "Strange," he said to himself out loud.

"What is strange?" Helene asked, overhearing him.

"Nothing, nothing at all," he replied, irritably.

"Sorry, I did not mean—" She did not finish her sentence. He gave her one look and Helene took the hint immediately.

Upon arriving home, Sigmund went straight to his study and closed the door. He just wanted to be alone and give himself some time. "Why this sadness, why this sense of loss?" he asked himself time and time again. He felt drained and tired. Everything was an effort. The doctor said he had found nothing wrong with him, but suddenly he remembered the blood test that he did not receive the results of, too busy talking to Freddy and trying to finish reading one of his books. And Helene could not remind him, for he had kept her in the dark. "Maybe I should go and see the doctor," he said out loud. "Maybe I am not as healthy as I am trying to make myself believe."

He lay back in his chair and closed his eyes, trying to silence his inner voice. Doctors are doctors. They are all the same. They go by the book, not by the individual. Your head hurts? Take an aspirin. They are so busy always rushing for time. When they are in medical school, they are told how sacred human life is, how compassionate and caring they must be towards their patients and how much time they must devote to each one in order to achieve this. That is in theory, in medical school. In reality, once they have their own practice or join up with other colleagues, or work in hospitals, they are overwhelmed. Too many patients, very tight schedules to accommodate them all, thus sacrificing the time and care given to each.

"Tell me your symptoms," they ask each patient between checking their blood pressure and listening to their lungs. Then the doctor goes back to his desk and writes out a prescription, hands it over and tells them to come back in a couple of weeks if the symptoms persist. The physical state is looked at and the mental state is fully ignored.

Sigmund could no longer bear listening to this inner monologue and he opened his eyes. If this continues, I might as well write a dissertation on medical care and laughed at the mere thought of it.

Helene, who was within hearing distance, rejoiced and decided that he must be in better spirits. Without giving it a second thought, she opened the door and walked in. "You must be in a good mood," she said, sitting down across from him.

"Actually, I am," he replied. "Ever since I came into my study and sat down, I have had this inner dialogue that at first was driving me crazy but now I find very funny," and then proceeded to share it with her.

She frowned as she listened then said, "You know, our bodies are miracles. I have been looking at a book on anatomy and it is amazing how every detail in our body is linked to another, how one action in one cell leads to a reaction in another. It is so perfect that man will never be able to copy or to really understand it."

"I realise that," said Sigmund. "This is why I do not trust doctors. They have the knowledge but that knowledge is limited."

"Only our Creator possesses the truth," said Helene. "For we are a copy of him. You go to a doctor and you might be told that you are really ill even though you feel fine, and you end up believing it and your body ends up with all the symptoms as a result of it. In a way, it is all in the mind. I am convinced of this.

But why are we having this conversation, are you feeling unwell?" she asked with a look of concern on her face.

"Not really, although it seems to me that I tire easily, I fall asleep over my reading and I've lost a little weight."

"How do you know? You look the same to me."

"The scale tells me. But anyway, I was just wondering about my health in general. And I must confess, and you are not going to like this, the doctor took some blood tests and I completely forgot about them until now."

"They might be the answer to all your questions."

"I hope so. What have you being doing?" Sigmund then asked his wife.

"I was tired so I had a short nap and then prepared dinner, your favourite meal and dessert. I thought you might be hungry."

"What time is it?" He looked at his watch. "Really…the older you get, the faster time seems to pass. I had not realised it was this late."

"I will set the table," said Helene, getting up.

"I will help you."

While she stirred the soup so it would not stick to the bottom of the pan, he set the table. She thought how charming and helpful he could be when he is in a good mood. Unfortunately, this was not often the case, more the exception, like when they began dating. She smiled to herself.

"You are smiling," said Sigmund, who had been watching her. "A penny for your thoughts?"

"Just being here together and you helping brought back memories of happy times gone by. We were dating then and when you came to my home for dinner, it was always teamwork, like now."

"Yes, those were happy times, indeed, and look at all that has happened since then. One could almost write a novel about it. In those days, nobody believed, or wanted to believe, that we would have to leave our beloved Germany in order to have a life and that we would become refugees."

"That is what we are, remember? Freddy and I both requested to be given the status of German refugees."

Sigmund's mind went over the parameters of the status of a refugee. It had been in accordance with the Convention of Recognition of the Status of German Refugees that was signed by Leo Blum, head of the French Government on 17 September 1936. At a later date, this would be changed to Refugees Coming from Germany, as the Jews would have been stripped of their nationality.

"I had forgotten about that, you are not only refugees by name but you have it confirmed on paper as well."

"I do not like the word. It means we are at the mercy of a country that has allowed us to settle here. The government of France can decide it no longer wants us and have us expelled. The French look down on us because we are a burden to the state and their tax money is being used to support us, not to mention that they are very much afraid we will take away their jobs and have nothing to offer in return. That is the reason why in the past, when I was looking for a job, as soon as the person interviewing me heard my French spoken with a German accent, they very politely told me I did not qualify."

Sigmund interrupted her. "You are forgetting the bad economic situation the country is in. The franc is becoming weaker and weaker and this is creating a lot of discontent among the population. We have seen some strikes, but I can assure you the worst is still to come. No government can hold its ground under these circumstances."

"Do you mean the government or the prime minister?" asked Helene.

"I mean both," replied Sigmund drily. "And just look at what is going on around us in Europe. Austria has proclaimed itself part of Germany, Hitler has his sights set on Czechoslovakia and was eyeing the Sudetenland like a hungry wolf. His argument was that the vast majority of the population in that region are German and therefore the whole border region should become part of Germany. He got away with that after long and heated discussions. Then Britain, France and Italy agreed to a settlement known as the Munich Agreements with Germany, whereby they would not defend Czechoslovakia if Hitler annexed the Sudetenland, not wanting to be dragged into another war once again Hitler got what he wanted."

"Do you think he is going to come after France?" asked Helene.

"He might, who knows?"

"Do you believe Britain and the rest of Europe would just stand by if that happened?"

"I cannot answer that question, Helene, only time will tell."

"I hope it does not happen," said Helene. "If it did, us leaving Germany would have been in vain."

Sigmund looked at her without replying, for he knew that if that were to be the case, he only had himself to blame. Abraham tried so hard to make him aware of what was happening and so had David, but his fear of the unknown and an uncertain future rendered him blind and powerless. Having brought up the subject of Abraham, Sigmund's thoughts went to Nellie. She wrote that she was dating somebody but had not given any details about him whatsoever, but seemed happy and content. Sigmund was certain that after her terrible experience with Andreas, which was still vivid in Sigmund's mind, she would not rush into a relationship. For Nellie's part, she knew that had she given any details about her boyfriend, she would have received a letter from her father rebuffing her behaviour. Arturo was 15 years older than she was and not only was he married, but he also had a daughter. Nellie met him at an office party and, initially not wanting to attend, one of her colleagues persuaded her to accompany her and in the end decided it was probably fate.

Arturo had a good sense of humour, a zest for life and loved all the things she did. He did not mention to her that he was married and when Nellie found out through a comment someone made within an earshot from her, she was surprised and hurt, but by then it was too late. She was head over heels in love with him.

She confronted him with the knowledge, but he simply shrugged his shoulders and said, looking her straight in the eye, "Nothing to worry about, little rose (as he had taken to calling her) there is nothing between, shall we say my *wife* and me. I was forced to marry her because she was pregnant, but I was never in love with her. You are the love of my life."

Of course, it had been a catholic wedding which meant he could not divorce her, but who cared about formalities? She was Jewish and he would never be accepted by the growing Jewish community anyway, so it was best they just kept their relationship to themselves and lived it to the fullest.

Nellie had, at first, thought she was wasting her time, nothing could come of it and when she sat quietly reading, her attention would wander towards Arturo and her inner voice would invariably make itself heard saying, "You are not only inflicting pain and sorrow on someone but you are playing with fire. Remember, there is no future to this relationship." She would feel remorseful and resolve every time to put an end to it but as soon as she heard his voice, she forgot her resolutions. It was a vicious cycle. She kept her relationship secret from Abraham and the family, for she knew that they would not only have voiced their disapproval but would have also put Sigmund wise to it.

However, she need not have worried about this aspect as the correspondence between Sigmund and Abraham had stopped long ago. One reason for it was that Abraham was really very busy with the brewery, which they had named Bavaria in honour of the Bavarian State known mostly for its beer and the beer festival, which took place every year on the last weekend of September and ended the first weekend of October. Everything went just as it had been planned, the deadlines had all been respected and they were selling more beer than they were able to produce, such was the demand. They were already thinking about expanding the factory and looking around for more land. Emmanuel had been a blessing in disguise.

Abraham had never felt better nor happier and, according to his wife, he even looked younger. They all felt very much at home in their adopted country, Germany and the friends they left behind belonged to the past, something Abraham reminded them of time and time again when they complained. "You cannot live in the past, you have to live in the present if you want to be happy and content," he would say.

It was Arturo who found the flat for her and she was overjoyed at leaving Abraham and his family's home behind. Hiding her relationship from them had been very stressful and at least now, she was on her own and did not have to report her whereabouts and who she was spending time with to anyone. Helene's voice brought Sigmund back to reality. "Where were you?" she asked. "You had such a far away, pained look on your face."

"I was just thinking about Abraham and Nellie and how fear can paralyse one."

"What do you mean?"

"Oh, Helene, I was thinking about your words, if France were to be invaded by Hitler, everything would have been in vain."

"I would not be blaming you," said Helene.

"I would be blaming myself. The fear of the unknown just gripped me and to tell you the truth, I, who have always been optimistic by nature, never, ever thought that this nightmare would happen."

"We are here now and we are making the best of it. Freddy is getting the best care money can buy and he is almost completely recovered."

"It won't be long now before he comes home," said Sigmund.

"We have each other, and everything in life has been good to us. For me, I feel very blessed and grateful for life."

The next morning, Sigmund left the house early but did not mention to Helene where he was going. He went for a stroll in the Luxembourg Gardens and even though the sun was out, there was a strong northerly wind blowing, which made it feel very cold indeed. However, the sky was a beautiful, deep blue and upon waking, he just felt that he needed some time with Mother Nature, some space and some air…but mostly silence.

There were people rushing along, some going to work, others carrying baguettes on their way from the baker's; there was such a diversity of people and one could hear various of languages being spoken. Human beings were all the same no matter what country they came from, sharing the same need for shelter, food, education and health. The four basic needs, and yet so difficult for so many to afford. How was France ever going to be able to fulfil their needs with the number of migrants arriving from Germany and Belgium increasing with every passing day, to say nothing of those arriving from the French colonies in North Africa, looking for a better quality of life? The government will be facing a lot of social unrest if things continue on this course. The prospects of the future were not looking too bright.

He continued his walk, but brought his attention back to the present and himself. Helene had pointed out all their blessings, which reminded him that he should be on his way to the doctor's to pick up his blood test results. He looked at the time; the nurse would be in by now and indeed, she looked up from her work as he walked into the office.

"Do you have an appointment?" she asked. Sigmund explained the situation to her. "The doctor is here and his patient is late. He will see you now."

"I sure am lucky," said Sigmund.

"You are indeed, it is so bitterly cold out there that everybody is staying home or waiting for a break in the weather." The doctor greeted him warmly. "I have been expecting you, Sigmund," he said.

"I guess you have. I forgot all about my blood tests," he replied sheepishly, "and I only remembered them when I started asking myself why I feel so tired."

"Well, you are here now and we have the answers, so let us go over them together. Your red blood count is low and you are still anaemic, which is part of the reason you are feeling so tired. So, I am going to prescribe another iron supplement for you and I would suggest you try and eat some good, red meat at least three times a week."

"I will," said Sigmund, getting up to leave.

"Please have a seat, I am not finished."

Sigmund looked at him in surprise. "Is there something else that is cause for concern?" he asked.

"Yes, I am afraid there is. I do not like that yellow colour of yours, it is an indication of something not right with either the liver or the pancreas and I would like to have them X-rayed. It will give us a clear picture as to what is going on, then we can proceed from there. Your red blood count has never been this low before and I would like to know if anything is causing it."

"What do you mean, doctor?"

"If there is any internal bleeding going on, a stool and urine test will answer that. The samples can be taken right now and I will see if the radiologist can take you this morning as well, that would save you having to come back later."

Sigmund nodded in agreement. Everything the doctor said made sense, but he could sense a kind of urgency in the way the doctor was acting. "Is there any cause for concern?"

"We won't know until we have the results, but I have always been of the opinion that not only time is money, but time is also health. The longer you wait, the harder it becomes to treat whatever is ailing the patient."

"Now that really makes sense doctor." He spent almost the entire day at the doctor's, but he now had the verdict. He was seriously ill. The doctor tried to spare his patient by keeping some of the most relevant information to himself, but Sigmund was determined he be told the whole truth, for as he made it clear to his doctor that it was his body, his life and he had a right to all the knowledge enabling him to decide on the course of treatment. Sigmund listened to the doctor without interrupting him. He had a large tumour on his pancreas, which must have been there for quite some time. There was no way of removing it due to its size and it was also very close to an artery. However, a biopsy could be taken, yet the results have always shown they are malignant.

"So what's the point?" asked Sigmund.

"Just to confirm the diagnosis," replied the doctor.

"I do not need confirmation," said Sigmund. "I will make the most of the time I have left, get my affairs in order and hopefully the Lord will have mercy on me and end my suffering."

"You are very coldblooded," said the doctor, admiringly.

"I was a soldier, once a soldier always a soldier, we are always aware that life and death go hand in hand and we are therefore more detached from life than most."

The nurse announced the arrival of the next patient and Sigmund rose to leave. The doctor handed him a prescription for morphine tablets, should the pain become unbearable. "These will help. Just drop by anytime and should you not be well enough to come, here is my number and I will attend to you in your home," said the doctor as he escorted him to the door.

Sigmund left the doctor's office in a daze. He recalled the monologue he'd had with himself, which he had also shared with Helene. He could not accuse the doctor of guessing his illness for he had seen a picture of the growth on his pancreas himself. His red cell count was low, nobody made that up either, it was a fact. How ignorant he had been, he chided himself quietly, he had not only discredited the doctors, but in the process completely forgot all the modern technology they possessed in order to make a correct diagnosis.

While walking home slowly, his thoughts were taken up with the doctor and his health. He had been open and kind to him and understood Sigmund's wish of not being turned in to an experimental guinea pig. Yes, he was very ill and his days were numbered, but he had the best medical adviser on his side. He was sure that as time went on, a complicity would develop between them. "It has already," said Sigmund out loud, thinking of the morphine tablets. A passer-by turned around to stare at him. *Another lunatic speaking to himself,* thought the stranger, another one who must be on drugs.

Helene had gone about her duties but was a little surprised that Sigmund had left early without mentioning where he was going but then, he was so absent minded sometimes. She let out a sigh of relief when she heard the front door closing. He debated whether to share his knowledge with Helene or not. Unable to find an answer for now, he decided to keep the information to himself. He was in a very thoughtful mood when he got home and gave Helene an absent-minded kiss before searching out the solace of his study, thus avoiding being questioned. Helene just stared after him without uttering a word.

He sure is getting moodier and moodier as time goes by. Her eyes filled with tears. No use crying, she scolded herself, tears are not the solution and feeling sorry for myself is not helpful, either. She had to admit that as time went on, she felt more and more lonely, longing for a companion to do things with, one that she was definitely not finding in her husband. She had no friends or family, yes there was Adele, but she was so taken up by her husband Gerald that she rarely had time. Not to mention that she was not one of Sigmund's favourite people. Stop complaining, she said to herself, Sigmund had seen to it more than once that she leave Paris and visit Freddy in Crans Monatana, so that she got a break from him and the city, even though it was an extra expense. The change of scenery always helped. Now all her hopes were placed on Freddy's return. His friends would come over to see him and once more, the days would be filled with laughter and activity.

Chapter 41

Unaware of his mother's thoughts and of Sigmund's dilemma, Freddy could not have been happier. His medical report was almost perfect. Dr Wolf was beside himself with joy about his young patient's progress. Indeed, he had become very attached to him and reminded him so much of his youngest son, with whom he unfortunately did not share in the complicity nor bond he had developed with Freddy. Neither one of them was to blame for it.

Dr Wolf was married when he was very young, having fallen in love with what, in his eyes, had been the most beautiful girl he had ever seen. She was tall and slender and had a gorgeous face, but it was her eyes that fascinated him. They were a very deep blue and reminded him of the sky on a very cold winter day, but they had the power to express everything, making words unnecessary. They were a reflection of her spirit. When she was sad, they would turn a cold metallic grey, when she was happy they would sparkle, and in the darkness, they reminded him of the stars. Her name was Emma and she had been the love of his life. Unfortunately, after the birth of his second son, who had not been planned, they drifted apart.

Emma demanded more and more time with him, complaining and nagging at him whenever he was home. He thought about leaving his profession several times, but deep down in his heart he knew that if he did, she would complain about something else. Sacrificing his profession for her was something he did think about, but it was so important to him and enabled him to give back to others, for he was a natural born giver, and he knew nothing would have changed. So in the end, when the baby was just a couple of months old, they parted ways in a very civilised manner.

Afterwards, she met a somewhat younger man who came from a wealthy family and therefore able to devote most of his time to her and her whims. His work consisted of looking after his fortune and because he could do that from anywhere in the world, it gave him the freedom to travel. They married soon after they met and his youngest son was closer to his stepdad since, in all fairness, he saw much more of him. *Yes*, thought Dr Wolf, *it will be a sad day when Freddy goes home. I will miss our long conversations but hopefully, we will be able to keep in touch.* All of a sudden, he smiled. "Yes," he said, speaking to himself in a loud voice. "Freddy's love of skiing will bring him back."

Freddy left Doctor Wolf's office with mixed feelings, having made it clear that his recovery was almost complete and that he would be ready to travel in the next week or two. He looked forward to seeing his friends again, to sleeping in his own bed, but it was not the correct timing. He had his mind made up to spend the whole season here and going back to Paris only in the spring. He did not have a clue as to how he was going to handle this subject with his parents, especially with Sigmund, and he could almost hear his father's voice telling him that he was definitely not going to pay for his skiing and other whims. Freddy still had not found a job, which would have enabled him to be independent and free. Yes, money gives you power, but it also enslaves you if you depend on someone else for it. This thought really depressed him. Time proved to him that it had been a huge mistake to turn down the full time job.

He arrived at the ski slope and his heart nearly skipped a beat, looking once more at the girl standing by the steps. It was not a mirage…it was Marianne. This was the breakthrough he had been looking for so he walked straight over to where she was standing and softly called her name.

"Why, hello, when did you arrive? I have been expecting you but then I thought something came up to ruin your return."

"Would you have been disappointed?" he asked.

She gave him a big smile. "Yes, I would have, you are a lot of fun to be with. But let us talk later and get ready."

"Let's go skiing!" they said in one voice.

They were having so much fun, the runs were very well groomed as it had snowed recently, the trees were white and it was winter at its best. They lost all sense of time and it was not until the sun hid behind the mountain did they realise how late it was. They also realised they were hungry. Freddy had not eaten since breakfast.

Saying good night to the slope, they headed into town. "This sure has been a lot of fun, Freddy, and you are such a great skier, I feel so safe just following you down."

"That is a complement," he replied. "Considering it hasn't been that long since I took up the sport."

"Yes, I know," said Marianne. "Skiing is all about balance, about having good balance, and you are very well balanced, I guess, in everything you do."

Freddy laughed. "It is almost as if you were reciting a poem, it has a rhythm to it and it rhymes."

"That is funny but, yes, you are right," said Marianne, giggling. They found a quaint little café Freddy could afford and ordered a little something to eat.

Marianne spent the entire year in Crans Montana, with the exception of a weekend in Lausanne with her parents last summer. They had gone shopping and she swam in the lake, but the water was freezing and she hated getting wet.

"So it was a short dip," said Freddy

"That is correct." She added that she was glad when the weekend was over and headed back home. Mountains surrounded Lausanne, but being a city, it was crowded and noisy and she missed the peacefulness but mostly the sunsets and sunrises. She was definitely not a city girl. "How about you?" she asked Freddy, "I am sure Paris is a much bigger city."

"It is Freddy," replied. "I miss the mountains as well, but what I miss the most is my freedom, up here I do not have to account to anyone. My parents mean well and I love them very much, but they are always prying into my business. I have nothing to hide, but it's the lack of privacy."

"I understand," said Marianne. "I can relate to that. I just hear what I want to hear and ignore the rest."

"That is a good way of dealing with it, but remember, I am an only child whereas…"

"Yes, there are three us and that makes a big difference as far as attention is concerned."

"I sometimes wished I'd had a brother," said Freddy. "I do have a sister, but she is much older than I am, by about 15 years, and she does not live with us. She lives in Colombia, South America."

"Have you ever been there?" Marianne queried. "No, I have not. Perhaps one day," said Freddy.

"My dream," said Marianne, "is to see the world, go to Nepal, see Mount Everest, see the wide Amazon River…yes, that is my dream."

"Well, hopefully one day, it will come true. But now I should be going, it is cold and—"

"Yes, I had forgotten you are recovering."

"I am almost recovered," said Freddy, looking a little sad.

"Anything wrong?" asked Marianne, noticing his expression.

"Not really, I just need to find a job so that I can be on my own and stay until the season ends. If I do not, I will have a very hard time convincing my parents."

"That sure is a predicament, I would not care to be in," said Marianne, looking serious. "I will try and help you, though I cannot promise anything."

"I know," replied Freddy, "just keep your ears and eyes open." They agreed to meet the following Saturday.

Freddy walked home deep in thought. He liked Marianne a lot and she was the only girl he had really spent any time with. She was pretty, intelligent and a lot of fun to be with. Most important of all, she shared his love for the sport he also loved. The day he would have to leave for Paris would be a sad day indeed. Hopefully Marianne, who seemed to know a great deal of people here or her parents, could help him find a job. "Stop building castles in the air," he scolded himself and decided he had better pay attention to where he was going, having missed the shortcut he usually took. Night was falling and the temperature was dropping, so he decided it would be faster if he retraced his steps.

He barely entered his room when there was a knock on the door. It was his landlady. "Your mother just called and asked that you return her call as soon as possible." Freddy thanked her and followed her down the hallway to the phone. He felt a little apprehensive, for his parents rarely called. His mother must have been standing by the phone for she picked up immediately and even though Helene tried to keep her voice calm, Freddy could tell something was wrong.

"Are you OK, Mama?"

"I am fine, Freddy, but it is Sigmund."

Freddy's heart skipped a beat. "Tell me, Mama."

"Your father has been feeling very unwell lately, he cannot hold down any food and he is asking for you. Not a day goes by without him asking me when I think you will be back. If Dr Wolf sees fit, I think you should come home." Freddy listened to her in silence. "Are you listening?" Helene asked impatiently.

"Yes, mama, I have not hung up, I am just overwhelmed. What can I say? I will come home with or without Dr Wolf's approval."

"No, your father would surely not want you to jeopardise your recovery, he does not know I am telling you about him being unwell, but I strongly believe your presence will help him recover from whatever it is that is ailing him. I have to hang up," said Helene. "I think he has just woken up."

"Wait, Mama, how are *you*?"

"I am worried and concerned, but nothing I cannot handle. I can be very strong when the occasion arises, but it would be nice if I could share the burden."

"I will be home, Mama."

With a very heavy heart, Freddy placed the phone back in its cradle then walked back to his room and pulled the chair to the window so he could see the sky and the stars. It was a cloudless night. He always found comfort in nature and this time was no exception. As he looked at the waning moon and watched the wind playing with the trees, he felt his body relax and the anxiety disappear. He remembered his father telling him that he tired easily and they had even gone to the doctor's together, but his father had not mentioned whether the doctor had given him the results of his blood tests or even if he knew what was ailing him. Could his tiredness be related to his not being able to keep any food down? He decided he would receive the answer to all these questions once he was back home.

Thinking of Paris brought him back to the present. What a great day it had been, he was so happy skiing with Marianne and taking her out for a bite to eat, but now he was going to have to cancel skiing for the following Saturday. He did not know where she lived, hopefully he would run into her in town or else he would have to write her a note, but to whom would he give it? He got ready for bed and his last thought before drifting off to sleep was that he would have to see Dr Wolf first thing in the morning. He held the key to his coming back.

Freddy tossed and turned in his sleep. He awoke early but did not feel at all rested, quite the contrary and thought to himself, "I am worn out and the day has only just begun. It's going to be a long one." Then he dressed and left for the clinic. Dr Wolf was an early riser and Freddy hoped that this morning would not be an exception.

They both arrived at the same time. Dr Wolf looked at him in surprise. "Why, Freddy what brings you here so early?"

"I need to talk to you. My father is very ill and I need to go back to Paris. I should get home as soon as possible. My mother needs someone to help her carry the burden and there is not a day that goes by without my father asking for me."

They were standing in the doorway of Dr Wolf's office.

"Come in, Freddy, and have a seat."

He did as he was told and covered his face with his hands. "I had so many plans."

"I understand," said Dr Wolf. "But let us look at your latest tests. Health-wise you are good to go, you are healed. That should be a huge relief to you and to your parents."

"It is, Dr Wolf."

"But tell me about her."

Freddy blushed. "We spent the day together skiing, but that is not what is troubling me. I had my heart set on staying for the season and now…"

"I understand you're being disappointed."

"That is not all. Now that I have fully recovered, how am I going to convince my parents that I have to return for a check-up in a couple of months' time? How can I justify the added expense?"

Dr Wolf was silent. "Freddy, I think you should deal with one thing at a time. Go home and spend time with your father, who knows, maybe you can persuade him to come back with you if he is unwilling or unable to come on his own. I will have to see you in a year's time anyway and by then, maybe things will have sorted themselves out and you will be able to spend the whole season here, in which case you could be my guest."

Freddy was taken aback by his offer. "That is very kind of you, Dr Wolf," said Freddy taking his leave. "I should be leaving now."

The doctor handed him a sheet of paper on which he had written that his patient was fully recovered and the date for his annual check-up was in a year's time. "This will put your father's mind at ease."

"Thank you, doctor, you do think of everything," said Freddy, shaking the doctor's hand. Freddy got to the door and looked back at the doctor who had also become a friend. "I will be back," he said, but he barely heard the doctor's reply.

"I will be expecting you."

Freddy left the clinic with a heavy heart, not paying much attention to where he was going. "Why, Freddy, I have been thinking about you these last few days and meant to come by and see you but I have been so busy that I kept postponing it." It was Father Christian. Freddy told him the latest developments. "Now I understand that unhappy look on your face."

"Dreams sure can change in a minute," said Freddy bitterly.

"I guess you understand the difference between dreams and reality then," said Father Christian.

"I have learned it the hard way." Freddy told him about Marianne and the date he would not be able to keep. "You do not happen to know her, do you?" he asked. "No, of course you would not know her, she is Jewish."

His friend thought for a minute. "I can make some inquiries if you like."

"No worries, I will find a way," said Freddy. "I need to be going."

"When are you leaving?"

"I have to go to the station now and get the schedule then buy my ticket. I am hoping to catch the night train from Lausanne to Paris tonight."

"You do not have much time, I will be your driver."

"Thank you," said Freddy. "That will really save time." As they walked into the ticket office, Freddy let out a gasp. Marianne was coming towards them and she looked at him in surprise. *Some guardian angel must be looking after my interests,* Freddy thought to himself.

Marianne gave him a surprised look. "Why are you leaving?"

Freddy explained the situation to her and she could sense his anger and disappointment. "I understand how you feel," she said, "but it is more important for you to attend to your father. I am sure you will be back." Then she scribbled her address on a piece of paper and gave it to him. "We can keep in touch," she said.

Freddy glanced at what she had written. "You are so lucky to live here year around," he said.

"We had better be going," said Father Christian, taking Freddy by the arm, and they drove to Freddy's lodgings in silence. It did not take Freddy long to pack his belongings. He gave Helene a quick call telling her of his travel plans, said good bye to his landlady, who wished him safe travels and a speedy recovery for his father, and before he knew it, he was back at the station bidding Father Christian farewell. Freddy boarded the train with a very heavy heart indeed.

Helene let out a sigh of relief. Freddy was on his way. How different his homecoming was going to be from that which she had imagined some weeks back. At least she would have someone to talk to and who would listen to her. Sigmund had become very introverted; he sometimes gave the impression he had lost all interest in life, except for Freddy. His books no longer seemed to appeal to him, either and he would just sit for hours on end looking into space. Helene had done her best to bring him out of what she had taken to calling 'the tunnel' but seeing her efforts go unrewarded, she soon gave up. Only the news of Freddy's complete reestablishment had brought the sparkle back into his eyes, but that, too, was of short duration. To be so close and yet so distant. She remembered her mother warning her that the age gap between them would become more and more noticeable as time went on.

How right her mother was, but Helene had to admit that she had absolutely no regrets. She'd had her child and had come to terms with the fact that Sigmund had not given in to her desire for a second, for time having proven him right. They had some very happy times together and in the hard times, there was a solidarity between them that had given them the strength to continue on their path. Life had not been easy for her, but who had it easy in these challenging times?

Sigmund calling for her interrupted her daydreaming. She hurried to him and looked at him in surprise. He was dressed and seemed about to go out. "Are you...?" Helene asked.

"No, no, I do not want to upset Freddy, what time will he be home? Are you going to the station to meet him?" he asked.

"I am not quite sure what train he is coming in on and I am not going to the station, he is old enough to find his way home on his own."

Just then, there was a sound of a key turning in the lock. They both hurried towards the front door. Freddy was home and he hugged his parents, horrified at how frail and aged his father looked. He was also aware that his mother was observing him, so he kept his face expressionless. On the way to Sigmund's study, Freddy excused himself, saying he would join them as soon as he had placed his suitcase in his room. He sat down on the bed and his head dropped into his hands. He could see that his father was seriously ill. When he went and opened the door to the study, he heard his parents talking.

Sigmund was reclining in his chair with his eyes closed, his face lined with pain. Helene was leaning over him, asking him if she should ring the doctor. "No need," he replied in a weak voice. "I have taken a pain killer and once it kicks in, I will be fine." He gave Freddy a smile. "It means so much to me that you are home and you are completely healed," he said, as Freddy handed him Dr Wolf's letter. "So, you don't have to go back for a check-up until a year's time; that is excellent news."

"It is, indeed," said Freddy, and mentioned matter-of-factly the invitation Dr Wolf had extended him. "Maybe you will both come with me. Mama can go skiing and I am sure that the mountain air will do you the world of good, Papa."

Sigmund shook his head. "I do not think I will be on this planet, but if I am, I will join you."

Helene and Freddy exchanged glances; taking his hand in hers she asked, "Is there something you have not told me?"

Sigmund let out a deep sigh. "I have cancer of the pancreas, it is inoperable and incurable. My days are numbered. I have had a happy life but my only regret is that I did not heed Abraham's advice. Yet, who knows if we would have been better off if I had. The only sure thing is that we would have all been together and Nellie would have been with us."

Helene and Freddy were stunned by what they just learned. "Freddy, I want you to promise me that you will look after your mother. I know that you will be very successful at whatever you choose to do and that you will remake the family fortune. I have one more wish and that is that you leave for Colombia and settle there once I am gone." The monologue exhausted him and so he closed his eyes and was soon sound asleep. Helene covered him up with a blanket, then signalled to Freddy and they both left the room.

They were both teary eyed. "Mama, you are in shock."

"Yes," said Helene. "This is the first I'm hearing of it. I now understand his insistence that you come home and I also realise he wanted us to be together when he unveiled his secret to us so we might find support in each other. One thing you can say about your father is that he never gives up control."

"That may be true," said Freddy, "but there is one thing he has no control over and that is his fate and destiny. He has had to surrender to his illness and I do believe he has accepted it."

"He could not do otherwise," replied Helene.

"He is calling you," said Freddy. "In the meantime, I will go and unpack," he said, heading for his room. He needed to be alone and as he unpacked, the tears started rolling down his cheeks, tears of sadness and frustration at knowing there was nothing to be done about his father's state of health. "Maybe he will pass on in his sleep, so that he does not suffer," he said aloud. He had spoken about them joining Nellie in Colombia, had he written her? Would she come to Paris to see him? He lay down on his bed and was soon sound asleep.

Helene helped Sigmund to bed. She had not realised how weak he was. "I seem to be losing strength, more and more every day," he said.

"It must have been very hard for you knowing the truth and keeping it away from me," said Helene.

"It was not easy, but I was able to come to terms with it all without any distractions, and that was of utmost importance to me. You must now accept and realise that you will be on your own with Freddy and you must let me go."

"Is Nellie aware of your situation?"

"I hope she is. I wrote her a letter some weeks back but I also made a copy of it, which I will give to you to hand over to her when you meet with her in Bogotá. My wish was to see her one last time but deep in my heart, I know that this one wish will not come true."

He took Helene's hand in his, kissed it gently and said in a whisper, "I thank you for all your love and kindness throughout these years."

Helene sat by his bedside, her hand in his until his hand went limp. From his breathing, she could tell he was sound asleep. She stood up and caught a glimpse of herself in the mirror, realising her tears had smeared the mascara all over her eyes. First, she went to the bathroom and washed her face then went to find Freddy.

He opened his eyes as his mother walked in. "I am sorry," he said. "I did not mean to doze off but I did not sleep at all last night. There was not an empty seat on the train and it was extremely noisy. I am glad I did not waste any time getting home."

"And I am so happy you are here, it has really been very difficult, not understanding, not knowing, not having anybody to share my misgivings with. It would have been a lot easier if your father had confided in me."

"Each one deals with his demons the best he can, and he has always been extremely private," said Freddy. "But it was very clever of him to wait until you and I were together to tell us the truth, he has always said, 'unity is strength' and he acted on that principal."

Helene stood up and began pacing the floor. "I am going to check on him, I have an uneasy feeling."

"Wait," said Freddy, "I will come with you." He was up in a flash and they walked in silence towards his parent's bedroom. Helene had closed the curtains before leaving the room, the sun had not quite set and was casting shadows on the wall. They walked over towards the bed, not a sound could be heard. Sigmund lay on his back with his eyes closed and he seemed to be smiling.

Helene whispered to Freddy, "Whatever that painkiller was, it must have worked, he is not in pain."

Sigmund did not stir. They stood by his bedside without saying a word, but they knew something was amiss. Helene walked over to him and took his hand in hers. It was cold. Freddy put an arm around her shoulders and said, "My wish came true. He left us in his sleep and it ended his suffering."

They stood in silence, the tears flowing freely. Helene broke the silence saying, "Sigmund was in control until the very end. He waited for you to come home, for us to be together, he gave us our instructions and then he left." The date 18 June 1939 would be engraved in their hearts for as long as they lived.

Without saying a word, they went into his sanctuary. On his desk lay what they were looking for: his burial instructions and a copy of his letter to Nellie. In accordance with his wishes, he was cremated and his ashes were placed in the columbarium of the cemetery at Pere la Chaise in Paris.

Part III – Life Without Sigmund

Chapter 42

Helene missed Sigmund very much and time hung heavily on her hands. Some acquaintances had come by to give their condolences, but their visits were short, which had been just as well since she put all her energy into taking care of Freddy and going through her late husband's belongings. It was in the study where she found the most peace. Since she could not be idle, she took out every book, cleaning the bookcase and dusting them off. Sigmund had forbidden everyone to touch his books, so one can imagine the amount of dust that covered them. But she did not mind, it gave her something to do and she could feel his presence.

Freddy, on the other hand, was getting very desperate. Try as he might, it was impossible to make his mother understand that he did not like being pampered and questioned all the time. He tried hard to keep his temper, but when it got to a point where he could not take it any longer, he would go for a walk. The last thing he wanted in this situation was to have an argument. His walks would invariably take him to Georges' house, but unfortunately he did not have much time to hang out with Freddy. The economic situation had gotten so bad that his father had been forced to lay off workers, at one time having employed 300 and now, between Georges and the few that were left, they just managed to fill the few orders they received. The demand for jewellery and silver items had diminished so much; they had to sell the beautiful country home they owned on the outskirts of Paris, much to the family's dismay.

His Aunt Adele came to their rescue when she dropped by unexpectedly one morning and announced that her husband Gerald had been offered a job with the New York Philharmonic and they would be leaving in two weeks' time. They had put in the required paperwork for the emigration papers at the same time as Gerald sent in his job application, which was very fortunate for they received their visas a couple of days earlier and there was nothing that could delay their departure. Helene felt a little jealous, but soon let the emotion pass and spent the next two weeks helping Adele get everything sorted. They would be sailing from Le Havre and would arrive at the Port of New York. Adele was very excited about the prospects of beginning a new life in America, the land of emigrants, in which new ideas and creativity were encouraged.

No, she had no regrets whatsoever about leaving Europe, in her opinion the continent was a mess and headed for war. After the annexation by Germany of Austria and the Sudetenland, Nazi Germany had not only given the rest of the world a glimpse of its expansionist policy, but with the British, French and Italians having signed a pact to defend Poland, as well as some other countries from German aggression, it would not be long before she would be proven right. Helene recalled her conversation with Sigmund in this regard and hoped that Adele's assessment of the situation was incorrect, but her intuition told her that Adele was right. Her only hope, if this were to come about, would be to fulfil Sigmund's wish of her and Freddy leaving for Colombia.

With his mother busy with Adele, Freddy now had time to concentrate on himself and bemoan his loss. His father had been very strict with him, but during the last couple of weeks after his return from Crans Montana, they had spent a lot of time together and really bonded. He regretted that it had been so short lived, but now, in his father's memory, he would do his very best to carry out his last wishes. Being an avid reader, he also kept abreast of the news, which became more and more depressing and worrisome with each passing day.

One evening, Helene came and sat down by Freddy's bedside as she used to do when he was little. She held a hand written letter in her hand and it was signed S for Sigmund. It was a letter he had written to Arthur, a close friend of his, which he had forgotten to mail…or maybe he had decided otherwise. It was very harsh indeed. He congratulated him on finally having left the pigsty that was Germany, referring to the Nazis as pigs, and told him that nobody would care about the Jews or their people. He saw them, forced to wear a yellow Star of David on their sleeve and living in Ghettos before being mass exterminated. But what struck the two of them most was his confession of how the developments in Germany had affected his health.

In an entire paragraph, he described how his nervous and digestive system were shattered, how he could not find peace and solace and one could feel the rage that was deeply in grained inside him. Freddy listened intently. When his mother finished, there were tears in their eyes. Helene broke the silence saying, "I regret him never sharing any of his emotions with me. Had I the knowledge and understanding, I might have been able to help him."

"I feel the same way," said Freddy. "But in the end, neither you nor I knew his most intimate thoughts. Together we might have been able to show him a brighter side of life, but was there a brighter side of life?" Freddy thought for a minute. "There are always opposites, dark and bright, happy and sad. One just has to look for them. But when one is blind, one does not see them, and that is what happened to Papa. He was so absorbed with what was happening in his homeland, he lost sight of all the rest."

"You are right," said Helene.

"And you know, the mind dictates to the body and all that negativity just sapped all the goodness from him and yet," Freddy went on, "he wanted me to have the best healthcare in the world and he neglected his own. Had I not insisted so many times that he go see the doctor, his journey on this planet might have been even shorter." Not having anything more to say about the subject, Helene left the room.

Nellie received Sigmund's letter, telling her about his illness. She had considered returning to Europe to be with him, but after looking into the costs of the plane fare, the length of the journey and, worst of all, the risks involved, she heeded Abraham's advice. Sad and very much withdrawn, she could feel her father's pain and suffering and cried a lot. Arturo took to calling her Maria Magdalena, for she could not stop weeping. Questioning her decision again and again about not having stayed with her parents and Freddy, and about listening to her father, she reminded herself about the nightmare with Andreas. Deep down inside her, she felt she had made the right decision.

She also had a very important mission, which she would not have been able to carry out had she stayed: To fulfil her father's wishes, as he had written in his letter, and be the go-between to bring Helene and Freddy to safety. She knew Sigmund was dying and she hoped that he would not suffer. He vividly described his health situation and made it clear he was very much fed up with life in general, but what he never mentioned was whether he had any regrets about not having left Europe. Now she would never know the answer. But it was not really important, he'd made up his mind that the trip was too hazardous, that he was too old and was still being optimistic that things would change and would never take the turn for the worse that they had taken.

She came home from work Friday evening and found a letter addressed to her in Freddy's handwriting. Her heart skipped a beat. She knew the contents without opening it or reading the message, the tears came to her eyes and started pouring down her cheeks. The sobs shook her body as she walked towards her flat. It took her some minutes to open the front door, for the tears blurred her vision and she could not find the keyhole. She turned on the light, splashed some cold water on her face hoping she would finally stop crying and sobbing, and sat down at her desk. Her hands shook as she opened the envelope and she took out the one and only neatly written page that read:

Dear Nellie,

I will have long have departed the planet as you read these lines. Even though we could not come face to face to take our departure from each other, I have felt your closeness and I trust you have felt mine. When there is love and caring, all distances are bridged and our subtle bodies come together and the communication is free and unbounded.

I am aware I did not choose right. I should have followed Abraham's advice to start a new life in Colombia. We all would have had a future and the family would have stayed together. I have paid for my mistake with my health and being deprived of your presence. And yet, I do not feel guilty. I chose what I thought was best for all of us at the time in good faith and yes by you heeding my advice, you found a complete new world, you learned another language, have learned to fend for yourself and are now in the position to carry out my wishes of reuniting the family in a peaceful and friendly country. There are not enough words to tell you how very, very proud I have been of you.

You have the sweetness of your mother but you also have my thick skin, which allows you to receive the blows without them infringing too much damage to your soul. Even though we are apart, before I sat down a day ago to write you this farewell letter, I had a dream and I would like to share it with you. Please do not be sad, it is a very happy one and as you read on you will understand.

I dreamt that I had already departed this world and had not been able to hold you in my arms and kiss you good-bye. I was in a beautiful valley and there was a stream running through it as well as some patches of trees. It was summer and all the flowers were in full bloom and colour. Out from behind a tree, you suddenly came towards me. I was in shock.

I was not expecting you, you were so, so far away. But you walked towards me with your arms outstretched, your beautiful smile lightening up your face and your eyes were sparkling—there was so much love in them. When you came towards where I was standing, you held out your arms towards me, we hugged and you placed your hand on my forehead and, looking me in the eye, said in that beautiful soft voice of yours, the one that has always reminded me so much of your mother: "Go in peace, Papa, please join Mama, she has been waiting all these years for you. The time has come for you to put an end to her longing for you."

I stood there dazzled and stunned, but you were no longer there—you had disappeared just as suddenly as you had come. Please do not feel sad, for this was our goodbye and it could not have been more beautiful.

When you feel sad, just think about the joyful farewell we took from each other and remember your words to me, 'It is time for you to re-join Mama' and the time will come when we shall all be reunited, Lovingly S.

Nellie reread the letter several times and then tenderly placed it back in the envelope. It was something she would treasure forever, the last communication with her father. And how beautifully he had phrased it and how honest he had been. Not only had he answered her questions, but he poured out his heart to her. She felt a revival of the complicity that had always existed between them. He was no longer on this earth but their bond could not be shattered by death. It was now much easier for her to accept his passing and although he was no longer here, his memory would live on in her, Freddy, and, in part, Helene. Now she had an important mission but no clue as to how to go about fulfilling it.

She took out a sheet of paper and an envelope and wrote Freddy a short note confirming reception of the letter and inviting him and Helene to come join her in Bogotá. As she wrote the date, 18 July 1939, she realised it was one month to the day since her father had passed on. One can definitely measure distances in time and it gives one a more accurate appreciation. She would probably have to wait a month for Freddy's reply.

Nellie showed the letter to Abraham and he read it thoughtfully. "I tried so hard to convince him, but my dear friend, whom I miss so much, was as stubborn as a mule. He would not listen to reason and he just did not want to see what I was seeing.

You can take a horse to water, Nellie, but you can't make him drink. It is sad that towards the end of his life, he was so unhappy but on the other hand, something good did come of it. Had they followed me to Colombia, who knows if Freddy would have been cured of his sickness."

"He had the best care money could buy," said Nellie.

"We shall now have to see what the formalities are in bringing Helene and Freddy over. But we had better move fast because with the political situation in Europe and all the uncertainty, they will have to come by ship like we did. Yes, it is not going to be easy to make Sigmund's wish come true, but we will do our best," said Abraham.

After a little less than a week, Abraham came back to see Nellie. She was delighted to see him. "Good news?"

"Yes, and no; they need a visa, of which there are a lot of formalities, and that we have to apply for here. Then they will have to make a reservation on one of the ships that sail, and I do not know which will be the easiest port for them to get to from Paris."

"Probably Le Havre, in Northern France," said Nellie. "But the formalities will have to be dealt with first."

That would not be a major problem. Colombia was a country that was open to emigration. There were Germans, Swiss, British, French as well as nationals from neighbouring Latin American countries living there and Germany was a major commercial partner. Colombia was its main coffee supplier and from there it was distributed all over Europe. This openness had brought a great deal of benefits to the country, like Scadta, the first Colombian airline that was founded by Germans. The German School had been founded first in Barranquilla, then later in Bogotá, mostly for children born of German parents. A lot of Germans had married into Colombian families as well. The only hitch now was the deteriorating situation in Europe. "With a little bit of luck and some influence, we might be able to get their visas without too much delay," said Nellie.

"I hope so," replied Abraham, but he was very apprehensive. While Nellie and Abraham were discussing their future actions, Freddy and Helene were trying to deal with the present as well as the future. They pondered whether to keep the flat in Paris or move. There were so many memories and a change of scenery might be a welcome respite from their grief, but where to? And what about the expense? And then, of course, should they decide to carry out Sigmund's wishes, they would need all their funds to pay for their travel expenses. So much had changed in their lives in such a short time, really leaving them in a limbo.

On 1 September, Germany attacked Poland and on 3 September, Britain and France declared war on Germany. The French government issued an order for all male foreign nationals to present themselves at their nearest police station. Freddy was stunned and Helene was speechless.

"I will go," said Freddy, "and see what they want."

Helene looked at him sadly. "Really? Must you go?"

"Yes, Papa always said, when the government calls, it is best to deal with it immediately. The sooner I leave, the sooner I will be back."

Helene watched him, her eyes brimming with tears, as he put on his jacket. She had a very uneasy feeling in the pit of her stomach, which she kept to herself. Freddy hugged her and as she kissed him gently on the cheek, he moved away from her and said, "Mama, don't be sad. No need to worry, I will be home shortly." Busying herself, she tidied up the flat and when she was finished, she sat down behind Sigmund's desk, wondering what the present held for them. With Germany at war with France, all refugees, especially those of German descent, would surely be looked upon with suspicion, resentment and anger.

She heard a key turn in the lock and let out a sigh of relief. It was Freddy. "I told you I would not be long, Mama."

Helene looked at her watch. "Yes," she replied, "you were right, you were only gone for three hours. But tell me, what did the police want?"

"I am starving. Once I have eaten, I will tell you."

Helene could sense that what she was going to hear would be anything but pleasant, so without prodding him further, she waited for him to finish his meal.

"Well, Mama, the news is unfortunately not good, neither for you nor for me."

"What do you mean?"

"Let me start from the beginning. When I got to the police station, there already was a huge line and there were only two people working. They registered us and before leaving, we were told to pack some clothing, some underwear, pants, a warm jacket or coat, etc., and to be back at the police headquarters in three days' time. We were also made aware that it would be a very serious offense if we did not show up."

"Where are they sending you?"

"No idea, they did not say."

"But do you really have to go, can't you just ignore it?"

"No way, Mama, I just told you it would be a very serious offense if we do not appear. They took our documents and they have each one of us on file, telling us to sign in as soon as we get there. If we do not come, they will search for us and we will be thrown into jail."

"What? In jail?" exclaimed Helene.

"Yes, Mama, they want to avoid us siding with the enemy at all costs and are firmly convinced we will make a lot of trouble if we are not under their supervision."

"That does not surprise me," said Helene. "I was just thinking about how difficult our lives as refugees were going to become, but it happened sooner than I bargained for."

They were both silent for a moment. Freddy did not want to admit it but he was scared, worried and concerned about his mother. What would she do without him? Who would help her? Not only had she recently lost her husband, but now he was leaving her for an unknown destination and doubted very much that they would be able to have contact. The police officer who had told them what to do had given him the impression he would take no nonsense. Helene's thoughts were not unlike Freddy's. She was concerned about herself living alone in this flat in Paris, but what worried her most was not knowing Freddy's whereabouts.

"Mama," said Freddy, seeing the worried look on his mother's face. "Do not forget, you can always count on Georges."

"I was wondering about him, he has not been around and you have not mentioned him lately, as a matter of fact I do not remember his coming to offer his condolences," said Helene as an afterthought.

Freddy was well aware that Helene disliked Georges, she had never criticised his background in front of him but sensed she felt he was not worthy of his friendship, and now he was really the only person she could count on. *Yes,* thought Freddy, *life can certainly be very strange at times.* Soon after finishing the conversation, Freddy excused himself and left to go find Georges.

Georges was home. He looked surprised seeing his friend standing by the gate. "What's up? You seemed to have vanished," he said teasingly.

"Not vanished, Georges, I have been quite busy with Papa gone, as you know, and now not only do I have to look out for myself but also for my mother, and sometimes it is not very easy. I never thought she would miss him as much as she does, but she gets moody and depressed and I try to keep her in good spirits."

"Yes, I have noticed it with my parents, as time goes by the bond deepens between them and it seems that one could not live without the other. Like swans. But do come in, my parents will be more then delighted to see you, as always."

"I know, especially your Dad so he can practice his German again."

"He is going to be very disappointed when I tell him you came over, for he just left to run an errand, and I do not know what time he will be back."

Freddy greeted Georges' mother affectionately and she gave him a broad smile. "I am glad you found your way back," she said. They made themselves comfortable in Georges' room. He had been looking at Freddy out of the corner of his eye and could tell that something was troubling his friend. "I can always tell when something is not right by the expression on your face, so tell me."

Freddy told him everything that was expected of him. "You are surprised, right?"

"Yes," answered Georges. "You of all people."

"No, it is not just me, it concerns all male refugees, ages 15 and older."

"Do you know where you are being sent?"

"I have no idea. All I know is I have to report back in three days."

"My Father is very well connected with the Chief of Police, so he may be able to find out some more details, so don't worry," Georges informed him.

"Good," said Freddy. "But please do have him look into it after I have left, not before. I do not want to be in trouble."

"You won't be, I can assure you."

"And if he finds out anything, could you please advise Mama? She is worried to death about my leaving and I am concerned about her as well. There are just the two of us."

"I understand and I will make a point of going by to see her, even though I have to admit and I have never told you this, I know she does not bear me much love and I have never been able to understand the reason."

"I have to admit that I am nervous and uneasy about leaving," said Freddy. "So many changes have happened in such a short time that it is hard to assimilate everything that is happening."

"I know," said Georges. "I hope it will not take us long to defeat the Germans, I really would hate to see them take over the country and I do not want to imagine German soldiers marching down the Champs Elysee."

"Well, I must be going," said Freddy, and he gave Georges a big hug.

"I am going to miss you," said his friend. "Even with all the travelling you have done, I still haven't gotten used to the thought of not having you around."

"I hope I will be back in a couple of days," said Freddy.

"We will do all we can to help."

On the way out, Freddy stopped to say good-bye to Georges' mother but she was fast asleep in her wheelchair. "Let's not wake her," said Freddy. Georges stood by the gate for a long time after Freddy had left. He hoped he would be safe and out of harm's way and would speak to his father as soon as he returned.

Freddy spent the next two days helping Helene, trying to distract her from his inevitable departure. He packed a small bag and without giving it a second thought, placed both his warmest winter coat and jacket in it. On the day of his departure, he rose very early, having slept badly the night before and there was no use staying in bed, listening to his mind painting all kinds of different scenarios.

Freddy ate a hearty breakfast before taking his leave for, as Helene so wisely put it, "You had better eat while there is food on the table, who knows when you will get your next meal." He came back again, much to Helene's surprise, to tell her not to worry and that Georges or his father would be in touch with her, reminding her not to hesitate to call on them should she need anything. Then he went on his way.

Helene was grateful she had been given a couple of days to get used to the idea, and even though she felt sad, she found some comfort in the thought that Freddy was taking responsibility for his life and that Sigmund would have been very proud of him. Thinking of her late husband, she also felt grateful that he had not lived to see France declare war on Germany.

Chapter 43

It did not take Freddy very long to reach his destination. Having done as he was told, he signed in and was given a number then was told to wait. The waiting room was not large enough for all of them so most of the young ones, including Freddy, decided to wait outside.

At about 4 pm, some buses pulled up. The Chief of Police ordered them to board the buses and everyone obeyed without asking any questions, except for a young man who asked the driver, "Where are they taking us?" But his question went completely ignored.

Freddy was one of the first to board and was able to settle down in a window seat. He looked eagerly out the window for a while but then fell sound asleep. When he opened his eyes and looked out, night had fallen and the only thing he could make out was that they were driving on a very narrow road on the countryside. He closed his eyes once more but the driver's screaming woke him up, ordering all of them to leave the bus and line up outside what looked like a gate. They did as they were told and the person in charge took out some cards with their names and numbers on them and told them to enter a huge courtyard.

A man was handing out work clothing that looked more like a prisoner uniforms than anything else. "Why are you giving us these?" someone inquired.

"You have arrived at a work camp and these are the clothes you will be wearing."

Freddy looked around him. *The elderly are going to be working here as well,* he thought to himself, *so it probably will not be too strenuous.* They were shown to a very large, one-story building and made their way inside. It was lined with beds and between each bed was a small metal nightstand, which had a door at the front and a padlock for them to keep their belongings. The beds were actually rollaway cots and on them lay two sheets that did not look too clean, as well as a well-worn blanket. Freddy emptied his bag and put everything away neatly, "It's a good thing I didn't bring much," he said out loud.

His neighbour overheard him and replied, "Not much room in there."

Then he went about making his bed. He was not very good at it, for as far back as he could remember, his mother had made his bed for him. Well, at least I am going to learn some new skills, he thought grinning. And new skills he really would learn, even though he was not aware of it at this time.

Someone came in screaming to make himself heard: "Dinner is served in the house next door." No one had to be told twice, they were all starving. Helene's words echoed in Freddy's ears. "Eat while you can, who knows where or what will be your next meal." A cook was standing behind a huge pot serving what looked like soup and there was a basket of baguettes for them to help themselves. They sat down on wooden benches around the longest table Freddy or anyone had ever seen and ate in silence. The soup could not have been worse, it was just some hot water with a piece of carrot and a leaf of cabbage swimming in it, and had no taste whatsoever. Freddy, who had a very delicate pallet, was unable to stomach anymore and had eaten just five spoonful when he gave up and embarked on the baguette. He dreamed of a fresh, hot baguette, but to his disappointment, it was stale and hard. *God only knows how long it has been waiting to be served,* he thought.

Freddy, and no one else to his knowledge, seemed to know in what part of the country they found themselves in. The only thing they really could say was that they were in some little village on the Atlantic coast. The person who seemed to be in charge was again screaming at the top of his lungs: "It is bedtime now for all of you; lights out in 15 minutes." They did not wait to be told twice and bolted to the exit.

Having donned his pyjamas, Freddy went looking for the washroom and finally found it at the other end of the corridor. After standing in line for what seemed like an eternity, his turn finally came to brush his teeth. Just as he was getting into bed, the lights went out. *No fooling around,* he thought, 15 minutes they were told and 15 minutes it was, on the dot. He also had trouble falling asleep, occasionally he'd shared a room with Helmut when he spent the night on Bunny Hill, but that was years ago, when he was still living in Germany, and once in a while when he stayed over with Georges. But here, it was a whole battalion he was sleeping with, at least 200 people or more must have been sleeping in there.

The person on his right was snoring so loud it almost sounded like a grunting pig, further down someone had a coughing fit and a little further down to his left, someone was talking in his sleep. Then, out of nowhere, a guy bumped into his cot, nearly landing on him. Freddy looked at the person in surprise. He was a middle-aged man as far as he could tell in the darkness, his eyes were closed, and he was sleepwalking. Once Freddy regained his calm, he spoke to the man softly and it was not long before the sleepwalker opened his eyes and looked at Freddy in the face.

"Sorry," he said.

"No worries," replied Freddy. "Do you know where your cot is? I will walk you to it."

"No need," replied the stranger. "I can find it. I am sure it is not very far from yours."

Freddy insisted once more but having received the same reply, he wished the stranger good luck and good night, then rolled onto his side. "I had better try to get some sleep, no telling what the morning will bring," was his last thought, and sleep he did.

A loud screaming voice woke them up, instructing them to put on their work clothes and go to the next building for breakfast, which was just as bad as the meal from the night before. It consisted of some very much watered down hot chocolate and, yet again, the stale baguette. Placed on the table was some butter and marmalade but that disappeared before you could say Jack Robinson. They were not given much time to eat, either, not that they would have needed more time to finish the meagre ration.

They were led outdoors and placed in groups of 20. Once all the groups had been formed, they followed the leaders down a narrow dirt road. Nobody knew where they were going. After having walked for 2 hours, they came to a clearing next to the road. "This is your work place," yelled the person in command. Freddy could not make sense out of what he was seeing until the boss explained that their job was to continue laying the foundation on which the railroad tracks would be set. Out of a nearby shed, they were given pails and shovels and the other tools needed to carry out their work.

Freddy's team was given the task of crushing stone. They worked all day, non-stop. Freddy felt really sorry for the elderly and thought, if *his* back and neck were hurting him, he could only imagine what a torture the others were going through. At five o'clock, one of the overseers told them to hand over their tools and start following the others back to headquarters. Their way back took them a little longer, as they were so exhausted, they could barely drag their feet.

Once back, they were given 10 minutes to wash up before going to dinner. The meal consisted of boiled chicken served with boiled potatoes and some turnips. Freddy and the rest were so famished they did not spend time pondering what they were putting in their mouths and just gulped down their food. That night, he had no trouble falling asleep and indeed slept soundly until the Foreman roused him by screaming at the top of his lungs that it was time to get up, breakfast would be in ten minutes.

They followed the same routine as the day before. "How long will I have to stay here?" Freddy asked himself. Some of the elderly had gotten sick, having come down with a high fever and were not fit to for the long walk. They were told to stay and given work in the kitchen or cleaning the bathrooms, there was no compassion for any of them whatsoever.

Freddy sat down one day and wrote Georges a note. "Have you forgotten me? This is living hell on earth," then went on to describe the life they were leading and the suffering of the elderly. They had been here since the middle of September and now it was mid-October. Fall had set in, bringing the winds that chill you to the bone, heating was non-existent and Freddy told him how badly he felt for the old men that were in his group. They tried to put on a brave front but their strength was leaving them fast, their defences were very low, thus leading to colds and bronchitis. He was especially worried about the sleepwalker. They had become friends and his sleepwalking adventures had become a joke between them. His name was John. He was very pale and told Freddy that he was coughing up blood. The next morning after their conversation, John walked up to Freddy at breakfast and told him that he was leaving; they were sending him to the hospital for treatment. Freddy let out a sigh of relief upon hearing the news. He ended his note begging Georges to please get him out of this prison.

With the note in his hand, Freddy went in search of the Foreman who replied to his request that there was no way; there was no one who could possibly deliver a message. Freddy was furious, but concealed his emotion very well. At work, he vented his frustration by crushing the stones with such force that bits and pieces went flying everywhere. One of his comrades who had been watching him remarked: "You sure are strong, mate."

"No," replied Freddy, "it is the rage that is seething in me that is giving me the energy."

His comrade was just about to continue the conversation when the Foreman came over. "Is your name Freddy?"

"Yes, that is my name."

"Come with me." He followed him down the road and back to their headquarters. "You have five minutes to pack your things; you are being driven back to Paris."

Freddy was jubilant. He packed in no time and, having said his goodbyes, was soon on his way back to Paris. It was a very long journey. When the driver dropped him off at Georges' house, for those were his instructions, it was 9 pm. Georges and his father kept looking out the window and as soon as they heard a car approach, they rushed down the stairs. They were both standing by the gate when Freddy got out of the car. "Good to see you," said Georges.

"You have no idea how wonderful it is to be back," said Freddy. He addressed Georges' father. "Thank you so much for all your help."

"I can imagine your ordeal," he replied. "But let us go inside, it is cold out here and I do have some issues to discuss with you."

As they walked up the stairs, Georges asked, "Tell me about your little adventure."

"You can read about it," replied Freddy. "I wrote you a note, but of course there was no one who would either post it, if there had been a post office, which I doubt, or deliver it." Reaching Georges' room, he opened his bag and gave his friend the note, watching his face as he read it.

"Man, you sure did have some excitement, no wonder you are looking so skinny."

"Had your father not rescued me, there probably would have not been much fat left on me," Freddy said, laughing.

"Come on, let's go find Dad, he has something to tell you."

"Yes," said Freddy. "Have you been over to see Mama?"

"I have, and she was doing well the last time I saw her, saying something about being busy packing boxes. I did not quite understand what she meant."

"Oh," said Freddy. "She was probably packing some of Papa's stuff to give away."

"It is about time you two showed up," said Georges' father.

"It is late and I am tired."

"Sorry we took so long," they replied in one voice. "Freddy, the Chief of Police was very gracious about exempting you from the labour camp—for now—however, he is of the opinion that you cannot stay in Paris or be free to roam around. You are a German refugee and you pose a risk to the security of the country."

Freddy gave him a surprised look. "In what way?"

"He is afraid you might commit an act of sabotage. It is not just you, it is every single refugee they are concerned about, any one of you could ally yourselves with the enemy, so you are to consider what you would like to do."

"Well," replied Freddy, "I would like to go and fight the enemy. This country was very kind and generous in taking us in, and I firmly believe that now the time has come for me to give back."

Georges looked at him in surprise. "You mean to say you want to join the Army?"

"Yes, that is what I want." Georges' father didn't say a word during this exchange. "Well," he finally said, "we would have to see if this is possible and, just for your information, I have to accompany you to police headquarters tomorrow at 8 am. Do you want to spend the night here?"

"No, I will go home and see how Mama is doing and it will really be nice to be able to sleep in my own bed with no one else in my room."

"We will walk you home."

The flat was in darkness when Freddy let himself in, but since Sigmund's passing, Helene had become a light sleeper and the turning of the key in the lock woke her up. Her heart beat faster, she was not expecting anyone. Freddy was gone, but it could only be him. She summoned all her courage and got out of bed to go and check. She saw a figure in the hallway and called out, "Is it you Freddy?"

"Yes, Mama, I am back." He walked her back to the room and sat down by her side. "How have you been?"

"OK, I got some boxes and have been putting Papa's things away. I have not yet made up my mind what I am going to do with all his books."

"You are not thinking of giving them away, are you, Mama?"

"I was considering it."

"No, no, you cannot do that, those were his treasures; they have to stay with us."

"We can discuss that later," said Helene, changing the subject. "Where have you been, what have you being doing?"

Freddy told her about his adventure and how grateful he was that Georges' father had gotten his release. "So, we can stay together from now on?" Helene asked, her eyes sparkling at the thought of not being left by herself.

"No, Mama, I do not think so. I have to go see the Chief of Police at his headquarters," said Freddy, "and a decision will be made."

"What do you mean?"

"Well, if I can convince him that I am harmless, I would like to enrol in the army and fight the enemy."

"Fight the Germans?"

"Yes, Mama, but let us leave it for now since it is late. I have been up since before dawn and it has been a very long day. And who knows what tomorrow will bring? We had better get some sleep."

"What time do you have to leave?"

"I am to be at Georges' house at 7:30 am and his father is going with me."

"Before I forget, it was very thoughtful of your friend to come by and ask me if I needed anything." Freddy did not answer; he just smiled to himself, knowing who he could count on.

"Good night, Mama," he said, but received no reply, as she was fast asleep.

Chapter 44

Freddy slept soundly until the clanging of his alarm clock woke him up. It took him a minute or two to realise where he was. As he got out of bed, he spoke out loud to himself. "One makes such a big to-do about things that are virtually unimportant and we just take for granted the little things that make life pleasant."

Helene was up and dressed when he came into the kitchen. "Have some breakfast," she said, "who knows what is in the cards for you today."

"You've never used that expression before, why now Mama?"

"Yes, Freddy, we do not know what card you will draw, maybe it will be a joker, or maybe the queen of hearts, but whatever card it is and whatever your destiny will be, I only pray that you may be safe."

"No worries, Mama, whatever I draw I will be back to tell you, now I must run."

He gave her a hug and was gone. Mr Bonse was at the gate waiting for him. "How is your mother?"

"She is fine, very surprised and relieved to see me."

"And I guess a little disappointed to see you leave so early this morning."

"Yes," replied Freddy.

There was a line outside the police station that surprised Freddy. "Are all these people refugees?"

"Yes," replied Mr Bonse. "But, come along, we do not have to stand in line, follow me."

The secretary looked up from her work as Georges' father spoke to her, "Yes, sir," she said, "he is expecting you." She ushered them into the Chief of Police's office and he introduced himself to Freddy as Mr Lancelot. He scrutinised Freddy for what seemed a long time and then, apparently satisfied with what he saw, finally spoke.

"I guess my dear friend has told you that you cannot stay in Paris that you must go into a labour camp for foreign refugees, am I right?"

"Yes," replied Freddy, "however, I would like to express a wish I have and maybe you can make it come true."

"I will not promise anything, what is it?"

"As you are aware, I am a German Jew who came here with my parents when Hitler was appointed Chancellor. I went to school here and have made many friends. As a matter of fact, my Father passed away a couple of months ago and was laid to rest in the Cemetery of Pere La Chaise. My parents and myself felt welcomed and we adjusted very well to life here, even though I did not speak

French at the time, everyone gave me a helping hand, which I have not forgotten. So, I would like to give back. I do not want to go to a work camp. I would like you to help me join the army, if possible. I want to fight the Germans. They are doing dreadful things and I firmly believe that one cannot stand by and watch and criticise and do nothing."

Mr Lancelot and Mr Bonse exchanged glances. "You are very wise for your age, how old are you?"

"I will turn 18 next February."

"I can only suggest that you go to the recruitment office here in Paris, but I cannot guarantee anything." He jotted down the address on a piece of paper.

"Do you know anyone there?" Mr Bonse asked.

"Not really," he said and, turning to Freddy said, "You will just have to state your case. Good luck," he said, as he escorted them to the door.

They said their good byes and left without another word.

"Well," said Freddy. "I think if you can spare the time, we should go to the address he gave us."

"I agree with you. I do not want you to be caught and taken God knows where for not complying with the rules."

The recruitment office was not far from where they were. Another line met them but this one was far longer. "We will just have to stand in line like the rest," said Freddy.

It took them three hours to get to the head of the line. The officer who greeted them was tired and very impatient. "What can I do for you?" Freddy stated his case. "No, Monsieur, there are no exceptions. Show me your documents."

Freddy showed him his refugee identity paper and read it out loud, "German," he said with disdain, "we have no place in our army for Germans. Sorry, you have to go to one of the labour camps for foreigners." Freddy looked at Georges' father in dismay. "I am assigning you to the camp located in Sables d'Olonne on the Atlantic Coast."

"When does he have to leave?" asked Mr Bonse.

"I will be generous and give you…" he turned to Freddy with a sneer… "Two hours to get your belongings and be back here."

Freddy was stunned. "How long will I be gone for?" he asked, his voice shaking with rage.

"I cannot answer that question, just bring everything and I expect to see you in two hours' time. Now, if you will excuse me." They did not speak much on the way to Freddy's house. Georges' father was very disappointed, he had hoped he could have helped Georges' best friend, but not only had he been unable to, he had witnessed the rage and contempt the German nationals living in the country provoked in his countrymen.

"It is not fair," he said, not realising he had said it out loud.

"What is not fair?"

"I do not think it is fair that because Germany is at war with France, the refugees who had been accepted by everyone until the war broke out are made into scapegoats and that the perception of them has changed so that they are looked upon as the villains, even though they came here as a last recourse to save their lives." Their arrival at their destination put an end to the conversation.

Georges met them at the door. He did not even bother to ask the question, he knew the answer just by looking at them.

"Yes," said Freddy, "not good at all. I have two hours to pack and to be back at the Military Recruitment Centre from which they are sending me to a labour camp for foreigners and refugees on the Atlantic Coast, a place called Sables d'Olonne."

"In other words, we are back at square one?"

"Yes, let's hope it is not the same camp. But now, I have to run and pack. I am bringing my typewriter with me, who knows, it might be useful to me."

"Once you are ready, come back here and we will come with you to see you off."

He let himself in and went straight to his room to pack. Once he was done, he went to the kitchen. Helene, who had heard him come home, was just setting the table for them. "No time for lunch Mama, I have to run. I am being sent to a camp somewhere on the Atlantic coast and no, Mama, I cannot join the French Army, all of us Germans are enemies of the Republic and we have to be put away, that is the bottom line."

"But…" Helene began.

"That is it, Mama. Georges and his father will be keeping an eye on you, but now I really have to go."

"I should have listened to Nellie and left when she invited me in 1938 to come and join her."

"Don't blame yourself for the choices you made, the circumstances were different, you were still dealing with your health issues and you did not want to leave Papa."

"I know, Mama, but had I known—"

"Had we *all* known," said Helene bitterly, "but there is no use crying over what could have been, it is what it is."

Freddy grabbed his bag. "Do not worry, Mama, I will be fine," he said over his shoulder and was gone.

Georges and his father were waiting for him. They did not speak much on the way. "Did you bring your typewriter?" Georges asked.

"Yes, that was the first thing I packed. I have a feeling having it will prove to be very handy. Do me a favour, once I have left, just go by and see my mother, tell her I am fine and write down the name of the camp where I will be. I told her where I was being sent, but I know for sure she did not write it down and will not remember. As an afterthought, you might want to show her where it is located on a map."

As they approached the Recruitment Centre, Freddy could see the buses pulling up at the curb, a scene he had witnessed before. "Let us hope it is not the same camp I was in before," he whispered to Georges.

The Recruitment officer nodded his head when Freddy signed in and said, "I had a feeling I could trust you, even if you *are* German." Freddy ignored the remark and, after giving Georges and his father a hug, made his way to the bus he had been assigned to. He did not sleep on this journey, he was very much intent on knowing where he was being taken. It was the same camp, nothing had changed.

The Foreman grinned at Freddy when he saw him. "So, we are back."

"Yes, I am back."

"Well, I am afraid you are damned to stay here," he said.

Freddy looked at him. "I do not think so. In fact, maybe you can help me." There was something about this young man that attracted him but he could not place his finger on it. Maybe it was his friendly and engaging manner, or the honesty that shone through his eyes.

"How do you think I might help you?"

"I just want to join the military and fight the Germans."

"But they are your countrymen."

"No, they are not. They do not represent my values. We refugees came to your country seeking refuge from a country in which the values of respect, tolerance and freedom have been replaced by wilfulness, scorn and disregard, subordination and incarceration, and where all dissent is punished."

"That is some statement you are making."

"No," said Freddy, "it is the truth. I would not like to see this beautiful country that welcomed my family and myself experience the same destiny. Just look at what is happening all around us, in Austria, the Sudetenland and now Poland. I hope and pray that France will be spared. The fate of the country lies in the hands of the Military and its government."

"I have a friend who works for the recruitment office. I will have a word with him." He was thoughtful for a moment then said, "I believe I have a recruitment form, do you think you could fill it out for me?"

"Sure," said Freddy.

"I won't be long."

Freddy waited and he was back shortly holding some papers in his hand. "Just fill them out and come see me in my office. It is in that building over there."

Freddy did as he was told and felt a tingle of excitement. Maybe, who knows, his wish might come true. He went to his cot and used the typewriter to fill out the form. He scanned it over one more time and went to deliver it. The Foreman looked at him in surprise, as he walked in the door. "That was quick."

"Yes," said Freddy.

He looked at it and said, full of admiration, "You have a typewriter with you?"

"Yes, I never go anywhere without it, one never knows when it might come in handy."

"Tomorrow is my day off, so I will go find my friend and deliver the paperwork for you. I hope you will not have to wait too long for a reply, but in the meantime, you will have to go about your work as usual."

"I realise that," said Freddy. "I will do my best."

After seeing Freddy off, Georges and his father went over to see Helene. Her eyes were red and it was obvious she had been crying. She was, however, a gracious hostess and tried to give them a welcoming smile. "He has left," she said.

"Yes," they both replied in one voice, then delivered their message. She wrote down the name of the centre or camp where Freddy had been sent and memorised its location. She asked if they thought Freddy would be away very long.

Mr Bonse took his time replying. "Yes, Helene, I believe so, as long as the country is at war, they will keep all male foreigners in labour camps. We can only hope that Germany is defeated so that at least some normality returns to our lives. Do not forget, there are many, many parents who are in the same situation you are in." And saying they would be back to see her soon, they took their leave.

"What a sad situation this is," Georges said. "She has not even finished mourning the loss of her husband and her son is made a prisoner in a refugee camp, her step-daughter is at the other end of the world, and her only sister, who lived here in Paris with her husband, has migrated to America. I am sure we are the only acquaintances she has."

"I would not say we are the only, but yes, one of the few," said Mr Bonse.

Helene did not belong to the type of person who felt sorry for themselves or who were idle. She found out early in life that the best cure for sadness and hurt is to keep busy, and that she did.

She continued with what she had started: sorting out Sigmund's personal items and books, what she would dispose of and what she would ship to Colombia, if that trip ever materialised. What a lot of things they had accumulated over the years, even though most of them stayed behind in Germany. As she went about her work, her mind kept repeating the name of the camp Freddy had been sent to. She decided to look up the nearest city. The name was Quimper, in the department of Brest. She also checked out Sables d'Olonne. It was on the Atlantic Ocean and was renowned for its beautiful long beach, about 350 kms away from Quimper.

An idea started taking shape in her mind. What if she were to leave Paris and move to Quimper? She would be closer to Freddy, even if she could not see him, and the mere thought gave her comfort. She would leave Paris with its grey and depressing weather that worsened as winter approached, and most importantly, she would get away from all the sad memories. No matter where she went in the flat, whether it be the living room or the kitchen, there was something to remind her of Sigmund and her loss. It did not take long to make up her mind.

About a week later, Mr Bonse and Georges came over to see her. Had they heard anything from Freddy? No not one word.

"Well," said Helene, "frankly, I was not expecting any news from him, given the situation, but," she said, turning to Georges father, "I have decided to go to Quimper and spend a couple of days in the town."

"That is an excellent idea, leave Paris, which is so gloomy this time of year, and discover another part of France. There you won't be too far from Sables d'Olonnes."

"Yes," said Helene. "I might go and see what the town is like. I understand it is known for its long and beautiful beach."

"That is correct. So, when are you planning on leaving?"

"I have booked a rail ticket for this coming Friday and found what looks like a beautiful bed and breakfast in the centre of town."

"You do not waste any time," said Georges admiringly.

She smiled at Georges. "You know, when you have an idea and it feels right, you go about making it happen. And anyway, it was not that difficult. I just went to the tourist information centre and asked all the right questions then, upon receiving the correct answers and in possession of the knowledge, I made my decision."

"I can tell you are looking forward to going," said Georges' father.

"Very much so," replied Helene.

"I hope you will be in touch with us, we promised Freddy we would keep an eye on you and we certainly do not want to let him down."

"No worries, I will only be gone for a week at the most."

Helene was a little apprehensive about her trip but she was also excited. Arriving at the Gare du Nord, she boarded the train and was reminded of all the trips she had taken to Crans Montana to visit Freddy. Sigmund had taken her to the station every time, then saw her safely on the train. She felt a lump in her throat and her eyes getting moist but quickly wiped away the tears. He had been so kind and generous, allowing her to visit, even though she knew how much he longed to be the one, but it was a question of finances. He taught her to take care of her money, not to have expenses that were unnecessary, and to justify every penny she spent. She asked herself time and time again if this trip was justified and she was convinced it was, a firm believer that sometimes, if one took the time to listen to oneself, the reason for making a choice would be unveiled.

It was a very long train ride, but she did not mind it. She sat in her seat looking out at the scenery, sometimes just daydreaming or listening to the conversations around her. The train slowed down as it pulled into the station and she looked at her watch. She had arrived at her destination.

A young girl was holding a panel with her name on it and she walked up to her. "My mother thought if I came to meet you, it would be a nice way to welcome you to our town."

"That is very, very thoughtful of you, thank you."

"Your lodgings are not very far from here, in the centre of town, although this is really the centre. We will only have to walk a couple of blocks, do you not mind?"

"Not at all," replied Helene. "I have been sitting practically all day and it will do me good to move. But do tell me, what is your name?"

"My name is Isabel, but everyone calls me Belle."

"What a lovely name," Helene said.

They walked alongside the river that reminded her not only of Paris but Frankfurt as well. Belle pointed out the cathedral to her, it was imposing and very old and it took many centuries to build, Belle informed her. "Well, here we are." The house was on a very quaint cobblestoned side street, just a block from the cathedral. "I hope you will enjoy the sound of the bells ringing." Just then, the clock struck 9 pm.

Belle's mother was waiting for them and she gave Helene a hearty welcome, bidding her to please join them for dinner once she had freshened up. Helene's room was small but very cosy and there was a view of the street, the façades of the houses giving it its character. She felt as if she had gone back in time to the middle ages. People sure are different once one leaves Paris. They are kind, thoughtful and genuine, not pretentious or obnoxious. Even though she had just arrived, she felt very much at home in her new surroundings.

Over dinner, Viviane, Belle's mother, told her about herself. Her family was originally from Quimper and went back to the middle ages. One of her ancestors was related to the first Archbishop of the town and, as Helene was surely aware, religion had been the cornerstone of it. "You will see tomorrow when you go for a stroll that the church was, and still is, predominant. The Benedicts founded a convent here and another order built a church. The architecture has contributed to the charm of the town and we have tried to keep its character. It is not very often that we have a tourist from Paris come and visit, may I ask what brought you here?" Helene told them the reason. "I understand. You and I are in a very similar situation, my husband did not wait to be called, he went to the recruitment office and they took him immediately."

"That is what my son would have liked, but as far as I know, he has not succeeded."

"There is a lot of distrust against Germans now that we are at war, but each person has a different story and one has to understand the individual reasons that brought them here."

"That is right," said Helene.

"I hope you feel at home here with us," said Viviane, who had taken an immediate liking to her.

"I do feel at home," replied Helene. "I believe it was meant for us to meet." As Helene lay in bed, she looked around her room. *So cosy,* she thought to herself, and for the first time in a long time, she felt her body relax and she drifted off into a deep sleep.

The couple of days she had intended to stay went by very fast indeed. She loved the feel of the town, it was small so she could walk everywhere and, most importantly, she felt very much at home. The people she encountered were friendly and talkative and she had to admit to herself she did not feel as lonely as she felt in Paris. Her idea of maybe leaving Paris was not so far-fetched after all and on the eve of her departure, she shared her thoughts with Viviane.

"Should you decide to move, I will be here to help you. You can stay with us for as long as you like. You would have a furnished room and all you would need to bring with you are your clothes."

Helene was thoughtful. It was a very valid point she was making, but on the other hand, she was used to having her independence and space and she could not envision giving it up. "I will think about it and we will stay in touch."

Arriving back in Paris, she again felt overwhelmed by the noise and traffic, with so many people everywhere. It was quite a change. She was just going to start unpacking her suitcase when there was a knock at the front door. She looked at the time, it was not that late but who could it be? She was absolutely sure it was not Freddy, he would never have knocked.

It was her neighbour. The postman came by this morning to deliver a registered letter to her. "I was just leaving and, knowing you were away, offered to sign for it so you would not have to waste time going to the main post office."

"That is very kind of you," said Helene, taking it from her. No sooner had she left than Helene tore open the envelope, eager to read what Nellie had written.

It was addressed to her and Freddy.

Dear Helene and Freddy,
I hope that when this missive reaches you, you are both safe and well.
Due to the news we are receiving from Europe, we are greatly concerned about your safety and wellbeing. Abraham and I, with our acquaintances, are doing everything possible to request your visas so you may come to Colombia. The process is far more complicated than we thought and due to the rogue and expansionist policy the German government is following, the Ministry of Foreign Affairs has restricted the number of visas it is issuing to German nationals considerably, no matter what their present situation might be.
I also have to say that for those who have been in the country for several years, the attitude of the Colombians has changed towards us and we are now viewed with distrust and misgivings. But we have our hearts set on making Papa's wish come true and bringing you to safety.
I hope to have better news in a couple of months.
Big hug,
Nellie

Helene read the letter once more with a heavy heart. It was now just a matter of time and patience and even if they had the required documents, they would have been of little service to them, with Freddy being held at a camp for foreign refugees.

Chapter 45

Four months had gone by since Freddy's arrival at the camp and still no news. When he asked the Foreman if there were any new developments, he said he had spoken to his friend but still nothing had been decided about incorporating refugees into the French army. Freddy was disgusted and disappointed. Breakfast was served at 7 am, their duties began at 7:30 and they worked for 10 hours without pay. The elderly suffered a great deal, there was no heating and it was very cold. Finally, they decided to let the elderly return home. This only made it worse for the young people, however, who were now looked upon to do the jobs of those who had left.

There was no kindness or compassion in the camp. The overseers were harsh and rude, and as the frustration and desperation grew among the refugees, so did their aggressiveness. The French were fighting the Germans, but their methods of punishment were no different from those used by Hitler and his cronies. The only decent human being in the camp was the Foreman, and Freddy had to keep their friendship secret in order to avoid repercussions. He whispered to Freddy that the person who made the decisions was a General headquartered in the city of Nantes.

Freddy went about his work and kept very much to himself, knowing he could trust no one. It was a dark, cold day and Freddy was in a bad mood when the Foreman came looking for him with a package in his hand. "Here," he said, handing it to him. "Someone has sent you this." Freddy looked at the sender.

"It's from my mother." Freddy grinned. "She has not forgotten me."

"But have a look at the postmark."

Freddy looked and read out loud: "Quimper?" He looked stunned. "But, my mother is in Paris."

"Apparently not, it looks like she posted it from Quimper. It is the nearest big city."

"Really?"

"Yes, it is only 340 kilometres away from here."

"I would not say that is very close."

"That depends on what perspective you see it from. It is closer than Paris."

Freddy wondered what Helene was doing in Quimper; they had never talked about that city. Georges would certainly know.

It was rumoured that the refugees would be given two weeks leave to go visit family and friends, and if that turned out to be true, Freddy was adamant about going back to Paris, but he would first stop in Nantes and look up the general to plead his cause.

As with life, everything can change at the spur of the moment without notice. Less than a week before the permission was to be granted, the Overseer announced at breakfast that day and weekly permissions had been cancelled until further notice. One refugee, seething with rage, demanded to know the reasons and was told that there would be a communication forthcoming and everyone was required to be in camp to hear it. Another wanted to know when it was happening. "Sometime in the near future."

Another inmate said under his breath, "It is horrible, the lack of respect, no feelings towards us, treating us like the worst scum, as if we were criminals, our only crime having sought refuge in this country…and being German."

All his hopes shattered, Freddy was really angry, but he kept his anger to himself. The Foreman caught up with him. "Really sorry for the bad news," he said apologetically.

"You are not to be blamed for it, it is what it is," replied Freddy, shaking his head.

"But I have some good news."

"What is it?"

"The person who writes up all the reports has had to leave because of an illness in his family. The reports are typewritten and he has not only left but taken his belongings with him. We are desperately looking for someone who can take his place and I thought of you. I trust your typewriter is in good working condition?"

"It is," replied Freddy, excitedly.

"Do you want the job?"

"Of course I want it, anything is better than labouring outside in the cold. When do I start?"

"Now."

Freddy hurried back to get his typewriter and walked to the Foreman's office with him. He could not remember the last time he had been so happy, working from early morning to late evening, typing sheet and sheets of reports. Having taught himself to type, he did so using just two fingers. It was a slow process but he was sure the more he practiced, the faster he would become. His boss was very impressed with his work, it was precise and very meticulous and he did not hesitate to tell him so. Freddy blushed with pride, there was not much praise around and one tended to forget what it sounded like as well as the good it did to the soul.

While in the office, Freddy also overheard the comments and conversations. He missed reading the newspaper and being informed, for they did their best to keep the refugees at the camp in ignorance, but here the news and point of views were openly discussed. That is how he heard about the atrocities being committed by the Germans on the Poles. So many had simply been shot and killed, or rounded up to work as cheap labourers in Germany.

He also heard about the invasion of Norway and Denmark by the Germans, and even though the British and the French tried to avoid it, Hitler had outwitted them. One office staff commented that Germany was so busy with the Scandinavian countries he had completely forgotten about the rest of Europe and it would surely be spared.

Freddy shook his head and said to himself, "It is just a matter of time before they come after France and Britain." A couple of days later, it was rumoured that the Germans were actively bombing Holland and the British and French had come to their rescue. The British bombed several cities in the Ruhr, the industrial zone of Germany and they were very concerned that should Holland, Belgium and France fall, the enemy would also be in control of the North Sea and the channel Coastline, making an invasion of Britain an easy target, which had to be avoided at all costs.

The mood in the office was one of gloom and everybody seemed to have forgotten that Freddy was a refugee, considering him one of their own. Freddy, in turn, kept his opinions to himself. He remembered a rhyme Sigmund had him memorise once upon a time:

A wise old owl
Sat on a tree
The more he saw
The less he spoke
The less he spoke
The more he heard
And it ended:
Why can't we be like that wise old bird?

Freddy smiled, fully identifying himself with that old bird. He heard so much, but kept his conclusions to himself.

Belgium, a country that had declared its neutrality in the war, surrendered unconditionally to the Germans, opening the way for the Germans to continue on to France. The British and the Allies kept on their fight, but were overpowered by the Germans. At Dunkirk, realising the Germans had surrounded them, the Commanders decided that their only chance was to cross the channel into Britain. Hitler delayed the attack he had planned by a day, thus allowing the Allies, meaning the Norwegians, Poles, British and French, to prepare an evacuation of all their soldiers. It was a terrible battle, a lot of lives were lost and tons of ammunition, tanks, vehicles and other equipment fell into the hands of the enemy, but the evacuation itself was successful. The French army was completely discouraged and the French Government was showing signs of weakness. The battle of Dunkirk was not only the topic of the conversation among Freddy's co-workers, but it made all the headlines in the newspapers as well.

Georges and his father were very busy and under a lot of stress.

377

Georges' two brothers had been recruited into the military and this was extremely hard on Georges' mother. Being blind, and having to depend on others, meant that she did not accept change easily. She was on a roller coaster of emotions, one moment she accepted the situation and was content, the next minute she was going into hysterics, which gradually gave way to depression. She refused to eat, have the curtains opened and would lie in bed for days at a time. It took all the gentleness and coaxing of Georges' father to get her out of that state of mind.

This situation took up a lot of their time and this was the reason, as they explained to Helene, why they had not been over to see her earlier. "No worries," said Helene, "the most important issue is that you can now leave her for a while without having to worry."

"And we do worry," said Georges. "That is why we will not stay long, but how was your trip?"

"It was meant to be," replied Helene, and proceeded to describe everything she had seen and how she had felt, as well as the kindness and warmth of the hostess and her daughter. She mentioned matter-of-factly that she sent Freddy a package but had no reply as yet, then wondered if he was still a prisoner in that centre. Georges replied that to his knowledge nothing had changed, he had received a postcard telling him they were going to give them some days off but that everything had been cancelled last minute without giving a reason for it.

"Well, at least we know he is safe."

"Yes, he is…for the time being."

No one said a word for a while, then Helene broke the silence.

"I've been reading the clippings my late husband cut out of both the French and German newspapers and I am very concerned with the developments happening around us, with the division that is becoming evident in the Government." Mr Bonse looked surprised and was about to say something but Helene went on. "I believe the time has come for me to leave Paris."

"Where will you go?"

"I will move to Quimper where I will be closer to Freddy. There really is no reason for me to stay here. When Sigmund was alive it was different, he chose to live in Paris, although it was not my choice, but with him gone, I am free to choose where I want to live."

"So, what do you intend to do?"

"That is what I wanted to discuss with you. I do not need all this furniture, most of it I will sell, but I would like to keep some pieces that have meaning for Freddy and myself, like my late husband's desk, his books and the paintings. Come along, I will point them out to you."

"Helene, you need not worry about them, we will store them for you in our house. I will have them well packed and if and when you leave for Colombia, we will have them shipped."

Helene let out a sigh of relief. "The flat is rented so all I have to do is write the landlord a letter advising him of my departure and sell the rest of the things."

"Are you going to rent a flat in Quimper?"

"No, Viviane, the owner of the guesthouse, very kindly offered me a room and I have not yet written her accepting her offer, but that is where I intend to stay."

"We will be sorry to see you leave," said Mr Bonse. "But I believe you are doing the right thing."

"I have given it a lot of thought," said Helene, "and I must say, I am very happy with my decision."

"When do you want us to take the items?"

"Everything is ready to go. I have packed the books in waterproof boxes."

"If you like, I can have a word with the movers to see when they are available, and…" Mr Bonse said, looking at Georges, "the day the garage sale takes place, Georges will be here to help you so you will not be alone with strangers."

"Thank you so much," said Helene. "I would really like to get the sale done no later than two weeks from now and be out of the flat by the end of the month, which is when the lease expires." Helene's decision had been very timely indeed and everything went according to her plans. Her landlord was delighted. He was now free to let the flat out at a higher rent, the movers had made themselves available immediately and the sale had gone very well. She sold everything; bed linens, table linens, silver (except for the family pieces) as well as all the kitchenware and some of her clothes that had hardly been worn and were only taking up space.

Viviane and Belle were delighted with her decision to come live with them and Helene herself felt very much at peace. Georges and his father came to take her to the station and just before leaving, she looked around at what had been her home for so long, so many memories, so much pain and so much joy lay in those walls. "Memories are memories," she said out loud, "they are unbounded, are in our hearts and accompany us wherever we go."

Freddy and everyone else in the Camp waited for days, then weeks and finally months for the General to show up and make his communication. He finally put in an appearance a couple of days after the battle of Dunkirk. There had been a great deal of speculation about what he would say. Some hoped they would be sent home, others who, through their families, had some information about what was happening in Europe, hoped they would be recruited, but most of them just wanted to return home and resume a normal life.

He was brief and to the point. All the refugees in the camp, regardless of their ages, were being accepted into the French military and would be integrated into different regiments. They would work as labourers without pay and would be armed with pails and shovels. The General looked around him and, noticing the office personnel, went on to elaborate that the persons who do office work will continue to do so, they will be part of one of the regiments and will move with it. This camp will be closed.

Having uttered this sentence, he turned on his heels and, escorted by his aides, disappeared. One of the refugees spoke, "When? He did not give a date." The Overseer heard him and replied, "What the General said is effective immediately," then ordered everyone to stay where they were. He returned shortly with military uniforms and pails and shovels that he proceeded to hand out. They were told to change quickly into the uniforms, pack their belongings and be ready to leave within the half hour.

Freddy did not waste any time doing as he was told. He never left his precious typewriter in the office and had made it a habit that once he was done with his work for the day, he would bring it back to his cot and place it under lock and key. It was the most valuable of his possessions and he was very much aware of it. He was ready to go long before the rest of them were and was sitting on his cot staring into space when the Foreman sat down beside him.

"Freddy," he said, "we will be leaving in trucks. You are part of the office team so you will be riding with us. Come with me to the office and bring your bag with you."

Freddy did as he was told. They were the last to leave and Freddy looked back as the Foreman closed the gate with a clatter and put the chain and padlock around it. "I hope I will never come back." He had spent six long months here and, with the exception of the food, which never improved and only got worse as time went by, the last two months had not been all that bad. Not only did he work in the office, but he'd had access to all the newest developments.

They sat huddled together on wooden benches in the back of the truck. It was not at all comfortable and when the truck swerved, they were jolted from one side to another. One time, the driver stepped on the brakes so hard that some of the men who were unable to hold on fell flat on their faces. Under different circumstances, it would have been a funny sight. There were not enough trucks so some of the other refugees were riding with them. One of them said under his breath, "This is the trip from hell."

Another replied, "We've now left hell and are heading for purgatory."

"I hope not," said one, overhearing the comment. It took them five hours to reach their destination. It was the camp of Meslay du Maine, which lay just outside the town.

The camp was crowded and there were about 2,000 prisoners, all from the Parisian region, some were intellectuals, some were Germans against the Nazis, some were Jewish. There was diversity. The new arrivals were tired and chilled to the bone. More cots were set up and everyone found a place to rest. Most of the newcomers were too tired to eat and just lay down and fell asleep.

Freddy was curious as well as sleepy. He could not understand why they were wearing military uniforms and had been brought here. He would have loved to have asked the question but thought it more prudent to mind his own business.

Dinner was served at the same time as in Sables d'Olonnes, nothing had changed except for their new surroundings and that there were a lot more of them and, if at all possible, the food was even worse. The next morning, they were woken up before sunrise and divided into companies. Freddy was told to join one of the labour companies, bidding farewell to his days in the office. His company was to work on laying the foundation for the railroad tracks. He had the impression that time stood still and he was back where it had all started: crushing stones. Even if you could not see the enemy, you could hear it.

It seemed as if the enemy planes were not very far from where they were working, or the wind carried the sound and gave them the impression they were within striking distance. They worked on in silence, hoping that they would not become the target, crushing stones for 10 hours a day with short breaks in between. Progressing very fast, the distance between their workplace and the camp had become so big that the decision was taken for them not to return but to set up camp where they were. Freddy, who took his typewriter with him everywhere he went, even though he had to admit it was very burdensome sometimes, was delighted. It was summer, it was warm and being able to sleep outdoors and not breathe in the stale air of more than 2,000 people was a blessing. No one complained and a sense of acceptance had settled over the company.

One day when they were out as usual, doing their work, a warning came that the enemy had been sighted and was not too far from where they were. The Commander ordered them to immediately drop what they were doing, leave everything where it was and move into formation. Freddy ignored the order and ran to get his typewriter, which he hid under his camouflage jacket, then hurried back to join the others. They marched for two long days, 90 kilometres all the way to the city of Angers.

Not one man had been taken prisoner, but it was a harrowing experience as the enemy was never far away. Every time they were alerted about enemy planes overhead, they hid in trenches they had quickly dug and waited, holding their breath until the all clear sign was given. There were several, and sometimes one alert after the other during the day until early evening, which had also slowed their pace. Finally arriving in the city of Anger completely worn out, they went directly to the train station.

There was no time to waste. The Germans were not far, the people of Angers were expecting the enemy any time now and the Polish government, that was in exile and had taken refuge, had left the day before. Aware that France was about to fall to the Germans, the Italians declared war on France and Britain on 10 June. The British bombed the cities of Genova and Turin and the Germans started putting even more pressure on the French. They entered Dijon, which is almost halfway between Paris and the Mediterranean, and were also south-west of Paris. The French troops fled and retreated and many were gunned down by the Germans. The government was forced to leave Paris and went to Bordeaux on that same date. Four days later, the Germans entered Paris.

The Prime Minister at the time, Reynaud, was unable to persuade his ministers to continue to fight from outside France, so he presented his resignation on 16 June 1940 and was replaced by Marshal Petain who declared an end to hostilities the following day and asked the Germans for an armistice which was signed on 22 June 1940. As part of the negotiations, it was agreed that the country would be divided as follows: The central and southern part of the country would be the unoccupied zone under the government of Marshal Petain, with the city of Vichy as its capital and the Germans would rule in the channel coast and northern industrial regions. The army and fleet would be demobilised and the French would have to pay for the costs of the German occupation.

Helene, who was safely in Quimper, could not believe her luck. She had left Paris just in time and mused, "Who would have thought the Germans would enter Paris without a shot being fired and the country would be divided?" Very concerned about Freddy, she decided that no news is good news, as the saying goes, but even so, the news about bombings, prisoners being taken and the Germans now ruling part of the country was not exactly meant to set a mother's mind at ease.

The worst time for her was at night when her fears surfaced and kept her awake for hours on end. She had given her address to Mr Bonse and Georges, for she was sure Freddy would contact them whenever he could. Not only did she worry about Freddy, but she was concerned for her own safety as well. Having read about the conditions of the signing of the Armistice, she was fully aware that Quimper came under what was to be known as the occupied zone. She had to leave, but where to? She knew she had to go south, towards the Mediterranean, but her handicap was that she knew no one. What she could not have known, however, is that Freddy was now comfortably seated on a train heading for the South of France himself, which belonged to the unoccupied zone.

No sooner had they arrived at the station than the train came in. They rushed to board it, as they were told, and barely had time to find a seat when the train was already picking up speed. Freddy had rushed on board and luck was with him again. He found an empty seat by the window. He smiled to himself, "Wherever I go, there is a window seat waiting for me," then thought of the truck ride and grinned, "with one exception."

There was not one empty seat and many people were standing. From the conversations he overheard going on around him, he surmised that most of the passengers were fleeing from the Germans. He heard someone mention that some German high-ranking officers had been seen walking the Champs Elysees and dining at Maxims, the renowned restaurant. Hearing this, he suddenly thought of Helene, with all that had been going on, he had not had time to even think of her. Where was she? Hopefully, she would have had sense enough to leave Paris. He felt a tight knot in his stomach, why had he forgotten her? He tried to calm his thoughts, saying that Georges and his father would most surely have seen to it that she left the city.

All of a sudden, he remembered the package and the postmark she had sent him. It had not been sent from Paris. He took out the little notebook he always carried with him and thought that if he remembered correctly, he had written the sender's address down. As he opened the book a paper fell out, it was part of the wrapping of the package, and upon looking at it closely, he saw very distinctly in Helene's handwriting, the address and phone number, as well as the name of Quimper, clearly on the postmark. He felt so guilty and confused, wondering how could he forget about his mother. "Not surprising," he said to himself. "With everything that was and is going on, the only thought one could have is of survival," and so far, they had all survived.

The train stopped, which it seemed to do at every station along the way, and Freddy heard someone say that Albi was the end of the journey, apparently everyone was heading there. More people kept getting on at each stop but none got off, there were people standing everywhere. At one of the stations, an elderly and very frail woman got on board and Freddy gave up his seat to her. His feet, which were full of sores, complained, but the thankful smile she gave him took the edge off the pain.

"One more stop," someone said, "and we will have arrived."

Just then, Freddy felt a hand on his shoulder; it was his friend, the Foreman. "I have been looking all over for you, have you been standing here the whole time?" Freddy told him that he had been seated for most of the ride.

"The next stop is our destination. Do you think I will have time to make a phone call? I am very concerned about my mother, as I have not heard from her since she sent that package. That was some time ago and with the Germans in Paris…"

"I understand your worries."

"It is also guilt, I did not think of her once." The train rumbled into the station and came to an abrupt stop. Someone said in a loud, clear voice, "Welcome to the city of Albi."

Everyone formed outside the station and waited for the others. One of the overseers shouted to make himself heard above the noise that they would have about an hour's walk to Camp de la Viscose. The Foreman walked besides Freddy. At the corner, he stopped and pointed out a phone booth to his friend. "I will be here waiting for you, go call your mother and hopefully the phone call will put your mind at ease."

Freddy shot him a grateful look and he took out some coins from his pocket and the paper he had carefully saved, and dialled the number. The phone rang and rang and he was just about to hang up when he heard a woman's voice on the other end. He identified himself and asked to speak to Helene. There was a slight pause and Freddy's heart skipped a beat, he thought the person had hung up.

"Is this her son?" asked a woman's voice.

"Yes, it is."

"Your mother has been waiting for days for this phone call, but unfortunately." She paused.

"Unfortunately what?" asked Freddy in a nervous and impatient voice.

"Your mother was staying with us, I mean my daughter and myself, but she left today."

"Today?" Freddy repeated in disbelief.

"Yes, she left just this morning."

"Did she say where she was going?"

"No, the only thing said was that if you called, to tell you she is safe and in good health and to ask if you have an address where you can be contacted."

Freddy thought for a minute. "Yes, I have an address."

"Bear with me, I will find a paper and a pencil to write it down." Freddy waited, concerned that the call would get cut off and he did not have any more small change to put in. "Tell me," said the voice.

"Camp Viscose." He repeated it one more time and the phone went dead. *That was lucky,* he thought. He walked over to where his friend was standing, "You were gone a long time, any luck?"

"Yes," said Freddy, and related the conversation to him.

"Now we had better hurry." And they soon caught up with the rest.

They walked past the city and in the distance, one could see the imposing bell towers, "Seventy-eight metres high from the cathedral," his friend whispered to him, almost in reverence, "Sainte Cecile."

"What?" Freddy asked. "Is that is the name of the cathedral?"

"I used to spend a lot of time here."

"Really?"

"Yes, my mother is from this city and we would come and visit my grandparents. It is a medieval city, the cathedral is built almost like a fortress, and I have very happy memories of the time I spent here." He did not elaborate any further and was pensive the rest of the way.

By the time they reached the camp, which lay on the outskirts of the city, night had fallen. All three camps were the same; the only changes were the location and the names.

Chapter 46

Helene made up her mind to leave since it was out of the question for her to remain in Quimper. *One more change,* she thought to herself, *yes, one more, better than going to prison or losing one's life.* She heard about everything going on in the countries that had been occupied by the Germans, how the Jews were being rounded up at times. Yes, it was imperative that she leave. She did not tell Viviane and Belle her reasons for leaving, the less information they had about her, the better off they would be. In its Sunday edition, Le Figaro had published a map detailing the division of the country into two zones and she studied it very thoroughly. She'd been right in her assessment of the situation, she had to go towards the Mediterranean. No, Marseille was a huge port city and did not appeal to her at all, but just between Montpelier and Marseille there was a small town or village with a name that caught her fancy. Sausset les Pins. It lay 40 kilometres before Marseille, directly on the coast and was part of the unoccupied zone.

She checked the map once more and told Vivianne she would be back shortly, then left for the tourist office. There she was told of one direct train per day that left early in the morning from Quimper and arrived in Sausset les Pins early evening. She would have travelled more than 1,000 kilometres. That suited her just fine, could they recommend a hotel? The person serving her was young and very obliging, she had grown up in Marseille and knew Sausset les Pins well, for it was not only a fishing village but it was also a well renowned beach town in the summer. She wrote down a name on a piece of paper and as she handed it to Helene, volunteered to make the call. "Do you have a date in mind?"

Helene thought for a minute. "Yes," she replied. "I will leave tomorrow so I need the room then if they have one available." There was no problem reserving it and, thanking the young lady for her kindness, Helene went to the station to purchase her train ticket. As she walked, her thoughts turned to Freddy. Where could he be? She had looked at the map and saw that Sables d'Olonnes was in the occupied zone and hoped that Freddy was not still there, feeling a slight unease. Only God knew if he was safe and well and she could only hope and pray, for he was all she had. After purchasing her train ticket, she headed back to pack her belongings, very relieved to find nobody at home. She saw a note on the kitchen table that read:

Sorry, Helene, we hoped you would be home in time to join us. We have been invited to dinner and will not be home till late. Hope you had a good day, Vivianne and Belle.

Yes, she'd had a good day but as she packed, her mood changed and she suddenly felt very sad. Then she looked back at her life, Wiesbaden, Frankfurt, Paris, Quimper, now Sausset les Pins and, with a little luck maybe Bogotá. The latest moves had taken place just a year after Sigmund's passing and thinking of Sigmund, she felt a wave of gratitude; thank God he had not lived to see the Germans occupy France. He would have died of remorse for not having heeded Abraham's advice.

It was late by the time she finished packing and heard the front door open when Vivianne and Belle returned. Seeing Helene's light still on, they knocked on her bedroom door, then looked at each other in surprise. "You are leaving?" they said in one voice.

"Yes, it is time to move on." Just then, Vivianne realised she was holding a paper in her hand. She looked at it then handed it to Helene.

"I am so sorry, I forgot to leave this with the note we wrote you." It was a telegram and Helene's heart skipped a beat when she saw it was from Nellie. It read:

Was told your visas would have been granted today but unfortunately more time is needed, very disappointed. Love, Nellie

She read the message one more time and tried to regain her composure. "Bad news?" Vivianne asked.

"No, no," replied Helene. "Nothing out of the ordinary. I must be up very early tomorrow."

"At what time?"

"I have to leave at 5 am."

"Then we had better go to bed for we will rise early as well to see you off."

Helene lay in bed, unable to fall asleep. She read and reread what Nellie had written and felt let down on the one hand but it had only confirmed that she'd taken the correct decision about leaving on the other. As she closed her eyes, she imagined hearing Sigmund's voice, saying that in due course, everything would turn out for the best, then fell asleep with a smile on her lips. She and the rest of the household were not the only early risers that morning.

The new Commander of the camp woke everyone up at 4:30 am. He was young and full of energy and as they rubbed their eyes and left their cots, the inmates could not understand what was expected of them at such an early hour. They were told to get into formation and stand at attention, then they were regrouped. The Commander had been informed in detail about each one of them and this was the reason why Freddy had been assigned back to the office team. His colleagues were amazed that his typewriter had made it this far.

"Yes," said Freddy, grinning. "It was awkward at times, having it under my camouflage shirt, and there were times when I felt so frustrated and uncomfortable that the thought was never far from my mind of just dumping it."

"It is a good thing you did not allow your emotions to control you," said the Foreman. "Had it been otherwise, you would not be sitting with us here today."

There was not much office work, so they spent most of their time playing cards. It all seemed like a huge waste of time. Freddy did not complain and kept his thoughts to himself, but he never could quite get rid of the persistent question of when and if he would ever be free again. Some of the inmates were sent on to other camps, others had been made prisoners and sent on to other cities. Seeing what was going on around him, Freddy was thankful for his good fortune. A couple of weeks had gone by since his arrival and they were all at dinner when the Overseer broke the silence by calling out Freddy's name. He hesitated for a minute then walked over to him. "Here," he said, and handed him a telegram. It was from Helene and it read:

I am in Sausset les Pins Hotel Val Mar
Love, Mama

Freddy was overjoyed. The Overseer interrupted his thoughts, "Good news?" he asked.

"Yes, thank you." Freddy felt as if a ton of bricks had been lifted off his shoulders. Helene was safe and well. His friend, the Foreman, came over to see him.

"I see you have received good news from your mother?"

"Yes, she is safe and well, and I am so relieved. Do you have a map?"

"There should be one in the office, come with me." They found what they were looking for. "What do you want to know?" Freddy took out the telegram he had folded neatly and placed in his pocket and showed it to him. The Foreman read out loud. "Sausset les Pins…why that is not very far from where we are. It is here," he said placing his finger on the map so Freddy could have a clear picture. "It is right on the coast. Have you been there?"

"No, never, how far is it from here?"

"I would say it is about 340 kilometres at the most."

Freddy thought, "If I ever regain my freedom, that is where I will go." Then he asked the Foreman, "What about you, do you have any plans?"

"Not really, I am a professional soldier. I will most likely stay in the military and go wherever they send me." Then, not a week after their conversation, the Commander called Freddy into his office and told him that he was now discharged.

Freddy looked at him in disbelief. "I am free to leave?"

"Yes, you are a free man. And let me express my gratitude to you for your help in the office. That typewriter of yours…"

Freddy finished the sentence for him, "Is invaluable."

"Good luck to you, and be safe," he said shaking Freddy's hand and handing him a travel permit that entitled him to go to Sausset les Pins. When he returned to the camp, he realised that he had not been an exception, all of them had been demobilised, owing their good fortune to the signing and implementation of the armistice. He would remember the date for as long as he lived: 17 August 1940.

Freddy did not have much to pack. Most of the clothing he had brought with him from Paris he'd gotten rid of along the way. He owned his raincoat, two long sleeved shirts, the boots he was wearing, a pair of sandals, a pair of pants and some underwear. That was it. On his way to the station, he decided to take a stroll through the town and as he walked, he kept repeating to himself, "I am free, I am free, I am free." Having always taken freedom for granted, now that he had lost it and regained it once again, he understood its full meaning.

He stood for a moment looking at the cathedral's tower, standing so tall that one could see it from afar, and remembered the name Sainte Cecile. He walked towards it and, looking at his watch, decided to go in. Once inside the main doors, he was startled to see how ornate it was. The frescoes and paintings were stunning. There were a few people standing near the choir, but the harmony and peace that engulfed him was an invitation for him to close his eyes and give thanks for the many blessings he had received within a couple of days from each other. The ringing of the church bells reminded him that he had a train to catch and he slowly made his way to the exit, arriving at the station with barely enough time to purchase his ticket and board the train.

He was very excited about seeing Helene. It was almost a year to that fateful day when he had had to report to the police headquarters. Neither one of them thought their separation would last so long. He thought of Georges and his family, how lucky he was to have such a trustworthy and loyal friend. Whenever he had been able to, he sent a postcard telling him about his situation. Unfortunately, this habit had been short lived, not because he was too lazy to write, but because of the circumstances. He hoped Helene would have some news about Nellie and their visa application, his only wish was for them to leave France sooner rather than later.

The controller announced in a loud voice: "Sausset les Pins! This train continues on to Marseille," interrupting his daydream. Freddy gathered his belongings and, having arrived at his destination, still had to find the Hotel. "This is a village," he said out loud, looking around. The station was small and the building was very old and in desperate need of repair. He stopped at the kiosk, bought a post card and asked for directions to the hotel.

"When you walk out of the station, just turn right and keep on walking for about two blocks."

He followed the instructions but one could not miss it. A huge sign that read Hotel Vale Mar hung over the entrance. Freddy felt the excitement mount up, in a couple of minutes, he would see his mother. The reception area was small but cosy and when he walked up to the receptionist and was about to speak, he heard her voice and turned around. Helene was standing behind him.

"Mama," he said softly under his breath. It took her a minute to realise that she was not dreaming or seeing a ghost, it was her son Freddy, standing before her. She opened her arms wide and held him to her while the tears streamed down her face. The receptionist was very moved by the scene she was witnessing. When both mother and son had regained their composure, Helene introduced him, and mentioned matter-of-factly that they had been separated from each other for a year.

She handed Freddy a room key and said, "The room on us, it is right next door to your mother's."

"Is that all you have?" Helene asked, looking at his bag.

"Yes, that is it, I travel light."

Helene explained that the hotel was family owned and not very big, but the owners were extremely nice and it was the owner's daughter who had handed them their keys.

"That really was a very generous and nice gesture," said Freddy. "I can't believe I will finally be sleeping by myself, or should I say *with* myself after having spent almost a year sleeping with 2,000 souls."

"We have a lot to catch up on."

"We can do it later," said Freddy. "There is nothing I would like better right now than a nice bath."

Once freshened up, he joined Helene in her room. "You sure have grown," she said, as he walked in. She stood beside him.

"Why, you are as tall as I am."

"Yes," said Freddy, "last time they measured me I was 1.75."

"You take after my side of the family."

"I know, Mama."

"But you look more like Papa. Come on, are you hungry? The food in the restaurant is very good, it is home cooking with local produce."

"No, Mama, I am not hungry. Are you?"

"No, not really…shall we sit down and catch up?" They talked until the wee morning hours. There were happy memories and sad ones, but they had one thing they wholeheartedly shared and that was the joy of having found each other. Helene told him about her time in Quimper and Freddy made her laugh, describing how sometimes he had been ready to dump the typewriter. He then described vividly how he had reasoned with his father, who was trying to convince him that it was an unnecessary luxury, and how, in the long run, he had been right all along. It truly made his life as a prisoner much more bearable.

A wave of sadness crept over them and they did not speak for a while. Freddy broke the silence with the question Helene was dreading. "What has Nellie said about our visas?" Helene did not answer, she just handed him the telegram. He read it twice then returned the paper to her. "I tell you, Mama, had I only left when she invited me to come in 1938…"

"Now, Freddy, we have been through that issue before, let us not bring it up again."

"Mama, you do not realise it, but we have to get out of here. We are not safe here."

"Yes, we are," said Helene.

"For the time being," said Freddy. "But do not fool yourself. The Germans will start issuing orders concerning the Jews in the unoccupied zone and they will be carried out, trust me, Mama."

"Let us think about the present," said Helene. "We cannot afford two rooms in this hotel."

"I am sure we will not be charged for the first couple of nights for my room," said Freddy.

"I know," said Helene, "but there is a cheaper option which will also be more practical."

"And that is?"

"We can rent a two-bedroom cottage. I have seen them advertised in the newspaper and there are quite a few to be had. I will be able to cook and do the housework, it will feel like having a home again and we will save some money."

"That is very good idea," said Freddy. "Let's look into it tomorrow." Then, as an afterthought, "Should those visas ever come through, we will need all our savings."

Helene was standing by the window from where she could see the sea. "The sun is rising over the horizon, we had better get some sleep," she said to Freddy, walking him to the door. "We are so blessed," she added, kissing him good night.

Neither one of them rose early and met around noon. Helene suggested they have lunch in the village, so Freddy could get acquainted with his surroundings and the area. Before going to bed, Freddy wrote Georges a postcard, giving him his address. Walking past the post office, he remembered he had it in his pocket and dropped it in the mailbox. "Both Georges and his father were wonderful to me; do you know if his brothers are back?"

"They were recruited." Freddy looked surprised. "He has been a true and loyal friend to you."

"To both of us," said Freddy.

"There are not many people as generous, compassionate and caring as they are," said Helene.

"It is a friendship that will last a lifetime, Mama. The same can be said for my friendship with Helmut."

"Do you still keep in touch?"

"The last I heard from him, he had been forced to join the Gestapo."

They found a quaint restaurant on the beach and had a wonderful meal of freshly caught fish. Freddy was starved. It was a sheer pleasure to watch him eat and when he finished, he just said, "What a difference a well-cooked meal with fresh ingredients can make."

They continued on their walk and came up to a very quaint villa that had a 'for rent' sign on it. The villa was surrounded by a beautiful garden and was just a block away from the beach. From where they were standing, they could hear the waves crashing. "The location is fantastic," said Freddy and just then, the front door opened and a gentleman walked out and towards them. "We were just admiring the garden," said Freddy.

"The last tenants took a lot of pride in looking after it," the man said. Freddy and Helene exchanged glances. "Allow me to introduce myself, my name is Mr Cohen and I am the owner of the Villa Marie Louise." Helene and Freddy gave him their names but did not give any more details. "Are you new newcomers to the region? Do you like it?"

"Very much, from what we have seen."

"I find there is no place in the world like the South of France, the turquoise blue of the sea, the wonderful sunsets and sunrises, its mild climate…"

Freddy finished the sentence for him: "And the food."

"Yes, I must say I feel very privileged to be able to live here, and with the current situation going on around us, even more so," said Mr Cohen.

Freddy and Helene took a liking to him. "Well," said Freddy, "we were actually taking a walk, getting our bearings. We only arrived yesterday and were looking for a place to spend the winter months."

"I would be happy to show you the villa if you like."

Helene agreed immediately. It was all on one floor and completely furnished in good taste. There were two bedrooms and two bathrooms, which surprised Helene. "I remodelled it when I bought it. When we moved in, it was just me and my wife, but you know how it is, the kids came and because there were three, we needed more space. Now we live in Montpelier, which, as you know, is not very far from here." As he spoke, they carried on with the viewing.

Helene was delighted. Mr Cohen asked her if she liked it. "Very much," replied Helene, "it feels like a home."

"I think you will be very happy here. You are close to the town centre and yet you do not have the noise, you are not far from the beach and can hear the surf."

"Yes," said Freddy, "it is very well located. Are you letting it out weekly, monthly?"

"It is up to you."

"I believe we would like to pay the rent monthly, but would also like to be able to leave on short notice," said Freddy, with the thought of leaving for Colombia at the back of his mind. "That would not be a problem if you could give me a month's notice."

Freddy and Helene exchanged looks. "How much is the rent?"

He named a figure. "There is no rush, take your time, and if you decide this is the property you are looking for, just give me a call. Here is my card." Freddy looked at Helene and could tell she saw herself already living there.

"Can I make you an offer?" Freddy asked.

"Sure, go ahead."

Freddy was extremely good at figures and offered him 25% less than what he had asked for. Much to Helene's surprise, Mr Cohen agreed to it.

The place was spick and span. Mr Cohen showed them how everything worked, where everything was and handed them the keys. Helene took them, smiling happily and placed them in her purse. They could move in immediately. There was just a small but important issue to sort out: The rent payment. They agreed it would be by bank transfer and Helene had just opened an account. Mr Cohen felt he could trust them and dispensed from asking for a deposit. He got into his car and drove off in a very good frame of mind. It had not been longer than a week since his tenants had left and he had only lost a week's income. He thanked his lucky stars for being at the right place at the right time.

Helene and Freddy went back into the house. They looked around one more time and Freddy chose the bedroom with the view of the garden, which somehow reminded him a little of his room in Frankfurt.

"Yes, indeed, it looked out on to the garden. But let us go and get our things, we have a lot of work ahead of us." They hurried back to the hotel, not believing their good fortune. "It was meant to be," said Helene.

"Everything has a way of sorting itself out," said Freddy.

"You sound just like Papa," Helene said, laughing.

Chapter 47

Life in Sausset les Pins was uneventful and boring. Helene was content to have a home once more and someone to care for. Freddy was happy just to sleep and eat and be looked after. Thanks to Helene's good cooking and his healthy appetite, he soon put on the weight he had lost and pretty much recovered from the ordeal of the past months. But as time went by, he began to feel restless and bored. There was really not much to do.

He would go down to the beach every morning and watch the fishermen leave in their boats. It was a very pretty sight, 10 boats all painted different colours going out to sea, and just before sunset, he would return to the beach to watch them come in, looking at the prizes they had caught. He befriended all of them and was often invited out to join them. Those were the times he enjoyed the most. He tried to find a job, and finally found one working with a carpenter. It was better than having nothing to do and it gave him a reason to get up in the morning. Even though the pay was not much, it helped towards their living expenses.

One day as he was going through the books in the library, he found a Spanish/French dictionary. He took it home with him and decided to learn Spanish since it would come in handy if they ever left for Colombia. They recently celebrated the arrival of 1941 and still no news about their visas. Nellie had written that they were all trying their hardest; they filled out more forms and had been to several interviews at the foreign office, but had been advised that it was just a matter of time. *But how much more time?* Freddy wondered.

Due to the war, food was becoming scarce and prices were rising. Freddy found an old fishing boat, which, with his newly learned carpenter skills, he was able to repair. Once he finished work for the day, he went out in it and sometimes, when luck was with him, two or three fish would bite which he would bring home.

Helene would prepare one and Freddy would exchange the other two for vegetables or potatoes. Meat was scarce as well.

Then he invested some of his savings in a couple of rabbits. Before purchasing them, he built the cages and since the garden was big, he was able to place them some distance from the house. He fed them well and in one of his letters to Georges, told him that he had one that weighed seven pounds, hoping he would be able to join them for a rabbit feast.

A hotel close by ordered one of his rabbits from him. Freddy went to deliver it and as he walked through the lobby on the way to the kitchen, he discovered a

Ping-Pong table with a ball and two rackets on it. As he was leaving, the concierge walked up to him and inquired if he played the game by any chance. They were organising a tournament and did not have enough players. Freddy was delighted and signed up immediately. It was during this event that he met Miriam.

She was beautiful, intelligent, had a wonderful sense of humour and was an only child living in Paris with her parents. Due to the recent events, and being Jewish, her family was forced to move to the unoccupied zone. As in Freddy and Helene's case, they were desperately trying to leave Europe, but so far, luck had eluded them.

It was love at first sight. She was one year younger than Freddy, had spent her summers in Switzerland and was an avid skier. They had a great deal in common. In the tournament, they played the mixed doubles together and won against a British couple. They were ecstatic. "Maybe our fortune is changing and we will be able to leave," said Miriam.

Freddy had told her about his sister and Colombia and Miriam said that her family had no relatives, both her parents had no brothers or sisters and her grandparents on both sides of the family had passed on. "In that case," said Freddy, "maybe you can come to Colombia."

Miriam laughed. "If even you, who has a relative there, have not been able to get your visas, what makes you think we will get ours?"

Freddy was thoughtful. "I get your point," he said. "Yes, it is all about having the right connections." Freddy would remember this conversation for as long as he lived. Life now had a meaning for Freddy, he was happy and content and his anxiety level diminished considerably, much to Helene's relief. He stopped brooding and enjoyed living in the now.

The hot summer months had given way to the cooler days of autumn. Freddy and Helene were sitting in the garden when the telegram delivery boy arrived on his bicycle. Leaning it against the wall, he walked over towards them and handed the envelope to Helene. Her hands were shaking and noticing it, the boy passed the book and pen for Freddy to sign. As soon as he left, Helene read it out loud, her voice trembling.

Good news, your visas have been granted, go to the
Colombian consulate in MARSEILLE
Love, Nellie

"Finally, the wait is over, Mama. Do you realise what this means? We can leave this country, this continent and get out of harm's way."

"Yes," replied Helene, "I realise all that, but…have you given any thought to everything that needs to happen before we can?"

"No, worries, Mama, whatever needs to be done will be taken care of. The most important thing is that the immigration authorities of Colombia have authorised our entry."

Helene was thoughtful. "Freddy, you do not have a passport."

"I do not even have citizenship anywhere," said Freddy.

"What?"

"I lost it when I served in the French army."

"You need some kind of travel document."

"I had not given the matter any thought but you are right, it poses a huge obstacle to us leaving." Freddy seemed light-hearted about it, not wanting to create more anxiety for his mother, but how on earth was he going to get a travel document? "Mama, Nellie told us to go to the Colombian consulate in Marseille, does she mention what documents we should take with us, if any?"

"I believe she mentioned something about documents. I have kept all her letters and telegrams and there are not many, so I will go find them."

Freddy was about to leave to go see Miriam and share his good news with her when Helene returned holding some papers in her hand. She read out the following: authenticated documents, birth certificates, marriage certificate and certificate of good conduct should be presented.

"I have the documents requested, but do you?"

"Yes, I do have a passport. So all you need, Freddy, is some kind of travel permit or document?"

"Yes, that is the complicated part, aside from finding a ship that will take us."

"Oh, yes, now that you mention it, she also wrote that we should go to a company called Ybarra located in Marseille, but she did not elaborate further."

"That might be the shipping company," said Freddy. He was pensive. *This is getting more and more complicated,* he thought to himself. "Well, Mama, I am going for a walk to think things over. I do not know if I will be back in time for dinner."

Helene watched him leave and thought how responsible for his age he was, how much he's been through and that he had no time to grow up. The years in which he had really been carefree were the ones when he was in Crans Montana recovering from tuberculosis. She walked over to her night table and picked up a picture. They were both on skis and looked so happy. Looking back at the past, she could almost compare their lives with the flow of a river, going steadily downhill, when all of a sudden, with no warning whatsoever, came the rapids and in between were the pools of calmness of short duration. She smiled to herself and asked out loud, "And how is the river flowing now?" It is getting closer to the mouth or the sea, but its path is going to be full of currents.

Yes, it certainly will not be an easy task, complying with all the requirements, but she seemed to hear Sigmund's voice one more time saying, "You can and you will fulfil my wish."

Freddy knocked on Miriam's door. "Ready to go for a walk?" he asked.

"Sure," she replied, getting her coat.

"I need some fresh air," he said. "Let's walk by the beach."

"Any news?"

Freddy was not sure he wanted to share his good fortune with her for he did not want her to feel bad, but on the other hand, he had been honest with her and had told her what his plans were. "Yes," he said, "but I have a problem, and a big one. I have no passport and I have no citizenship, so I will need a travel permit or document, and I do not know anyone in the French government who might help me."

"Does your mother have a passport?"

"Yes, she has one, but I was deposed of my citizenship for having been in the 317th company of the French army."

"I do not see the problem. All you have to do is go to the army headquarters and have them issue a permit for you."

"You are so smart. They will probably give me a travel permit to go to Marseille, but I am sure they will not be able to issue one for international travel."

Miriam was thoughtful for a minute. "I will share some very private information with you, but you must promise to keep it to yourself. As you are aware, us Jews are being persecuted not only in the occupied countries but here in France as well."

"Yes, I know, I do read the newspapers," said Freddy sarcastically.

"Well, there is an underground movement that is trying to get as many of us out of the country as possible. As a matter of fact, my parents are working with them, as it is our only chance."

"Do you have a name?"

"I can ask my parents if they know someone."

"That would be fantastic. And I, in turn, might be able to get you a visa for Colombia with my sister's help and connections. Close your eyes for a moment and just imagine, us leaving together on the same ship and discovering a whole new country together."

"It would be a dream come true," said Miriam, "if only we could make it come true."

Freddy took her in his arms and whispered in her ear, "We will both try our hardest." Then he escorted her back to her room. Freddy wished her sweet dreams.

"I will dream of a beautiful future in a far off land," said Miriam. Tears came to her eyes as she sat down on her bed and went back over the day's events. Her parents and her own situation were very difficult indeed. They had applied for entry to the USA but their application had been rejected, her father tried to get more information, but the people at the consulate refused to see him. He was very much discouraged, until just by chance he had encountered a gentleman by the name of Mr Cohen. It was a very strange encounter indeed, they were both just leaving the synagogue when he walked up to him and introduced himself. "You look very, very sad," said the stranger.

Miriam's father gave him a surprised look. "You have hit the nail on the head," he replied. "I am not only very sad but I am also extremely upset."

"Would you care to share the reasons with me?" he asked. Miriam's father, whose name was Simon, thought for a minute then he looked at the person facing him one more time and thought to himself, why not, and said out loud, "What have I got to lose?" Mr Cohen was an attentive listener and interrupted just once.

"The Americans refused to grant you a visa, yes? And no reasons given? I will try to help you. I am part of a Jewish organisation and I will see what we can do. Here is my card." And Simon gave him his. "I will get in touch with, you but I will need some time."

"No worries," said Simon, and gave him a smile. Nothing uplifts the spirit more than a glimmer of hope. Miriam was falling asleep when she heard a knock on the door. She knew who it was; her father had always come to her room and kissed her good night, no matter how late. Simon saw she was in a talkative mood. "So how was your day?" he asked.

"It was brilliant."

Simon smiled. "I guess that handsome young man came over to see you, am I right?"

Miriam blushed to the roots of her hair. "Yes, and this is what he told me," and she related the conversation to him.

"So basically," said Simon, "if we can help him get the travel document he needs to go abroad, he would then help us get the visas for Colombia?"

"Yes."

Simon was thoughtful. "It is worth a try."

"But even if he can't help us, we might be able to help him, and you know when one gives, one always receives in one way or another."

Simon took the card Mr Cohen had given him and wrote the name and phone number on a piece of paper. "When you see him again, give it to him, but please do keep this information to yourselves, I would not want to cause anyone any trouble."

Helene was already in bed and fast asleep when Freddy got home. *Just as well,* he thought to himself. "I need some time to think," he said out loud. If this person Miriam had mentioned could really get him a travel document, that would solve his problem, but would Nellie be able to make a visa application for a completely unknown family? Be honest, Freddy, he heard his inner voice telling him, you do not know anything at all about them and you have met her parents only once. You know they are Jewish, they must be well to-do if they could afford vacationing in the winter in Switzerland, and you have a crush on Miriam. A crush? "It is more than a crush, I am really madly in love with her," and said it out loud as if he needed to convince himself that by hearing the words, it would be so. His thoughts went back to Nellie and the visa request; he decided he would send her a short telegram.

He awoke early and did not wait for Helene to prepare breakfast. "Where are you going?" she asked.

"I am just going to run an errand, I will not be long." The telegraph office had just opened and there was no line. He wrote the text which read:

We are both delighted with the good news, trying to find some kind of travel document to travel abroad with. Can you help a family of three who have nowhere to go?

Love, Freddy

If everything went according to plan, she would receive it by late afternoon. He left the office feeling pleased with himself and was thinking of asking Miriam to join him for breakfast when he suddenly remembered her mentioning an underground Jewish movement. He decided to head for home instead and ask Helene if she knew anything about it. As he came around the corner, he saw a car parked in front of his house. He wondered who could possibly be visiting his mother at such an early hour and felt a pang of apprehension.

When he entered the house, he saw Mr Cohen sitting with Helene in the living room having a cup of coffee. "This is the most pleasant surprise," said Freddy, greeting the guest and hoping that he had not come to tell them to vacate the property.

"The pleasure is entirely mine. I have some business to attend to in the neighbourhood, and since I was a little early, I decided to stop by and say hello."

"Mr Cohen was just telling me—"

He interrupted her saying, "I will tell him."

Freddy looked from one to the other in surprise. "Tell me what?"

"Your mother has told me about your good fortune." Freddy shot his mother a questioning look, which Mr Cohen also saw. "No need to worry, I might be able to help. You see, and this is for your information only, I am a member of the Armee Juive, the Jewish Army, which is a Zionist resistance movement, and one of our missions is to try and get as many members of our community out of France before it is too late."

"I guess you are aware of the situation."

"Yes, I am," replied Mr Cohen.

"I am planning on dealing with the local authorities and doing everything out in the open, however, should I feel I need your help, I will come back to you."

Mr Cohen stood up to take his leave, thanking Helene for the coffee he shook Freddy's hand and left.

The door had hardly closed behind him when Freddy turned to his mother. "Why did you confide in him?"

"Because someone I met in Quimper mentioned the resistance group to me. I did not know our landlord was a member of it but we were making small talk and when I asked him if he had any hobbies or what else he did, he told me he was very well aware that we were part of the community and should we need anything, we could count on him and his organisation."

"I see." Then Freddy said, "So you told him the whole story. I do not understand why women always have to gossip, we men are so discreet and quiet."

Helene burst out laughing. "That is definitely not true, men gossip more than women. I observed it time and time again when your father and I used to attend the different venues in Frankfurt. Our spouses would go into the library to smoke their cigars and one could hear a never ending hum of conversation," she said.

"Those must have been the days," said Freddy.

"Yes, they were, and they did not last long, either. Everything seems to move at a very fast pace."

"Especially now that I am free. But, I had better get into action," said Freddy.

"I take it you have something planned?"

"Yes, I sure do. You said that all the paperwork Nellie requested is authenticated, are you sure?"

"Let's look at it together," said Helene.

"OK," said Freddy. "Once that is taken care of, we'll have one thing less on the list, then I will see about getting a travel permit, which will allow me to go to the consulate in Marseille."

"But shouldn't you wait until you have a Document of Safe Passage?" asked Helene.

"No, one thing does not exclude the other and I still do not know how I am going to go about it. But now I really must to be leaving."

"I do not know your destination but I wish you the best of luck," Helene said.

"I can really use some," replied Freddy, grinning, then hurried to the bus just as it was pulling up to the curb. *Lady Luck must be with me,* he thought. There were not very many people on it and it was just a short 10-kilometre ride to Martigues, a place he had never been before.

He thought about Miriam and remembered the conversation they'd had. It would not surprise him at all if Mr Cohen were the person she mentioned. *Life works in strange ways,* he thought. The driver interrupted his thoughts, "Last stop, Martigues, everybody off."

Freddy stood on the main square for a minute taking in his surroundings, facing the church. He found what he was looking for: the police headquarters. As it was close to lunchtime the Chief of Police ushered Freddy into his office immediately. He listened sympathetically as Freddy stated his case. Upon hearing that he had been in the French Military and therefore lost his citizenship, he surprised Freddy by saying he might be able to help him get a safe passage permit. "That would be really helpful," said Freddy. "But why would you do that? There are not many people who care."

"My father was killed by the Germans in the battle of Dunkirk. He did not enlist in the army, he was recruited. The day before he left, he called me aside and said, 'I want you to promise me one thing, as you know violence only incites violence, I have not chosen to go and fight and kill Germans or other human beings, it goes against my nature, my values, and my beliefs. Therefore, I want you to promise me that if someone turns to you for help, you will help him, regardless of his nationality, religion or colour of his skin.' You have come to seek my help and you are the means for me to keep my promise, just like you are working towards keeping your promise to your father."

Freddy was stunned. He had come to ask for a travel permit to Marseille and now it seemed as if he might…no, he dare not think about it. He looked at the Chief of Police, who was waiting for Freddy to answer. "Sorry, what did you say?"

"I was asking you to come back in a week. I will have everything sorted by then." Freddy agreed and thanked him very much, wishing him well.

Freddy did not know what to think. A week was a long time to wait. If nothing came of it, he would have wasted seven days and there was no time to waste. More and more people were fleeing the occupied zone, everything was being rationed, and there was just a general sense of unease within the population. He was in a hurry to get back and talk to Miriam, to see whom this mysterious person was she had spoken about. He was so busy with his own thoughts that he lost track of time and felt as if he had just boarded the bus when he was getting off. Instead of going to Miriam's, he decided to go home first and tell Helene about everything that had happened. She was just as surprised as he was, but said it was worth giving it a chance and if push came to shove, they could still seek Mr Cohen's help.

She spent the morning sorting out things, writing letters and yes, a telegram had arrived for him from Nellie. She had not opened it as it was addressed to Freddy. He felt very uneasy, then read:

I will try, Freddy
Love, N

He read it twice and Helene had been watching him out of the corner of her eye but refrained from making any comment. "Well, I got my answer."

"Was it the one you were expecting?"

"Yes, Mama, she said she would give it a try." He did not elaborate further and Helene knew better than to ask. "I am going to run some errands and I may go out on the boat."

"Yes, some fish for dinner would be a nice change," said Helene.

Due to the food rationing, they were only eating meat once a week. The rabbits were doing very well indeed, they now had 20 of them including the babies. Freddy had created quite a reputation for himself as a rabbit dealer and had his loyal clients who placed their orders in advance, knowing they would not be let down. Helene, who had gone out to the garden to feed them, wondered if Mr Cohen would take them when they left.

Nellie was really looking very much forward to her family coming and was beside herself with excitement when she was finally handed the document that confirmed that their visas had been granted. She felt deeply grateful to Abraham and so many of his acquaintances who had made it possible. If they hadn't known the right people in the government, it never would have happened. The Colombian government was extremely sceptical of German Nationals and one could not blame them. But the Jewish community was quite a large one and had contributed substantially to the industrialisation of the country and thus created a great number of jobs.

She read Freddy's telegram and had just shaken her head and smiled. Her little brother has such a big heart and even though he had not mentioned it, she surmised it was his sweetheart and her family he was trying to help. She saw Abraham a couple of days later and mentioned Freddy's request to him. He looked at her and said, "I will raise the issue. Do you have a name?"

"I do not as yet."

"You can always get the details later, but let us not raise any hopes. You know Nellie, it is all turning out the way I thought it would, and it just makes me sick to my stomach to see the humiliation, suffering and hardship our people are having to endure. We are just seeing the tip of the iceberg, though. I do not know if I will be around to hear the details, but history will be the judge and I am sure that the perpetrators will not go unpunished. I will be very relieved once I have confirmation that they are on their way."

"So will I," said Nellie. "Although everything is very time consuming, I know Freddy is doing everything he can to leave as soon as possible."

"I was told yesterday that he still has not been to the consulate," said Abraham.

"He must be waiting for some document or other," said Nellie.

"We will know in due course, but the ball is in his court and we have to be patient," said Abraham taking his leave.

What he did not say was that the situation in France was becoming bleaker and bleaker as the days went by. The government had moved to Vichy and was in fact only a puppet government. It would not be long before the Germans occupied the whole of the French territory. Abraham just hoped Helene and Freddy would be gone before that happened.

Chapter 48

Miriam had been waiting for Freddy all morning. She was a little concerned about him, for if she remembered correctly, he had said something about them having breakfast together. It was now mid-afternoon and there was no sign of him. She tried to concentrate on her reading, but every once in a while, she would look up from her book until finally giving up. Getting up from where she was sitting, she decided to walk in direction of the port where he kept his boat and had done so for about five minutes when she heard his familiar voice.

"Wait for me!" She turned around and he was smiling broadly. "Sorry," he said, "I know I have kept you waiting most of the day."

"How could I be mad or upset at someone who gives me such an engaging smile? No worries, I have been reading and frankly, I lost the notion of time."

"That book must really be full of action," said Freddy, laughing and not believing one word about her losing the sense of time. "I have been watching you from a distance and you were looking in my direction every five minutes."

Miriam just said, "I guess one can keep nothing from you."

"That is right, and I will only listen to the truth. I am very sensitive to lies and storytelling," he said, taking her hand. "Do you want to come on the boat with me? You will bring me luck, so I might catch some fish. Mama and I are so tired of our vegetable and rabbit diet."

Miriam laughed out loud. "We are also tired of our fish and vegetable diet, but," she said, getting serious, "let us be thankful that we still have something to eat, there are a great many people out there who have nothing and would give everything to have a turnip on their plate."

It was cold on the water. Freddy took out his fishing gear and did not have to wait long for his first catch. "I guess it was the bait." He unhooked the prize. "This will be our dinner tonight, my mother will be pleased. All I need is one more and then we can talk," he said.

Miriam was cold. She did not complain but Freddy noticed that she was shivering and placed his jacket over her shoulders, then turned his attention to his fishing rod. "That's it, I have met my goal."

"And they really are a nice size," said Miriam, looking at them. "I, for one, will not be having fish for dinner."

"Why?" asked Freddy, looking up in surprise.

"I just feel sorry for them. They were happy, seemingly carefree, judging from how fat they are, and now…"

"They end up in the food chain!" Freddy said, laughing. "I think now that we are done, we should go back to shore and get a warm drink, it is really cold."

The sun was about to set and a cool breeze had come up. Once on land, Miriam handed him the piece of paper her father had given her. "I promised you this," she said. "My father asks that you be discreet with the information."

"No worries, I will," he said, taking it from her and placing it in his wallet, deciding to read the note later. They had no sooner finished their drinks that Freddy stood up. "I am sorry, but I had better take the fish home." He was about to invite her to join him and Helene for dinner, but changed his mind for he suddenly remembered that he had never mentioned Miriam to his mother. Miriam looked a little disappointed, he kissed her goodbye and was about to leave when he remembered the telegram. "Oh, I kept forgetting to tell you, my sister wrote back and said she would try to get your visas."

"You know, Freddy, where there is a will there is a way, who knows? We might just see our dream come true."

Helene was delighted with Freddy's catch and made a beautiful big salad to go with it. Freddy watched her as she expertly prepared the main dish and over dinner, he told her about Miriam. Helene could not resist teasing him. "You know, Freddy, I always surmised there was a girl in the background."

"Really, why?"

"Well, you know a mother is intimately connected to her offspring and the connection starts with the pregnancy, continuing after birth. This bond lasts a lifetime, it is not as intimate, but women, as you may know, are very intuitive and it is this intuition that allows a mother to perceive and therefore surmise circumstances that have not been clearly manifested. So tell me about her? What is her name?"

"Her name is Miriam."

"She must be very pretty and intelligent," said Helene.

"Yes, she is, Mama, but why what makes you think that?"

"Because you will never settle for less. You have set the bar very high for yourself and those around you."

"That is quite a statement."

"It is the truth. Ask her over sometime, I would like to meet her."

"As a matter a fact, she gave me this," he said, taking out the paper she had given him. He read out Mr Cohen's name, his telephone, number and address.

"I am lost," said Helene, "could you kindly explain?"

"It is quite simple, Mama, she is an only child, Jewish, and they are trying to leave France. They have been rejected by USA and Mr Cohen is trying to help them. I had mentioned to Miriam that I have no travel documents and she kindly asked her father to help us by giving us the name of the person who is helping them."

"And what do they want in exchange?" asked Helene, who knew that there were always some strings attached.

"She did not ask for anything," said Freddy, going on the defensive. "But I offered to see if Nellie could help get them visas for Colombia."

"What was Nellie's reply?"

"She said she would try. But that is beside the point."

"Our Landlord must be very well connected."

"He is, I can assure you of that," said Helene.

"I hope so, because we may have to turn to him and his organisation."

"Are you changing your mind?"

"No, but one never knows."

Just then, the doorbell rang. "I wonder who it is," said Helene in a worried tone of voice. "I will get it."

It was just one of their neighbours and a very good client. "Freddy, I saw you go out on your boat this afternoon, and I was just wondering if you would exchange some potatoes for some fish with me. My wife and I cannot stand to eat another bite of rabbit."

Freddy laughed out loud and went to the kitchen. Helene looked on in dismay as Freddy wrapped the fish and walked to the door and handed it over to his neighbour. "What did you exchange it for?" Helene asked, trying to keep the anger from her voice.

"Look." And Freddy showed her a pail full of potatoes. "But, Freddy, we already have so many."

"I know, Mama, don't worry, we will exchange them for something else. He left a happy man and his wife is going to be even happier."

"You have such a good heart, Freddy."

"Thank you, Mama, it is all about putting yourself in the other person's place, and about empathy, there sure is not much around these days."

Freddy was becoming impatient, toying with the idea of going back to Martigues before the deadline, but after discussing it one evening with Helene, she pointed out to him that it did not make much sense to rush the Chief of Police and risk alienating him because of his impatience. "Since time is hanging heavily on your hands right now, why don't you bring Miriam over for tea? I would very much like to meet her."

"That is a great idea, I will ask her. But before I leave, Mama, I am going to write Georges and ask him to ship the furniture to Nellie." Helene looked at him in surprise.

"Why?"

"Mama, things are going from bad to worse here in France. We do not know what can happen so let us suppose for a minute that we cannot leave. Do you not think that Papa would like for Nellie to have that which you were able to salvage when you left Frankfurt?"

"I agree with you wholeheartedly, Freddy, and Nellie would then have something that would remind her of her father, like his desk and his books."

"Once I have written Georges and posted the letter, I will go by and invite Miriam for tea."

"That sounds like an excellent plan, and I will bake a cake in the meantime."

What Freddy did not tell Helene was that an edict titled 'Recensorship of Jews' had been issued by the city of Marseille, obliging all Jews to make a declaration on a special form that could be found at the city hall. This declaration rendered all others invalid and had to be done before 31 July. Freddy looked at the date of issuance, 22 July 1941. It only gave them a week to comply. Freddy was furious, but as he walked towards Miriam's hotel, his mood changed. He wondered if she would accept the invitation and what she would think of Helene, hoping they would get along.

Miriam agreed immediately. He noticed, however, that she had a sad look in her eyes. "Is anything troubling you?" Freddy asked. She unfolded a newspaper clipping and Freddy glanced at it. "I've read it," he said.

"Do you think the Chief of Police is going to keep his word?" she asked.

"I hope so. I was thinking about going to Martigues today, but I thought it was best to wait. I will go tomorrow. But what about you? Are you going to comply with the edict?"

"My father is going to discuss it with Mr Cohen, but I think we have no choice but to do what is expected of us."

They walked in silence. Freddy hoped Nellie would be able to help, but deep down in his heart, he knew he was asking for a miracle.

Helene greeted her guest warmly and took an immediate liking to her. As for Miriam, who was in fact very shy, soon felt comfortable in her presence. The two of them forgot about Freddy and were soon talking about Switzerland and skiing, discovering a common ground.

Freddy listened to them for a while then busied himself with his own thoughts. The cake Helene had baked was out of this world and she was delighted when Miriam asked for a second helping. "My mother loves to cook," said Freddy, "and nothing pleases her more than a guest with a hearty appetite. But now, my dear, I think we must be going."

"Why are you in such a hurry to leave?"

"It is getting late and I have to be up early."

"So do I," said Miriam.

"Feel free to come again any time, you will always be welcome," said Helene, giving her a hug.

"Thank you so much, I will bear that in mind."

Freddy gave his mother a thankful look for without knowing it, she had distracted Miriam from her worries.

"I was very impressed by Helene," said Miriam, without even waiting for Freddy to ask her.

"You do not even have to tell me, you hit it off so well you even forgot about me."

"Oh, come on, I could never forget about you," said Miriam. "How could I? And besides, you were sitting there facing me and I had your charming smile to look at."

"Now you are really being funny."

"Not at all, and of course, you had my sweet face to look at as well."

"But then, even when you are not facing me, I close my eyes and I see your beautiful smile," said Freddy, pulling her towards him.

"Good luck tomorrow," said Miriam.

"I will come and give you the news."

"It had better be good."

"I hope it is. Good night," he said and went home.

Helene was asleep when he got there. It was late and he had to be up early. He felt so tired and no sooner had he gotten under the covers, he was sound asleep, then waking up early and well rested the next morning. Helene remarked over breakfast how much she liked his girlfriend and would have made more small talk but could tell that her son was in one of his 'leave me alone' moods, so fell silent.

"I must be going."

"Are you going to Martigues?"

"Yes, I am."

"I hope he has kept his word."

"So do I," said Freddy, closing the door.

Helene was worried, but she could not put her finger on the reason, although she drew some comfort from the thought that if things did not work out the way expected, they could still count on Mr Cohen.

Freddy boarded the bus with a great deal of apprehension. The Chief of Police had yet not arrived and one of his assistants asked him to take a seat in the reception room. It was very small, just a couple of chairs and no window. *This looks more like a dungeon than a waiting room,* Freddy thought. He did not have to wait long. The door opened and the Chief of Police walked in.

"Come, let us go to my office." *What a difference a window and some light can make,* he thought, but was wise enough to keep the remark to himself. "I will give you your travel permit to Marseille." Freddy's heart sunk but waited in silence, he must have forgotten his promise, and he dare not ask the question. "Are you aware of the edict that has been issued?"

Freddy looked at him. "Yes, I am, but it does not concern me for I am Christian, not Jewish," said Freddy.

"Can you prove it?"

"Of course I can, I have my baptismal certificate."

"That is a good thing. I am unable to issue your certificate of safe passage, but my friend, the Chief of Police in Marseille promised to do so as long as you can prove to him that you are not Jewish. I am really sorry about this, but if we get caught helping Jews and people get wind of it, we can end up in jail."

"I understand," said Freddy. But had he not made Freddy wait a week, he might have it. It was, however, of no use making him aware of this. The Chief of Police handed him the travel permit, which read:

Permission valid for one week to travel to Marseille, reason to organise his trip to Colombia.

"I am sorry I have let you down."

"It is OK. I just hope your friend will fulfil the promise you made me."

"I am sure he will if, as I say, you have the paper you mentioned. I wish you good luck."

Freddy was very, very disappointed. He believed and even trusted him, but on the other hand, he could not blame him. The Government of Vichy had issued the edict and all they were doing were obeying orders. He looked at the time. It was mid-morning.

Helene looked up in surprise as he walked in. "I have to go to Marseille and I need my baptismal certificate."

"I will get it." He explained the situation to her in one sentence. She was horrified.

"I have always said that the situation was not going to get any better, only going to get worse as time goes by, and this edict proves it." Freddy took the envelope from her and left without saying another word.

Helene thought of Sigmund, how stubborn he had been, and how blind he had been. No, it was not a matter of being blind or stubborn, it was just a matter of how one perceived the country. Abraham's vision was realistic; he saw the facts, the unemployed and a government completely incapable of dealing with the whole situation. Sigmund was the eternal optimist for whom change would come. Change did come, but not the change he had dreamed of. Hitler had expanded the German borders all the way to Eastern Europe and was now almost at the gate to Moscow.

The closing of the front door startled Helene. Freddy had left and she was the only one in the house, sure he had locked it behind him. She was trembling all over, as she walked into the hallway only to catch a glimpse of Freddy. "You scared me," said Helene, letting out a sigh of relief.

"I just thought of something that might prove useful and came back to get it. But now I have to run or else I will miss the bus."

She walked to the door and made sure she locked it after him. The hardships of war were becoming more and more noticeable as time went by, even a bar of soap had become a luxury item and then, of course, one never knew. The town's population had more than doubled and the people who were born and raised here used to talk about the better times, when everyone knew each other and nobody locked their front doors and one's word was worth gold. But not any longer, trust had been lost and she knew all too well how hard it was to be gained. It was all a sign of the times. Her thoughts turned to Freddy, it surely was some important document he had returned for, but try as she might, she could not name it.

He just barely made the bus and at each stop, there were a few more passengers waiting for it. Then he realised that they were all Jews heading for the city to comply with the order. It saddened him deeply to see how his people were being stigmatised while at the same time, he was thankful for being baptised. He could only hope that he would be given the document that would give him his freedom. He did not waste any time finding the police station, being the only passenger not headed for the city Hall.

A pretty secretary was sitting behind the reception desk and upon hearing his voice, she looked up from the newspaper she was reading and asked in a soft tone of voice, "What can I do for you?" Freddy mentioned the name of the person he wanted to see. "I believe he is expecting you."

Freddy looked surprised but did not say a word. She ushered him into the Chief of Police's office. "Please take a seat; he will be with you shortly."

Just then, a tall, heavy-set man walked in. "What can I do for you, sir?" He sat down behind his desk and Freddy mentioned the Chief of Police of Martigues. "Oh, yes, I have been expecting you. Can you prove to me that you were in the French military?"

"Sure," said Freddy, showing him not only the travel permit that had been issued him to travel to Sausset les Pins, but also the reference given to him by the Commander of the Regiment in which he had served. The Chief of Police was impressed; he had played a wild card and had been outwitted. But he was not to give up that easily.

"Can you prove to me you are not Jewish?"

"I sure can," said Freddy, handing him the required document. Freddy sat quietly in his chair watching him. He read it, turned it over he saw it had been authenticated and, try as he might, could not find a flaw. "May I see your travel permit to come to Marseille?" Freddy handed it over to him. The Chief of Police took his time and Freddy did not break the silence. He finally spoke. "The paperwork I have requested from you is all in good order, I have no reason to withhold your Document of Safe Passage, here it is," he said, handing it to him. "Please read it carefully and make sure the spelling of your name and destination are correct and when you have finished, kindly sign your name here as proof that it has been handed to you."

Freddy did as he was told then stood up to leave. He did not trust the Chief of Police, there was something menacing in his attitude. He shook Freddy's outstretched hand and wished him safe travels. Freddy thanked him and left.

He was just going to get on the bus when he changed his mind. He felt that he was unable to trust anybody in this town so, taking out a map of the city, he located the Colombian Consulate. It was not far from where he stood, just a 15-minute walk. The receptionist was a Colombian national and spoke French with a charming Spanish accent. He greeted her in Spanish and she inquired politely, "What can I do for you?" She asked him to sit down then went to a file cabinet and took out a file. "The Consul will see you. But first, we have received some documents for you. Actually, we received them about two months ago," she said.

"I am aware of it," replied Freddy. "But there were some unusual circumstances that did not allow me to come in sooner."

"No problem, better late than never, as we say in Spanish."

Freddy gave her his most engaging smile. "He will see you now."

The Consul was tall, in his early forties, and greeted Freddy with a warm smile. What a difference this person was from the one he had just seen. "We have received no end of telegrams asking us to please help you and your mother, but why has it taken you all this time to come?"

Freddy explained his situation and handed over his Document of Safe Passage. The Consul looked it over. It was issued by the Government of Vichy and had all the stamps and seals and signatures required and allowed Freddy to travel to Colombia. It was valid for just six months. "I can give you your visa and stamp on it," said the Consul, "but what about your mother?"

"She has a valid passport but I believe it is best if she comes on her own. I am under the impression that I am being watched and I would not like to give them any pretext."

"You are right. Marseille is getting more and more complicated. Here is my card."

"I will arrange for her to come see you tomorrow or the day after."

"That is fine with me, I will be expecting her. Is there anything more I can help you with?"

Freddy thought for a minute. "There is a Company called Ybarra."

"Yes, their ships sail to South America. They used to sail from Marseille but those days are over, now they only sail from Spain. Their offices are in this same block, just two doors down. I actually have a friend who works there. I can put you in contact with him."

"Please do," said Freddy.

"I will give him a call, who knows, he might be able to see you now."

"Thank you, you are most kind."

His phone call was answered almost immediately. "His name is Juan, he is expecting you."

"I thank you for your kindness and understanding," said Freddy, taking his leave.

"It is my pleasure, I am a strong believer that our purpose for being here is to help others and I live by that belief."

The Ybarra offices were just as the Consul had said, literally two doors down. Pictures of the different steamers hung on the walls as well as the picture of the two founders. Freddy took a moment to look at them while he waited for Juan. "I am very grateful you could see me," said Freddy. "I live in Sausset les Pins."

"It is a beautiful place, I go there in the summers and enjoy the beach," said Juan.

"Summers are the best time," said Freddy. "But I am glad you were in the office today, it has saved me time and money."

"I was noticing you look at the pictures."

"I have always been attracted to boats and the sea," said Freddy, "but I am also very much of a mountain person."

"It really is nice when you enjoy nature and have no preferences. I will tell you a little about the company. It was founded in northern Spain by two gentlemen, starting out as, shall we say, a shuttle between Seville and Bilbao. They used a small sailboat called Dolores in honour of one of the wives, the company itself was called Ceres and Basilia. During the First World War, they took freight and a few passengers to North America but due to the Great Depression, the route was cancelled. However, in 1927, the route to South America was inaugurated and a ship that took both passengers and freight served it. The ship was called Cabo Tortosa that had made the maiden voyage."

"What an interesting story… Is it still sailing today?"

"Yes, it is, as a matter of fact and it left the port of Seville just last week."

"How long does it take it to do the crossing?" Freddy asked.

"To where?"

"Colombia."

"It takes approximately 4 to 5 weeks."

"That sure is a long time."

"Is that your destination?"

"Yes, and I was told the port of entry is Barranquilla."

"That is correct."

"What are the dates you have in mind?"

Freddy thought for a moment. "A month from today?"

"Let us go into my office." Juan led the way and Freddy was impressed. His office had a huge window from which there was an amazing view of the Port of Marseille. Juan looked up from the paper he was studying. "The next ship is due to sail in two months' time that means two months from today from the port of Seville."

"Can I make a reservation on it? There are two of us, my mother and myself."

"Sure, but you will have to share a cabin."

"That is not an issue," said Freddy. "My Document of Safe Passage is valid for only six months, which is not much time."

"It definitely is not, considering everything that needs to be done."

"But my mother and I are a very good team." Freddy smiled to himself; good team? He was the one who would bear the burden, but who cared, the main thing was to get on board that ship.

Juan was gazing at Freddy, "Are you all right?"

Freddy looked at him, startled. "Yes, yes, I am all right, I was just making a list in my mind," he said laughing. His laughter was contagious and soon they were laughing together.

When their fit of laughter subsided, Juan said, "You know, there is nothing like a good laugh to release all the tension."

"Yes," agreed Freddy. "Can you give me a price?"

"The only double cabin that is left is on the main deck towards the stern, which means if the sea gets choppy, you will most likely not get seasick."

"How much will it be?" Freddy scowled upon hearing the amount. It was very expensive and exceeded their budget by a lot.

"Shall I book you, or do you want to wait? There might be a cancellation, one never knows and you could—"

Freddy interrupted him. "No, no, it's fine, I will pay the price."

Juan took down all his details and made the booking. "I will need to see your mother's passport and her visa for Colombia."

"That is not a problem," said Freddy. "She will be coming to Marseille either tomorrow or the day after."

"Are you going to come with her?"

"I have not made up my mind."

"Well, I do not care if both of you come or just one of you, but I do need a deposit in order to hold that one cabin for you."

"No worries, Juan, if you give me your bank details—"

"We only take cash. But the Bank of France is just down the street from us."

"Good, one thing less to worry about."

"I will hold the booking for you until you return with your mother and the cash. Bear in mind that I cannot hold it for more than two days," Juan added.

"You have my word," said Freddy and, looking at the time said, "I must be going."

"You had better," replied Juan. "The next bus leaves in ten minutes, and I believe it is the last one."

As Freddy walked to the bus station, his thoughts turned to Miriam. What would her destiny be? She had not been on his mind at all, how selfish of me, he reprimanded himself, I might have mentioned her case to the Consul. But he reminded himself that he would be back with Helen and would bring up the subject, the thought appeasing his guilt.

There was not one empty seat on the bus and hardly any standing room, all of the passengers engulfed in an eerie silence. Everyone, without exception, had a very sad look on their face. Freddy felt very fortunate, he had a country that had agreed to take him and Helene in, but what about all these people? What was behind this new edict, which only mentioned re-censorship of the Jews, but what about the Christians and all the other faiths? Why were they not mentioned? It would not be until many years later that Freddy would receive the answer to his unspoken question.

Chapter 49

It was late when he finally arrived home but Helene was up, waiting for him. She kept herself busy, but felt very uneasy about him going to Marseille, having heard so many awful stories, of people getting robbed, mugged and even murdered. "Does it live up to its reputation?" she asked.

"What are you talking about?" asked Freddy, "No, I do not think it is as bad as people claim, although one does feel a little threatened, even if there is no one in sight. But you will see for yourself, you are expected at the consulate with your passport. We will go together."

"So, you did get your Document of Safe Passage."

"Yes, and my visa is stamped on it *and* I have booked the ship, it leaves in two months from today. While you are at the consulate, I will go cash a check at the Banque de France to pay for our trip."

"They only take cash?" asked Helene, very much surprised.

"I am afraid so."

"You sure did accomplish a lot."

"Thanks for the compliment, but there is still a lot more to be done and time is really running short."

"Do you know where the ship leaves from?"

"I believe it is the port of Seville."

"Oh, it leaves from Spain not France?"

"That is what I have been told."

Helene was silent. "Freddy, how are we going to get to Spain from here, have you forgotten that north of us lies the occupied zone?"

"You are right Mama, I had not thought of that," then he muttered under his breath, "I can't think of everything."

Helene heard him. "I am not criticising you, you have done a wonderful job, but we are a team and I can be of some help, don't you agree?"

"Like pointing out to me that I have forgotten something and making me feel guilty?" replied Freddy.

"Come on," said Helene, "you are tired have had a very long day, let us not quarrel." Freddy nodded his head and kissed her good night. "I thought you might be going over to see Miriam."

"No, Mama, I am exhausted. I will see her tomorrow." And having said that, he hurried to his room. "Man, she sure does have a way of irritating me," he said out loud. "Nothing is ever good enough, always finding fault with something, the 'way' she has of making me feel guilty. I hate that feeling. I do the best I can

412

and she just does not get it. All she has to do is keep the house clean, cook and amuse herself and I have to do the thinking the organising." As he was undressing, a thought suddenly crossed his mind. He could not go over to see Miriam in the morning because he had to be at the consulate with Helene. Then he remembered he was going to take her and her family's case up with the consul and see if... Oh, yes, if only they would give them the visa, their dream would come true.

Miriam spent the day hoping the same thing and waiting for Freddy to show up. Her mother went to no end of efforts to point out to her how unreliable he was. "See, I told you so," she said, joining Miriam on the beach. "He only thinks about himself, no consideration and no caring. All he cares about is himself." Miriam tried hard to keep her temper in check. She knew her parents did not care much for Freddy, and his behaviour towards her made them dislike him even more.

"Mama," she said, hoping to end the incessant criticism, "these days one never knows what might happen, his mother might have gotten sick or he might have had an urgent errand to run. I am sure that when he finally puts in an appearance, it will justify his not coming and I will be understanding and supportive."

"Well, I shall leave you to it," said Miriam's mother, exasperated with her daughter's passive attitude.

"See you later," said Miriam, letting out a sigh of relief. Her mother would never, ever understand, but how could she? She always had to be in control and could not understand how her daughter was able to just live in the moment, the now.

Miriam felt hurt and frustrated. At times, she thought Freddy did not care about her at all, but when they were together, they not only had a good time, but he always showed his concern for her and made her feel important. She was sure that something unexpected had come up and as soon as he could, he would come to her. Deciding to make good use of her time, she picked up the book she had just started. Once she had read a sentence: 'When one reads, one flies', and this was so true. Captivated by the story, her surroundings, worries and concerns were soon forgotten, soon losing all track of the time.

Suddenly, she felt a hand on her shoulder. She looked up from her book into Freddy's smiling face. "You startled me," she said.

"I called your name but you did not hear me, that must be a pretty good story you are reading," he said.

"It is, and it has captivated me all day."

"What time is it?"

"Time for tea," said Freddy. "Come on, I have had no lunch and I doubt you have." He helped her to her feet and, taking her hand in his, walked towards their favourite restaurant on the beach. "I am sorry I have not been able to spend more time with you but I have really been very busy."

"Last time I saw you, you mentioned something—"

Freddy interrupted her. "I went to Marseille and I got my Document of Safe Passage."

"When was that?" she asked.

"Yesterday, and then we were both in Marseille. I went with my mother to City Hall then to the police station, and I went to the Colombian consulate and went back with my mother again today. The Consul is a kind and compassionate person and I mentioned you and your family and our dream, hoping that he would be able to help."

"What did he say, Freddy, can he help us?"

"I am afraid not, the visa request has to be authorised by the Colombian foreign office and the request can only be made directly to that office. Once the visa is approved, he can issue it here."

"I see," said Miriam. "Well, thank you anyway, at least you gave it a try. But I guess our dream is not meant to come true. So you are now free to travel, when are you leaving?"

"My mother and I are booked on a ship that is supposed to leave on the 12 of November."

"That really does not give you much time, it is in two months."

"Yes, I am very much aware of this."

They found a table and ordered their lunch. Miriam looked at him sadly. "I guess our time together is coming to an end," she said.

"Let us not look at the glass as if it were half empty, let us look at it as if it were half full and make the most of the time we have together. It is about today, we do not know what tomorrow, if there is one, might bring. Miriam, just to end this conversation, I promise you that as soon as I arrive in Colombia, I will do everything that is in my power to get that visa for you and your parents."

"I know you will, Freddy, but let us hope it won't be too late.

Is your mother happy?"

"Very much, yes, and she sends you her regards, she really liked you."

"And I like her as well, she is a fine lady."

"Yes, she is, and she has been through a great deal. I believe she is very much looking forward to new surroundings and seeing my half-sister, but all this comes at a price."

"And that is?"

"I will be the one doing all the work."

"Really?"

"Oh, yes, she gave me a number of letters to write for her."

"Why does she not do it herself?"

"Because I can type them for her. I tried to teach her how to use the typewriter but she messed up the ribbon. I still cannot understand how she did it, so I decided it was best I type them for her."

"Will I see you tomorrow?" Miriam asked.

"Sure, we will see each other every day, no worries," he said, hugging her. "And please, do not be sad, it will all work out for the best." He put on a good front for her but the Consul had made it very clear to him that the amount of paperwork involved made it totally impossible for her and her family to be granted the visas.

As Miriam walked towards her room, she ran into her mother who did not have to ask, the answer was written on her face. "I am glad he came."

"I told you he would." She thought about telling her what Freddy said but decided against it, knowing her mother's reaction and she really was not in the mood to listen to her. But she would tell her father in due time. After kissing her mother good night, she went to her room and had just gotten in to bed when her father walked in after nearly knocking the door down. "I thought you were asleep," he said, "sorry about the noise."

Miriam just smiled. "Have you got any news, Papa?"

"No, actually I have not been to see Mr Cohen, I decided to wait a couple of days and see how things develop, have *you* got any news?"

Miriam's eyes filled with tears. "I do. Freddy and his mother will be boarding the ship in two months from today, from Spain. He did make an inquiry with the Colombian Consul but the visas have to be requested directly at the Foreign office in Colombia."

"Well, in that case, I will have to see what other options we might have. Did you tell your mother?"

"No, I decided to leave it up to you and I do not even know if—"

"I haven't shared the information with her yet. Sometimes it is best to leave her in the dark."

They both smiled at each other acknowledging the complicity they shared. "Now, do not worry your little head about this, a solution will be found, I am sure."

"You are always so positive, Papa."

"One has to be, this journey is full of obstacles and one always has to make the best of it, it is of little or no use what so ever to always see the dark side of life, there is always a light somewhere. Just remember that."

"I will," said Miriam, "good night." Then she fell asleep and dreamt of a huge rainbow lighting up her entire room. She woke up the next morning to the sun shining in and remembered her dream. Yes, she would be positive and joyful, she was sure that just like the rainbow, a ray of light would show her the path she and her family were to follow.

Helene's words still rang in Freddy's ears, "We have to get to Spain." How were they going to get there? The Occupied Zone went from the north all the way to the centre of France. Maybe by train? He would have to do some research. A couple of days later, Helene brought up the subject again.

"Freddy, have you given the matter some thought?"

"I have, Mama, but there is still some time."

"I do not think we have that much time, it is already mid-August and one has to be prepared for the unforeseen."

"I know, Mama, but I have been so busy. I wrote a postcard to Georges telling him about our good fortune and asking him if he has shipped the furniture, and believe it or not, I still have not gotten around to mailing it. I keep forgetting to do so." Helene did not answer. "There is so much to be taken care of and put in order before we can leave. The rabbits have to be sold or eaten and maybe I can sell my boat; that would bring in some money. Our ship fare was very expensive."

"I know," said Helene, "and we still have at least two months of rent to pay. I am going to see what I can sell," said Helene. "The issue is that nobody has any money."

"What about Miriam and her family? Have they found a solution?"

"As far as I know, they are still waiting."

"Waiting for what?"

"To get a visa."

"It looks as if several countries are granting visas, I read it in the newspaper and I believe Mexico is one of them."

"Really?"

"Yes," said Helene, "I even cut out the article. I will give it to you to give to her. It would be a blessing for them."

Freddy read the article. "You are right, Mama, I am going to give it to her straight away."

"And don't forget to mail the postcard," Helene called out after him. Freddy did not look back, he just nodded his head.

He found Miriam at her usual spot by the beach reading her book. "Why, Freddy, I was not expecting you this early," said Miriam looking up.

"Here, I have something that might be of great interest to you and your family," and he showed her the newspaper clipping.

She took her time reading it. "You are right, this might be the light."

"Light?" Freddy asked. Then she explained her dream to him and her knowing that a ray of light would show them the path and this was it. "I do not quite understand," said Freddy, but was interrupted by Simon, Miriam's father.

"You could not have timed your arrival better," said Miriam.

"Why? What is going on?" She handed him the newspaper clipping. "This certainly is worth exploring. Thank you so much, Freddy. I will go make some phone calls. Just think, if you could get an entry visa for Mexico, you could come and visit me in Colombia. It is in the same hemisphere and maybe then you could apply for a Colombian visa."

"Now that is taking it a bit far," Miriam said, always the practical one. "Let us be grateful for whatever visa we receive. Just as long as we can leave France," she said under her breath.

Her parents tried very hard to conceal their anxiety from her, but she knew how precarious the situation was and also very much aware that it was only a matter of time before the Nazis took over the whole of the country. No one in the Jewish community had any illusions and they all shared the same goal, to leave the country as soon as possible.

Simon came back shortly and told them he had been granted an interview at the Mexican consulate for the following day. "That is wonderful news, Papa."

"Now do not get your hopes up too high, child, we have been disappointed once so let us wait and see what they tell us. I was told to bring all our personal documents and luckily, the American Consulate handed them back to me so the paperwork is in good order. Thank you again, Freddy."

"Actually you should thank my mother; she was the one who saw the advertisement."

"Miriam has spoken very highly of her and I look forward to thanking her personally one day."

Freddy looked at the time. "I will leave you two," he said, "I am behind with my work, but I will come over tomorrow."

"No, Freddy," said Simon. "I do not know what time we will be back."

"So, I will see you the day after then…and good luck." He shook Simon's hand, gave Miriam a hug and left.

What a thoughtful and nice young man he is, and he is very responsible as well.

"Since his father passed away, he has had to care for his mother," said Miriam.

"Now I understand why he is so mature," said Simon.

Freddy arrived home as the telegram delivery boy was leaving. Helene was still at the door holding it in her hands. "Who is it from?" Freddy asked.

"It is from Ybarra, the shipping company. I do hope our trip has not been cancelled."

Freddy opened it and read aloud:

Please be advised your departure has been rescheduled, the ship will now be departing on 11 November from the port of Lisbon. If you have any questions, please call.
Juan

"It must be due to the current political situation," said Freddy.

"The port of Lisbon… Now how are we going to get *there*?" Helene asked.

"I think we should plan on leaving as soon as possible and waiting in Lisbon for our ship to leave," said Freddy.

"But why Lisbon?"

"It must be the only port on the continent now from which one can get to the Americas."

"Everything changes, one cannot even plan ahead."

"I know," said Freddy, "but you have to realise, Mama, that we are living in uncertain times. By the way, Miriam and her father are very grateful for the information."

"I am glad it was useful."

"Yes, it sure was, and they have an appointment tomorrow at the Mexican consulate."

"I am glad I could be of some help," said Helene.

They were each busy with their own thoughts. The silence was suddenly broken by Freddy saying, "We have a problem and a big one. We will need a visa for Portugal."

"There must be a Consulate in Marseille," said Helene, "all we have to do is go to there."

"Mama, you never see the bigger picture. You are just looking at the consulate, but have you even thought that we need a travel permit to go to Marseille and mine was only valid for a week and has expired?"

"Oh, Freddy, you always accuse me of not being smart."

"I have not said that, I just said…oh, never mind."

"Well, can't you go back to Martigues and ask for one?"

"No, Mama, I will not go back, it is too much of a risk."

"I have an idea. Remember Mr Cohen, he said if we needed anything he might be able to help."

"Mama, that is an excellent thought, I will call him and ask if he can come by." Freddy felt much better now that he thought they had found a solution.

Helene went into action immediately. Mr Cohen was home and picked up the phone and said he would come by for a cup of coffee in the afternoon as soon as he had finished with some business he had in Martigues.

"Mama, do you have any idea how we are going to get from Sausset les Pins to Lisbon?"

"I haven't got a clue, but ask Mr Cohen when he comes, he might be able to give us an itinerary."

Freddy looked at his watch. He did not feel like spending the rest of the morning and afternoon with his mother and Miriam was in Marseilles. "I am going to the post office to mail the postcard to Georges and then I think I will take the boat out and see if some fish will bite."

"That is a lovely thought," said Helene, "fish for dinner, and maybe you can give one to Mr Cohen to take home with him." Helene could hear Freddy whistling to himself happily, as he walked towards the front door.

Left to herself, she sat down to digest the latest news. She felt very tired and sad and it seemed to her as if she had lived all her life through periods of uncertainty. *This is not true*, she said to herself, *the uncertainty started just after Sigmund left us.* It has been a little over a year, but she had to admit it's been very intense. I hope that if and when we get to Colombia, we can lead a calm and peaceful, normal life, because here, well, it really has not been all that bad, we have had plenty to eat…plenty? Rabbit and more rabbit and once in a while fish. She was silent but her inner voice rambled on. "Do not be ungrateful, Helene, that is more than most people have had. You have had a roof over your head, you have been warm in the winter, you have been able to go out. No, Helene, you have been far better off than most people, and you have not been separated from your son. How many mothers can say that today? Look at the uncertainty Miriam and her family are having to live, and you are complaining, forgetting how blessed you have been?"

Her inner voice was annoying her. The only way to stop listening to it was to busy herself with something, so she stood up and went to the kitchen and started preparing a salad to go with the evening meal, be it rabbit or fish. One thing she was certain of, and spoke out loud giggling, once I leave Europe, I hope I will never have to look a living rabbit in the eye again.

She looked in the cupboard but there were no cookies to offer Mr Cohen so she hastily baked a cake and was just taking it out of the oven when the doorbell rang. It was her guest and just as she opened the door, Freddy arrived. He had a huge smile on his face. "I caught four fish," he said, beaming.

He handed two to Mr Cohen who said, "What a treat, thank you!"

Over coffee and cake, Freddy described their situation to him and he listened attentively, at the end saying that the visa for Portugal was easily solved.

"How?" they asked in unison.

"You see, the Portuguese government is doing the best it can to help all the Jews leave France and the other countries, which are under German rule. It is very much aware of the fate the Jews and they do not want to be a part of it. Portugal is a neutral country but is very friendly towards the allies."

"So," asked Freddy, beginning to get impatient.

"You are Jewish, are you not?"

"Yes, we are one hundred percent Jewish."

"I have a friend at the consulate in Marseille, I will ask him to issue the visas for you and your mother. When does your ship leave?"

"It leaves the 11 of November."

"If I were you, I would leave as soon as you have your visas and wait in Lisbon until your departure."

"That is an excellent idea," said Helene. "But how are we going to get to Lisbon?"

"There is a train, which leaves from Marseille to Barcelona and goes on to Madrid. You would have to change trains in Madrid, but there is no other alternative."

"Do we need a permit… I mean a visa?"

"No, I will provide you with the train tickets and the visas, and you should have no problems. But time is of essence, the longer you wait, the more complicated it is going to become. The Germans are getting impatient with the government of Vichy, they, I mean the Germans, want it all, and it is just a matter of time before they take control of this unoccupied zone. We will be lucky if that does not happen until next year, which is why my organisation and myself are working so hard to get our people out of harm's way."

"When do you think we will be able to leave?"

"I would plan to leave in three to four weeks from today."

"Well, at least that gives us time to get ready to sell what we can."

"But please," said Mr Cohen, "you must be very discreet about it. After that decree was issued, the authorities have become very suspicious of the Jews and are keeping a close eye on them."

Helene and Freddy exchanged looks. They both were having the same thoughts; Mr Cohen did not have to be told they were not on the list.

"How much is this all going to cost?" asked Freddy.

"You will not have to pay a cent towards the visas, our organisation takes care of that through a fund that has been set up, you will only have to pay for the train tickets and I can assure you, they will cost less than you ship fare."

"Undoubtedly," said Freddy.

"I will, however, need a copy of your travel documents."

Helene and Freddy handed them over to him. He was not surprised to see that Freddy did not have a passport. "Are *you* planning on leaving?" asked Freddy.

"Yes, I will be leaving in due course, but for the moment I am happy being able to help others. I am fully convinced that my purpose in life is to serve others and by so doing, I am the happiest person in the world."

He stood up to take his leave. "I will be in touch with you as soon as I have the visas and can give you travel date." They walked him to the door. "It will be a joyful yet a sad day for me, returning here once you have gone."

"Yes," said Helene, "Villa Marie Louise has been a lovely home for us and we will share the fond memories with others."

"Three weeks from today, give or take. And I wonder how Miriam and her parents fared today," said Freddy.

"You will have to be patient until tomorrow, but I do hope it went well."

"I hope so too," said Freddy. "Well, I will help you in the kitchen since you still have to prepare the fish."

"No, just one fish, the other is going in the refrigerator. The salad is ready and I just hope once we leave here that I will not have to eat another morsel of rabbit for the rest of my life."

Freddy burst out laughing. "It has not been all that bad."

"No, I have cooked that meat in different ways, but at the end of the day, it is and remains what it is."

"One cannot transform it into something else," said Freddy with a grin, "and regardless of how you cook it, rabbit it shall remain."

Helene burst out laughing. They had a relaxed and enjoyable meal, the conversation filled with their plans for the next couple of weeks and…the thought of being reunited with Nellie filled their hearts with love and hope.

Chapter 50

Miriam and her parents were very late getting back from the Mexican consulate and were exhausted. The rumour had spread that not only was the Mexican government issuing visas, but that it was issuing passports to all those who did not possess one as well. It was not until late afternoon when they were finally called into one of the consul's offices. In view of the wave of people that were seeking travel documents, the government had transferred some personnel from other cities that were less busy to help out, but they were still understaffed. The Consul was friendly and very straightforward; he looked over their application and their documents and told them to be prepared for a long wait as they were giving the visas out on a first come first served basis. Simon asked how many people were ahead of him and he was fully unprepared for the answer. It was more than 500. His reply was barely audible. "That means it will be a very long wait."

"I am afraid so," said the official, "but have faith and hope."

On the bus ride home, they were quiet and sad. Miriam hoped that Freddy would stop by, but after waiting for him until ten o'clock, she decided she was wasting her time and went to bed.

Simon was up bright and early and rang Mr Cohen. He recounted his experience of the day before and asked for his advice. Mr Cohen listened sympathetically and told him to be patient, the consulates had a way of sorting things out, but that there was no way he could speed things up for them as he did not know any one there. He did have some other connections, but it was best not to go knocking on all the doors at once, since that could only hold up matters further.

Simon hung up the phone feeling very desperate. Were he and his family doomed to stay in France and be held captive under the Nazi regime? Was there no hope? Why was there hope for some and not for him? He shared his thoughts and feelings with his wife. Unbeknownst to him, Miriam was pouring out her heart to Freddy.

"Life is so unfair," she said. "Why do you and your mother get to leave and we are we stuck here? What are we being punished for? My parents and I, we have been honest, kind and compassionate people. Why not us?"

Freddy was deeply moved and he wished he could do more, but his hands were tied. "Miriam," he said gently, "there is hope. Two days ago, you had no other alternative but to wait and see what the future would bring. Suddenly, a door opened and you walked through it, now it is just a matter of waiting."

"You are right," said Miriam, "but all we have done is wait and be patient, when is something going to give? When will the day come when we as a family, just like you and your mother, can say we are leaving?"

"We have a future, we are blessed, a country has opened its doors to us so that we can start a new life, away from discrimination and maybe death, where we will be looked upon as normal human beings and not be despised for our religion and race. I wish I could give you a time and a date but it is not in my hands, it is only in the hands of the Almighty ones. Do not lose faith and do not despair. Let us enjoy our being together NOW, being able to share our joys and sorrows. Just having each other is a blessing in and of itself, let us not take it for granted. Together we will help each other calm our despair and impatience."

Miriam listened to him with tears rolling down her cheeks. "You are so right," she said between sobs. Freddy asked her to come home with him and see Helene, talking about Switzerland and skiing would surely take her mind of her troubles. Helene was delighted to see her and just as Freddy had predicted, they were soon laughing together.

Georges smiled as he read Freddy's short postcard. It did not come as a surprise to him that he would want a follow-up on his instructions, for his friend was not only very precise but sometimes acted like a general. Yes, a full-fledged general. His father had passed his military discipline on to him and this had only been enhanced by his service in the Regiment. He sat down and wrote a short report:

Your orders have been dutifully carried out, shipment on the way to port, who knows, maybe it will be travelling on the same ship as you.
Georges

Deciding to make a lasting impression on his friend, he sent the note as a telegram. He looked at the date on the card…no, he was sure he would still be at his address. They had always loved playing pranks on each other and he could just imagine Freddy's face and hear him laughing. He rejoiced for them, but he felt very sad. Looking again at the map, he thought about what a long distance they would be travelling, and he would never be able to afford such a trip, much less with the circumstances they were living under in Paris. Yes, Freddy wrote about his rabbits, about going out fishing in his boat and about his girlfriend.

His life, on the other hand, was completely different. There was a curfew in the city that went from nine in the evening to five in the morning and whoever was caught breaking it went to jail. There were shortages of food and clothing. The best produce went to feed the occupiers and what was left over was sent to Germany. Yes, Freddy was lucky to be living in the South of France, spared the humiliation all Parisians had to endure. His brothers, who had been taken prisoners, were released and the family was again reunited. There would always be one missing, though, the one that had been killed in the Spanish Civil War.

If only he could have gone to visit his friend, but that too, was out of the question. He reread the card again, the part where Freddy wrote: 'As soon as I am settled in Colombia and have found a job, I will send you my address and hopefully you will be able to come, not just to visit but maybe to settle there.' It was wishful thinking, but one had to have an open mind, for the future was completely unpredictable.

Freddy was surprised to see the telegram delivery messenger a week later. Who could it be from this time? He opened it and laughed out loud. "What is so funny?" asked Helene.

"It is from Georges, reporting back that he has done what I asked him to do."

"He could have sent a card, why a telegram?"

"He was in teasing mode and signed it 'Your loyal servant'."

"Are you going to reply?" Helene asked, amused.

"Yes, I will send him a telegram with our forwarding address, which will be Mr Cohen's. I am sure he will not mind forwarding any mail for us to Nellie's address."

"I do not know who is going to bother writing us," said Helene.

"I do not know either, but one never knows."

Freddy took inventory of his possessions; there were ten rabbits, his bicycle, his boat and his fishing gear. He could sell the rabbits, that would not cause any suspicion, but selling the other items would be signalling that they were leaving and Mr Cohen had cautioned that discretion was of essence. Helene did not share those worries, as with every move she had given away the items she no longer needed and all she had now was what she had kept to take with her.

It had been a week and a half since their meeting with Mr Cohen when they suddenly received the phone call they had been waiting so impatiently for. He had their visas and their train tickets; they would be leaving on the 15 October, which barely gave them three more weeks in Sausset les Pins. Helene was delighted; the long wait was slowly coming to an end. Freddy, on the other hand, had very mixed feelings. Leaving Miriam with the uncertainty of not knowing what her fate would be hung heavily over him. How he wished he could do something or that the Mexican government would finally reply to their application. She avoided discussing his departure and refrained from inquiring if there was any news. It was as if both of them made up their minds to live in the moment and enjoy their time together, leaving out all the unpleasantness of life and it was probably the most beautiful time of their relationship.

Quite late in the afternoon, they were strolling on the beach and arrived at the port where Freddy kept his boat. "Miriam, do you think your father would like to have it?" She looked at him without replying. "I asked you if you thought your father might like to have the boat?"

"I am sure he would. Are you giving it away?"

"Yes, we are leaving a week from today." He had not meant to tell her.

"When did you find out?"

"It does not matter, does it? Had I told you before, there would have been a shadow cast over our happiness," he replied.

"Yes, but now it has been cast."

"No, it has not, for who knows, maybe you might have some good news to share with me in the next couple of days."

"Do you know something I don't?" asked Miriam.

"Everything is in the realm of all possibilities, right?"

"Yes, I agree."

"So should I offer the boat to Simon?"

"Yes, he will be delighted."

"Well, then, that is taken care of. My bicycle I shall give to Mr Cohen since he has children and they will get a lot of enjoyment out of it."

"I am quite sure it he will be the one using it, with the shortage and price of fuel, it will enable him to leave the car at home."

They walked back in silence. Miriam felt very sad and tried hard to keep her emotions in check. Her inner voice repeated incessantly: "In a week he will be gone, in a week he will be gone." And there was no way she could quiet it.

As they approached the hotel, they encountered Simon who had been looking for them. "Miriam, I have been looking for you for the past hour."

"We were down by the port looking at Freddy's boat, of which you are now the proud owner."

"What do you mean?" Miriam explained.

Simon shook his head. "Sorry Freddy, I cannot accept your gift, you see, our application has been approved and we should be receiving our visas for Mexico in the next week or so."

Miriam was beside herself with joy. "Are you sure, Papa?" she asked, putting her arms around his neck.

"Yes, see for yourself," he said, handing her the telegram.

Freddy read it over her shoulder. He was very happy for them and very relieved to know that Miriam and her family would finally be out of harm's way.

Simon invited Freddy to join them for dinner. They were all in a celebrating mood and he was uncertain whether to stay or leave, but Miriam's pleading look persuaded him to accept. Simon noticed his hesitation and, realising what his problem might be, suggested he invite Helene. "This would really be the occasion for us to meet her and to thank her for what she did for us." Freddy was touched by his thoughtfulness and, asking Miriam to come with him, went home to invite her.

"I will do my best to convince her," he said, taking his leave, "but my mother believes in getting a good night's sleep and goes to bed early."

Miriam spoke the whole way; she was so happy and excited, making plans for the future, imagining what the Mexicans would be like, when Freddy interrupted her. "You are definitely not going to miss me, once I get on that train next week and it leaves the station, you will not lose another thought over me."

Her eyes filled with tears. "You are wrong. I will miss you very much. We have shared everything together, the sad and the happy moments; you have given me strength and persuaded me not to lose hope. We are both following our destiny, but unfortunately the paths we are walking are taking us in different directions."

"For now," said Freddy. "But maybe someday, our paths will cross again and if that happens, we will be together forever." They arrived at Villa Marie Louise and all the lights were off.

"It looks as if there is nobody home," said Miriam.

"I think it is more likely that my mother has gone to bed." Helene was in her room reading. "Miriam is here with me," he said, as he walked in. "We have come to invite you for dinner with my family."

"Any luck?" asked Helene.

"Yes, our application has been accepted and we will be leaving as well. And…we have you to thank. My parents would really like to thank you personally and they would also like to meet Freddy's, mother."

Helene gave her a warm smile. "I am very relieved and happy for you, but I will stay here. I am tired and I would not be good company."

Miriam was about to insist but Freddy gave her a look that meant let it be. "I understand," said Miriam.

"I am so glad you came over to give me the good news yourself, thank you."

"I would walk back with you," said Freddy, "but if I am honest, I myself am very tired, it has been an intense couple of weeks, I know your parents will understand."

"You are not coming?"

"No, Miriam, I will see you tomorrow."

And Miriam went to join her family. They were all waiting for her arrival to place their food order. "Freddy and his mother asked that they please be excused," she said.

"I understand," answered Simon, "there are no hard feelings."

Nellie was eagerly counting the days, waiting for a word from Freddy giving her their travel information. The wait seemed eternal. The weeks and months had gone by and not a word. She made up her mind not to think about it anymore, which really helped. And so, it came as a small surprise to her when Abraham rang her one evening with their travel information. She was so happy and excited, rejoicing at the idea of all of them being reunited and knowing that she was no longer on her own but that she had a family close by. It sure would make a great difference. But she decided they would not move in together, she was used to having her space and her freedom. However, she would try to find a flat for them that would be within walking distance from hers.

While some were busy with their departure preparations, others were busy planning for the arrival of their loved ones. There was sorrow and rejoicing and uncertainty, the core ingredients of life.

Freddy was debating on what to do with his rabbits. He shared his dilemma with Miriam who found the perfect solution. "Why don't you offer them to the hotel chef?"

"That is a wonderful idea."

"And he can pay cash for them, for if anyone has money around here, it is the hotel. With everyone fleeing the occupied zone, the hotel has been fully booked and I am sure they have raised their prices as well."

"You sure are becoming business-wise," said Freddy, laughing. "But come on, let us have a word with him." Freddy refrained from giving him the real reason, only saying that they took up a lot of his time and he was busy with another project. The chef was delighted, as he was having a great deal of trouble getting ingredients. Delicacies like rabbit meat had become a high-end luxury.

The days of their last week in France went by extremely fast. Freddy spent as much time as he could with Miriam, trying his best to cheer her up. They avoided speaking about her departure for Mexico since, due to the lack of news from the Mexican consulate, Simon was so anguished that it had become his only topic of conversation and it was putting a lot of stress on both Miriam and her mother. Freddy had hoped that the call would come before his departure but it was not meant to be. He gave Miriam, Georges' address and made her promise that she would send him a telegram and he in turn would pass the information on to Freddy.

Helene had been very busy herself. She cleaned the house and left it spick and span, extremely happy and having no regrets about leaving Europe whatsoever, as well as looking very much forward to the trip and seeing Nellie again. She wondered if they would get along better now that Nellie had been on her own for so long.

The day of their departure was finally upon them and Mr Cohen arrived right on time. He told them that he had been in contact with Juan from Ybarra and that their departure had been moved forward. The ship would depart Lisbon in two days. "Why is that?" asked Helene.

Freddy said spontaneously, "That's wonderful news! It cuts our stay in Lisbon short and saves us money *and* keeps us out of harm's way."

Miriam and her parents were at the station waiting for them. "We have come to see you off and wish you safe travels," said Simon and, turning to Helene, "I cannot thank you enough for the information you passed on to us."

Helene blushed. "I am glad it was useful."

"Yes, the applications have been accepted but we are still waiting for them to grant us the visas."

Helene sensed his anguish and said, "You know it is all a matter of time, but my experience has been that in the long run, everything always turns out. Just be patient."

Freddy and Miriam had said their goodbyes the night before. They both felt that it was not a farewell but just a short separation and that their destiny was to be together sometime in the future.

The train came into the station and Mr Cohen placed the luggage in their compartment. The controller was yelling 'all aboard' at the top of his lungs, not leaving much time for goodbye hugs and kisses. The lovers embraced one last time and Freddy followed Helene into the train. Miriam, her parents and Mr Cohen stood on the track until the train disappeared from sight. "I am sure it won't be long now before I will be here bidding you farewell," said Mr Cohen.

"I hope so," replied Simon. Unbeknownst to Simon, Mr Cohen had made some inquiries and the visas would be granted them in the next couple of days, after which he would issue them with their transit visas via Spain to Lisbon.

Helene and Freddy looked out the window. Helene was in excellent spirits, but looking over at Freddy, she could tell that he was in one of his 'leave me alone' moods and could understand it. He was sad at leaving Miriam, they were madly in love with each other and they were a beautiful couple. But, as her mother told her a couple of times when she first started dating Sigmund, there are a lot more fish in the sea. She smiled to herself and thought that also held true for Freddy, surely with his good looks and wonderful personality—

Freddy interrupted her chain of thought. "Mama, I completely forgot about my boat."

"What do you mean?"

"I offered it to Simon and he did not accept my gift, but I never offered it to anybody else."

"No worries, I am sure once the fishermen see it has been abandoned—"

"You are right, I am sure someone will make good use of it."

The train stopped, having arrived at the border town of Portbou. The border police came on board. Freddy and Helene handed over their documents and after studying them for what seemed an eternity, the policemen returned them. They both breathed a sigh of relief. One passenger was asked to leave the train and follow them, not possessing the transit visa for Spain. After a long and very tiring journey, they finally arrived in Lisbon.

Mr Cohen had booked a small hotel for them within walking distance of the station. They would spend two nights there. He told them to keep a low profile and not speak to strangers since the city was a hub for spies from different countries like Germany, Spain and was common knowledge that the Gestapo had been kidnapping prominent Jews off the streets. The hotel restaurant was closed. Luckily, Helene, who thought of everything, had made some sandwiches. They ate them in their room then went to bed. They slept in the next morning and after a late breakfast, Freddy suggested going for a walk.

"Do you think it is safe for us to go out?" asked Helene.

"Sure, what a shame to be here and not see the city. We probably will never return, so come let's go."

"What a difference from Sausset les Pins and Marseille!" Helene remarked. The city was bustling with activity and since Portugal was not at war, the food stalls at the market were full of fresh produce. You sure can tell that there is no rationing here. They walked up to the city walls and to the castle from where they had a magnificent view of the city and port. They found a small, quaint looking restaurant where they had a late lunch then made their way back to the hotel.

"Freddy," said Helene, "what a nice day we have had."

"Yes, it was a lot of fun, and a nice way of saying goodbye to Europe," replied Freddy.

There was somebody waiting for them in the lobby. The stranger introduced himself, "I am from the HICEM (An organisation formed by the Hebrew Immigrant Aid Society, Jewish Colonisation Association and Emigdirect, its goal to help European Jews emigrate). It is the same organisation Mr Cohen works for. Your ship is leaving tomorrow but, if you like, you can go on board tonight. Or would you rather wait until tomorrow?" Freddy and Helene said in one voice, "We will go now." They picked up their belongings and were soon on their way. It was about a good 40-minute drive from where they were staying. As they arrived at the port, their driver, who never told them his name, pointed their ship out to them. "I was expecting a small ship," said Helene, feeling very relieved that it was not what she had imagined.

"It is a mid-size ship, built for transatlantic crossings."

He escorted them through emigration where their documents were thoroughly checked. The officer took a long time with Freddy's Document of Safe Passage, then asked to see his visa for Colombia. Freddy pointed it out to him. "Everything is in good order," he said, giving him back the documents. The stranger then bade them good-bye and good luck and left them in the care of the ship personnel.

They were not the only ones who had decided to board that evening, on the way to their cabin, they encountered several passengers who looked at the newcomers curiously. Their cabin had two bunk beds, a small bathroom and a pothole. "Not much of a view," said Freddy.

"I can do without the view," said Helene, "we are on our way. Your father would be very pleased, his wish is about to come true." They took a tour of the ship that would be their home for several weeks and decided to call it a day.

They were up early the next morning, more and more passengers were coming on board and the two of them stood on the deck watching the crew at work. "So many hands to get the ship ready," said Helene. "And when you think about the distance we will be travelling."

"Yes," said Freddy. "But we will be stopping at different ports-of-call and supplies will be brought on board."

"I am glad…" said Helene, laughing, "that we will not go hungry."

Freddy teased her, "You are right, no more rabbit, no more fish and thinking about it, that steak we had yesterday, what a delicacy.

I can't remember having eaten a better one."

"Of course not, it was so very long ago."

The ship was due to depart at 12 noon. When the engine roared into life, the last deck hands jumped on board, the moorings were removed and Helene and Freddy stood with the other passengers on the upper deck, watching as the ship slowly headed out towards the Atlantic. No one spoke. Freddy put his arm around his mother's shoulders, her eyes brimming with tears and he barely heard what she said, "Sigmund stayed behind."

It would be a new beginning in a new world and, as the two of them watched the old continent disappear from sight, they wondered what life would have in store for them.

Epilogue

They reached Colombia four weeks later. Nellie and Abraham were at the port of Barranquilla to welcome them. It was a very joyful and gratifying reunion. Sigmund's wish had come true. The city of Bogotá was completely different from any other. It was nestled on a huge plateau at 2650 metres above sea level, surrounded by the Andean Mountains. It took them some time to get used to the altitude. This did not overshadow their joy of being free and safe. Freddy's knowledge of Spanish came in very handy and Helene's knowledge of French was a great asset to her learning the country's language.

The flat, Nellie had found for them, was within walking distance of Nellie's and they loved it. She would walk over to see them after work and enjoyed the evening meal Helene prepared for them. She had forgotten what a wonderful cook her stepmother was. A couple of weeks after their arrival, the furniture was delivered. Seeing her father's desk and his few mementos, as well as his books, brought tears to Nellie's eyes. If only, yes, if only… She did not speak her thoughts out loud. Freddy, who had been watching her out of the corner of his eye, walked over to her and said gently: "It was meant to be." She just nodded her head. The shadow did not last long.

Freddy thought about his friends, Georges in Paris and Helmut in Frankfurt, and wondered how they were faring. Europe was still at war. True to his promise, Georges sent the telegram.

Miriam and her family never received the visas they had been promised and had tried to flee over the Pyrenees. They were caught by a German guard who sent them with other prisoners in a convoy but no one knew its final destination. After seeing Freddy and Helene off at the train station, Mr Cohen was never seen or heard of again. This was Georges' last message.

It was not until the end of the war that, after turning to the International Red Cross for help, Freddy received news that both his friends were safe and well. He also found out that his beloved and her family had been murdered in Auschwitz Concentration Camp.

In the summer of 1953, Freddy returned to Europe as a Colombian national. He met with Helmut in Frankfurt and Georges in Paris. It was a very joyful reunion indeed. Georges accepted Freddy's invitation to come to Colombia and travelled there several times, but Freddy was unable to persuade him to settle there. For many years, he sent Freddy and his family a huge box of crystallised fruit, which was a huge success.

Helmut, however, did not relish the long trip and never left Germany, managing the bed and breakfast he set up on Bunny Hill. Freddy would invariably stop over on his way to Switzerland to spend a couple of days with him and his family. A true friendship that had endured the hardships of separation, war and distance, at whose core was gratitude, generosity and compassion, came to an end with Freddy's passing in September 1990. Helmut outlived him by a couple more years. Georges was the last to leave the planet. They live on in the memories that Freddy shared of them with his family.

Bibliography

The Weimar Republic by Stephen J Lee
The Twilight Years Paris in the 1930s by William Wiser
Geschichte eines Deutschen by Sebastian Haffner
A Social History of the Third Reich by Richard Grunberger
Guernica Booklet from the Reina Sofia Museum in Madrid
A History of the Twentieth Century Volume two 1933-1951
By Martin Gilber
Rough Guide History of France by Ian Littlewood
Occupation: The Ordeal of France by Ian Ousby
Night by Elie Wiesel
Wikipedia Armee Juive
The Underground Movement
Among others
Private letters and personal stories